AF560236

STATE FORMATION IN RAJASTHAN

Mewar during the Seventh-Fifteenth Centuries

State Formation in Rajasthan

Mewar during the Seventh-Fifteenth Centuries

NANDINI SINHA KAPUR

MANOHAR
2002

First published 2002

ISBN 81-7304-429-5

Published by
Ajay Kumar Jain for
Manohar Publishers & Distributors
4753/23 Ansari Road, Daryaganj
New Delhi 110002

Printed at
Rajkamal Electric Press
Delhi 110033

TO
THE LOVING MEMORY OF
MY FATHER
SHRI SATYAJIT KUMAR SINHA
(18-3-1931–18-6-1991)

ALSO FOR
MY MOTHER, SMT. DIPALI SINHA
AND
MY BROTHER, RAJU (ABHIJIT SINHA)

Contents

Maps

Acknowledgements

This book is an expanded version of my Ph.D. thesis submitted to Jawaharlal Nehru University in 1997. I owe a debt of gratitude to my supervisors Professor Romila Thapar, Emeritus and Professor Kunal Chakrabarti for having supervised this work at a crucial stage. I must thank Prof. B.D. Chattopadhyaya who not only supervised it initially but had introduced me into the studies of early medieval Rajasthan at M.A. and M.Phil. levels. I am grateful to Prof. Shereen Ratnagar without whose constant encouragement and moral support I would not have been able to complete this work. Thanks are due to my friend Supriya. I express my gratitude to Professor Dilbagh Singh, Professor Muzaffar Alam and Professor Bhairabi Prasad Sahu for their insightful comments on different aspects of this research. I must thank Prof. Pratipal Bhatia, Prof. Mrinal Miri and Dr. Devnathan for inviting me to the departmental special assistance seminar, 'Government and Society', department of History, University of Delhi (sponsored by the University Grants Commission) and national seminar 'Tribe to Caste' at the Indian Institute of Advanced Study, Shimla where parts of this work had been presented. I take this opportunity to thank Prof. Susanne Rudolph, Prof. Lloyd Rudolph, Prof. Dirk H.A. Kolff, Prof. Julia Leslie, Dr. Daud Ali, Dr. Maxine Weisgrau, Prof. James Scott, Prof. Ann Grodzins Gold, Dr. Bishwamoy Pati and Prof. Sumit Guha for their appreciation of important aspects of this monograph. I thank Sanjeeb Behera, Himanshu Behera and Kalyan Das for the help received in the making of maps for my Ph.D. thesis and Kamal Singh for my book. I must not forget to thank Bholaji, Chaubeji, and Bhupnathji of the National Museum Library, Tekramji and Teghbahadurji of the Central Library of the Archaeological Survey of India, and the staff of Pratap Shodh Pratisthan, Sahitya Sansthan, Rajasthan Prachya Vidya Pratisthan, Library of the Maharana Mewar Foundation, Maniklal Verma Tribal Research Institute, Udaipur and the staff of Rajasthan State Archives, Bikaner. I must thank Prof. Sibesh Bhattacharya and Prof. Aloka Parasher Sen for the encourgement I have received in the publication of this book. I acknowledge with thanks the financial help that I have received from the University Grants Commission and Indian Council for Historical Research towards the completion of this monograph. I thank my typist, Omprakashji.

This book is dedicated to the loving memory of my father who inspired me to study further but did not live long to see the completion of this monograph. Words fail me to express my gratitude to my mother and brother, Raju who have been the pillars of support throughout the course of this research. This book is also dedicated to my mother and brother. My maternal grandmother, Dimma who is no more would have been happy to see this book. Although it would be a formality yet I take this opportunity to thank my husband, Vijay who has been a source of moral support at the time of finalization of this book. His interest in my research-work helps me negotiating between my domestic responsibilities and my academic committments. I thank my father-in-law, Brig. H.L. Kapur and my brother-in-law, Vikram for making me feel at home in my new household. I thank my sister-in-law, Molly (Raju's wife) who has been supportive and helpful. Finally, I must acknowledge the fruitful interaction and enjoyable time I have had teaching History to my students at PGDAV College and Department of History, Delhi University (South Campus).

NANDINI SINHA KAPUR

Abbreviations

ASI	Archaeological Survey of India, Report
An. Rep. of ASI	*Annual Report of Archaeological Survey of India*
ARIE	*Annual Report of Indian Epigraphy*
ARRM	*Annual Report of Rajputana Museum*
Bom. Br. RAS	Bombay Branch of Royal Asiatic Society
BSOAS	*Bulletin of the School of Oriental and African Studies*
CII	*Corpus Inscriptionum Indicarum*
CPSI	Corpus of Prakrit and Sanskrit Inscriptions
DRI	G.H. Ojha, *Dungarpur Rājya Kā Itihāsa*, Ajmer, 1936
EI	*Epigraphia Indica*
EIAPS	*Epigraphia Indica: Arabic and Persian Supplement*
IA	*Indian Antiquary*
IESHR	*Indian Economic and Social History Review*
IHR	*Indian Historical Review*
IHQ	*Indian Historical Quarterly*
JESHO	*Journal of Economic and Social History of Orient*
JIH	*Journal of Indian History*
JNSI	*Journal of Numismatic Society of India*
MK	Ram Vallabh Somani, *Mahārāṇā Kumbha*, Jodhpur, 1968 (Hindi)
PIHC	*Proceedings of Indian History Congress*
PRAS, WC	Progress Report of Archaeological Survey, Western Circle
RPVP	Rajasthan Prachya Vidya Pratisthan
RTA	Dasharath Sharma, *Rajasthan Through The Ages*, Bikaner, 1966
Sharda, *MK*	H.B. Sharda, *Mahārāṇā Kumbha*, Ajmer, 1922
URI	G.H. Ojha, *Udaipur Rājya Kā Itihāsa*, Ajmer, 1936

CHAPTER I

Introduction

The objective of this study is to trace the process of state formation in the region of Mewar in Rajasthan between the seventh and fifteenth centuries. This study attempts to chart out the distinct stages in this process, beginning with the local state polities which ran parallel to the growth in the political career of the Guhila ruling family of Mewar. Evidently, political and administrative structures at the local and sub-regional levels crystallized in particular between the tenth and thirteenth centuries and led to the emergence of a regional state structure in Mewar. Evolution of the political structure of the state of Mewar and expansion of Guhila sovereignty all over Mewar involved territorial and political integration. The extension of this study up to the fifteenth century has its own significance. Firstly, the political structure of the fifteenth-century state of Mewar will be shown to have been different from that of the thirteenth century. Secondly, the fifteenth century marks a decisive point in the history of Mewar: massive territorial expansion took place and Guhila sovereignty reached new heights. Finally, the fifteenth century also marked a culmination of the ideological apparatus of the state of Mewar, for, the royal epithet of *Ekaliṅganijasevaka* (later, Diwan of Ekaliṅga) evolved in this period.

II

State Formation: General Theoretical Discussions

Ronald Cohen and Elman R. Service discuss the problems of definition and theories of state formation. The 'Conflict Approach' focuses on increased centralization of governmental institutions, because of competition between groups with limited access to scarce resources, ultimately leading to the dominance of one group. For instance, Morton Fried points out that the state receives its 'key impetus' from the need to protect the stratification system.[1] On the other hand, the 'Integrative' approach, while admitting that state formation involves conflicts, emphasizes the increased capacities of state systems in coordinating a large number of people of different ethnic and ecological backgrounds. The organizational benefits of a centralized government serves to legitimize its exercise of power over the subjects.[2] In other words, the 'integrative' approach identifies government with state.

A historiographical note on the study of state formation opens up a vast arena of theoretical approaches to the early state. I restrict my discussion to a brief and hopefully substantial representation of the spectrum. Henri J.M. Claessen and Peter Skalnik in *The Early State*, conclude, on the basis of a few case studies (mainly anthropological) that there were essentially three types of early state: 'the inchoate', the 'typical' and the 'transitional'.[3] The last leads to the 'mature state' with a fully developed class society.[4]

Scholars contributing to *The Study of the State* discuss the wide range of possibilities of formation of states in Africa and the concept of 'sacred kingship', pastoralist states, etc., with general theoretical discussions on the origins and mechanisms of state formation including that of warfare.[5] Romila Thapar in her essay 'The State as Empire' develops the idea of a metropolitan state with reference to the Mauryas ruling over a number of differentiated socio-political, economic systems.[6] These differentiated systems were very much retained by the Mauryas and they merely attempted to control the revenue which these differing systems provided.[7]

III

Historiography of State Formation in India as Representing a Shift from Simple Dynastic History

Romila Thapar pointing out the inadequacies of the theories on the earliest formation of states in India, highlighted possibilities of processes and distinct changes in the stages of state formation in the areas with a long history of state systems. 'The transition from lineage to state was not the only pattern of change, nor was conquest the only avenue of state formation as has been asserted by many commentators on the pre-modern Indian past. Areas with a long history of state systems underwent intensive historical changes through time, the varying forms being integrated to the nature and the role of the state.'[8]

Romila Thapar discussed the origin of state formation in early Indian history as a process of change from lineage based social formation to that of a predominantly peasant state system.[9] In *From Lineage to State: Social Formations in the Mid-First Millennium B.C. in the Gaṅgā Valley*, Thapar highlighted the socio-political, economic and ideological processes that helped transform a lineage based society into a state system disintinguished by the emergence of monarchy.[10] However, kingship remained central to the emergence of state system. Both Brāhmaṇical sources including the *Rāmāyaṇa* and *Mahābhārata* and Buddhist sources depict powerful kings in eulogistic tones.[11] Abhorrence of the absence of monarchy is clearly discernible in *Rāmāyaṇa*.[12]

Kumkum Roy develops the importance of the idea of 'Rājā' and 'Rājya', among others, as the central theme in the Brāhmaṇical sources between eighth and fourth centuries BC.[13] On the other hand, R.S. Sharma discusses in detail the intensification of productive forces and their social implications giving rise to a large number of territorial states called mahājanapada characterized by a stratified society.[14] Elsewhere, he states, 'It is, therefore, clear that the growth of the state apparatus was closely connected with the increasing supply of various taxes.'[15] The process was facilitated by brāhmaṇa-kṣatriya alliance through control over distribution of 'surplus' and the ideology of the varṇa system. Among significant contributions towards the study of local state formation in early historic period, Sudarshan Seneviratne's study on early Kaliṅga and Andhra needs mention. Seneviratne analyses the internal factors of state formation (such as growth of the local chiefs) accelerated by the presence of external factors such as the culture of the metropolitan state of Mauryas and the role played by the trade routes.[16]

IV

Historiography of Local and Regional State Formation in the Early Medieval Period

In protest against the model of political disunity projected by British imperialist hitorians, there arose the theory of strong, united empires of ancient India with equally strong, centralized bureaucracies.[17] A product of the heyday of nationalist upsurge, this 'conventional-bureaucratic' model highlighted centralized empires, particularly of the post-Gupta period.[18]

If the nationalists looked at the post-Gupta regional states as highly centralized polities, in which early kings began their careers with power concentrated in their hands, their critics came up with the notion of 'Indian Feudalism' to explain medieval states and empires.[19] Emergence of local or regional states in the early medieval period was seen as a by-product of the break-up of erstwhile empires, those of Harṣa or the Pratihāras in the North and the Cālukyas or the Rāṣṭrakūṭas in the Deccan.

Based on a vast corpus of epigraphical data from the Rāṣṭrakūṭa, Pāla and Pratihāra period, R.S. Sharma's *Indian Feudalism* offered a picture of a highly decentralized and fragmented political structure for early medieval India.[20] The decentralized political structure was supposed to be the result of a widespread practice of religious and secular land grants made by the imperial powers in the far-flung areas of their mighty empires. The religious donees emerged as the intermediaries in the countryside exploiting the peasantry with ever increasing demands and leading to the latter's gradual impoverishment. The economic origin of the land-based system in early medieval times was traced in a definite decline in foreign trade and commerce (echoing Henry Pirenne's theory on early medieval Europe) while culturally, the period is stated to have witnessed the emergence of seemingly demeaning practices like tāntric cults and obnoxious representations in the arts.[21]

In a fresh approach to the study of state in early medieval times, Burton Stein put out the concept of 'segmentary state' in 1973. Stein derived his paradigm from A. Southall's study of the Alur society in Eastern Africa. In this new scheme, Stein viewed the entire structure of the Cola state as a pyramid made up of segments in which the king had the maximum authority at the core or political centre and is increasingly represented by mere ritual sovereignty and not by actual power, in the segments at the periphery.[22]

A major departure from the above formulation was offered through the application of the idea of 'integrative polity' to the study of state formation and structure. This model essentially looks at the phenomenon of state formation as 'processual'.[23] Kulke questioned the very basis of the political decentralization of the post-Gupta period, which fails to explain the growth of the great regional kingdoms and the long duration of their rule in certain cases. He rightly observes that 'structural interpretation of the post-Gupta era reveals that this period of North-Indian decentralization coincided with a very intensive process of state formation on the local level, subregional, and regional levels in some parts of Northern India, in many parts of Central India, and in most parts of Southern India'.[24] Although Kulke forcefully challenged the concept of fragmentation and segmentation, he was silent about the political mechanisms of 'integration' that were crucial to his own formulations.

B.D. Chattopadhyaya in 1983 noted two bases of state formation in early medieval India, illuminating the composition of the so-called feudatories. Finally, the emergence of the overlord or feudatory had its basis mostly in the lineage power of the local ruling elites. The transformation of the lineage into a regional power was through command of military resources and other forms of support from other lineages.[25]

Secondly and more significantly, the command of military resources and allegiance not only required a redistribution of resources but also called for a system of ranking. Ranking was based on services which could be worked out between such roles as the *dūtaka*, *sāndhivigrahika*, *daṇḍanāyaka*, etc., and also ranks in the *sāmanta* hierarchy. The political basis of integration was brought about by the inter-lineage and intra-lineage network of power. These political processes operated simultaneously with parallels in contemporary economic, social and religious processes. To quote Chattopadhyaya:

> The essence of the economic process lay in the horizontal spread of rural agrarian settlements. The process of caste formation remained the essence of the social processes which drew widely dispersed and originally outlying groups into a structure which allowed them in a large measure to retain their original character except that this character was now defined with reference to the structure. In the related religious process too the major trend was integration of local cult, rituals, and sacred centres into a pantheistic supra-local structure. The mechanism of integration was by seeking affiliation with a deity or a sacred centre which had come to acquire a supra-local significance. Applied to the study of the political processes, these parallels would suggest consideration of three levels: presence of established norms and nuclei of state society, horizontal spread of state society, implying transformation of pre-state polities into state polities, and integration of local polities into a structure that transcended the bounds of local polities.[26]

The spread of state society was realized only through the process of local state formation which also brought a measure of cohesion among local elements of culture by providing them with a focus.[27] Although some of the recent related notions such as those of 'Imperial formations' put forth by Ronald Inden,[28] and Andre Wink,[29] for early medieval Indian empires do not emphasize the phenomenon of regional state formation, they do highlight important political proceses in the early medieval period.

The historiography on state between the thirteenth and the fifteenth centuries is dominated by monographs on Delhi Sultanate. It ranges from traditional approaches of dynastic history to an analysis of the nature of the state.[30] This historiography ranges from Khaliq Ahmad Nizami's concept of a broad-based state characterized by transformation of the Turkish state,[31] Upendra Nath Day's characterization of the sultanate as a sectarian state,[32] S.B.P. Nigam's discussion of nobility and its transformation from a 'tribal elite' to a heterogeneous group,[33] and H.C. Verma's evaluation of *iqta* and *kharāj* that is supposed to have distinguished the sultanate from 'its predecessor Rajput feudal states'[34] to Peter Jackson's study of the 'mamluk institution'[35] which was firmly rooted in a long, tradition of muslim military activity with legitimizing connections with the present and past ruling dynasties and Afghan rule characterized by the 'Khalji Revolution'.[36]

The bias towards Delhi-Agra grid was corrected to some extent by those historians who focussed on formation of regional sultanates in Malwa and Gujarat. Although based on dynastic approach, we need to mention the works of U.N. Day on Malwa,[37] and Edward Clive Bayley[38] and S.C. Misra on Gujarat.[39] Recently, the works of Burton Stein on Vijayanagara Empire[40] and Richard M. Eaton on the spread of Islam in Bengal[41] have filled the gap by highlighting the importance of regional states in southern India and Bengal. However, these monographs continued to focus on the post-twelfth-century period.

But the historiography that highlights the continuity of the processes of regional state formation cutting across the conventional divide of the early medieval and medieval periods is yet to find its place. The fact that autonomous spaces with uneven changes from within witnessed processes of state formation beyond the early medieval period has been recognized. 'Transactions from the pre-state to the state-society have been documented through medieval to modern times.'[42]

We must take note of the formation of states in different regions of Orissa, central India, Bihar, Bengal, and Assam from the early medieval to the late medieval periods. Orissa witnessed a stepwise continuous process of territorial integration of nuclear areas from the sixth to the sixteenth centuries.[43] None of the rulers during the fifth-sixth centuries was able to extend his power into neighbouring nuclear areas, nor socio-economic developments of these areas had yet reached a stage which could sustain political power. Bhaumakaras of Uttara Tosala were the first dynasty which integrated the whole coastal region of Orissa, northern parts of Uttara Tosala, Dakṣiṇa Tosala and Koṅgoda in the south into their state with its capital at Jajpur.[44] They were also acknowledged by several rulers of smaller nuclear areas in the hinterland such as the Śulkīs of Kodālaka Maṇḍala and the Bhañjas of Khiñjali Maṇḍala.[45]

Somavaṁśīs of Dakṣiṇa Kośala conquered Khiñjali Maṇḍala and coastal Orissa and integrated them for the first time with their state in western Orissa. When King Anantavarman Coḍagaṅga (one of the eastern Gaṅgas of Kaliṅga) in *c.*1112 conquered central Orissa and extended his rule from modern Midnapur district in present West Bengal up to the northern banks of Godavari in Andhra Pradesh in the subsequent period, Orissa witnessed the emergence of the 'great regional kingdom' under the Gaṅgas and the Sūryavaṁśīs (AD 1112-1568).[46] James Heitzman's studies on south India[47] focussing on the processes of state formation under the Cọlas and the later Gaṅga state in Orissa are examples of chronological specificities.[48]

Gonds formed large kingdoms in central India mostly covering parts of present Madhya Pradesh around the fourteenth and fifteenth centuries.[49] Four kingdoms of the Gonds with their capitals at Garha, Deogarh, Kherla and Chanda ruled for nearly four hundred years.[50] 'Nevertheless, there is evidence of a certain degree of development of bureaucratized centralized machinery cutting across the principle of sub-infeudation, in the kingdoms of Garha and Chanda.'[51] Process of 'Rajputization' associated with the ruling elite amongst the Gonds is clearly evident from the two aristocratic subdivisions, the Rāj Gonds and Khatolas while Dhur Gonds came from the mass of the ordinary peasants.[52] Rāj Gond rulers of Goṇḍwānā also formed kingdoms in medieval Chattisgarh.[53] The largest of Chattisgarh states, Bastar had a Rāj family which claims descent from Pāṇḍu king, Bīrabhadra of Indraprastha.[54]

Similarly, Bhumijs in Barabhum[55] and Mundas in Chhotanagpur had formed kingdoms in the medieval times. Surajit Sinha rightly observes that, 'the actual process of the formation of the states, as far as could be ascertained, has taken varied courses in the different instances discussed above. Some, like the Munda Rājās of Chhotanagpur, the Bhumij state of Barabhum and the Rāj Gond kingdoms of Gondwana, appear to have emerged mainly through internal developments out of a tribal base. There are also cases of immigrant Rajput adventurers gaining powers in the tribal tract by manoeuvring the narrow-range, clan-bound tribal chieftaincies, and in a few cases, even by conquest (for example, Bastar, Surguja, Jashpur and so on).'[56] Hence the regional states formed by the

Nāgavaṁśīs in Chhotanagpur in which the Mundas played an important role,[57] by the Mallas in Bankura and Surbhum areas of Bengal with significant Bagdi connections,[58] by the Tai-Ahoms in Assam from the thirteenth to the sixteenth centuries,[59] and by the Dimasas in the Cachar area of Assam from the thirteenth to the early nineteenth centuries[60] are also worth noting in the historiography on state formation in early medieval and medieval India. The present work on Mewar highlights amongst others, the importance of the study of those processes of regional state formation which went beyond the twelfth century in the making of the regional state of Mewar.

V

The other major problem tackled in the present work concerns the origin of the Rajputs and their states. Rajputs, have variously been considered to have descended either from Kṣatriya-Vedic origin[61] or from Scythian (Central Asian) stock[62] or from a varied caste origin such as brāhmaṇa, kṣatriya, etc.[63] This is a result of separate treatment meted out to the Rajput dynasties of western India. Similarly, Rajput states including that of the Guhila of Mewar have either been viewed as mere dynastic houses with endless military achievements,[64] or post-tribal feudal states[65] or 'that Rajasthan had been divided into a number of small kingdoms'.[66] The other popular perspective on the medieval Rajput state is that of *Bhāī-bant*.[67] However, some early traditional accounts of the history of Mewar and Rajasthan, such as the writings of Gauri Shankar Hirachand Ojha, Kaviraj Shyamaldas and Harbilas Sharda, are of immense value as they abound in local legends, contemporary accounts, topographical details and unpublished inscriptional records.[68]

Although some of the recent monographs on the fifteenth-century Guhilas such as Ram Vallabh Somani's *Mahārāṇā Kumbha* (Jodhpur, 1968), Tara Mangal's *Mahārāṇā Kumbha aur Unkā Kāl* (Jodhpur, 1984), Neelam Kaushik's *Rājasthān ke Cūṇḍāwaton kā Itihāsa* (Jaipur, 1988), etc., are well-researched, their perspective remains dynastic and confined to a particular point in time. Even a recent anthropological study on the tribal population of Mewar in the historical period fall short of expectations, as historical sources from early medieval Mewar have been ignored.[69] Finally, what has been neglected is that the important political developments characteristic of early medieval India and reflected in the exaggerated genealogies of the small kingdoms, find a parallel in the inflated claims of origin made by different Rajput royal houses. In fact, mighty claims made by the Rajput ruling families may be seen as attempts to get away from the actual origin rather than to reveal it. After all, the category of 'Rajput' like other varṇa categories have been assimilative in time and space.[70] In spite of the few developments which may have been peculiar to western India, the rise and emergence of the Rajputs should be seen in the context of the main political process characterizing early medieval India, viz., the phenomenon of state formation.

The Guhilas of Mewar having begun their career as kings in the Nāgdā-Āhaḍa[71] locality laid the foundation of a state structure in the region of Mewar. Processes of state formation (political, economic and ideological) characterized the history of the Guhilas of Mewar for a long period of seven hundred years (seventh to thirteenth century): in distinct stages from a local state to a sub-regional state of Mewar hills in the tenth century, graduating into the regional state of Mewar by the thirteenth century. The banner of the Guhila royal family carved out a state structure through gradual territorial integration, incorporation of local and trans-local chiefs from non-Guhila Rajput lineages (the term lineage is used in the sense of *vaṁśa*) as well as Guhila royal families, along with a growing material base. New heights in territorial achievements and political growth were reflected in new claims to prestigious origin which validated Guhila power through a variety of motifs. Thus, the Guhilas of Mewar were not dynastic entities alone; nor was the Guhila state a break-away feudatory power of the Pratihāra Empire. Neither did it represent a decentralized political structure; feudal or *Bhāī-bant*. Through the processes of incorporation, a Guhila local state grew into the regional state of Mewar.

Finally, but not the least, the present work contributes to the recent spurt on the study of regional identities in India, notably in Rajasthan. Two impressive volumes of, *The Idea of Rajasthan: Explorations in Regional Identity* probe into important facts of historic and modern Rajasthan. Enquiries range widely from the Harappan culture in Rajasthan, the political process of the rise of the Rajputs in early medieval period, Rāṭhaur state formation in medieval period, royal portraits, popular musicians, pilgrimages, panchayati raj in contemporary times to the ecological problem of desertification.[72] However, Lodrick's discussion on regional identity of Rajasthan seems to be one of the important contributions where he probes into the identity of Rajasthan as a political space. He highlights the contributory role of the Rajputs and Rajput ethoes that helped Rajasthan evolve its own political identity between the thirteenth and the sixteenth centuries.[73] If Rajputs contributed to the making of political identity of Rajasthan between thirteenth and the sixteenth centuries, Rajput state formation at the regional levels such as the Guhila state of Mewar, between the tenth and the fifteenth centuries can certainly be considered to be a precursor of the political identity of Rajasthan.

VI

I have drawn my sources for the present work from the following cateogires:

Archaeological

(a) Archaeological Excavation Reports.
(b) Inscriptional Records of the Guhilas and contemporary powers referring to Medapāṭa, Citrakūṭa and the Guhilas.
(c) Inscriptional Records of the non-Guhila Rajput powers in Mewar.
(d) Inscriptional Records of the Jains from Mewar, Mount Abu and surrounding localities.
(e) Numismatic Finds of the Śākambharī Cāhamānas in Mewar.

Literary: Sanskrit Texts

Ekaliṅgamāhātmyam (*Sthala Purāṇa*) of Ekaliṅgajī, Mewar (fifteenth century), Rāṇā Kumbha's *Saṅgītarāja* (fifteenth century), Sūtradhāra Maṇḍana's *Rājaballabha Maṇḍana* (fifteenth century), Raṇachoḍa Bhaṭṭa's *Amarakāvyam* (seventeenth century), Raṇachoḍa Bhaṭṭa's *Rājapraśasti Māhākavyam* (seventeenth century), Jinaprabha Sūri's *Vividhatīrthakalpa* (fourteenth century), Jayasiṁha Sūri's *Hammīra-madamardana* (thirteenth century), Nyāyacandra Sūri's *Hammīra-mahākāvyam* (fourteenth century), Jinapāla's *Kharataragacchabṛhad-gurvāvalī*, and Jinavijayajī's *Kharataragacchapaṭṭāvalī* (collections range from the twelfth to the seventeenth centuries); *Jain Pustaka Praśasti Saṁgraha* (twelfth-fifteenth centuries).

Persian, Arabic and Turkish Texts: English Translations

Amir Khusrau's *Khazain-ul-Futuh* (fourteenth century),[74] Babar's *Tuzuk-i-Baburi* (*Babar Nama*) (Turkish) (early sixteenth century),[75] Yahyabin Ahmad Sirhindi's *Tarikh-i-Mubarakshahi* (mid-fifteenth century),[76]

Muhammad Qasim Ferishta's *Tarikh-i-Ferishta* (early seventeenth century),[77] Ziauddin Barani's *Tarikh-i-Firuzshahi* (mid-fourteenth century),[78] Ibn Battuta's *Kutabur Rehla* (Arabic) (mid-fourteenth century),[79] and Abul Fazal's *Akbar Nama* (mid-sixteenth century).[80]

Rajasthani Texts

Muhaṇot Nainsī rī Khyāt, an historical account of Rajasthan (mid-seventeenth century).

Vaṁśāvalīs: Genealogical accounts of the Guhila dynasty as well as of the royal kinsmen compiled by the Bhāṭs are vast in number. Following have been consulted: (a) *Sūryavaṁśāvalī*, (b) *Baḍvādevīdān Khyāt* (*Vaṁśāvalī*), *Bāṅkīdās rī Khyāt*, *Murārī dān rī Khyāt*, and *Rāṇājī rī bāt*, etc., have been utilized for the study of the Rāṭhaurs in Mewar.

Cāraṇ Traditions: (a) Girdhar Āsiā's *Sagat Rāso* (seventeenth century), (b) *Rāṇā Pratāp rā Jhulnā*, (c) *Bagḍāvat Devanārāyaṇa Mahāgāthā*, an epic tradition of the Gujars of south-central Rajasthan and Malwa of the medieval period.

Local bardic traditions recorded in secondary works like Col. James Tod's *Annals and Antiquities of Rajasthan* as well as Bhil songs published in Bhili dialect with Hindi translations are also important.

Chronological Use of the Sources

The Early Historic Period in Mewar before the Rise of the Guhilas

It is possible to delineate a cultural profile of early Mewar with the use of excavation and exploration reports, structural remains, numismatic finds, as well as short Prakrit inscriptional records, and Sanskrit inscriptions. These sources illuminate the settlement pattern, and possible socio-political and economic profiles of localities in proto-historic and early historic Mewar. Specially, the nature of the settlements helps us formulate an idea of the nuclear centres, but the sources do not allow a detailed profile of rural society in Mewar of the pre-Guhila period.

The Early Medieval Period: Seventh to Thirteenth Centuries

The sources for this period mainly include inscriptional records of the Guhila royal families of Mewar and those of the Rāṣṭrakūṭas of Hastikuṇḍī, the Pratihāras of Kanauj, the Rāṣṭrakūṭas of Māniyākheta, and the Paramāras of Malwa and Citrakūṭa. Guhila inscriptions offer scope for reconstructing the various stages of state formation in early medieval Mewar. Guhila inscriptions, when contrasted with pre-Guhila inscriptional finds in Mewar, clearly point towards the emergence of new political centres, help profile the ruling elite, and reveal the structure of rural society. We explore the presence of the non-Guhila Rajput chiefs, the extent of rural settlements, the emergence of urban centres at particular points of time, patterns of taxation, etc. Most of the inscriptional records were found near habitations, rural or urban. But the Samoli Inscription of AD 646, recording mining activities in forest and hilly localities helps in locating the tribal population in the Nāgdā-Āhaḍa belt. The limitation of the inscriptional records as a source for the history of the tribal population has necessitated utilization of Col. James Tod's *Annals and Antiquities of Rajasthan* for the early medieval period, supplemented by the contemporary inscriptional records. For instance, a thirteenth century Guhila inscriptional record refers to the Bhils for the first time. However, such information is scarce. It must be remembered that Tod's *Annals and Antiquities*, essentially a late eighteenth-early nineteenth centuries account of Rajasthan, is a rich mine of local oral traditions, particularly those of the Bhils. Hence, an analysis of Tod's account along with Guhila royal sources help us in placing the Bhils in their historic setting.

Inscriptions of the contemporary Rajput ruling houses are even more useful in reconstructing Guhila-Chittaurgarh relationship and hence facilitate retracing the stages of regional state formation in Mewar. A few of these records, such as those of Kalacuris of central India, reveal Guhila matrimonial relations beyond Rajasthan. Non-Guhila Rajput records from late fourteenth-century Mewar are helpful in cross-checking the reigns of the possible contemporary Guhila rulers.

Medieval Period: Thirteenth to Fifteenth Centuries

Besides Guhila inscriptions of thirteenth and fifteenth centuries, important sources include Raṇachoḍa Bhaṭṭa's *Rājapraśasti* (a seventeenth-century Guhila royal inscription), *Amarakāvyam* (a seventeenth-century text) and *Ekaliṅgamāhātmyam* (*Sthala Purāṇa* compiled in the court of Mewar in late fifteenth century). Seventeenth-century royal inscriptions and texts are helpful in constructing the royal image perceived by the ruling house after 1500 and when contrasted with the preceding century, prove that the self-perception of the state continued to evlove after the fifteenth century. Vaṁśāvalīs and Cāraṇ traditions such as Girdhar Āsiā's *Sagat Rāso* reflect popular perception of the state and royal family in the seventeenth century, which is corroborated by a seventeenth-century historian from Marwar, Nainsī (chief minister at Jodhpur court). However, the post-fifteenth-century sources have remained marginal to our study.

Jain texts of the thirteenth-fourteenth centuries such as Jinavijayajī's *Kharataragacchapaṭṭavali*, Jayasiṁha Sūri's *Hammīramadamardana* and Nyāyacandra Sūri's *Hammīra mahākavyam*, contemporary Jain Grantha *praśastis*, etc., are essential to list the Jain functionaries in the administrative apparatus of the Guhila state of Mewar. They also reveal when they were first incorporated as administrative functionaries. But Jain texts need to be carefully handled as they present their perception of the Guhila state only at particular points of time. We learn from the vast corpus of Jain inscriptions and texts about the status and wealth of the Jains; they speak of the Jains incorporated into the political structure of Mewar in important capacities. Hence, Jain texts and inscriptions are utilized to construct the Jain image of the state and the Guhila royal family between the thirteenth and fifteenth centuries.

Persian texts such as Amir Khusrau's *Khazain-ul-Futuh* (fourteenth century), Yahyabin Ahmad Sirhindi's *Tarikh-i-Mubarakshahi* (mid-fifteenth century), Ibn Battuta's *Kutabur Rehla* (mid-fourteenth century), etc., are not only helpful in constructing the relations of Mewar with contemporary powers but also reflect the importance of Chittaurgarh, and hence the Guhilas, in western India. Babar refered to Rāṇā Sānkā (the Guhila Rāṇā Sāṅgā of the early sixteenth century) in the *Babar Nama*. However, Persian texts have to be carefully scrutinized for the history of Mewar as they possibly project ideas from the point of view of Delhi Sultanate. Unlike the tenth to thirteenth-century Guhila inscriptions, fifteenth-century records are absolutely silent (two exceptions: Rāṇā Mokal's Śṛṅgiṛṣi Inscription of 1429 refers to a Baghelā queen and Rāimalla's Ekaliṅgajī Temple Dakṣiṇadvāra Praśasti of 1488 refers to his Gauḍa mother)[81] about the possible family-affiliations of the Guhila queens. *Baḍvādevīdān Khyāt* (a manuscript lodged in the Sahitya Sansthan, Udaipur and edited/published by the same institution) comes to our rescue as it lists some of the fifteenth-century Guhila queens and hence provides some clue to possible family affiliations. Baḍvā Bhāṭs were traditional genealogists of the royal house of Mewar. *Bāṅkīdās rī Khyāt* and *Murārī dān rī Khyāt* help in reconstructing the history of the Rāṭhaur chiefs of Mewar. Finally, but not the least, Guhila inscriptional records and the *Ekaliṅgamāhātmyam* make excellent sources for a study of the ideological apparatus of the state of Mewar. However, the latter incorporates both royal and popular perceptions. The Purāṇic section of the *Ekaliṅgamāhātmyam* seems to have been composed after the fifteenth century.

Having introduced the scope of the present study, limitations of current historiography and the sources to be utilized, I now proceed to a discussion of the physical features of Mewar in terms of its sub-regions, routes of communication, mineral wealth, etc. An attempt is also made to reconstruct the cultural profile of Mewar in the early historic period. This chapter concludes with a study of the beginnings of the process of regional state formation and the emergence of Guhila states in the localities of Nāgdā-Āhaḍa and Kiṣkindhā between the seventh and tenth centuries.

The second chapter deals with the process of regional state formation in Mewar that intensified between the tenth and thirteenth centuries. The Guhila state graduated from a local state to a sub-regional state of Mewar hills by the tenth century. The sub-regional state finally developed into a regional state through processes of territorial and political integration. Hence, the chapter enquires into the mechanisms of territorial and political integration including royal patronage of a regional cult that facilitated cultural integration.

The third chapter explores the political structure of the state of Mewar (thirteenth to fifteenth centuries): the position of the Guhila kinsmen *vis-à-vis* the Guhila king, incorporation of new social groups such as Jains, a new set of Rajput chiefs as the Hāḍās of eastern Mewar, and the tribal population, particularly the Bhil chiefs of the Nāgdā-Āhaḍa belt into the political and administrative structure. It also enquires into the problems of defence faced by the state of Mewar and hence the social mechanisms (including matrimonial relations) through which the state created allies in its immediate neighbourhood.

The fourth chapter enquires into the qualitative changes in the administration and military apparatus of Mewar in terms of growing administrative and military problems between the thirteenth and fifteenth centuries. The chain of fortresses controlled in the fifteenth century not only secured strategic routes for Mewar but also diverted resources to the Guhila state.

The fifth chapter makes a survey of the ideological apparatus of the state of Mewar. In other words, it explores the sources of legitimization of royal power: from religious land grants to the brāhmaṇas to the royal patronage of a regional cult, *Ekaliṅga* as well as the importance of the cult of goddess in Mewar. It also attempts to analyse the origin myths of the Guhila royal family and their territorial connotations.

The sixth chapter makes an attempt at situating the image of the Guhila royal family as well as recognition of the Guhilas as sovereigns of Mewar in the perspective of the locally, important social groups such as Jains, the Ṭāmṭarāḍa family from Chiravā (near Ekaliṅgajī-Nāgdā) and popular perceptions till the nineteenth century. However, the study begins with the royal perception of the state of Mewar and the attempts of its rulers at identifying themselves with the sovereignty of Mewar. The final chapter concludes the investigation with the essential findings of my study.

VII

An introduction to the geography of the region of Mewar will provide an initial understanding of the evolution of early settlements in the area.[82] Such an understanding is indispensible for the study of the processes of state formation in the region. Geographical variations within Mewar suggest differentiation in space. In other words, even within this given region, we can differentiate several sub-regions, with their own nuclei of core areas and peripheries. It is with such a perspective of differentiated space that it is possible to highlight effectively the integrative role of a royal family in transforming a local power into a regional power. The model of centre and periphery applied to analyse the contemporary political structure can thus have a historical utility.[83]

The 'non-state organized' target area has a limited capacity to maintain an appropriate infrastructure with economic and political modification of its institutional environment caused by the expanding state.[84] A state successfully does so by draining resources from the periphery into the centre by keeping the former in a continual condition of ecological instability and political dependence.[85] When the process picks up momentum, it inevitably leads to territorial conquests and economic and political subordination of formerly independent societies. Thus, a state grows and expands generally by incorporation, rather than replacement of populations, regardless of their cultural background. Such a process had indeed been at work in the state formation of Mewar as it incorporated the tribal groups of the peripheral zones.

The mountainous chains of the Aravallis diagonally divide the present state of Rajasthan into north-western and south-eastern division. Mewar lies in the south-eastern division of Rajasthan. The geographical sub-regions of Mewar hills and upper Banas plain comprise the territory popularly known as 'Mewar'.[86] It consists of the modern districts of Udaipur, recently carved out Rajasamand, Chittaurgarh and Bhilwara. Towards the south of Mewar hills lies the region of Vagod (districts of Dungarpur and Banswara in middle Mahi basin).

The major route of communication during the early medieval period ran from Delhi-Agra to Malwa and Champaner-Dohad in Gujarat, via Udaipur in Mewar.[87] This route included both main and link routes. A second link route to Gujarat passed from Chittaurgarh-Udaipur through Dungarpur to Idar (north-east Gujarat) and finally to Ahmedabad. A third link route almost ran parallel from Ajmer through Khamnor and Gogunda in Udaipur district to Idar and then Ahmedabad.[88] This route in turn was again parallel to the more frequented route running from Jodhpur to Ahmedabad via Sirohi, Abugarh, Sidhpur, and Mehsana.[89] Thus the prosperous sea ports of Gujarat could easily be approached through Mewar. On the other hand, Malwa could be approached both from Banswara and Chittaurgarh.

Before we discuss the physical features of Mewar, we shall highlight it links with the other major regions in terms of cattle tracts and animal husbandry, and minerals. On the north-western part of the Aravallis are reared Rajasthan's best cattle, sheep, goats and camels.[90] Camel rearing is a monopoly of this part of Rajasthan. The cattle tract of Great Hariyana breed runs from Bikaner via Churu, Sikar, Jaipur, Ajmer, Pali and Udaipur to Chittaurgarh.[91]

Today, the south-eastern division to which Mewar belongs contains two-thirds of the population of Rajasthan because of its congenial climate, rainfall, vegetation and considerable number of rivers and their tributaries. It is, therefore, quite obvious that the region of Mewar must have had a dependency on the north-western division of Rajasthan for dairy provisions, draught animals and above all for the Mallani horses.[92] Cattle fairs are a common feature in the Tharparkar tract. From Mewar, following the Tharparkar tract through the Gogunda pass-Abugarh-Jalor section one can reach the cattle fairs in Barmer.

A brief note on the mineral resources of Rajasthan not only highlights her general wealth but also potentialities of her different regions. Iron ores are concentrated in the north-eastern and south-eastern parts of this state. Udaipur district leads in lead and zinc concentrates. The Zawar mines, situated 40 km south-east of Udaipur, are famous for lead-zinc concentrates.[93] It is also important to note that silver traces might also occur in such deposits. The other places of lead-zinc concentrates in south-east are Rikhaldeo and Debari in Udaipur district, Ghughra and Mando in Dungarpur district, and Wardalia in Banswara district. In the north-east, Chanth-ki-Barwara in Sawai Madhopur district and Gudha Kisoridas in Alwar district are the two major fields of lead-zinc concentrates. Beryllium is found in districts of Udaipur, Jaipur, Tonk and Bhilwara. A rich copper belt is also found in Delwara-Kerovli and Dariba-Debari near Udaipur in Mewar.[94] Copper ore is found in scattered spots in Bhilwara, Churu and Jhalawar districts. Mica is scattered in Dungarpur, Bundi and Sikar, but the mica belt runs through Tonk and Jaipur districts in the north-east and Bhilwara and northern Udaipur districts in the south-west. Nearly all the emerald is confined to the northern part of Udaipur district in a narrow belt that stretches between Deogarh in the north to Kankroli (Udaipur district) in the south.[95]

The above survey suggests possibilities of a regular flow of trade between the north-western and south-eastern division of Rajasthan with Mewar constituting a major part of the latter, provided we assume that these resources were all utilized in our period. The distribution of shell bangles in Jodhpura, Rairh and Āhaḍa, sandstone sculptures in Nāgarī, rock crystal beads in Rairh, sandstone rubber stones in Āhaḍa, carnelian beads in Nāgarī and Rairh, etc., during the period between 1000 BC and 200 BC indicates that at least some local resources and routes were developed in the early historic period.[96]

Sub-regions of Mewar

(i) Mewar Hills

The Mewar hills (see Map 1) at present, cover the whole of Udaipur district except its two eastern tahsils (Mavali and Vallabhnagar), and the south-eastern margin of Pali district and parts of Gujarat state.[97] It touches the northern portions of middle Mahi basin, which is largely occupied by the Bhil and Gerasia tribes. Thus the southernmost portion of the Mewar hills is also likely to have had the potential of a nuclear area because of the Mahi. This sub-region is situated between the Banas plain and the Abu block: it is the most distinctive hill region covering 17,007 km.[98] The highest part of the region is called the Bhorat plateau (1,202 m). The rainfall is moderate (50-100 cm). Its south-eastern part contains dense forest and the south-western is densely covered with scrub jungle and grass, close-packed ridges and valleys ridden with boulder strewn river beds.[99] The sub-region has red and yellow soil in

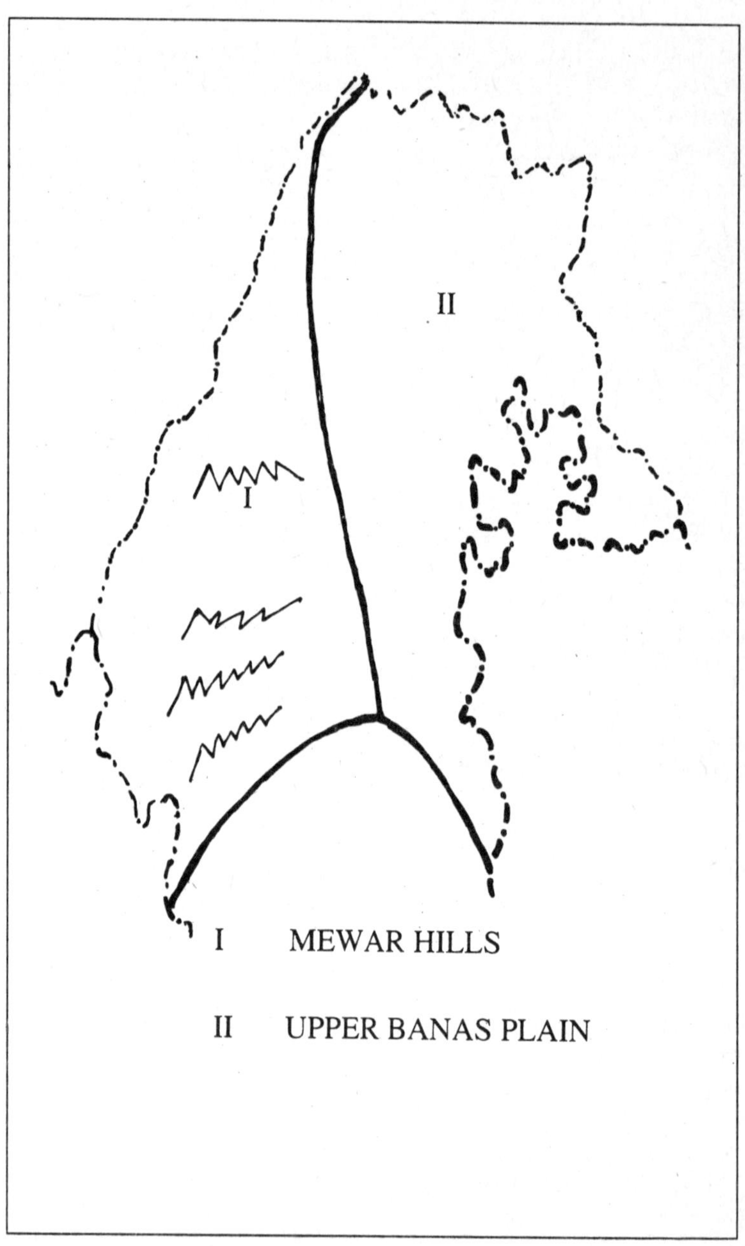

Map 1: Sub-regions of Mewar.

the north-west and ferruginous red soil in the southern parts.[100] It produces crops like maize, wheat, barley, gram and oilseeds. The agricultural activities are mainly confined to the valley of the Berach and its smaller tributaries. On the other hand, its western and southern hills are unable to sustain agricultural activities because of forests and an inhospitable terrain. Thus it is clear that it was the valley of the Berach which could have emerged as the nuclear area, while its south-western hills might be considered peripheries. The other feature which helped the Berach valley emerge as a nuclear area could be its rich mineral wealth mentioned above. The other significant feature of this sub-region was the concentration of tribal population on the Bhorat plateau and adjoining hills. Here lay the land predominantly of the Bhils. Even today, many of them practise shifting agriculture.[101] The Bhil-occupied territory of Mewar hills are popularly known as Bhomat. Bhomat is again divided by a massive mountain range into a south-western division known as the Kotra Bhomat and a part of the Merwara region is inhabited by the tribe of Mers (Medas).[102] Merwara is that portion of the Aravalli chain that runs between Kumbhalmer (Kumbhalgarh) and Ajmer.[103]

(ii) The Upper Banas Plain

The upper Banas plain comprises the three districts of Bhilwara, Chittaurgarh and Rajsamand and the two eastern tahsils of Udaipur district, Mavali and Vallabhnagar. It is an elevated plain drained by the Banas and its tributaries, the Khari, Kothari, Berach, Gambhiri and Wagan. The average annual rainfall is 85.21 cm.[104] The variety of soils range from thin and stony in the west to mixed red and black in the western and southern parts. Extensive cultivation of maize, wheat, cotton, sugar cane, etc., is the dominant feature of agricultural activities. Cotton is predominantly grown on the black soil belt of Bhilwara and Chittaurgarh districts. The agricultural potential may be gleaned from the present pattern of land use. While the northern and central parts of Mewar have high cropping incidence, the same for its western part (covering almost the whole of Udaipur district) is as low as 52 per cent or even less.[105]

VIII

Our area saw very early human activity, as is evidenced by a scatter of palaeolithic sites. As for early farming communities, they may have been established soon after 2500 BC in about 50 settlements, along the

Banas and Berach systems. These 'chalcolithic' sites show evidence of cereal agriculture and cattle keeping and also sometimes, skilled copper technology.[106]

Early historical period in Rajasthan is characterized by the rise of settlements with remains of brick structures, ornaments, terracotta figurines, etc. Coins and short inscriptions have also been excavated at Bairat, Rairh, Naliasar-Sambhar and Karkota-Nagara in eastern Rajasthan and Nāgarī in Mewar.[107]

The settlement at Nāgarī (17.6 km to the north of the present city of Chittaurgarh) became the first known political centre of ancient Mewar. Nāgarī was the capital town of the janapada of the Śibis. It is known from the Śibi coins with the legend, *Majhyamikāya Śibijanapadasya* that the town was called Madhyamikā. Discovery of punch-marked coins of the pre-Śibi period and coins with Prakrit legends at Nāgarī[108] suggest that ancient Nāgarī had already emerged as a nuclear centre in the southern upper Banas plain.[109] Discovery of a coin with the legend Mālava at Nāgarī may point to commercial contacts with the Mālavan kingdom of Nāgara or Karkoṭā Nāgara (Jaipur region).[110] The presence of the cult of Śaṅkaraṣaṇa-Vāsudeva in early historic Mewar is evident from the Hāthī-bāḍā inscription (first quarter of first century BC).[111]

The geo-political centre of ancient Mewar gradually shifted from ancient Nāgarī to the present site of Chittaurgarh. The site of Chittaurgarh was favoured because of its advantageous location on a hill top, commanding a major route of communication passing below the hills.

The new political status of Chittaurgarh in the sixth century AD is borne out by the grants of a *rājasthānīya* (governor or a government official) made at a temple of Manorathasvāmī.[112] The fact that Chittaurgarh had already emerged as an important centre in the upper Banas plain is further attested by inscriptional reference to a family of merchants moving into Chittaurgarh. The family is described as *vaṇijam śreṣtho* (best among merchants).[113] It suggests traffic from neighbouring Mandasaur to the ancient region of Madhyamikā.

Nandsa-yupa Inscriptions of AD 226 from Nandsa (Sahara tahsil) in Bhilwara district indicate the emergence of another centre in the northern upper Banas plain.[114] Another important area of settlement was Chhoti-Sadri, situated in the southern part of Chittaurgarh district bordering Mandasaur. The Bhawarmātā inscription and an epigraphical record, both dated round the end of fifth century, point towards Chhoti-Sadri and its surrounding localities in the south-eastern parts of the upper

Banas plain as areas under the control of the kings (e.g. Mahārāja Gauri) of the Māṇavāyaṇi family.[115]

We do not have any evidence to suggest the existence of settlements in the Vagod region on the scale of the Mewar hills during the early historic period. We can possibly suggest, on account of the discovery of a big hoard of Śaka-Kṣatrapa coins in Banswara district that Vagod during this period served as a transit point on the trade route between Mewar and western India.[116]

The above discussion briefly sketched the topography of Mewar on the eve of the rise of Guhila ruling families in the early medieval period. Although a number of terracotta plaques and a Śaiva temple at Nāgarī have been claimed as pieces of Gupta art, it is important to note that the political history of the region of Mewar begins only with the Guhilas.[117] There is no evidence to suggest that Mewar was included in the Gupta states prior to seventh century. It is evident that Mewar was yet to experience state formation on a significant scale at the local level. It is against this largely obscure cultural map of early historical Mewar that I will discuss the processes and stages of state formation in Mewar during the early medieval period. The disparate cultures in various nuclear and peripheral zones in Mewar had to be integrated to effectively forge it into a territorial state. This process can be traced with the advent of the Guhilas, who later came to be regarded as one of the major clans of the Rajputs, on the historical scene of Mewar.

IX

The Guhilas between the Seventh and the Tenth Centuries

Evidence of the beginnings of state formation at a local level in Mewar can be traced to the seventh century. Two centres of Guhila royal families at Nāgdā-Āhaḍa and Kiṣkindhā in the Mewar hills, and a small Guhila chief at Dhavagartā (Dhor in Jahazpur tahsil, Bhilwaṛa district) in the upper Banas plain under the suzerainty of the Morīs (later Mauryas of eastern Rajasthan and western Uttar Pradesh) of Chittaurgarh appear on the map of seventh century Mewar (see Map 2).[118] We identify this royal family as the Guhilas of Nāgdā-Āhaḍa not on the basis of their initial or later capital towns but on the basis of the area under their control in the seventh century. Nāgdā is only 22 km north of Āhaḍa

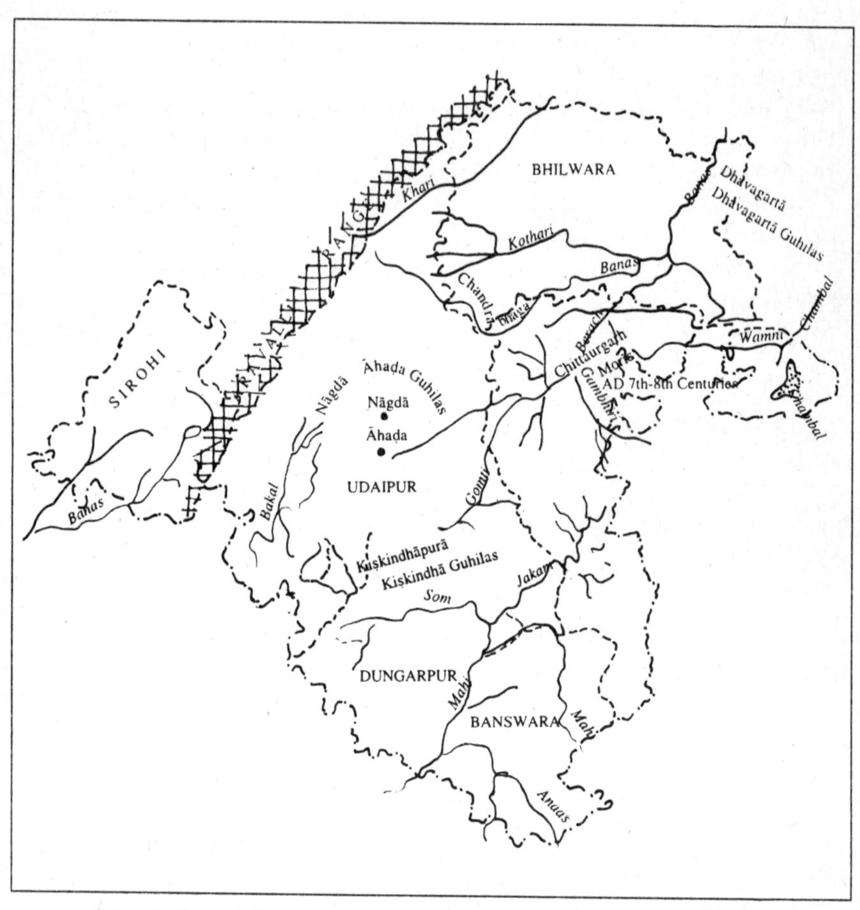

Map 2: Local Guhila States and Guhila Chiefs Inscriptionally Located in Mewar: AD Seventh Century.

(modern Udaipur). It is beyond doubt that this family based at Nāgdā must have controlled a territory that lay 22 km south of their seat of power during this period.[119]

These Guhila chiefs began their career in the Nāgdā-Āhaḍa belt of the western Berach valley in Udaipur district.[120] In the seventh century, Guhila power was confined to this belt. The Guhilas of Kiṣkindhā based themselves in the southern portion of the Mewar hills touching Bagar (tribal pocket of the Bhils) locality in the middle Mahi basin (northern part of Dungarpur district).[121] Kiṣkindhā is identified with present Kalyanpur in southern Udaipur district, bordering Dungarpur.

Guhila acknowledgement of the Morī sovereigns is evident from the subordinate titles of the Kiṣkindhā Guhilas, such as *vāpt-aśeṣa-mahāśabdah*,[122] *samadhigata-pañc-mahāśabdah*,[123] *samupārjjita-pañc-mahāśabdah*,[124] etc. It is also reflected that Dhavagartā Guhila chief Dhanika's reference to his overlord as *paramabhaṭṭāraka mahārājā-dhirāja parameśvara śrī dhavalappadevapravardhamānarājye*[125] as well as in the title of *rāval* for the legendary Bāppā Rāval (ancestor of the Nāgdā-Āhaḍa Guhila family). Their limited territorial control is obvious not only from the proximity of the Morīs of Chittaurgarh but more importantly from their simple claims to social status. If a small Guhila chief of Dhavagartā referred to himself merely as *guhilaputrāṇām śrī dhanika*,[126] Guhila kings of Kiṣkindhā and Nāgdā-Āhaḍa introduced themselves simply as *guhilaputtrānavaye*,[127] *guhilanarādhipavaṁśe*,[128] and *guhilānvaya*.[129] However, Guhila acknowledgement of Morī sovereignty did not minimize the Guhila predominance in the seventh-century Mewar. There is no evidence in the records to prove that the Morīs settled these Guhila rulers in these three different nuclear centres. On the contrary, there is Morī acknowledgement of Mewar as the domain of the Guhilas. The fact is evident from the following expression in the Dabok inscription: '*guhilaputrāṇām śrī(dh)anikasyopabhu(jya)mānāyām (dha)-vagartāyām*'.[130] This literally means that the village of Dhavagartā lay in the domain (or in the enjoyment) of Guhilaputra Śrī Dhanika. The family was not settled by the Morī sovereign through the system of land grants. Therefore, the term *bhujyamāna* indicates that the Morīs formally recognized the Guhilas as the most prominent political element in the locality of Dhavagartā.

The emphasis upon *guhilaputra*, *guhilānvaya*, *guhilanarādhipavaṁśe*, etc., made both by the Kiṣkindhā and Nāgdā-Āhaḍa Guhilas also indicates an attempt to highlight their lineage (in the sense of *vaṁśa*) identity. Hence, the Mewar hills had emerged as the domain of the Guhila royal families and their kinsmen.

The creation of lineage domain and mobilization of lineage power in areas of pre-state polity (absence of local states) such as the Mewar hills of the pre-seventh century period evidently involved change of the economic pattern of the region by expansive lineages. In this case, the emergence of 'ruling lineages' (royal families originating from different *vaṁśas*), would correspond to 'primary state formation' and introduction of monarchical rule.[131] Evidences have been cited from early medieval north Rajasthan, Gujarat, south India and the Deccan in which close relationships between lineage and territory were expressed through territorial names, e.g. Gurjarabhūmi, Gurjaratrā, Gurjaradharitrī and Gurjaradharā for the Gurjaras in north Rajasthan and Gujarat, Cola-nāḍu, Cera-nāḍu, Toṇḍai-nāḍu, Gaṅga-pāḍi, Nolamba-pāḍi, etc., for the south and the Deccan. Undoubtedly, such lineages originated from agrarian bases.[132]

Richard G. Fox in his discussion on the formation of a lineage, views the lineage ancestors as agricultural entrepreneurs.[133] Marc Bloch traces the origin of some of the seigniorial families in medieval Europe to a similar process. 'The ancestors of others, perhaps, were among those rich peasants of whose transformation into landlords, each with group of tenements, we catch a glimpse in certain documents of the tenth century.'[134] Thus, formation of lineage domains entailed a process of transformation of the rich peasants of a particular lineage into landlords. The ultimate success in the growth of these landlords would manifest itself in their assumption of political or royal power.[135] In other words, it is the assumption of 'kingship' which would distinguish these lineage heads from the rest of society. Once a family of the dominant lineage transformed itself into a royal house in its domain, the process of state formation began at the local level.

Neither contemporary nor succeeding Guhila sources speak of matrimonial relations between the three Guhila ruling families. Lineage exogamy suggests possible ancestral connections, however remote, between these Guhila families. But the process of the political rise of the Guhila lineages and the formation of Guhila royal houses was uneven, leaving its mark on the phenomenon of state formation.

The beginning of the process of state formation at a local level in Mewar is amply borne out by a prosperous agrarian base of the local Guhila states in the seventh century including settlements in the tribal belt. It is also corroborated by the evidence of political incorporation of the local chiefs through a system of ranking and distribution of roles and services, and through royal patronage of local sects and cults. The agrarian base of the Dhavagartā Guhila is evident by the Guhila grant of *śāradyagraiṣmkakṣetram* (fields that can be tilled in autumn as well as in summer).[136] The boundaries of the donated plots touched the fields of many other individuals, indicating the presence of many more well-cultivated fields in the village.[137] What is most significant are the references to the *araghaṭṭa* (or Persian wheel).[138]

These irrigational works were owned both by individuals and by the royal family. Just like *vāhiyālīnām araghaṭṭakṣetram* (field irrigated by *araghaṭṭa* named *vāhiyālī*), reference is also made to *rājakīya araghaṭṭa kullyā* (*araghaṭṭa* owned by the royal house).[139] These references are indicative of royal and individual initiative in expanding agricultural fields, within the spatial limits of the village. Such initiatives point to conscious attempts to strengthen the resource base of the locality.[140]

In addition, the emergence of Dhavagartā as an exchange centre by the seventh century is evident from the grant of two shops situated in the marketplace, as well as some coins.[141] Proximity to Chittaurgarh, lying on the major trade route to Malwa and Gujarat, must have also contributed to the development of exchange networks at Dhavagartā. The cults of Śiva and Durgā, the latter representing a local goddess, Ghaṭṭavāsinī, appear to have been patronized in Dhavagartā (*ghaṭṭavāsinī nāmaśrīdurggādevyā* . . .) by the local chiefs.[142]

The most significant aspect of the economic process of state formation in the Guhila state of Nāgdā-Āhaḍa is perhaps the foundation of new settlements in the peripheral areas. The Samoli inscription of the Guhila King Śilāditya (AD 646) records the opening of a mine at a place called Araṇyakūpagiri by a migrating community (mahājanas), headed by Mahattara Jentaka.[143] It also records the building of a temple (devakula) of goddess Araṇyavāsinī by Mahattara Jentaka at the command of the community (mahājanas).[144] Both the terms Araṇyakūpagiri and Araṇyavāsinī indicate hilly and forested terrain. In the context of Mewar, hills and forest are the abode of the Bhils. The building of the temple of Araṇyavāsinī (goddess who dwells in the forest) also proves that this settlement was created in the country of the 'forest dwellers' (Bhils in case of the Mewar hills). Although very close, Bhil territory was still peripheral to the core of the Nāgdā-Āhaḍa state. The entire operation indicates the creation of a workshop-cum-manufacturing centre either in the copper belt around Āhaḍa or at zinc-lead-silver concentrates at Zawar (south of Udaipur). It is important to note that Zawar mines came back into operation in the seventh century, precisely the period of the beginnings of local state formation in Mewar.[145] Such settlements seem to have mobilized both raw materials as well as manufactured items for the nearest nodes, Nāgdā or Āhaḍa or both. Araṇyakūpgiri itself seems to have emerged as an exchange centre during the period, for, the temple of Araṇyavāsinī is stated to have been thronged with wealthy people.[146]

The foundation and operation of a mine which became the source of livelihood to many people[147] presumes the creation of an agricultural pocket at Araṇyakūpagiri necessitating some degree of deforestation. The very process of deforestation and agricultural activities changed the nature of tribal settlements in the core-area (Nāgdā-Āhaḍa belt is surrounded by Bhil settlements in its north-western, south-western and southern sides) of the Nāgdā-Āhaḍa principality. The territorial expansion of what came to be known as Rajput power was achieved, at least in certain areas, at the expense of the erstwhile tribal settlements.[148] Hermann Kulke also points out in his study of Orissa that the *rājās* (kings) needed tribal land for the gradual extension of peasant agriculture, which alone could yield sufficient crops for the maintenance of the court.[149] Thus began the gradual process of transformation of few of the core-area Bhils (Bhils close to Nāgdā-Āhaḍa locality) from hunter-gatherers to agriculturists in these tribal pockets. A part of the core-area Bhils might have been mobilized as miners. This is evident from the discovery of charcoal retort dumps (smelting) at Zawar. Charcoal preparation has been one of the major economic pursuits of the majority of the Bhils engaged in non-agricultural activities.[150]

Local Bhils were indispensable also for communications through Mewar hills. Hills and forests restrict the capacity of governments to move men and goods through their territories.[151] The Bhils of the core area, once integrated, could be expected to facilitate communications throughout the Bhil country because they guarded the forests, caves, passes and hill routes. Such popular names of the Bhils as Vanaputras (the children of the forest), Māirote (born of mountain), Goind (land the caves) and Pāl Indra (lord of the pass) indicate this.[152] A vast corpus of bardic literature from Mewar associates the Guhilas with the Bhils in the days of Guhila (Guha or Guhadatta), the founder of the Guhila dynasty of Mewar.[153] Baleo and Dewa, Bhil chiefs of Oghna Panarwa and Undri respectively, are traditionally known to have put the *ṭīkā* of sovereignty (with the blood of Baleo's thumb) on the forehead of Bāppā Rāval. Since then the Bhil chiefs have been putting *ṭīkā* of sovereignty on the forehead of each of the succeeding Guhila kings.[154] The annals affiliate Guhadatta to the Bhils of Gujarat (Idar in north-east Gujarat). The Bhils are known to have selected Guhadatta their leader with a *ṭīkā* of sovereignty. Guhadatta is stated to have subsequently killed his benefactor, the Bhil chief Māṇḍalika, and seized all power.[155] The legend signifies the military conquest of the Bhils by the Guhilas. It indicates that the transfer of power was not smooth.

The political process of incorporation of chiefs in the Nāgdā-Āhaḍa kingdom is amply corroborated by the title of *mahārājā* for the Guhila Commander-in-Chief Varāhasiṁha. His father Śiva did not bear any political title.[156] The case of Varāhasiṁha clearly shows that he was inducted into the military apparatus and conferred the title of *mahārājā*. That the process of political incorporation was gradual is evident from absence of any title for Śiva, Varāhasiṁha's father. Here is an instance of incorporation into *sāmanta* circle and also being given the role of a military commander. Secondly, upward mobility of Varāhasiṁha clearly indicates the processes of incorporation of chiefs through a system of ranking as well as distribution of roles and services. Thirdly, there is no evidence to disprove that Varāhasiṁha was a local chief. Hence, Varāhasiṁha was a local chief who neither received any land grant from the Guhilas nor was brought from outside through land grants. Since the lineage identity of Varāhasiṁha is not revealed, it is difficult to ascertain his actual family identity. However, in the initial stage of the emergence of local monarchy, kinsmen of the Guhila royal family are likely to have been integrated and accommodated in the military apparatus of the local Guhila state. Our suggestion is further buttressed by later evidences of the Guhilas of Nāgdā-Āhaḍa referring to the non-Guhila Rajput families for the first time in the tenth century. The way Guhilānvaya (the lineage of the Guhila) is eulogized in Varāhasiṁha's record, this evidence possibly indicates that the Commander-in-Chief Varāhasiṁha, belonged to a family of the Guhila lineage.

The agrarian base of the Guhila kingdom of Kiṣkindhā is amply corroborated by the extent of royal land grants. Villages like Mitrāpallikā had well cultivated plots belonging to different individuals.[157] The fact that plots were well assessed is evident from the mention of specific yields of grains; *pañcikāparimāṇa* (five standard measures of land) from the donated plots.[158] The number of villages within the territory of Kiṣkindhā was not insignificant if one considers the boundaries of the granted plots. As in the case of Dhavagartā, the plots in the charters of Bābhaṭa touched smaller hamlets like Śakapālī indicating the gradual spread of the rural settlements. The presence of *gamāgamikas* (messengers for villages?) and mention of the *uparikara*[159] (tax on the temporary tenants) also suggests the existence of considerable number of villages. The initiative to sustain and expand agricultural yields within the spatial limits of these villages can be seen in the irrigation works owned by individuals attached to these fields. The main methods of irrigation seem to have been wells, tanks and similar other reservoirs (*kūpakaccho*, *pāniy-opāvarttaḥ* and *pāhaka taḍāgikā*).[160]

While trying to consolidate their power, the Guhilas of Kiṣkindhā were in the process of integrating the chiefs of this locality. Incorporation of chiefs into the administrative apparatus is evident from the Dungarpur plates of Bhāvihita. These are addressed to the following classes of subordinate chiefs and functionaries: *rājan* (subordinate king), *rājaputra* (son of a *rājan*), *rājasthānīya* (viceroy), *pratihāra* (guard of the palace or capital), *pramātṛ* (officer-in-charge of measuring the king's share of the grains), *balādhikṛta* (commander of forces), *caudroddharaṇika* (police magistrate dealing with cases of theft), *daṇḍapāśika* (head of a group of policemen), *śaulkika* (collector of customs duties), *prātisāraka* (gate-keeper and collector of tolls), *gamāgamika* (messenger), *cāṭa* (chief of group of paiks), *bhaṭa* (paik), and *sevaka* (attendant).[161] Dūtaka (messenger) of Dhulev plates of King Bhetti is Sāmanta Bhāvihita.[162] Besides functionaries, the chiefs in the Kiṣkindhā grants such as the '*nṛpa*', '*nṛpasuta*', '*rājan*', and '*rājasthāniya*', point towards incorporation of some local chiefs into a *sāmanta* circle (through distribution of ranks), and rest of them in the administrative hierarchy. One may assume that the chiefs addressed in the land-grant charters were of local origin, for, these land charters do not specify the chiefs by their place of origin or as land donees. Hence, the set of local Rajput chiefs seems to have consisted both of Guhila (royal kinsmen) and non-Guhila lineages.

The Guhila kings were addressing the entire circle of local *sāmantas* including administrative functionaries at the time of making land grants. Two important functions were being performed by the series of land-grants made by the Kiṣkindhā Guhilas. Firstly, the Guhila kings of Kiṣkindhā introduced themselves as the sovereigns of Kiṣkindhā to the various sections of rural population including chiefs and local notables. The royal standards and dues were going to be fixed by the Guhila kings of Kiṣkindhā. Secondly, the long list of addresses indicate the Guhila kings desired, and were in the process of, incorporating the chiefs. The point is further proved by one of the land grant charters of the Guhilas of Kiṣkindhā which refers to the permission taken from a local *sāmanta* (Sāmanta Bhartṛvaḍḍa) before the Guhila king donated land in a locality called *tambulikaniveśa.*[163] It is natural that the Guhila kings acknowledged the chiefs of the locality of Kiṣkindhā by their royal titles such as *nṛpa* and *rājan* in the initial stage of state formation. It is equally important to mention that the Guhila kings of Kiṣkindhā distinguished themselves at this stage, just like the Guhilas of Nāgdā-Āhaḍa and Dhavagartā, by referring to themselves as members in the royal lineage of Guhila—'Guhilanarādhipavaṁśe'[164] and not simply as *nṛpa* or *narādhipa*. When the Guhila kings of Kiṣkindhā addressed locally important chiefs as '*nṛpa*' during the process of political incorporation, distinction for the royal dynasty was sought through the title of '*guhilanarādhipavaṁśe*'.

The beginnings of royal patronage of local Śaiva *ācāryas*, through the construction of temples of Śiva and grants for their maintenance in the Guhila kingdom of Kiṣkindhā, can be traced back to this early phase of state formation. In the eighth century, King Kadachi's Queen Voṇṇā, at the instance of her preceptor, Kuṭukkācārya, made a grant of 40 *dramma* coins to a temple of Śiva.[165]

Finally, one more important factor that contributed towards the making of these local states in Mewar seems to have been warfare.[166]

I need not go into the physical descriptions of warfare in the seventh-century records of Mewar to suggest that military operations also contributed to the process of territorial incorporation at the local levels. As noted, the Nāgdā-Āhaḍa state had a military apparatus headed by Commander-in-Chief Varāhasiṁha. It is equally significant that Balādhikṛta (commander of forces) repeatedly figures in all the charters of the Guhilas of Kiṣkindhā. Samoli inscription refers to the strength of Guhila king Śilāditya of Nāgdā-Āhaḍa against his enemies.[167] It may be important to point out that much later in the tenth century when a sub-regional state in Mewar under the Guhilas of Nāgdā-Āhaḍa was trying to establish itself, there are very few actual inscriptional references to battles being fought between the Guhilas and their opponents.

The above section surveyed the spatial distribution of the Guhila royal families on the map of early medieval Mewar, between seventh and tenth centuries. Three centres of Guhila power were located within Mewar. All these ruling families claimed descent from Guhila. It is obvious that by the seventh century the lineage of Guhila had acquired a prestigious status in western India. A number of ruling families even outside Mewar, in other parts of Rajasthan, started claiming descent from the Guhila. Secondly, evidence from Kiṣkindhā and Nāgdā-Āhaḍa point to the beginnings of the political process of state formation, and integration of local chiefs into the emerging political structure. Thirdly, there is distinct evidence of increased agricultural activities as a foundation for these developments; at the same time, trade and commerce also appear to be getting more organized. Besides the Guhila ruling families, local notables and individual landholders characterized the rural society in Mewar in this period. Finally, the ideological dimension of state also appeared for the first time in the seventh century. The use of symbols of royalty such as titles of *mahārājā* and *narādhipa*, and *praśastis* of the Guhila rulers testify to the formation of local states. The other important facet of ideological dimension, royal patronage of popular cults, also started in this period.

NOTES

1. R. Cohen and E.R. Service, eds., *Origins of the State: The Anthropology of Political Evolution*, Philadelphia, 1978, p. 6.
2. Ibid., p. 7.
3. Henri J.M. Claessen and Peter Skalnik, eds., *The Early State*, The Hague, 1978, pp. 22-3.
4. Ibid., pt. III, 'Synthesis', p. 589. Also see Lawrence Krader, 'The State in History', *Studies in History*, vol. IV, no. 2, 1982, pp. 167-80. Krader also looks at state as an expression of antagonistic relations between classes in a period when public and private spheres of economy became distinct and production relations came to be characterized by wage labour.
5. *The Study of the State*, The Hague, 1981.
6. Ibid., pp. 409-26.
7. Ibid., pp. 414-15. For a further discussion of the theme, also see, H.J.M. Claessen and P. Van de Velde, eds., *Early State Dynamics*, Leiden, 1987.
8. Romila Thapar, 'State Formation in Early India', in *International Social Science Journal*, vol. XXXII, no. 4, 1980, p. 666.
9. Ibid., p. 668.
10. Romila Thapar, *From Lineage to State: Social Formations in the Mid-First Millennium* B.C. *in the Gaṅgā Valley*, Bombay, 1984.
11. Ibid., pp. 115-18.
12. Romila Thapar, *Exile and the Kingdom: Some Thoughts on the Rāmāyaṇa*, Bangalore, 1978, pp. 17-18. 'Saptāṅga' theory of state in Kauṭilya's *Arthaśāstra* lists king at the top of the seven essential limbs of a state besides *amātya*, *janapada*, *durga*, *kośa*, *daṇḍa* and *mitra*. See R. Shamasastry, ed., *Arthaśāstra of Kauṭilya*, 3rd edn., Mysore, 1924, Ch. IV.1.
13. Kumkum Roy, *The Emergence of Monarchy in North India: Eighth-Fourth*

Centuries B.C. as Reflected in the Brāhmaṇical Tradition, Delhi, 1995, pp. 103-302.

14. R.S. Sharma, *Material Culture and Social Formations in Ancient India*, Delhi, 1983.
15. Idem, 'Taxation and State Formation in Northern India in Pre-Maurya Times', in his *Aspects of Political Ideas and Institutions in Ancient India* (3rd rev. edn.), Delhi, 1991, p. 219; idem, 'From Gopati to Bhūpati', ibid., pp. 185-95.
16. S. Seneviratne, 'Kaliṅga and Andhra: The Process of Secondary State Formation in Early India', in H.J.M. Claessen and Peter Skalnik, eds., *The Study of the State*, op. cit., pp. 317-38.
17. Vincent Smith, *Early History of India: From 660 B.C. to the Muhammadan Conquest*, 1906; also see, idem, *Oxford History of India*, 1919.
18. K.A.N. Shastri, *Colas*, rpt. of 2nd edn., Madras, 1975; R.C. Majumdar, H.C. Raychaudhuri and K.K. Datta, in *An Advanced History of India*, Calcutta, 1961; R.C. Majumdar, *The Age of Imperial Unity*, Bharatiya Vidya Bhavan Series, Bombay, 1960; R.C. Majumdar, *Caulukyas of Gujarat: A Survey of the History and Culture of Gujarat from the Middle of the Tenth to the end of the Thirteenth Century*, Bombay, 1956; H.C. Raychaudhuri, *Political History of Ancient India*, 6th edn., Calcutta, 1953.
19. D.D. Kosambi, 'Origins of Feudalism in Kashmir', *Journal of the Bombay Branch of the RAS*, Commemoration Volume, 1956-7, pp. 108-20; idem, 'On the Development of Feudalism in India', *Annals of the Bhandarkar Oriental Research Institute*, vol. XXXVI, pp. 258-69; idem, *An Introduction to the Study of Indian History*, Bombay, 1956; Daniel Thorner, 'Feudalism in India', in R. Coulborn, ed., *Feudalism in History*, Princeton, 1956, pp. 133-50; R.S. Sharma, *Indian Feudalism c. 300-1200*, Calcutta, 1965; idem, 'Problem of Transition from Ancient to Medieval Indian History', *IHR*, vol. I, no. 1, March 1974, pp. 1-9; idem, 'Methods and Problems of the Study of Feudalism in Early Medieval India', in ibid., pp. 81-4; S.K. Maity, *Economic Life of Northern India in the Gupta Period (c. AD 330-550)*, 1st edn., Delhi, 1966; B.N.S. Yadava, *Society and Culture in Northern India in A.D. 12th Century*, Allahabad, 1973; idem, 'Immobility and Subjection of Indian Peasantry in Early Medieval Complex', *IHR*, vol. I, no. 1, 1974, pp. 31-63; R.S. Sharma, 'The Segmentary State and the Indian Experience', *IHR*, vol. XVI, nos. 1-2, 1989-91, pp. 90-2; Kesavan Veluthat in his work, *The Political Structure of Early Medieval South India*, Delhi, 1993, develops the idea of 'south Indian feudalism'.
20. R.S. Sharma, *Indian Feudalism*.
21. Critiques of a few aspects of the concept of Indian feudalism have been substantially offered by D.C. Sircar, *Land System and Feudalism in Ancient India*, Calcutta, 1966, pp. 57-62; Harbans Mukhia, 'Was There Feudalism in Indian History?', Presidential Address to Medieval Indian Section, Indian History Congress, 40th Session, Waltair, 1979; Also see D.N. Jha, 'Early

Indian Feudalism: A Historiographical Critique', Presidential Address to Ancient Indian Section, Indian History Congress, 40th Session, Waltair, 1979.

22. Burton Stein, 'The Segmentary State in South Indian History', in R.G. Fox, ed., *Realm and Region in Traditional India*, New Delhi, 1977, pp. 3-51; idem, *Peasant State and Society in Medieval South India*, Delhi, 1980; Also see Kenneth R. Hall, *Trade and Statecraft in the Age of the Colas*, Delhi, 1980. For a very good critique of the concept of 'Segmentary State' on the Colas, see R. Champakalakshmi, 'Peasant State and Society in Medieval South India: A Review Article', *IESHR*, vol. XVIII, nos. 3 and 4, July-December 1981, pp. 411-26; D.N. Jha, 'Relevance of "Peasant State and Society" in Pallava-Cola times', *IHR*, vol. VIII, nos. 1-2, 1981-2, pp. 74-94. For a slightly revised version and the basics of the concept of Segmentary State, see Burton Stein, *The New Cambridge History of India: Vijayanagara*, vol. I, no. 2, Delhi, 1991.
23. Hermann Kulke, 'Fragmentation and Segmentation versus Integration? Reflections on the Concept of Indian Feudalism and the Segmentary State in Indian History', *Studies in History*, vol. 4, no. 2, 1982, pp. 237-63; idem, *Kings and Cults: State Formation and Legitimation in India and Southeast Asia*, Delhi, 1993, pp. 245; also see, idem, 'Royal Temple Policy and the Structure of Medieval Hindu Kingdoms', in A. Eschmann, H. Kulke and G.C. Tripathi, eds., *The Cult of Jagannath and the Regional Tradition of Orissa*, Delhi, 1978, pp. 125-38; idem, 'Early State Formation and Royal Legitimation in Tribal Areas of Eastern India', in R. Moser and M.K. Gautam, eds., *Aspects of Tribal Life in South Asia, I: Strategy and Survival*, Berne, 1978, pp. 29-38; idem, 'Legitimation and Town-planning in the Feudatory States of Central Orissa', in J. Peiper, ed., *Ritual Space in India: Studies in Architectural Anthropology*, London, 1980; idem, *The State in India: 1000-1700*, Delhi, 1995.
24. Hermann Kulke, 'Fragmentation and Segmentation versus Integration', p. 245.
25. *PIHC*, Burdwan, 1983; also see its reprint in B.D. Chattopadhyaya, *Making of Early Medieval India*, Delhi, 1994, pp. 219-20.
26. Ibid., p. 204.
27. Ibid., p. 215.
28. *Imagining India*, Delhi, 1990, p. 29.
29. Andre Wink, *Al-Hind: The Making of the Indo-Islamic World*, Leiden, 1990, p. 219. Also see Sunil Kumar's Review of *Al-Hind* in *Studies in History*, vol. X, no. 1, pp. 147-52; Vishwa Mohan Jha, 'The Artless Pirennian, Review of Wink's *Al-Hind*', in *IHR*, vol. XVIII, nos. 1-2, pp. 93-103.
30. A.B.M. Habibullah, *The Foundation of Muslim Rule in India*, 2nd edn., Allahabad, 1961; Mohammad Habib and Khaliq Ahmad Nizami, *The Delhi Sultanate (A.D. 1206-1526): A Comprehensive History of India*, vol. V,

Delhi, 1970; K.S. Lal, *History of the Khaljis A.D. 1290-1320*, 3rd edn., Delhi, 1980.
31. Khaliq Ahmad Nizami, *State and Culture in Medieval India*, Delhi, 1985.
32. U.N. Day, *The Government of the Sultanate*, 2nd edn., Delhi, 1993.
33. S.B.P. Nigam, *Nobility under the Sultans of Delhi, A.D. 1206-1398*, Delhi, 1968.
34 H.C. Verma, 'Aqta Praṇālī', in his *Madhyakālīn Bhārat*, vol. I, Delhi University Publication, 1989 edn., pp. 384-408.
35 Peter Jackson, 'The Mamluk Institution in Early Muslim India', in *JRAS*, 1990, pp. 340-58.
36 Peter Jackson, *Delhi Sultanate: A Political and Military History*, Cambridge Studies in Islamic Civilization, Cambridge, 1999.
37. U.N. Day, *Medieval Malwa: A Political and Cultural History,* AD *1401-1562*, 1st edn., Delhi, 1965.
38. E.C. Bayley, *The Local Muhammadan Dynasties: History of Gujarat*, Delhi, 1st Indian rpt., 1970.
39. S.C. Misra, *The Rise of Muslim Power in Gujarat: History of Gujarat from* AD *1298 to* AD *1442*, Bombay, 1963.
40. *The New Cambridge History of India: Vijayanagara.*
41. Richard M. Eaton, *The Rise of Islam and the Bengal Frontier, 1204-1760*, Berkeley-Los Angeles-London, 1993.
42. B.D. Chattopadhyaya, 'Political Processes and Structure of Polity in Early Medieval India', in his *Making of Early Medieval India*, p. 205.
43. Kulke, 'Fragmentation and Segmenation versus Integration', p. 258.
44. Ibid., p. 258.
45. Ibid.
46. Sisir Kumar Panda, *The State and Statecraft in Medieval Orissa under the Later Eastern Gaṅgas (A.D. 1038-1434)*, Calcutta, 1995, pp. 120-1.
47. James Heitzman, 'State Formation in South India, 850-1280', *IESHR*, vol. 24, no. 1, 1987, pp. 35-61.
48. B.P. Sahu, 'The State in Early India: An Overview', in *PIHC*, 55th Session, Aligarh (1994), Delhi, 1995, p. 91.
49. Surajit Sinha, 'State Formation and Rajput Myth in Tribal Central India', in Hermann Kulke, ed., *The State in India*, op. cit., p. 326.
50. R.V. Russel and Hira Lal, *The Castes and Tribes of the Central Provinces of India*, vol. III, London, 1916, pp. 44-7; Bishop Eybe Chatterton, *The Story of Gondwana*, London, 1916, p. 9.
51. Sinha, op. cit., pp. 327-8. Also see C.U. Wills, 'Territorial System of the Rajput Kingdoms of Medieval Chattisgarh', in *JRAS*, *Bengal*, vol. 15, 1919, pp. 257-8.
52. Sinha, op. cit., p. 328.
53. Sinha, op. cit, pp. 329-31.

54. Sinha, op. cit., p. 332.
55. Sinha, op. cit., pp. 306-22.
56. Sinha, op. cit., pp. 324-6.
57. K. Suresh Singh, 'Chhotanagpur Raj: Mythology, Structure and Ramifications', in Surajit Sinha, ed., *Tribal Politics and State Systems in Pre-Colonial Eastern and North-Eastern India*, Calcutta, 1987, pp. 51-72.
58. Hitesranjan Sanyal, 'Mallabhum', in Surajit Sinha, ed., *Tribal Politics*, pp. 73-142.
59. Amalendu Guha, 'The Ahom Political System: An Enquiry into State Formation in Medieval Assam: 1228-1800', in Surajit Sinha, ed., *Tribal Politics*, pp. 142-76.
60. J.B. Bhattacharjee, 'Dimasa State Formation in Cachar', in Surajit Sinha, ed., *Tribal Politics*, pp. 177-211.
61. C.V. Vaidya, *History of Hindu Medieval India*, vols. I-II, Pune, 1924, vol. I, pp. 70-2.
62. Col. James Tod, *Annals and Antiquities of Rajasthan*, vol. I, Delhi, 1971 (Preface by Douglas Sladen, rpt.), vol. I, pp. 48, 450, 471 (henceforth, *Annals*).
63. Relevant bibliographical references may be seen in the following standard works on the subject. Dasharath Sharma, *Early Chauhan Dynasties* (2nd rev. edn.), New Delhi, 1975; J.N. Asopa, *Origin of the Rajputs*, New Delhi, 1976.
64. Harbilas Sharda, *Mahārāṇā Kumbha* (henceforth Sharda, *MK*), Ajmer, 1922; idem, *Mahārāṇā Sāṅgā*, Ajmer, 1930; G.H. Ojha, ed., *Early History of Rajputana*, vol. I, 2nd edn., Ajmer, 1937; idem, *Udaipur Rājya kā Itihāsa* (henceforth *URI*), vols. I and II, Ajmer, 1930; idem, *Jodhpur Rājya kā Itihāsa*, Ajmer, 1938; idem, *Pratāpgarh Rājya kā Itihāsa*, Ajmer, 1940; *Dungarpur Rājya kā Itihāsa* (henceforth *DRI*), Ajmer, 1936; idem; *History of Banswara State*, Ajmer (1937); idem, *Bikaner Rājya kā Itihāsa* , Ajmer, 1939-40; H.C. Ray, *Dynastic History of Northern India*, vol. II, Calcutta, 1936; R.C. Majumdar, ed., *The Age of Imperial Kanauj*, Bharatiya Vidya Bhavan Series, Bombay, 1964, G.C. Raychaudhuri, *History of Mewar*, Calcutta, n.d.; Dasharath Sharma, *Early Chauhan Dynasties*; R.R. Halder, 'The Guhila Kings of Mewar', in *IA*, 1927, pp. 169ff.; G.C. Raychaudhuri, 'A Note on the Early Guhilas', in *Indian Culture*, vol. II, pp. 219-22.
65. *Annals*, pp. 107-71.
66. Dasharath Sharma, *Rajasthan Through the Ages*, Bikaner, 1966 (henceforth, *RTA*).
67. G.D. Sharma, *Rajput Polity*, New Delhi, 1977; idem, 'A note on the rise of the Guhilots in Chittor', in *PIHC*, vol. III, pp. 813-17.
68. Kaviraj Shyamaldas, *Vir Vinod*, vol. I, Delhi, 1986; G.H. Ojha, *Early History of Rajputana*; Ajmer, 1937; idem, *URI*, Ajmer, 1930; idem, *Pratapgarh Rājya kā Itihāsa*, Ajmer, 1940; idem, *History of the Banswara State*, Ajmer, 1937; idem, *Bikaner Rājya kā Itihāsa*, Ajmer, 1939-40; idem, *Dungarpur*

Rājya kā Itihāsa, Ajmer, 1936 (henceforth *BRI*); Sharda, *MK*, Ajmer, 1922; idem, *Mahārāṇā Sāṅgā*, Ajmer, 1930.

69. Rima Hooja, 'Contacts, Conflicts and Co-existence: Bhils and Non-Bhils in South-eastern Rajasthan', in Bridget Allchin, ed., *Living Traditions: Studies in the Ethnoarchaeology of South Asia*, Cambridge, 1995, pp. 125-42; see its critique by Shereen Ratnagar, *Book Review*, September 1995.
70. B.D. Chattopadhyaya, 'Origin of the Rajputs: Political, Economic and Social Processes in Early Medieval Rajasthan', in his *Making of Early Medieval India*, p. 59.
71. Āhaḍa or Āhar. See index, in *The Making of Early Medieval India*, p. 253.
72. Karine Schomer, Joan L. Erdman, Deryik O. Lodrick and Lloyd I. Rudolph, eds., *The Idea of Rajasthan: Explorations in Regional Identity*, vol. I, *Constructions* and vol. II, *Institutions*, Delhi, 1994.
73. Deryik O. Lodrick, 'Rajasthan: Myth or Reality', in *The Idea of Rajasthan*, vol. I, ibid., pp. 6-12.
74. Muhammad Habib (Eng. tran.), *Khazain-ul-Futuh*, Madras, 1931; H.M. Elliot and John Dowson, *History of India As Told by its Historians*, vol. III, Allahabad, 1973, pp. 67-92.
75. H.M. Elliot and John Dowson, vol. IV, ibid., pp. 218-87.
76. K.K. Basu, *Tarikh-i-Mubarak Shahi* (Eng. trans.), Baroda Oriental Institute, 1932.
77. J. Briggs, *Muhammad Qasim Ferishta's Tarikh-i-Ferishta*, in *Bibliothica Indica*, Calcutta, 1913.
78. Maj. A.R. Fuller, *Ziauddin Barani's Tarikh-i-Firuzshahi*, Extracts translated in English from *Bibliothica Indica*, Calcutta, 1862.
79. Agha Mahdi Hussain, *Rehla or Travels of Ibn Batuta* (Eng. trans.), Baroda, 1953.
80. H. Beveridge, *Akbar Nama of Abul Fazal*, Delhi, 1973.
81. *EI*, vol. XXIII, p. 237; *Vir Vinod*, vol. I, p. 424.
82. *RTA*, pp. 1-10, and K.C. Jain, *Ancient Cities and Towns of Rajasthan* (*A Study of Culture and Civilization*), Delhi, Varanasi, Patna, 1972, pp. 80-130. Unfortunately, studies on the historical geography of Mewar have so far been confined to its general features in the broader context of Rajasthan, and to a list of its urban centres.
83. T.C. Champion, ed., *Centre and Periphery—Comparative Studies in Archaeology*, London, 1989, p. 4.
84. Barbara J. Price, 'Secondary State Formation', in Cohen and Service, eds., *Origin of State—The Anthropology of Political Evolution*, Philadelphia, 1978, p. 183. In the context of state formation of Mewar, 'non-state organized' target area would relate to areas peripheral (occupied by the tribal population) to core (area of operation) of the local Guhila states.
85. J.F. Cherry, 'Power in Space: Archaeological and Geographical Studies of the State', in J.H. Wagstaff, ed., *Landscape and Culture: A Geographical and Archaeological Perspectives*, London, 1992, p. 160.

86. R.L. Singh, *India: A Regional Geography*, Varanasi-New Delhi, p. 557; See also Maj. K.D. Erskine, *Rajputana Gazetteers*, vol. II-A and vol. II-B, Mewar Residency, first published in 1908, reprinted in 1992, Gurgaon, p. 1. Mewar Residency was defined in the early nineteenth century (Col. James Tod was appointed the first Political Agent of Mewar Residency where he served from March 1818 to June 1822) as a state that was situated in the south of Rajputana. It was bounded on the north by Ajmer-Merwara and the Shahpura chiefship; on the west by Jodhpur and Sirohi; on the south-west by Idar; on the south by Dungarpur, Banswara and Partabgarh, on the east by Sindhia's district of Nimach, the Nimbahera district of Tonk, and Bundi and Kotah, on north-east, near the Cantonment of Deoli, by Jaipur.
87. V.K. Jain, *Trade and Traders in Western India: AD 1000-1300*, Delhi, 1990, p. 111 (map on important ports, towns and trade routes in western India). Henceforth, *Trade and Traders.*
88. R.K. Dhabai, 'Regional Structure of Mewar', M.Phil. Dissertation (unpublished), Centre for Studies in Regional Development, Jawaharlal Nehru University, 1975, see map on the link routes.
89. *Trade and Traders*, p. 111.
90. V.C. Misra, *Geography of Rajasthan*, Delhi, 1967, p. 92.
91. Ibid., p. 94.
92. Ibid., p. 3.
93. Ibid., pp. 110-11.
94. H.D. Sankalia, *Archaeology in Rajasthan*, Udaipur, 1988, p. 74.
95. Ibid., pp. 122-3.
96. Nayanjot Lahiri, *The Archaeology of Indian Trade Routes (up to c. 200 BC)*, Delhi, 1992, pp. 285-6.
97. Singh, op. cit., p. 557.
98. Ibid.
99. Morris Castairs, 'The Bhils of Kotra Bhomat', *The Eastern Anthropologist*, vol. VII (nos. 3-4), 1953-4, pp. 169-81.
100. Misra, op. cit., p. 173.
101. O.H. Spate, *India, Pakistan and Ceylon*, London, 1972, p. 621.
102. Morris Castairs, op. cit., p. 169.
103. Ibid., p. 181.
104. *Gazetteer of Chittaurgarh*, 1977, p. 15.
105. Dhabai, op. cit., p. 110. There are three main sources of irrigation in Mewar: wells, tanks and canals. Ninety-eight per cent of the gross irrigated area is covered by wells. Tank-irrigation is low but is important as rainfall is deficient. Canals dominate in tahsils of Salumbar, Bhilwara, Asind and Chittaurgarh.
106. Personal communication. Prof. Shereen Ratnagar, Centre for Historical Studies, Jawaharlal Nehru University.
107. *RTA*, p. 40.

108. A.C.L. Carllyle, ed., *Report of a Tour in Eastern Rajputana*, ASI, 1871-2, p. 197.
109. Ibid.
110. *RTA*, p. 54. Such relationship seems to have existed also with the janapada of the Arjunāyanas of Bharatpur-Alwar belt. The extent of the trading network of ancient Nāgarī can be further surmised by the discovery of two coins of Śaka-Kṣatrapas, Bhatṛdāman and Yaśodāman.
111. *EI*, vol. XXII, pp. 198-203.
112. *EI*, vol. XXXIV, pp. 53-8.
113. Ibid.
114. *EI*, vol. XXVII, pp. 252-65. The inscription records the performance of Ekaṣaṣṭirātra sacrifice by a Mālava chief Śrī Soma of Sogi clan, commemorating his victory over the Śakas.
115. *EI*, vol. XXX, pp. 120-7. The kings are stated to have carried out the building of a temple dedicated to a goddess (described as a consort of Śiva), excavation of a tank, etc., in the vicinity of Chhoti-Sadri-Daśapura (Mandasaur) belt.
116. Adris Banerji, op. cit., p. 111.
117. D.L. Paliwal, *Mewar Through the Ages*, Udaipur, 1969, p. 12.
118. Rule of the Morīs at Chittaur in the seventh-eighth centuries is evident from the Chittaurgarh inscription of king Māna Morī of AD 713. See *Annals*, vol. I, pp. 625-7.
119. K.C. Jain, op. cit., p. 233. Nāgdā is known to have been founded by the Guhila King Nāgāditya in the seventh century. Also see, *URI*, p. 98.
120. Udaipur Praśasti of the reign of Guhila King Aparajitā (AD 661), *EI*, vol. IV, pp. 29-32.
121. Copper Plate Grant of Guhila King Bābhaṭa of AD 688, *EI*, vol. XXXIV, pp. 174-6.
122. Bhāvihita of AD 653, ibid., pp. 171-3.
123. Ibid., 1.8. The subordinate allies often claimed to have obtained the five great *śabdas* from their overlords, in which *śabda* means either 'a title' or 'a sound'. 'In some west Indian records, the five titles appear to have been Mahārāja, Mahāsāmanta (feudatory), Mahākartākṛtika (probably, a royal agent or remembrances), Mahādaṇḍanāyaka (commander of forces) and Mahāpratīhāra', in D.C. Sircar, *Indian Epigraphy*, Delhi, 1965, pp. 341-2.
124. Grant of Bābhaṭa, op. cit., p. 174, 1.9.
125. Dabok Inscription of the Reign of Morī King Dhavalappadeva of AD 644, *EI*, vol. XX, pp. 122-5, ll.1-2.
126. Dabok Inscription, p. 122, l.2.
127. Grant of Bhāvihita, p. 171, l.2.
128. Grant of Bābhaṭa, p. 174, l.1.
129. Udaipur Praśasti of the reign of Aparājita, vv. 1-2.
130. Dabok Inscription, p. 122, l.2-3.

131. Chattopadhyaya, 'Political Process and Structure', p. 208.
132. Ibid., p. 210. 'Generally, the mobility upward was from a base which can be broadly characterized as agrarian.... We have noted that Gurjaratrā or Gurjarabhūmi was the base from which several lineages claiming descent from the Gurjara emerged, the separation of the ruling lineages from the common stock is suggested by the general name Gurjara-Pratihāra used by the lineages, and while the base of one such lineage in Jodhpur area seems to have been established by displacing pre-existing groups, in the Alwar area in eastern Rajasthan there is clear indication of a sharp distinction which had developed between Gurjara cultivators and the Gurjara-Pratihāra ruling lineage. It is on this basis that Gurjara-Pratihāra supra-regional power, which had begun with the expansion of one of the lineages and extended at one stage as far east as Bengal, was built up.'
133. Richard G. Fox, *Kin, Clan, Raja and Rule: State-Hinterland Relations in pre-Industrial India*, Bombay, 1971, p. 69.
134. Marc Bloch, *Feudal Society*, vol. II, tr. L.A. Manson, Chicago and London, 1962, pp. 288-9.
135. Perry Anderson discusses the point that the secular struggle between classes is ultimately resolved at the political not at the economic or cultural level of society. See his *Lineages of the Absolutist State*, London, 1979, p. 11.
136. Dabok Inscription, p.123, l.6.
137. Ibid., p. 123, ll.6-8. '*uttara (to) vartmā | tathā nagādityabhaṭāsya cāgrate śāradyaigraiṣmika kṣetram | purvvato brahmasomabāuṭakakṣetram vakaṭā ca || dakṣiṇataḥ tatākodakam || uttarato bharmmakabhakakṣetram . . . kāśyapeyakṣetram | purvvato viṣṇusomakṣetram*'.
138. For a discussion on *araghaṭṭa*, see Chattopadhyaya, *Making of Early Medieval India*, pp. 43-5.
139. Ibid., l.7.
140. Samuel Beal, ed., *Buddhist Records of the Western World Travels of Hiuen Tsiang*, vol. II, Book XL, Delhi, p. 271. Hiuen Tsiang's following remarks during his visit to Chittaurgarh around this time is noteworthy: 'The soil is celebrated for its fertility, it is regularly cultivated and yields abundant crops; it is specially adapted for beans and barley, it produces abundance of fruits and flowers. The climate is temperate. The king honours and rewards those who are distinguished for virtue. Very many learned men from distant countries congregate in this place.'
141. Dabok Inscription, op. cit., pp. 124-5, l.9. '*tathā haṭṭa-madhye-vīthī*' as well as few *dramma* coins '*(śāradya kṣetrādih sapta dramīṇa-kahala kuṭakana kṛ(ka)ṣ(arṣa) niyā(yah) dvāvapi . . . catu(dra) mmī(mi) ṇako(māsi) dātabyoh.*'
142. Ibid., p. 122, l.1.
143. *EI*, vol. XX, pp. 97-9.

144. Ibid., ll.8-9, '*tatra jentaka mahattarah śrī araṇyavāsinyā devakulam cakra mahājanādiṣṭah devo ca pratiṣṭhāpyamanupālayatu*'.
145. Paul T. Craddock, et al., 'The Production of Lead, Silver and Zinc in Early India', in A. Hauptmaun, E. Perinicka and G.A. Wagner, eds., *Old World Archaeometry*, Bochum, 1989, p. 56. I am grateful to Prof. Shereen Ratnagar, Jawaharlal Nehru University, for providing this article to me.
146. Samoli Inscription, p. 99, 1.8. '*dhanadhānya hrṣṭapuṣṭa (pra) viṣṭajana nityasambādham*'.
147. Ibid., p. 99, ll.6-7.
148. 'Origin of the Rajputs', p. 63.
149. Kulke, 'Royal Temple Policy and the Structure of Medieval Hindu Kingdom', in Anncharlott Eschmann, Hermann Kulke and Gayacharan Tripathy, eds., op. cit., p. 128.
150. Sukhvir Singh Gahlot and Banshi Dhar, *Castes and Tribes of Rajasthan*, Jodhpur, 1989, p. 221.
151. Henry J.M. Claessen and Peter Skalnik, eds., *The Early State*, p. 35.
152. *Annals*, vol. I, p. 39.
153. *Annals*, vol. I, pp. 258-68. Guha, a Rajput boy, brought up by the Bhil chief Māṇḍalīka, of Idar (north-east Gujarat), was granted chiefship of the local Bhil villages, following application of *ṭīkā* of sovereignty (*ṭīkā* of blood). In due course, the Bhils revolted against the Guhila rule, killing Guha's eighth successor Nagāditya and deprived the Guhilas of Idar. Nāgāditya's infant son, Bāppā (legendary Bāppā Rāval) fled to Mewar hills, following his stay with the Bhils of Yadu lineage, accompanied by equally legendary Bhil chiefs of Oghna-Panarwa and Oondri (located in south-west of Udaipur). Having mastered the loyalty of chiefs of Mewar, Bāppā Rāval snatched away the crown from the reigning Morī king and himself became the king of Mewar.
154. Ibid., p. 268.
155. Ibid.
156. Ibid., v. 4, '*śivātmajokhaṇḍita-śakti saṁpa dhuryah samākrānta-bhujaṅga-śatru(h)/ten=endravat=skandaiva praṇetā vṛto mahārājā-varāhasiṁhah*'.
157. Dungarpur Plates of Bābhaṭa, p. 175, ll.12-15.
158. Ibid., p. 175, l.13.
159. Ibid., l.14. '*uttare śakapālī-śodhanasyasva (stha)-vanamārggastathā*'.
160. Ibid., pp. 175, ll.14-15.
161. D.C. Sircar, ed., *EI*, vol. XXXIV, pp. 171-3. Also see D.C. Sircar, *The Guhilas of Kiṣkindhā*, Calcutta, 1965. Similar list of addresses figures in other land grant charters of the Guhilas of Kiṣkindhā, see p. 74, ll.9-10. 'Nṛpa (subordinate ruler), Nṛpasuta (son of a subordinate chief), sāndhivigrahika (minister for war and peace), senādhyakṣa (leader of forces), Purodha (priest), pramātṛ, mantrīn (minister), Pratihāra, Rājasthānīya (viceroy), Kumāramātya (officers enjoying the status of a

prince) . . . Viṣaya bhogapati (district magistrate or officers in charge of district and sub-regions), Caurodharaṇika, Śaulkika, Rājapuruṣa (royal agent),Vyāpṛtaka (head of administrative division or department), Daṇḍapāśika, Cāṭa, Bhaṭa, Pratisāraka, grāmādhipati (head of village), Drāṅgika (the agriculturist householders) as well as the people of the area in question headed by the kuṭumbīs (peasant-householders), vaṇiks (merchants), and brāhmaṇas and also the karaṇikas (members of the scribal community).'

162. Sircar, *The Guhilas of Kiṣkindhā*, ibid., p. 73, l.7.
163. Ibid., ll. 4-5.
164. Ibid.
165. Kalyanpur Fragmentary Inscription of Guhila King Kadachi, p. 77, vv. 7-9.
166. The situation of the local Guhila states of Nāgdā-Āhaḍa and Kiṣkindhā in the seventh century reminds us of Robert L. Carneiro's observations on the stages of state formation. 'In this stage of struggle instead of village fighting village, it was now chiefdom against chiefdom. The stronger again prevailed, and in this manner larger political units were formed. . . . The political unit thus formed, so much larger, stronger and more highly organized than the small chiefdoms out of which it had arisen, warranted being called a state.' Robert L. Carneiro, 'Political Expansion as an Expression of the Principle of Competitive Exclusion', in Ronald Cohen and E.R. Service, eds., *Origins of the State—The Anthropology of Political Evolution*, p. 208.
167. Samoli Inscription, op. cit., l.4, '*jayati vijayī ripuṇām deva dvijagurujaṇān-nandī | śrīsīlāditya narapatih svakulāmbaracandramāh pṛthvīḥ*'.

CHAPTER II

Mewar as the Locus of a State

A. CONSOLIDATION OF GUHILA: TENTH-THIRTEENTH CENTURIES

The tenth century in Rajasthan may be considered a crucial phase in the history of the Guhila dynasties as it witnessed the crystallization of a state apparatus among them. In order to highlight the integrating role of the Guhilas of Nāgdā-Āhaḍa in the process of state formation in Mewar, it becomes necessary to make a brief survey of the more important of contemporary Guhila families. The comparison would bring out the contrasts in the history of different Guhila ruling families in the period (see Map 3). Contemporary with the Nāgdā-Āhaḍa Guhilas were the Guhilas of Chāṭsu (near Jaipur, Jaipur district), the Guhilas of Unsṭrā (north-west of Bāgoḍiā, Jodhpur district), the Guhilas of Bāgoḍiā (north-west of Pipar, Jodhpur district), the Guhilas of Nāḍol (Pali district) and the Guhilas of Māṅgrol (Saurashtra, Gujarat).

The Guhila dynasty that successfully transformed itself into a regional power by the thirteenth century. In this chapter, I will consider its changing material base, patronage of religious institutions and cults, genealogical structure and new political symbols, and administrative apparatus.

Finally the proliferation of branches of the Nāgdā-Āhaḍa Guhila royal family, its impact on the contemporary principality of the Mewar hills and other centres of Guhila power beyond Mewar hills will be discussed to examine the role of Rajput kinship structure in a period of state formation and growth.

(i) The Guhilas of Chāṭsu

The Guhilas of Chāṭsu initially started their political career in the area of Tonk in the seventh century.[1] They seem to have extended their power up to the area of Chāṭsu near Jaipur by the tenth century. Their growing territorial expanse and political power is evident from prestigious claims made in the Chāṭsu inscription of Guhila ruler Bālāditya (tenth century). They laid claims to the status of Brahmakṣatrānvita and to the lineage of Guhilavaṁśa.[2] Bālāditya took pride in his overlords,[3] the Gurjara-Pratihāras who controlled eastern and southern Rajasthan till the tenth century. Yet their subordinate political status as allies of the Pratihāras was no deterrent to their prestigious social linkages. They consolidated their power in eastern Rajasthan through matrimonial alliances with contemporary Paramāra and Cāhamāna chiefly families.[4] However, it is important that no record of this Guhila family appears beyond the tenth century. It seems that the Guhilas of Chāṭsu had been integrated into the growing kingdom of the Cāhamānas of Śākambharī who held major parts of eastern Rajasthan by the late tenth century.

(ii) The Guhilas of Unsṭrā

Memorial Stone Inscriptions of 1179-80 and of 1190-7 at an ancient Jain temple at Unsṭrā suggest the existence of a pocket of Guhila power in this arid tract of Marwar. The inscriptions record the deaths of Rāṇā Tihunapāla[5] and Rāṇā Motīśvara, both of the Guhilautra (Guhila) lineage.[6] The Inscription of 1179-80 also records that Rāṇā Tihunapāla's wives, Pālhanadevī (of the Bodana lineage) and Mātādevī, became satīs.[7] Rāṇā Motīśvara's wife, Rājī of the Mohili lineage, also became a satī.[8]

The title of *rāṇā* and the limited territorial control of the Guhila chiefs of Unsṭrā suggests that they served in the capacity of subordinate allies and probably died fighting for the cause of an overlord.[9] The overlord could be a Nāḍol Cāhamāna ruler as an inscription of King Sāmanta Siṁhadeva of 1202 is found at a nearby site at Bali, Bamnera.[10] The presence of Bodana and Mohili Rajputs also suggests that Unsṭrā was a part of the Cāhamāna state of Nāḍol as Bodana and Mohili are the two subdivisions of the Cāhamāna clan. Unlike the contemporary Nāgdā-Āhaḍa Guhilas, the Guhila *rāṇās* of Unsṭrā made no claim to exalted origin. They simply referred to themselves as Guhila.[11] This may have been in keeping with their subordinate status.

(iii) The Guhilas of Bāgoḍiā

A Bāgoḍiā Tīrthamba Inscription of 1054 points to the existence of chiefly Guhila families at Bāgoḍiā, near Jodhpur (Marwar). It is also a memorial stone inscription: it refers to the death of one Dhalavana, son of Alaja Vichāri, a Guhilaputra.[12] Its recording of the construction of a *devalī*

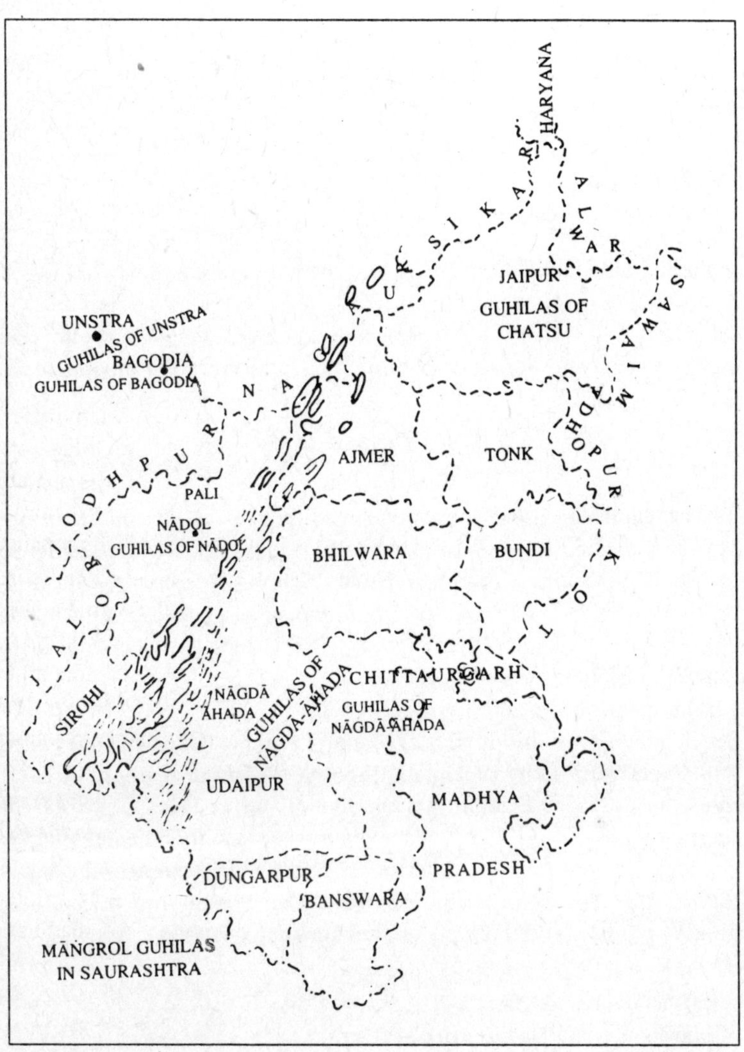

Map 3: Distribution of the Guhila Royal and Chiefly Families: AD Tenth-Thirteenth Centuries.

(temple), further suggests the association of the Guhilas with this area.[13]

(iv) The Guhilas of Nāḍol

A Guhila base of power at Nadūlaḍāgikā, Nāḍol (Pali district) is evident from the Jadvaji Jain Temple Inscription of the Reign of Nāḍol Cāhamāna Ruler, Mahārājaputra Rāyapāladeva (1137-8) and from the Adināth Temple Inscriptions of the same Guhila family. Both inscriptions record grants of grains, shares from oil-mills, incense, flowers, etc., by Ṭhakkura Rājadeva, son of Udhāraṇa of the Guhila lineage.[14] The donations were granted from Nadūlaḍāgikā.[15] In addition, the grants included parts of the duties levied on pack oxen going to and from Nadūlaḍāgikā.[16] Ṭhakkura Rājadeva is described as 'holding Nadūlaḍāgikā'.[17] Both these charters suggest the position of the Guhila family as subordinates of the Cāhamānas of Nāḍol.

(v) The Guhilas of Māṅgrol

The Sobhadi Vāo Stone Inscription of 1146 takes us to a Guhila centre of power outside Rajasthan: Māṅgrol, in Saurashtra. The genealogical list in the inscription eulogises Guhila Sahajīga's sons as protectors (military officials) of Saurashtra.[18] In the same genealogical line, the contemporary Guhila Mūlaka bears the title of *nāyaka* (chief) of Saurashtra.[19]

The progenitor of the family, Śrī Sāhāra is simply referred to as a Śrī Guhila.[20] Thus the Guhilas of Māṅgrol seem to have been integrated into Caulukyan polity of Gujarat through a system of distribution of roles and services evident in such administrative titles as *nāyaka* of Saurashtra. However, the absence of any other claim indicates that the Guhilas of Māṅgrol enjoyed territorial and political power only within Saurashtra. The limited political power is also evident from the political ranking of Guhila Mūlaka in the Ṭhakkura category.[21]

(vi) The Guhilas of Nāgdā-Āhaḍa and State Formation in Mewar, Tenth-Thirteenth Centuries

It was the Guhila family of Nāgdā-Āhaḍa which appears to be directly connected with the rise of a state. It is with the history of this family that we shall be concerned now.

The imperial Pratihāras held their sway over southern Rajasthan in the ninth century but their continuous military campaigns kept Pratihāra Bhoja I (836-92) occupied in the north, with Devapāla of Gauda in the east, and with the Rāṣṭrakūṭas of Deccan for most of his reign.[22] There was no direct annexation of southern Rajasthan by the Pratihāras in the period. Like their contemporary neighbours, the Nāgdā-Āhaḍa Guhilas are likely to have acknowledged Pratihāra supremacy over northern India. But such acknowledgement must have been temporary in their case as is apparent from the decline of the Pratihāra power in southern Rajasthan by the mid-tenth century. The presence of Pratihāra representatives at the strategic fortress of Chittaur (as is evident from the Sirur inscription of the time of Rāṣṭrakūṭa Amoghavarṣa I[23] of 866 and Karhad Plates of Kṛṣṇa II of 959) could not therefore, effectively interrupt the political career of the Nāgdā-Āhaḍa Guhilas.[24]

The Guhilas of Nāgdā-Āhaḍa not only consolidated their power in their base region but also territorially integrated the central part of the Mewar hills and possibly touched the northern Mahi basin. For this, we have a circumstantial evidence: the total disappearance of the Guhila house of Kiṣkindhā after the eighth century. The Nāgdā-Āhaḍa house might have expanded southwards at the expense of the Kiṣkindhā-Guhilas. It is equally significant to note that, of all the Guhilas of southern Rajasthan, it is only the Guhila house of Nāgdā-Āhaḍa which figures as political subordinates of the Pratihāras in Mewar along with a small ruling family of the Cāhamānas at Pratapgarh in district Chittaurgarh bordering Mandasaur (upper Banas plain) in tenth century.[25] There is no trace of the Guhilas of Dhavagartā or those of Kiṣkindhā in Pratapgarh Inscription (942-6), the only epigraphical record from Mewar dating to the reign of Pratihāra Mahendrapāla II. This extension of Nāgdā-Āhaḍa Guhila territory was achieved through military superiority. In fact, grants made by Bhartṛpaṭṭa II at Pratapgarh indicate that the Nāgdā-Āhaḍa Guhilas held some territorial claim in the southern part (Pratapgarh) of the upper Banas plain before 950. The title of *mahārājādhirāja* for Guhila Bhartṛpaṭṭa (II)[26] in the Pratapgarh records (as against the title of *bhūpo* or *mahāsāmantas* for the Cāhamānas[27] of Pratapgarh) is significant in this respect.

The consolidation of Nāgdā-Āhaḍa Guhila power is corroborated by the long genealogical lists occurring in their official records for the first time in the tenth century. The Āṭapura inscription of the Guhila, Śaktikumāra contains an interesting genealogical information. Śaktikumāra is stated to have obtained the glory of Bhartṛpaṭṭa (II) and consolidated his kingdom.[28] The reference to King Śaktikumāra as the prince who consolidated the kingdom also indicates the point of time (the second half of the tenth century) when the early Guhilas consolidated power in their central area and beyond. This may be taken as the second phase in the growth of the processes of state formation in Mewar. Āghaṭa or Āhaḍa was made the new capital by Śaktikumāra: he is stated to have established himself at Āghaṭapura.[29] It is important to note that Sāraṇeśvara Inscription of 953 does not eulogize the town of Āhaḍa unlike the Āṭapur Inscription of 977.[30] This evidence indicates that Āhaḍa had not acquired political importance or status of a capital till 977. Even Kailash Chand Jain comments that Allaṭa, the son and successor of Bhartṛpaṭṭa II, probably transferred his capital from Nāgdā to Āhaḍa.[31] Transfer of capital from Nāgdā to Āhaḍa was apparently due to the latter's increasing economic significance[32] in the tenth century and did not signify any territorial acquisition.[33] Guhila King Bhartṛpaṭṭa (II) bears the title of *mahārājādhirāja* in the Pratapgarh inscription of Pratihāra Mahendrapāladeva (II) of 945-6.[34] It is again Bhartṛpaṭṭa (II) who is eulogized in the Āṭapura inscription as the 'ornament of the three worlds'.[35] Thus new political titles and a genealogical list are claimed in the tenth century by the Nāgdā-Āhaḍa Guhilas.

The new heights of political power are expressed in ambitious claims about origins. The records now for the first time speak of the ancestor, Guhadatta as a brāhmaṇa belonging to a family of Ānandapura (*Ānandapuravinirgataḥ Viprakulāhnandanoḥ-mahīdeva jayati Śrī Guhadattaḥ prabhavaḥ Śrī Guhilavaṁśasya*).[36] Ānandapura is identified with present Vadnagar in Idar, north-east Gujarat. It is a very significant development when contrasted with the simple expression of Guhilānvaya of seventh-century records. The same genealogical list and origin myth are repeated in the eleventh century, as is evident from the Kadmal plates of 1083 of Guhila Vijayasiṁha.[37]

The Pratihāra power in southern Rajasthan had by this time begun to decline. Pratihāra hold over the strategic fortress of Chittaurgarh weakened by the second half of tenth century. The Rāṣṭrakūṭa invasions into northern India had undermined the Pratihāra power militarily as it is evident by Karhad plates[38] and Deoli Plates of Kṛṣṇa III.[39] This was also the period when powerful rulers like Paramāra Sīyaka II, Mūlarāja Caulukya, and Candella Dhaṅga were making intrusions into the Pratihāra dominion from central and western India.[40] In the weakening of the Pratihāra hold over the fortress of Chittaurgarh, the Guhilas of Nāgdā-Āhaḍa are likely to have played a significant role as is evident from an unpublished inscription of the reign of Guhila King Allaṭa (Ālu

Rāval of tradition). King Allaṭa is said to have been killed in the battle-field, by a strong enemy named Devapāla[41] (identified with Pratihāra King Devapāla of Kanauj of the late tenth century).[42] Thus, the extent to which the Nāgdā-Āhaḍa Guhilas helped in weakening the Pratihāra hold over Citrakūṭa remains a matter of conjecture. The fact that the Guhilas of Nāgdā-Āhaḍa had become a power to be reckoned with is borne out by the Paramāra invasion of Āghaṭa, their capital. The Bijapur Inscription of Dhavalā Rāṣṭrakūṭa of Hastikuṇḍī records that Prince Dhavalā gave shelter to the armies of a king whose name is lost and the army of the Gurjaras when Paramāra Muñjarāja had destroyed Āghaṭa, the pride of Medapāṭa and caused them to flee.[43] Thus they figure in the official records of their contemporaries for the first time in the tenth century. Paramāra Muñja was the contemporary of Guhila King Śaktikumāra. As is evident from the Hastīkuṇḍī record, Guhila Śaktikumāra was given political refuge by the Rāṣṭrakūṭa prince of Hastīkuṇḍī at the time of the sack of Āghaṭa (Āhaḍa). It was on this occasion that the fortress of Chittaur passed into Paramāra hands. Muñja Vākpati's nephew Bhoja is known to have often resided at Chittaur. Construction of the temples of Tribhuvana-Nārāyaṇa[44] (now known as Mokaljī's temple) and Samāddhīśvara is attributed to Paramāra Bhoja.[45] Next to the Paramāras, it was the Cāhamānas who continued to keep up pressures on the Nāgdā-Āhaḍa Guhilas. Guhila Śaktikumāra's son Ambāprasāda is known to have been killed by his contemporary Cāhamāna, Vākpati II of Śākambharī in an attack on the capital.[46]

However, these occasional inroads into Nāgdā-Āhaḍa might be considered as minor setbacks in the political career of the Guhila dynasty without seriously jeopardising the processes of state formation at this point of time.[47]

Increasing political power had to be supplemented with higher social claims. There were matrimonial alliances with the contemporary Rajput families of different lineages in the tenth and eleventh centuries. Some of these families not only belonged to respectable lineages but were also important political powers. Allaṭa had a queen from a royal Hūṇa family of central India.[48] Hūṇa Princess Hariyādevī (the name seems to suggest that this Hūṇa family had already been absorbed into the Rajput fold, which facilitated a Guhila-Hūṇa marriage) is also called the founder or an associate of the town of Harṣapura (Harshuada, district Hoshangabad). The Hūṇas may have sought matrimonial alliance with Guhilas of Nāgdā-Āhaḍa to thwart the rising Paramāra power of Malwa. The alliance also secured for the Guhilas a political ally in the Hūṇas of central India against the Paramāra. Bhartṛpaṭṭa's queen Mahālakṣmī is stated to have been of Rāṣṭrakūṭa ancestry (most probably from Rāṣṭrakūṭas of Hastikuṇḍī, Marwari),[49] Naravāhana also had a Cāhamāna queen.[50] Not only the ruling family but their important functionaries also began to seek matrimonial alliances with respectable Rajput families. Two epigraphical records of 1000 and 1008 refer to the two wives of Guhila *mahāsāmantādhipati* of Nāgadṛaha (Nāgdā) as Mahārājñī Sarvadevī, daughter of a *mahāsāmantādhipati* of the Sūrya-vaṁśī family and Mahārājñī Jājukā, daughter of a *mahāsāmantādhipati* of another Sūryavaṁśī family of Bharukaccha.[51]

Territorial expansion of the Guhila state occurred in the late eleventh century to the north, beyond the traditional boundary of Mewar, into the Godwar region (see Map 4). Kadmal plates record the grant of the fifth part of the produce of the village Pallī, embracing all its receipts, by Guhila King Vijayasiṁha to a brāhmaṇa Unanalācārya.[52] The village of Pallī has been identified with the modern town of Pali in the district of Pali (Godwar region).[53] Godwar region was commercially strategic to Rajasthan as the trade route to the seacoast of Gujarat from northern India passed through it in this period.[54] The credit for annexing Godwar is likely to go to Vairīsiṁha, father of Vijayasiṁha, as is evident from eulogies and military exploits of Vairīsiṁha recorded in the Kadmal plates.[55]

It is likely that enmity with the Paramāras of Malwa continued into the late eleventh century. But by this period the Paramāras were a declining political power and Vairīsiṁha's military exploits must have put an end to Paramāra ambitions in Mewar. A small Paramāra power which had ruled in Vagod (Dungarpur-Banswara districts) with its political centre at Arthuna (Banswara district) during the eleventh century does not seem to have existed in Vagod beyond 1100.[56] Arthuna Inscriptions of Paramāra Cāmuṇḍarāja dated 1078 and 1080 seem to be the last of the Paramāra records in Vagod. Therefore, with fast changing political configurations in western and central India, the Guhilas of Nāgdā-Āhaḍa entered into matrimonial relationship with the Paramāras of Malwa at this juncture. The Bheraghat Inscriptions of the Chedi dated 907 (AD 1155) mention that Guhila King Vijayasiṁha married Śyāmaladevī, the daughter of Paramāra King Udayāditya of Malwa (AD 1060-87).[57] This alliance seems to have been utilized as a joint front against the threatening ambitions of Caulukyan ruler Bhīma I (AD 1022-64). The Bheraghat inscription also states that Śyāmaladevī was the mother of Alahaṇadevī, the queen of Kalacuri Gayākarṇa of Dahala.[58]

The early twelfth century witnessed a significant development for

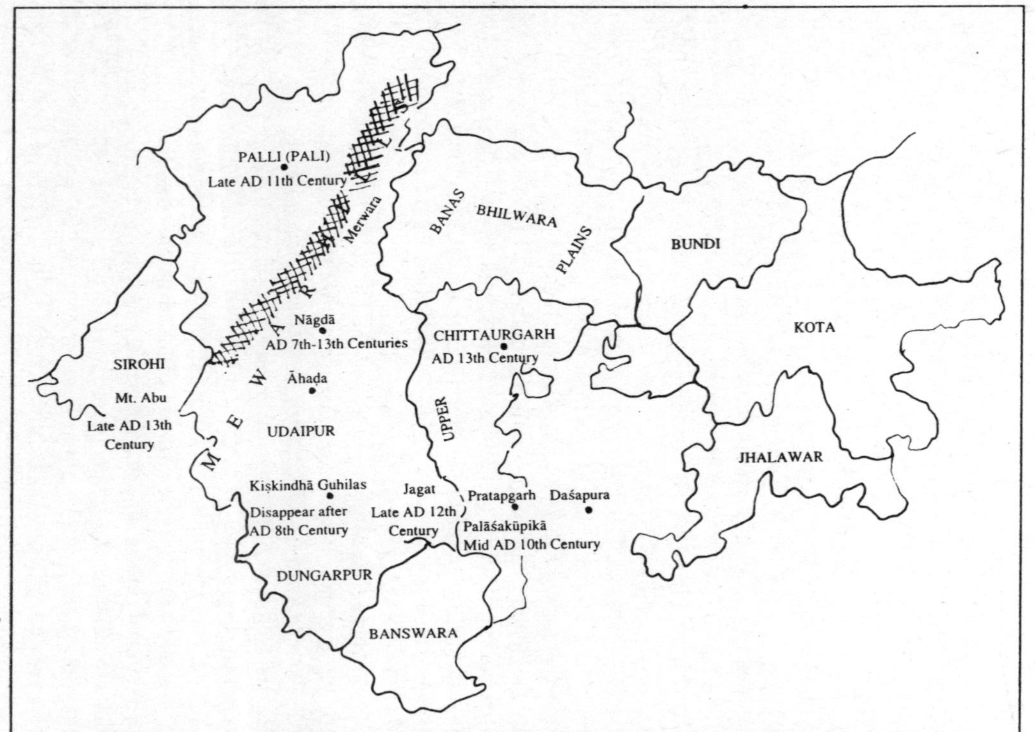

Map 4: Territorial Integration and Expansion by the Nāgdā-Āhaḍa Guhilas: AD Seventh-Thirteenth Centuries.

the Guhilas of Nāgdā-Āhaḍa. The Guhilas, for the first time in their history identified themselves as the sovereigns of the region of Mewar implying territorial integration, and hence, an important step towards regional state formation was taken. The Paldi Inscription of Guhila Arisiṁha (son of Vijayasiṁha) of 1116 proclaimed the king as the ruling prince of Medapāṭa (Bhūpāle Medapāṭamahīmām).[59] Thus, the identification of the Guhila king with the king of Mewar is a proof of the claim of the Nāgdā-Āhaḍa Guhilas on the region of Medapāṭa at this point of time.

To be sure, there was a brief Caulukyan intrusion into Mewar and Vagod regions (districts of Dungarpur and Banswara in middle Mahi basin), as suggested by Kumārapāla's Chittaurgarh Inscription[60] of 1.150, Bhīmadeva II's short inscriptional records of 1196,[61] Āhaḍa grant of 1207 from Gujarat[62] and another record of Siddharāja Jayasiṁha from the last decade of the twelfth century.[63] Yet, the Nāgdā-Āhaḍa Guhilas came to command southern portion of the upper Banas plain in the late twelfth century.[64] If Pratapgarh records prove that they held some territorial claims in the southern part of upper Banas plain in the mid-tenth century, they seem to have integrated this territory into their state by the second half of the twelfth century as is evident from the Jagat Inscription of 1172 of Guhila Sāmantasiṁhadeva.[65] It is significant that unlike the status of the Pratihāras in the tenth century in the upper Banas plain, the Guhilas in Jagat inscription figure as sovereigns on their own.

The thirteenth century witnessed the height of territorial expansion for the Guhilas. It was then that the traditional political landmark of Mewar, the fortress of Chittaur, was finally occupied by the Nāgdā-Āhaḍa Guhilas. A number of Guhila records were issued during the reign of Tejasiṁha from Chittaur.[66] Jaitrasiṁha is eulogized in the Achaleśvara Inscription of Samarasiṁha (his grandson) as the protector of the earth through the exploits of his arms and also as the destroyer of Naḍūla.[67] He is also eulogized as occupant of a throne along with the monarch of the gods, Indra.[68] As to the age of Jaitrasiṁha, two inscriptions of AD 1213 (Pillar Inscription near Ekaliṅgajī) and AD 1222 (Nadesama Village Inscription) refer to the reign of Guhila King Jaitrasiṁha, who is spoken as ruling from Nāgadṛaha.[69] Thus from all the available evidences it seems that Jaitrasiṁha was possibly the first Guhila king who annexed the fortress of Chittaur briefly: whereby the political sovereignty of the Nāgdā-Āhaḍa Guhilas all over Mewar was sealed. Chittaur was the ancient political landmark of Mewar. Chittaur which began its political career at Nāgarī, the capital of the Śibis, went on to be the political centre of ancient Mewar under the Aulikāras, the later Morīs of eastern Rajasthan and western Uttar Pradesh. It is already noted that Chittaurgarh later came under the control of the Cāhamānas, Pratihāras, Paramāras and Caulukyas, before passing into the hands of the Guhilas. The special mention of the rooting out of Naḍūla by Jaitrasiṁha implies the occupation of the Godwar region (Pali district) by the Guhilas.[70] As noted, it is evident from the Kadmal plates that the Guhilas had established their sway over Godwar by the late eleventh century. But because of the rise of the Nāḍol Cāhamānas, the Guhilas had to reassert themselves again in Godwar in the thirteenth century. The occupation of Chittaur formally integrated greater part of upper Banas plain into the Guhila state. The end of the Imperial Cāhamāna power in central Rajasthan (with the defeat of Pṛthvīrāja III at the battle of Tarrain in 1192) evidently facilitated the conquest of Chittaur. The Cāhamāna occupation of Chittaur and the upper Banas plain in the late twelfth century is evident from Bijolia and Menal stone inscriptions (both in Bhilwara district) of 1168 and 1170 respectively of the reign of Pṛthvīrāja III.[71] However, the Achaleśvara Inscription of Samarasiṁha proves the sway of the Guhilas over the Mount Abu region (the inscription was issued from the temple of Achaleśvara, Mount Abu) as well as much of Godwar, controlling routes to sea-ports of Gujarat by the late thirteenth century.

Thus the thirteenth century was a decisive period in the history of the state: Mewar finally came to have its own political identity as a regional state. The Guhila acquisition of Chittaurgarh extended their sovereignty over Vagod (districts of Dungarpur and Banswara) as well. The fifteenth-century official claim that Jaitrasiṁha ruled over Citrakūṭa, Medapāṭa, Āghaṭa and Vagod,[72] reflects the actual political configuration of the region in the aftermath of the acquisition.

Thus in contrast to the Guhilas of Kiṣkindhā and Dhavagartā (seventh-eighth centuries), the Guhila royal family of Nāgdā-Āhaḍa stands out as the effective sovereign of Mewar. It was the Nāgdā-Āhaḍa family, of all the Guhila ruling families of Mewar and beyond, which successfully laid the foundation of a state structure.[73]

Inevitably, there were further, new, and prestigious genealogical claims along with claims of sovereignty over Mewar. The Guhadatta legend of tenth-eleventh centuries was dropped from the records and instead the new legends of *Bappaka Hārītarāśi-Ekaliṅga-Medapāṭa* were adopted.

B. RESOURCES OF THE STATE

We begin with a brief scrutiny of the strategic importance of Mewar in contemporary western India. Mewar formed an important part of the regional circuit of trade in western India. Between the tenth and fourteenth centuries, the Gujarat coast saw an increasing maritime and coastal trade; this stimulated commercial activities in the hinterland.

Arab settlements in western India are evident if one looked at Persian and Arabic inscriptions as well as the accounts of such travellers as Al-Masudi, Al-Biladuri, Ibn Battuta and Al-Qulqashandi.[74] Not only foreign trade but an equally vibrant network of internal trade in western India is evident both from literary and epigraphic sources of the period. Merchants in western India traded in both essential and luxury commodities, ranging from grains, salt, jaggery, oil, ghee, textiles, leather goods, metal goods, animals, spices, betel-leaves and areca nuts to saffron, ivory, coral, gold, semi-precious stones such as carnelian, onyx and cat's eye.[75] Some of these commodities found markets in West Asia. The initiative of the local states in helping the trade to thrive can be seen in the political measures undertaken. The kings always ordered the local residents of the land to provide protection to all the merchants and pilgrims passing through their region, and provided them with financial assistance whenever required.[76] In a similar spirit, rulers quelled disruptive elements which were impediments to free flow of commercial traffic. In *Prabandhacintāmaṇi* Merutuṅga described the defeat of the Bhils in Malwa by Caulukyan King Siddharāja, as the farmer had obstructed a road.[77] It is evident from such texts as *Prabandhacintāmaṇi*[78] and *Tilakamañjarī*[79] that some rulers and ministers constructed rest-houses, water-reservoirs, and charity houses for food, drink, beds and medicines for the needy (mainly pilgrims) at Anahilavāḍa, Pāṭṭana, Stambhatīrtha (Cambay), Śatruñjaya, Ujjayanta (Girnar), Darbhavali (Dabhoi), etc. Such measures must have helped the traders too.

The crucial question is how Mewar figured in this western trade network. In this context, the importance of Mewar is its location between northern India and western-central India. Mewar became critical for the passage of trade and traffic. True, one could bypass Mewar by travelling through the chief artery, the 'Palanpur gap' and Mt. Abu. This route ran from Anahilapura through Siddhapura, Candrāvatī, Abu, Bhinmal, Nāḍol, Jalor, Bali, Pali, Ajmer and Naraina to Mathura.[80] However, even in this context, western Mewar was very important because it provided the link route to the major artery through passes in the Mewar hills and forests. V.K. Jain points out that another route ran through Āhaḍa (near present Udaipur, the Āhaḍa of Nāgdā-Āhaḍa), Pol and Idar, joining the Mount Abu route (the chief artery).[81] Western Mewar provided routes to Malwa and central India as well. The route from Ujjain ran through Dhora, Dohad, Arthuna (district Banswara), Āhaḍa, Nadlai, Nāḍol and Pali to Ajmer and Naraina.[82] But what has not been highlighted by V.K. Jain is the strategic importance of eastern Mewar. The route through Chittaur was equally important as it linked northern India with central and western India. The Mount Abu route being a popular trade route (on a vast plain and unguarded) was always vulnerable to the threat of Mongol attacks right from the thirteenth century. This seems to be the compelling reason which forced both the sultans, Iltutmish[83] and Alauddin Khalji to make a passage through Mewar to Gujarat in the early thirteenth century and through central India in the early fourteenth century respectively.[84] The Chittaur route was defended by the Aravallis and thick forest as it ran through Mewar and Vagod to Gujarat and Malwa. Much has been said about the imperial designs of Sultan Alauddin Khalji in invading Mewar in the early fourteenth century. Undoubtedly, he had to contain the ambitious Rajput rulers; but the move to annexe Mewar had a strategic importance as well. And it was the same reason that compelled Iltutmish to ask for passage through Mewar. Alauddin Khalji was not content with the riches secured from Gujarat and with its incorporation into the sultanate. As one historian has pointed out, 'most of Alauddin's other ventures were mainly directed at securing his communication lines against the Rajputs and safeguarding the empire against repeated inroads of the Mongols. The attack on Ranthambhor and Chittor and his invasions of Sevana and Jalor were mainly for this purpose.'[85] Mewar continued to command increasing commercial importance throughout the period specially in the fourteenth and the fifteenth centuries. An epigraphic study of exchange centres such as Ghatiyala, Manḍor, Haṭhuṇḍī, Jalor, Nāḍol, Dhalop, Narlai, Sevadi, Kiradu, Candrāvatī, Arthuna, Panahera, Shergarh, Āhaḍa, Khamnor and Chittaur (the last three in Mewar), as well as *praśastis* put up by merchant families, testify to commercial transactions in early medieval Rajasthan.[86]

The Guhila centres of power had been built on a rural resource base in the seventh century.[87] This material base gradually entered the age of commercial and urban epoch by the tenth century. Some important settlements figure for the first time in the Guhila records of the tenth century. The following is a list of a few important settlements between the tenth and the thirteenth centuries (i) Āṭapura,[88] (ii) Ekaliṅgajī,[89] situated 22 km to the north of Udaipur, (iii) Paldi, situated near Udaipur,[90] (iv) Jagat,[91] situated on the border of Udaipur-Chittaurgarh districts, (v) Dariba[92] near Kankroli (famous for zinc and lead mines), Udaipur district and (vi) Chiravā near Āhaḍa (Udaipur).[93] Because of the strategic location of western Mewar, a part of the commercial traffic of western India was regularly passing through Āhaḍa. The traffic was either on its way to Nāḍol to join the arterial route, or to Malwa through Arthuna (Banswara), or to Gujarat. An idea of the nature and volume of trade passing through Āhaḍa is provided by the inscriptions. The Nāgdā-Āhaḍa kingdom was regularly visited by merchants from distant places such as Karnāṭa (Karnataka), Madhyadeśa, Lāṭa (southern Gujarat and northern Konkan) and Ṭakka (Punjab).[94] Sāraṇeśvara temple inscription of Guhila Allaṭa of 953 records the grant of a number of commercial cesses levied on these merchants and travellers. Merchants and travellers entering Āhaḍa were asked to pay one *dramma* on the sale of an elephant, two *rūpakas* on a horse, one-fortieth of a *dramma* on a horned animal,[95] one *tulā*[96] from *lāṭa* (the division of crops between a peasant and the state is called *lāṭā* or *lāṭa* in Mewar) and so on. It appears that every item entering the market of Āhaḍa was assessed and duly taxed. Therefore, the state exchequer now came to receive commercial revenue in the form of tolls and custom in considerable amount.

Occupations such as *randhanī*[97] (probably refers to a feast held for the entertainment of the members of a community), *dyūtam dharāṇām* (a gambler), etc., at Āhaḍa also distinguished it as an urban centre, as does the list of grants made by different categories of residents of Āhaḍa to the temple of Sāraṇeśvara. The list runs as follows: one *ghaṭikapala* (unit of measurement for milk) from every iron saucepan (of confectioners), one *peṭaka* (this probably means the amount of money won by a gambler at one venture) from each gambler, one *pala* (a ladle generally containing four *tolās*) of oil from every oil mill, one *rūpaka* from *randhanī* (for a feast held for the entertainment of the members of a community), one *catuḥsar* (four-stringed garland) from flower-sellers everyday, one *tulā* from the shop of seller of worn-out clothes and one *āḍhaka* (a measure of grain containing three-and-half *seers*) from a *hāṭa* (weekly fairs or a market place).[98] Such a list of residents contrasts remarkably with the list we get from the village settlements in the epigraphic records of the seventh-century Guhilas.[99] Grant of a specialized amount of grain from the *hāṭā* is indicative of the fact that peasants from neighbouring villages converged on Āhaḍa with rural produce and took back goods from Āhaḍa. Thus Āhaḍa must have accounted for the bulk of the income of the central exchequer both from non-agricultural and agricultural items. Donations of commercial levies for religious purposes did not necessarily mean 'feudalization of trade and commerce'[100] but indicates royal share in the proceeds of commercial transactions.

Strangely, this busy commercial scenario is not matched by an availability of a proportionate number of coins of the Guhilas. The few finds of the Cāhamāna coins in northern Mewar and Dhoda inscriptions of AD 1168 and 1169 (records that the 'silver Ajaya Deva coins' were subjected to careful scrutiny and examination and became legal tender) suggest that local transactions were carried out in Cāhamāna coins.[101] John Deyell rightly states that commerce continued in the more popular denominations in a trans-territorial context.[102]

The direct inscriptional reference to the establishment of King Śaktikumāra[103] at Āṭapura should indicate the possibility of transfer of capital from Nāgdā to Āhaḍa and of a fortress being built at Āhaḍa. Āhaḍa seems to have been named as Āṭapura and acquired political and administrative importance as the capital of the Guhilas during Śaktikumāra's reign. The above suggestion seems plausible in view of the eulogy of this town for the first time in any Guhila record.[104] The presence of the ruling elite in Āhaḍa must have accelerated further demand for high-value items.[105] Therefore, the new political status of Āhaḍa might have been an additional factor in increasing the commercial traffic at this centre. We hear of Āhaḍadurga as an important political and commercial centre in the thirteenth century.[106]

Resources were also mobilized from other areas of control such as Pratapgarh in southern part of upper Banas plain.[107] Ekaliṅgajī, Paldi, Jagat and Dariba with their temples and monasteries were emerging as important religious centres. Occasional fairs and festivals at these centres undoubtedly encouraged periodic markets which contributed to the resource base of the Guhila state. Chiravā was a thriving rural settlement with new temples.[108] Because of its proximity to Āhaḍa, Chiravā must have entered, by the thirteenth century, into the circuit of commercial transactions centred in Āhaḍa. Finally, continued mining at Zawar, evident from zinc smelting retort dumps dated between AD 1025-1280, and once again between AD 1325-1690,[109] contributed towards the intensification of the commercial transactions at Āhaḍa in our period of study and later.

Territorial extension in the eleventh century expanded the availability of land. Northward expansion of the Nāgdā-Āhaḍa, evident from Kadmal plates of Guhila King Vijayasiṁha (AD 1083), diverted some of Godwar's resources towards Mewar. The fact that the state was mobilizing resources from the Pali locality is evident from retainment of half of the taxes and income from the irrigational channels for the royal donor.[110]

The accounts of Hiuen Tsiang,[111] Chittaurgarh Inscription of King Māna Morī of AD 713,[112] Chittaurgarh Inscription of Caulukya King Kamārapāla of AD 1151 recording grants at Samaddhiśvara temple[113] and Dhavagartā Inscription of Guhila Dhanika[114] testify to the wealth of Chittaurgarh and the eastern Berach basin in the pre-Guhila period. The Ghaghsa record of AD 1265 referring to the building of a *bāvrī* (step-well) by a member of Dindu community in the reign of Guhila King Tejasiṁha,[115] Jain records such as the Ghaghsa Praśasti of AD 1265[116] and the Chittaur Stone Inscription of AD 1267 referring to the *ācāryas* of the Caitragaccha,[117] inscriptions from Menal and Bijolia recording the grant of *drammas* to a temple of Mahānāl (Śiva),[118] and the grant of a village to a Jain temple of Pārśvanāth[119] respectively point towards the range of economic activities in Chittaurgarh locality in the Guhila period. Mobilization of resources by the Guhila state from the local commercial transactions is evident from the royal dues levied on the *maṇḍapikā* (custom houses) in Chittaurgarh belt. The Chittaurgarh Inscription of AD 1274 of Samarasiṁha records a royal grant of a few *drammas* and such items as ghee, oil, etc., which were made from the *maṇḍapikās* (see Map 5) of Talhaṭṭī, Āghaṭa (Āhaḍa), Khohar and Sajjanpura to a Jain temple of Pārśvanāth.[120] Except Āghaṭa (Āhaḍa, Mewar hills), the other places were all located near Chittaurgarh. Āghaṭa evidently came to acquire a *maṇḍapikā* for the first time in the thirteenth century (definitely after the tenth century). Further, increasing mining activities in the Mewar hills, incorporation of important mining centres other than Zawar within the commercial network (evident from Kankroli road-station inscription of the period of Samarasiṁha[121]) and control of the Mount Abu region,[122] accelerated the process of resource mobilization particularly in terms of commercial revenue for the Guhila state.

In contrast, the two Guhila houses of Unsṭrā and Bāgoḍiā (Marwar region) clearly had poorer resources as they operated from a semi-arid locality. Although the grants made by the Nāḍol Guhilas consisted of agrarian and commercial levies, the limited area of control restricted their resource base. The Guhila chiefs of Māṅgrol in coastal Saurashtra were evidently able to tap greater wealth from the continuous flow of commercial traffic. The *per diem* grant made by Gūhila Mūlaka to the

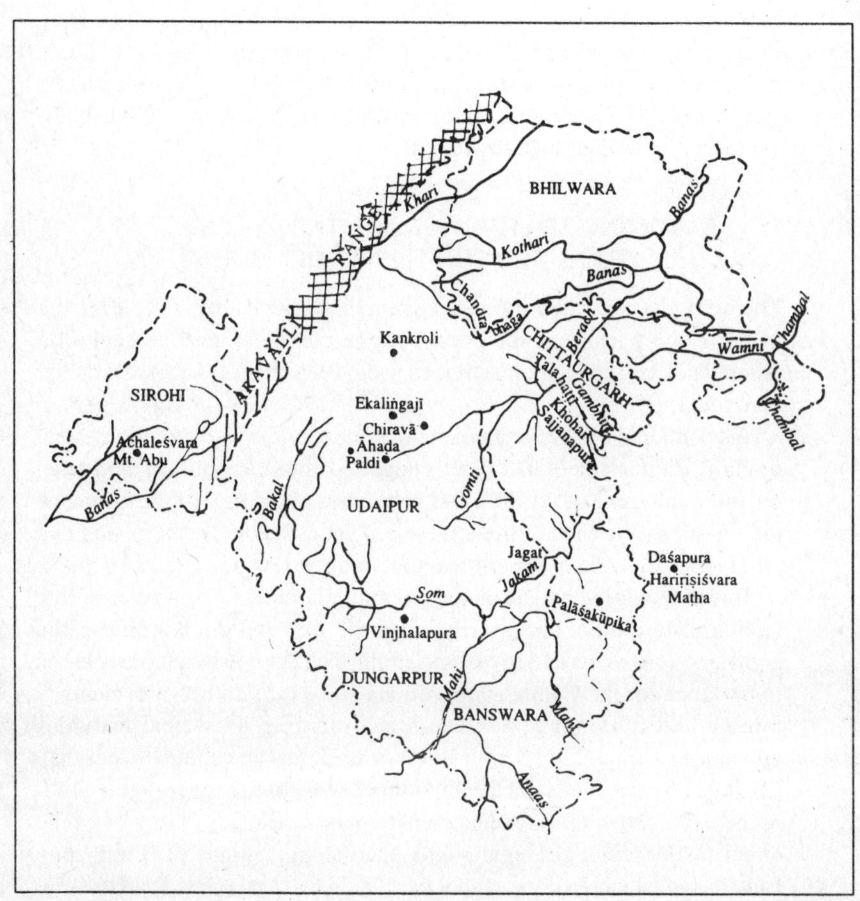

Map 5: Guhila References to the *Maṇḍapikās* in the Thirteenth Century and Religious Centres having Occasional Fairs: AD Tenth-Thirteenth Centuries.

temple of Sahajigeśvara comprised one *kārṣāpaṇa* from *maṇḍapikā* of Śrī Māṅgalapura, one *kārṣāpaṇa* from the revenue of Talāra (Talarakṣaka of Māṅgalapura) and one *kārṣāpaṇa* on every *mānaka* (unit of load) from a pack-bullock, four *kārṣāpaṇas* on every cart-load of grain, and one silver piece from the transit duties at *maṇḍapikā* on the road to Lalhevada.[123] The mahājanas of Choravad also donated a *vāo* (well) called Deguna to the same temple.[124] However, the actual control and mobilization of resources was defined by their exercise of political power as *nāyakas* of Saurashtra. Their resource base seems to have been essentially confined to Māṅgalapura.

C. ADMINISTRATIVE AND MILITARY APPARATUS: TENTH–MID THIRTEENTH CENTURIES

The administrative and military apparatus of the Guhila state evolved in the same period, as the state became complex, and the scope of administrative and military activities widened, as befits a regional (rather than local) power.

Inscriptional evidences indicate that most of the important local and migrant Rajput chiefs had been integrated into the political structure by the tenth century in different capacities. It is important to locate the chiefs as officials at the strategic points. Secondly, there was the emergence of various departments of administration.

It is noteworthy that the centres of administrative importance for the Guhila state did not necessarily mean the capital town with its court, courtiers, fortresses and royal household. The centres of administrative importance for the Guhila state would also be the centres of exchange, mining and religious activities. Areas merging into tribal territory commanded importance for economic, ideological and strategic reasons. Chattopadhyaya points out the importance of fortresses as foci of control in the early phase of ascendancy of Rajputs.[125] The possibility of a few small fortresses at strategic points such as beginnings of routes into forests and tribal territory cannot be ruled out. The exchange centres of importance in the Guhila state, as evident from inscriptional records, were Araṇyakūpagiri,[126] Āhaḍa,[127] Pratapgarh,[128] Khohar,[129] Sajjanpura,[130] Talahaṭṭī,[131] Mount Abu,[132] and Chittaurgarh.[133] Inscriptional evidence for important religious centres map out the following sites: Araṇyakūpagiri,[134] Āhaḍa,[135] Pratapgarh,[136] Paldi,[137] Jagat,[138] Chiravā,[139] Chittaurgarh.[140] Centres of mining included Araṇyakūpagiri near Nāgdā-Āhaḍa, the copper belt of the Mewar hills, Dariba near Kankroli (zinc and lead mines), and Zawar (zinc-lead-silver concentrate, 40 km south of Udaipur city). While most of these important centres are in the Mewar hills, the rest lie in the upper Banas plain. Hence, the Guhila state seems to have had effective control not only of Nāgdā and Āhaḍa but also of the centres listed above (inscriptionally attested). These centres would not have appeared in the records of the Guhilas had they not been controlled.

Although the absence of direct inscriptional evidences do not permit us to locate the non-Guhila Rajput chiefs, references to the lineages and fathers of some of the Guhila queens in the Āṭapura inscription indicate the presence of Caulukya, Cāhamāna, Rāṣṭrakūṭa, Paramāra and Hūṇa chiefs at least at few of the strategic points. It may be assumed that some of these chiefs were entrusted with special responsibilities of negotiating with the local Bhil chiefs. These Rajput chiefs were indeed administratively crucial to the state. Some of these chiefs could be of local origin and might have territorially integrated into the Guhila domain. Rest of the chiefs could be migrants such as the Hūṇas from Hoshangabad. Undoubtedly, the presence of kinsmen of some of the queens facilitated consolidation of the Guhila power through the administrative and military network.

The sources of the period throw light on the important offices of administration and the nature of personnel at the seat of power, Āhaḍa. The Sāraṇeśvara Temple Inscription of AD 953 refers to the members of a *goṣṭhika.*[141] *Goṣṭhikas* were usually the administrators attached to religious institutions. In the case of royally patronized temples, the *goṣṭhikas* seem to have been appointed by the state to administer the affairs of these institutions (Ādivarāha,[142] Viṣṇu,[143] Sūrya,[144] Nānigasvāmī,[145] and a number of Śaiva temples constructed by the Guhila royal house).[146] Pratihāra and Hūṇa Rajputs appear as officials in the *goṣṭhikas* at the temple of Ādivarāha at Āhaḍa.[147] The other important offices of administration evident from Sāraṇeśvara inscription are those of town gate-keepers or door-keepers (pratihāri) and managers of ecclesiastical affairs (dharma). Pratihāra Rudrahāsa and Rahata appear as Pratihārīs. Hūṇa Kāṣṭika and Śrīdhara occupy the office of ecclesiastical affairs.[148] Hūṇa Maṭṭaṭa appears as King Allaṭa's minister (*amātya*).[149] Thus, important members of the Pratihāra and Hūṇa lineages were integrated through important administrative ranks.

Since Guhila Allaṭa had a Hūṇa queen from central India,[150] matrimonial alliances of the Nāgdā-Āhaḍa Guhilas in the early phase of their rise seems to have helped them organize a network of power.[151]

Hūṇa, the member of *goṣṭhika* could be a kinsman of Queen Hariyādevī. Mayura and Samudra appear as a *akṣapaṭalas* (accountants or depositories of legal documents) and Durlabharāja as *sāndhivigrahika* (an officer for peace and war).[152] While Nāga figures as the chief bard, Rudrāditya and Mammaṭa appear as the chief of medical men and minister respectively.[153] It is significant that someone named Hūṇa[154] and Yaśahpuṣpo of Pratihāra lineage figure as members of this *goṣṭhika*.[155]

Cāhamānas appear as important officials in the eleventh century. It is evident from the Kadmal Plates that a *dūta* (messenger) Raṇadhavala, son of Sagamḍā, was a Cāhamāna *rājaputra*.[156] A Saulaṁki (Solaṁkī) *rājaputra* figures as an important member of the *goṣṭhika* in the twelfth century. The Paldi Inscription of AD 1116 refers to Saulaṁkī Rājaputra Śrī Salakhaṇarā, the son of Rājaputra Śrī Upala.[157] As late as the early thirteenth century, Rajputs continued to occupy the top ranks in administration. It seems from the Chiravā inscription that Bhīmasiṁha and his son Rājasiṁha served Jaitrasiṁha and Tejasiṁha respectively as ministers (*pradhānyam prāpya*).[158] It is also noted that Bhīmasiṁha had to die fighting for the state of Mewar against Gujarat (ministers were diverted to military functions during external invasions).[159] Two Kāyasthas also figure, Pāla and Vellaka, as the writers of Sāraṇeśvara Inscription of AD 953.[160]

Local Level Administration

Given the extensive rural base of the state, local level administrative bodies can be expected to have expanded. However, the term *pañcakulika* figures in only one royal record of the period. The scribe of the Kadmal plates of Guhila Vijayasiṁha (AD 1083), Nāgapāla the son of Pandita Unhila, belonged to the *pañcakulika* caste.[161] This stray evidence does not speak for the absence of the *pañcakulika* throughout the expanse of the territory. The members in such corporate bodies were likely to be the notables of the rural society. Appointments made from amongst local population ensured continuity of tenures at the local level, irrespective of dynastic change.[162] The rural notables of the earlier period such as kuṭumbins, vaṇikas, etc. (e.g. the list of witnesses in the Kiṣkindhā Guhila grants) may not have necessarily dominated the local administrative bodies in the later period, as pointed out by Chattopadhyaya in the case of early medieval Bengal.[163] Some other social groups such as mahattaras in early medieval Bengal might have grown powerful and dominated the local, corporate bodies. Mahājanas made their appearance in rural Mewar as early as the seventh century.[164] However, notables as individual members of rural society (brāhmaṇas, mahattaras, mahājans, vaṇikas, etc.), remained administratively important even in between 1100 and 1300 without a formal *pañcakulika*.[165] Even if *pañcakulikas* were appointed by the kings for supervision of cesses from *araghaṭṭa*-fields, transferred lands and *araghaṭṭas*, the fact remains that the choice fell on the local level notables.[166] Thapar also observes the presence of local persons in *pañcakulas* in post-Gupta period.[167] Chattopadhyaya discusses the presence of *pañcakulas* in early medieval towns as well, such as Siyadoni in the Gurjara-Pratihāra realm.[168] However, *goṣṭhikas* appear to be important in early medieval towns of Mewar such as Āṭapura (Āhaḍa).[169]

Military Apparatus

The Āṭapura inscription of King Śaktikumāra of AD 977, which lists the Guhila queens of the Rāṣṭrakūṭas (Rāṣṭrakūṭa of Hastīkuṇḍī), Cāhamānas, and Hūṇa[170] lineages indicates the presence of these Rajput chiefs in the Mewar hills. We have already stated the possibility of the presence of these Rajput chiefs at strategic points. Therefore, the most obvious support that the Guhilas received from these local, Rajput chiefs was military in nature. B.D. Chattopadhyaya notes the presence of similar military support from the Cāhamānas, Caulukyas and minor Pratihāra lineages to the Gurjara-Pratihāra royal family in a much larger territorial context. The settlement of external Rajput elements not only indicates political integration of the local chiefs but also a system of checks against the local chiefs. Matrimonial alliances with Rajput royal families from Hastīkuṇḍī and central India are likely to have drawn some affinal kin to Mewar, facilitating the organization of a network of Guhila power. However, kinsmen of the royal family evidently occupied higher posts in the military apparatus. The point is supported by two epigraphical records of AD 1000 and AD 1008. They speak of a Guhila *mahāsāmantādhipati* (chief of the big *sāmantas*) of Nāgahṛda (Nāgdā).[171] If Guhilas occupied the posts of *mahāsāmantādhipati*, non-Guhila Rajput chiefs were the other *sāmantas*. Secondly, unlike the simple reference to the chief leader (apparently commander of troops) in the seventh century record,[172] Nāgdā-Āhaḍa records refer to the formal title, *mahāsāmantādhipati* for the first time in the late tenth and early eleventh century.

The other significant facet of the military apparatus would be the chain of fortresses newly constructed, or captured to guard both the core-area of the state as well as the peripheral belt. Āṭapura, the newly constructed capital town at Āhaḍa in tenth century,[173] must have necessitated a chain of fortresses particularly on its northern, north-eastern and southern sides (the western side was guarded by hills and forests). Unfortunately, the lack of direct evidence except for the presence of Kiṣkindhāpur in the Chhappan area, deters us from mapping out such centres. However, the presence of newly inducted Rajputs such as the Hūṇas (central India), Pratihāras or Rāṣṭrakūṭas (Hastikuṇḍī) may indicate the construction of new strongholds. The repeated fall of Āhaḍa in the late tenth century to Cāhamāna and Paramāra incursions possibly suggest that the line of defence was still not strong. Yet, the state territorially expanded in the late eleventh century, and some of the local strongholds were definitely annexed in the Godwar region, to hold the strategically and commercially important Pali.[174] Nāḍol (seat of Nāḍol Cāhamānas) was captured by Jaitrasiṁha in the early thirteenth century which apparently extended the line of defence particularly for the Nāgdā-Āhaḍa belt.[175] Finally Jaitrasiṁha's capture of Chittaurgarh evidently brought a number of neighbouring local fortresses under Guhila control.

D. POLITICAL AND RELIGIOUS SYMBOLS AND THEIR RELATIONSHIP WITH GUHILA MONARCHY

Āṭapura inscription of King Śaktikumāra claims Guhila ancestor Guhadatta as a son of a brāhmaṇa family which had emigrated from Ānandapura (*Ānandapuravinirgatah Viprakulāhnandanoh-mahīdeva jayati Śrī Guhadattah prabhavah Śrī Guhilavaṁśasya*).[176] The Kadmal Plates of King Vijayasiṁha of late eleventh century also repeated the tenth century claim to the brāhmaṇa status of the Guhila.[177] Now the question is why it was necessary to invent a myth of migration from Gujarat to Mewar. We must remember that the Guhilas never associated themselves with Ānandapura or Gujarat before 900. The answer lies in the desire to legitimize the hold of the Nāgdā-Āhaḍa Guhilas over their recent territorial acquisition.

The details of the answers are hidden in the popular annals of Mewar. The transition of power from the Bhils to Nāgdā-Āhaḍa Guhilas recorded in the traditions of Mewar have already been mentioned.[178] It was imperative for the state to officially ignore the fact of subjugation of the Bhils as they had been made subordinates in their own land. Secondly, the Guhilas had also established their predominance over a number of non-Guhila Rajput chiefs of the locality through territorial integration by the tenth century. Hence, the introduction of a migration myth linking the Guhilas with the prestigious Ānandapura brāhmaṇas furnished the task of legitimization of Guhila power over the entire sub-region of the Mewar hills and parts of upper Banas plain. Legitimization was sought by association with a respectable brāhmaṇa family from Ānandapura in Gujarat officially proclaimed for the first time in Āṭapura Inscription of AD 977.[179] The popular annals of Mewar claim that Guhadatta, the founder of the ruling lineage, was the posthumous son of the last Maitraka King Śilāditya of Valabhi. This not only lent respectability to the Nāgdā-Āhaḍa Guhilas but also helped in tracing migration roots from outside Mewar hills. It is interesting that legends also claim that Guhadatta was brought up by a brāhmaṇa of Birnagar (Kamlāvatī) of Nagar *gotra*. She was instructed to bring him up as a brāhmaṇa, but to be married off to a Rajputani.[180]

Religious Symbols

Just as it was necessary for the Nāgdā-Āhaḍa state to take recourse to political symbols to legitimize power in Mewar hills in tenth century, it was equally expedient to associate itself with a religious landmark, signifying beginnings of religious dimension of the process of state formation. The Guhilas sought affiliation with Nāgahṛda, an emerging Pāśupata centre in Mewar hills and through patronage of their cult, Ekaliṅga.

The construction of the royal and magnificient temple of Ekaliṅga is recorded in inscription of AD 971.[181] It was constructed in the reign of Naravāhana at the instruction of Pāśupata *ācāryas* such as Supujitarāśi, Viṁścitarāśi, etc., on the Trikūṭa hills at Nāgahṛda.[182] This inscription mentions the famous Kāyāvarohaṇa episode (the story of Śiva's incarnation at Karvana, Gujarat), the story of the origin of Lakulīśa Pāśupata sect.[183] The episode is a description of Śiva incarnating himself on the earth at Kāyāvarohaṇa in Bhṛgukaccha (Broach district, Gujarat). This incarnation evidently refers to Lakulīśa, the founder of Pāśupata sect of Śaivism. He was followed by disciples Kuśika and others.[184] The inscription records another very significant statement. It states that Śrī Bappaka established himself at Nāgahṛda.[185] For the first time, the Bāppā Rāval of the legends, figures in official records of the Guhila. He is mentioned in association with Nāgahṛda, a Pāśupata centre in tenth century. Another Stone Inscription of King Naravāhana at the Temple of Nātha (AD 970-1) repeats the Kāyāvarohaṇa episode: 'They (Guhilas) sought the protection of Śaṅkara, the lord of Pārvatī . . . , who favoured Bhṛgukacchah. . . . There came Kuśika and other munis, who possessing knowledge and pure bodies took crowns of *jaṭā* (braided hair).'[186] The physical descriptions undoubtedly are those of Pāśupata sages.

Political and Religious Symbols: Thirteenth Century

The acquisition of Chittaurgarh bestowed political sanctity on the Guhila royal family as the sovereigns of Mewar. As noted, Chittaurgarh had evolved into a symbol of political eminence in southern Rajasthan since the beginning of its career as Nāgarī, the capital of the ancient Śibis.[187] As it was annexed and integrated into the expanding Guhila state, the Guhilas of Nāgdā-Āhaḍa could legitimately call themselves the kings of Mewar. Thus was completed the process of territorial unification. So, it was with the Guhila acquisition of Chittaurgarh that the region of Mewar could identify itself with the Guhila royal family of Nāgdā-Āhaḍa.

The culminating phase of this process found echoes in the new political and religious symbols. It was in the thirteenth century that the Guhilas acquired new political and religious symbols. They were no longer the Guhilas of Nāgdā-Āhaḍa; they were formally transformed into Guhilas of Medapāṭa (Mewar).

The point of reference for legitimization, with new territorial acquisitions, was no longer just the Mewar hills for the Guhilas, but all Mewar. A significant turn in their genealogical structure in thirteenth century changed the political and religious symbols. The Chittaurgarh Inscription (AD 1274)[188] and the Achaleśvara Inscription (AD 1285) of Samarasiṁha claimed Bappāka and not Guhadatta, as the founder of the royal house of Medapāṭa.[189] Guhila (Guhadatta) merely appeared as his son.[190] Thus, Guhadatta of the tenth-eleventh century was dropped from the thirteenth century records as the founder of the royal family. The records claimed the bestowal of the state of Mewar on Bappā by the Pāśupata sage Hārītarāśi with the favour of Ekaliṅga.[191] The sage also gave Bappā, a brāhmaṇa by caste, a golden anklet[192] and Bappā got his brāhmaṇahood exchanged for kṣatriyahood which was obtained by the blessing of god Ekaliṅga, who was happy with the devotion of the Pāśupata sage, Hārītarāśi.[193] Thus, the new political and religious symbols of the thirteenth century revolved around the legends of

Bappaka-Hārītarāśi-Ekaliṅga-Medapāṭa and the status of bramha-kṣatra (Brāhmaṇa Bappa receiving kṣatriyahood from Hārītarāśi).

Kinship Structure, Proliferation of the Branches of Nāgdā-Āhaḍa Guhilas, Expansion of Nāgdā-Āhaḍa Guhila Power in Vagod (Middle Mahi Basin) and Emergence of Centres of Power in Upper Banas Plain and Vagod claiming Guhila Lineage

The first evidence of segmentations of the Nāgdā-Āhaḍa Guhila royal family comes from a late eleventh century record, the Kadmal Plates of Guhila Vijayasiṁha (AD 1083). The list reads:

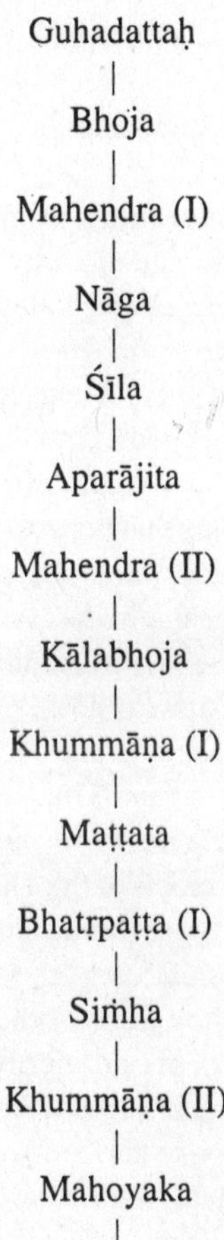

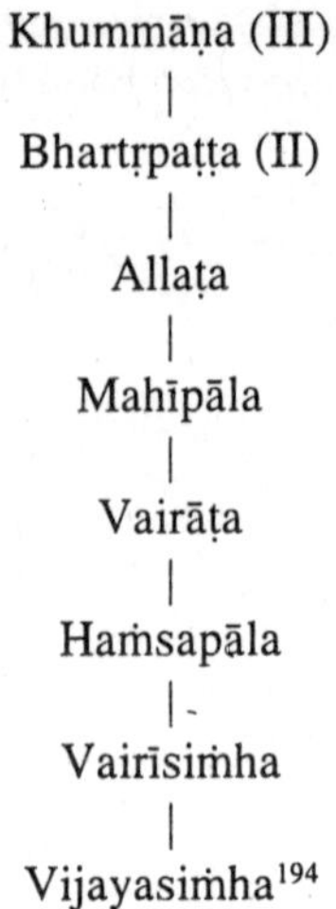

The relation of each succeeding prince with his immediate predecessor in the description got mentioned from Siṁha (the twelfth ruler) onwards in contrast with the earlier rulers.[195] For instance, Siṁha is Bhartṛpaṭṭa (I)'s son (*siṁho = bhava . . . daku{nu}va{ta}sya suto = tha{tha} yāje*).[196] It is significant that instead of Naravāhana of tenth-century records, Allaṭa is succeeded by Mahīpāla in the present record. Naravāhana, the successor of Allaṭa, is not mentioned by the above record. Therefore, it is obvious that both Naravāhana and Mahīpāla were sons of the same father, Allaṭa. Naravāhana being the eldest, succeeded to the throne in regular succession after Allaṭa. This is the main reason why all the known epigraphic records of the Guhilas of Mewar mention Naravāhana. The question arises, however, as to why this particular record omits the mention of Naravāhana and proclaims instead, Mahīpāla as the son and successor of Allaṭa. The question becomes important in view of the fact that Mahīpāla never succeeded to the throne of Nāgdā-Āhaḍa in the tenth century. None of the Guhila records except Kadmal plates mentions Mahīpāla as a Guhila prince. One may assume that only if Vijayasiṁha (the Guhila king issuing Kadmal plates) belonged to a branch of the Guhila ruling family other than that of Naravāhana's, would he have mentioned his immediate ancestors (rather than Naravāhana). In other words, it it likely that Vijayasiṁha belonged to a junior branch of the ruling house. Evidently, this junior branch originated with the younger son of Allaṭa, Mahīpāla. This is evident from the fact that Vairāṭa who preceded Haṁsapāla in the genealogy had obtained rulership elsewhere, i.e. outside his paternal place (*anyatra labdha rājyasya*).[197] The fact is corroborated by the third slab of Kumbhalgarh inscription, which stated that the progeny of Yogarāja (who figures in the main list of the rulers), the predecessor of Vairāṭa, did not attain regal status, and that the lot finally fell on Vairāṭa who was a descendant of a branch of Allaṭa's lineage.[198] The above genealogical variations as culled from all the extant and important records are presented below.[199]

ALLAṬA (vs 1010 = AD 953)

Senior Branch	Junior Branch
□	□
1. Naravāhana (vs 1028 = AD 971)	1. Mahīpāla
□	□
2. Śālivāhana	
□	□
3. Śaktikumāra (vs 1034 = AD 977)	
□	□
4. Ambāprasāda	
□	□
5. Śucivarman	
□	□
6. Naravarman	
□	□
7. Anantavarman	
□	□
8. Yaśovarman	
□	□
9. Yogarāja	
□	□
10. Vairāṭa (vs 1083 = AD 1026)	

In the Kumbhalgarh slabs, the second major segment of the ruling house which branched off with Yogarāja's son in the early eleventh century is mentioned. Since Yogarāja's son could not succeed to the throne, the scion of the immediate junior branch, Vairāṭa was the next legal claimant. Thus, Vairāṭa succeeded Yogarāja. A fragmentary inscription of vs 1083 (AD 1026) preserved in the Victoria Hall Museum at Udaipur can probably be assigned to the reign of Vairāṭa (the major portion containing the name of the ruling prince and other details are lost).[200] It is important that neither a fifteenth-century literary source like the *Ekaliṅgamāhātmyam* (Section: Rājavarṇana) nor a seventeenth-century epigraphic or literary source such as *Rājapraśasti* and *Amarakāvyam* provide any clue to early junior branches. The question arises as to what necessitated these segmentations of the royal family that led to proliferation of its junior branches. A.K. Vyas is probably right when he points out that it might have been a case of some internal family feud of the Guhila state in this period (tenth-eleventh centuries). Formation of new branches seems to have been the most plausible consequence of the ranking system which was the basis of political integration. As the very system of ranking was open-ended, political mobility was implicit. 'Since the basis of territorial and political hold was not static, rank was not static either. In fact, even inadequate studies available so far would suggest that ranks held by individual families underwent changes that ranks varied from one generation to the next and that aspirations for higher ranks were operative within the individual political structures.'[201] The formation of Mahīpāla house is a good instance of competition for higher ranks by junior members of the Nāgdā-Āhaḍa Guhila royal family resulting in formation of junior branches. However, it is very important to note that Mahīpāla's house did not remain a separate branch after with Vairāṭa's accession to the throne in early eleventh century.

A new junior line branched out from Yogarāja's successor in early eleventh century. In both the cases, the records are silent about the actual geographical location of their domain. Therefore, it is difficult to locate their areas of control. Nor can it be expected to be mentioned by the official records of the Guhila state. However, formation of new branches would inevitably locate new areas of control. Only one expression refers to the new locality of control by Yogarāja's successor: *anyatra labdha rājyasya* (Yogarāja's successor obtained rulership elsewhere outside his paternal kingdom).[202] This expression may help us tentatively locate these new areas of control. The expression explicitly points towards a locality outside the tenth-century Guhila state. If ranking was the basis for political mobility, aspirations for higher ranks could not possibly operate within the givern Guhila domain. It was not possible to assign a higher rank to Mahīpāla in preference to his elder brother Naravāhana: the only option was to form a new domain elsewhere in the mid-tenth century.

Is concept of political fragmentation at all relevant for the Guhila state, in view of evidences cited above for the tenth-eleventh centuries? Could newly founded small principalities at the periphery of the state contribute to fragmentation? The new centres of power at peripheries were in fact likely to have contributed towards formation of a chain of immediate allies. Secondly, in the tenth-eleventh centuries there still must have been ample space available in the periphery to settle, and initiate a new dynastic order. Finally, if the junior branches had equal political rights *vis-à-vis* the Guhila king then would not Vijayasiṁha have mentioned his immediate predecessors between Mahīpāla (the founder of the junior house) and himself in his official record, Kadmal plates. The very fact that Vijayasiṁha, a member of the junior branch, remained silent about his immediate predecessors in a royal charter even after becoming king (and presented a single genealogical list of the Guhila dynasty) is indicative of the actual power and status of the junior branches. This is further corroborated by Paldi Inscription of Arisiṁha (Vijayasiṁha's son and successor) which mentioned Vairīsiṁha, Vijayasiṁha and Arisiṁha in succession along with a *praśasti* of the Guhila.[203] Arisiṁha did not even mention Mahīpāla, founder of the house, in his official record. He named his grandfather Vairīsiṁha instead. Even Vairāṭa, an actual ruler of the Guhila throne who probably happened to be Arisiṁha's greater grandfather, did not find a place in the Paldi inscription.

The fact that expansion of kinship networks, leading to formation of junior branches became phenomenal in this period is evident from the following expression in Paldi Inscription: *hārivistāriśākhah prājyaih patrai guhilanṛpatera (śrī) tottapaharī* (the expanding branches of the Guhila kings).[204] Thus, new centres of power did not disrupt the process of state formation initiated by the main line; instead expansion of the kinship network caused rivalries, rather than diffusing them.[205]

Pratapgarh Guhilas from Nāgahṛda

Expansion of kinship network in the period witnessed emergence of Guhila centres of power in south-eastern part of upper Banas plain. Localities in Pratapgarh region of Chittaurgarh district (south-eastern part of upper Banas plain) were held by members of Nāgdā-Āhaḍa Guhila royal lineage (see Map 6). It is evident from the three inscriptions of Guhila Vigrahapāla of vs 1053, 1065 and 1066 inscribed on the *chhatrī*-pillar of Mahārāvat Bhānasiṁha (Bhāna), a ruler of Deolia-Pratapgarh.[206] The find-spot of these inscriptions is Jiran in the Neemach tahsil of district Gwalior. Guhila Vigrahapāla proclaimed himself *mahāsāmantādhipati* of Nāgahṛda.[207] The claim to both 'Guhila' and 'Nāgahṛda' along

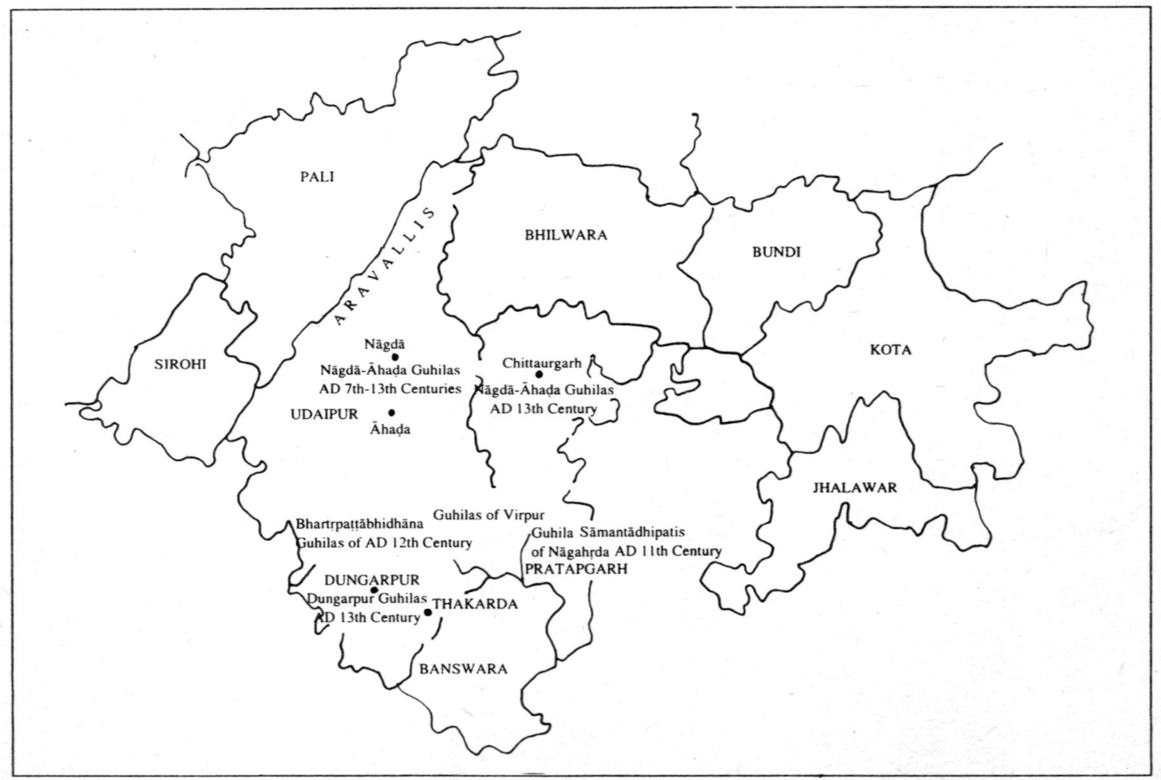

Map 6: Inscriptional Location of the Branches of the Nāgdā-Āhaḍa Guhilas: Eleventh-Thirteenth Centuries.

with the rank of *mahāsāmantādhipati* suggests that the settlements of Guhila kinsmen were proliferating. These Guhila chiefs might have been incorporated into the Guhila state in the mid-tenth century as is evident from their rank of *mahāsāmantādhipati*. Guhila King Bhartṛpaṭṭa's territorial rights in Pratapgarh and his title of *mahārājādhirāja* before mid-tenth century seem to support our suggestion. However, G.H. Ojha opines that Pratapgarh Guhilas of early eleventh century were probably the subordinate allies of the Paramāras of Malwa.[208] This suggestion is plausible in view of Paramāra incursions into southern Rajasthan in the late tenth century and their occupation of Chittaurgarh.

Bhartṛpaṭṭabhidhāna Guhilas of Vagod and Ingnoda

The emergence of a kingdom claiming Guhila lineage in the Vagod region by the late twelfth century is evident from the discovery of three inscriptions. A chronological study of these three inscriptions clearly reveals a significant process in which a local ruling family in Vagod from an obscure background claimed lineage with the Guhilas. King Vijayapāla in his Ingnoda (western Malwa) Inscription of AD 1133 declared himself to be a grandson of King Pṛthvīpāla who bore the title of Bhartṛpaṭṭa (*samastarājavalīvirājitabhartṛpadābhidānamahārājādhirājā parameśvara śrīpṛthvīpālapādānudhyāta paramabhaṭṭāraka mahārājādhirājādhirājāparameśvara śrī tihuṇapāladevapādānudhyāta mahārājādhirājaparameśvara śrī vijayapāladeva*).[209] Vijayapāla donated the village of Agāsiyaka to the god Gohadeśvara situated within the division to the south of Iṇgaṇapaṭa.[210] Interestingly, there is no mention of the Guhila lineage in this record. But the reference to the title of Bhartṛpaṭṭa points towards beginnings of claims of kinship connections with the Nāgdā-Āhaḍa Guhilas. We have already noted that Bhartṛpaṭṭa II had consolidated and extended the Guhila power in the tenth century. Claiming kinship lineages to a famous Guhila king of the tenth century would have legitimized their power in the domain of the Guhila lineage. They possibly claimed the kinship linkage for the first time in Ingnoda record and hence refrained from claiming Guhila lineage outrightly at the point.

The next epigraph Ṭhākarda (Dungarpur district) Inscription of AD 1155 records the grant of land of one plough to the god Siddheśvara by Mahārājāputra Śrī Anaṅgapāladeva, Vijayapāladeva's grandson.[211]

This record too refers to the title of Bhartṛpaṭṭa for Pṛthvīpāla but not to the Guhila lineage.[212] The above two records give us an idea of the area of control under this ruling family. Pṛthvīpāla's successors seem to have controlled an area between Vagod (districts of Dungarpur and Banswara) and Iṇgaṇapaṭa (modern Ingnoda) in western Malwa. In view of the decline of the Paramāra power in Malwa in the twelfth century, Vijayapāladeva seems to have extended his sway up to the western part of Malwa. The last of the records, Virpur (in southern part of Udaipur district) inscription of AD 1185 refers to the grant of a well (*araghaṭṭa*) called Lasādiā and a land of two *halas* (ploughs) in the village of Gāṭauḍa in the province of Saht(a)-pañcaśat (Chhappan in Udaipur district) to a brāhmaṇa, Madana by Amṛtpāla, son of Vijayapāla alias Bhartṛpaṭṭa of the lineage Guhadatta (*śrī guhiladattavaṁśa śrīmadbhartṛpaṭṭābhidhānamahārājādhirāja śrī vijayapālasuta mahārājādhirāja śrī amṛtapāladeva*).[213] Thus, the three records demonstrate the gradual process through which the ruling family of Vagod in the twelfth century claimed lineage connections with the Guhilas. It is significant that Vijayapāla too bears the title of Bhartṛpaṭṭa in Virpur record.

I shall now mention the views of the epigraphists and historians who have extensively discussed the above records, to make our position clear on the Bhartṛpaṭṭabhidhāna Guhilas. Asoke Kumar Majumdar, on the basis of Ingnoda and Ṭhākarada inscriptions opines that an independent line of kings existed within 80 km of Ujjain.[214]

> These two inscriptions show that members of a petty dynasty took advantage of the decay of the Paramāras and asserted their independence. Probably they brought under their control territories in western Malwa, but were later driven out and forced to assume their humbler rank in their now obscure principality near Dungarpur . . . most likely driven out of Mālava by Siddharāja or Chandella Madanavarman and content as feudatories.[215]

R.R. Halder, the editor of the Ṭhākarda Inscription of the time of Mahārāja Surapāladeva, comparing this record with Surapāladeva's Ingnoda Inscription, observes that the genealogical lists are common to both the records. But Ṭhākarda Inscription does not mention the epithets of *mahārājādhirāja*, *parameśvara* and *paramabhaṭṭāraka*. Halder opines that they were probably, though not necessarily independent kings at first, and ruled over certain parts of Rajputana and central India.[216] He finds it difficult to assign a dynastic origin to them as none of the records mentions the name of the family. Gauri Shankar Hirachand Ojha initially included them in the Kacchavāha rulers of Gwalior[217] but later on changed his opinion and remarked in the *Annual Report of the Rajputana Museum* that these kings were possibly the descendants of the Pratihāra kings of Kanauj and ruled over parts of central India and Rajasthan.[218] Halder accepts the latter view.[219] D.C. Ganguly opines that Vijayapāla was a governor of the Paramāras in control of Ingnoda and its surrounding localities.[220] Vijayapāla seems to have declared his independence after the death of his master, Paramāra King Naravarman.[221]

Pratipal Bhatia, discussing the Ingnoda Inscription of Vijayapāla, observes that since Ingnoda is only 80 km to the north-west of Ujjain, this record reveals the presence of a kingdom, the princes of which seem to have claimed independent position.[222] Not only the Chandellas but also the family of Vijayapāla were encroaching upon the borders of the Paramāra kingdom of Malwa.[223]

Our suggestion that Bhartṛpaṭṭābhidhāna Guhilas extended their sway over western Malwa from Vagod in the twelfth century during the decline of the Paramāra power does not contradict the views of Majumdar, Ganguly, or Bhatia. But none of the three inscriptional records of the Bhartṛpaṭṭābhidhāna Guhilas supports Ojha's contention or Halder's views that this ruling family was a descendant of the Pratihāras of Kanauj.

The rise of the family of the Bhartṛpaṭṭābhidhāna Guhilas seems to be an instance of formation of a dynasty from an obscure background, claiming Guhila lineage, and controlling an area south of the territory of the Nāgdā-Āhaḍa Guhilas. The area under the control of the Bhartṛpaṭṭabhidhāna Guhilas is likely to have stretched from the south-eastern part of Dungarpur to western part of Malwa. Possibly they also held parts of Chhappan—south-eastern part of Udaipur district. The fact that the ousted Guhila King Sāmantasiṁhadeva could found a principality around the locality of Dungarpur in the end of twelfth century indicates that the Guhilas of Nāgdā-Āhaḍa were yet to control Vagod.

The Guhilas of Dungarpur

A major house of the Guhilas of Nāgdā-Āhaḍa that was born in late twelfth century was that of Dungarpur. This branch, known to have originated with Guhila Sāmantasiṁhadeva, continued to hold the whole of Vagod as a separate kingdom throughout the medieval period. G.S. Ojha in his monumental work, *History of the Dungarpur State* constructed the following genealogical table on the basis of epigraphic records, legends and gazetteers of the colonial period:

KṢEMA SIṀHA (KING OF MEWAR)

Vagod Branch	Mewar Branch
Sāmantasiṁha (previously king of Mewar and later king of Vagod (vs 1228-36)	Kumarasiṁha
	Mathanasiṁha
Jayatasiṁha	Padmasiṁha
Sīhaḍadeva (vs 1277-91)	Jaitrasiṁha (vs 1271-1309)
Vijayasiṁhadeva (Jayasiṁhadeva)	Tejasiṁha (vs 1317-20)
(vs 1306-1308) Devapāladeva	Samarasiṁha (vs 1330-58)
Vīrasiṁhadeva (vs 1343-59)	Ratnasiṁha (vs 1359-60)[224]

The Jagat (AD 1172)[225] and Soloj (Dungarpur district) Inscriptions (AD 1179)[226] show that Sāmantasiṁha ruled in Mewar and Vagod respectively in the eighth decade of twelfth century. How did he acquire Vagod? Was it territorial extension of the Guhila state of Nāgdā-Āhaḍa or was it another case of segmentation of the royal family due to kinship pressures? To answer these questions, we shall examine the evidences of two royal sources, Achaleśvara Inscription of AD 1285 and Kumbhalgarh Praśasti of AD 1460. Achaleśvara Inscription states that Sāmantasiṁha snatched away everything from the *sāmantas* and that Kumārasiṁha had to win back the royalty for his ancestral kingdom which had been lost to the enemies.[227] Kumbhalgarh Praśasti states that Rāṇāsiṁha was succeeded by Kṣemasiṁha, the younger brother of Mathanasiṁha who evidently predeceased his father and then Sāmantasiṁha became the ruler of Mewar.[228] It records further that Sāmantasiṁha was succeeded by his brother Kumārasiṁha who threw a person called Kītū out of Mewar because the latter had somehow taken hold of the country. He also made Āghaṭapura his own by acquiring the favour of the ruler of Gujarat.[229] Thus, some external factor seems to have influenced the course of political history of the reign of Sāmantasiṁha and accession of Kumārasiṁha.

Some other near contemporary sources outside the house of Guhilas also throw light on the history of Sāmantasiṁha's reign. The Luṇavasahī Temple Inscription of AD 1230 (record of the Paramāras of Abu) states that Prahlādan, younger brother of Paramāra King Dhārāvarṣa, saved the life of a ruler of Gujarat when he was badly defeated by Sāmantā-siṁha.[230] Since Paramāras of Abu were the subordinate allies of the Caulukyas of Gujarat, they must have joined forces against Guhila King Sāmantasiṁhadeva. Ojha identifies Ajayapāla (Kumārapāla's successor) as the Caulukya contemporary of Guhila Sāmantasiṁha.[231] Therefore, Guhila Sāmantasiṁha must have defeated Caulukya Ajayapāla in the battlefield. In the fifteenth canto of *Surathotsavakāvya* composed by Gurjareśvara Purohita, Someśvara (composer of Luṇavasahī Inscription) states about one of his ancestors, Kumāra, that he cooled the many wounds of King Ajayapāla caused at Raṇakheta.[232] Ojha places the defeat of Caulukya Ajayapāla by Guhila Sāmantasiṁha around AD 1174.[233] It is obvious from both the Luṇavasahī Inscription and *Surathotsavakāvya* that although Sāmantasiṁha had inflicted defeat, the Caulukyas soon avenged themselves and Guhila Sāmantasiṁhadeva was forced to abdicate.

Invasion by the Caulukyas of Gujarat (combined with cliques of their *sāmantas*) seem to have been the determining factor in the ouster of Sāmantasiṁha in the 1180s. Thus, lineage fission/segmentation during political turmoil in the royal house helped the consolidation of royal power, while opening up Guhila centres of power beyond its immediate frontiers.

However, after the abdication, Sāmantasiṁha sought his fortunes in Dungarpur locality of Vagod. Ojha places the defeat of Sāmantasiṁha by the Caulukyan forces around AD 1175.[234] Finally, as noted, the Achaleśvara inscription says that in Sāmantasiṁha's abdication, the *sāmantas* of the Guhila state played an important role by projecting the former's younger brother, Kumārasiṁha as their candidate. Kumārasiṁha seems to have consolidated Guhila power in a period of turmoil with the help of Guhila *sāmantas*. Details of the history of external invasions juxtaposed against Guhila inscriptional evidence throw significant light on the political process of state formation in which *sāmantas* contributed to the preservation of the Guhila throne in Mewar. The above suggestion possibly answers as to why one of the main official records of Mewar of AD 1285 should highlight the *sāmantas* in the reign of Sāmantasiṁhadeva after hundred years of the actual event (eighth decade of the twelfth century) ? *Sāmantas* played a decisive role in the politics of Mewar in the latter half of the twelfth century. The Acaleśvara Inscription suggests that some of the *sāmantas*—local as well as neighbouring chiefs—had been accommodated but suffered loss of power at the hands of Sāmantasiṁhadeva.

To quote verses 36 and 37 of Acaleśvara Inscription,

> From him was born the protector of the earth named Sāmantasiṁha . . . who took away the possessions (everything) of neighbouring princes (sāmantas). Afterwards, winning (again) Fortune who was embarrassed by her separation from the lineage of Shommāṇa (and) who clearly was pining for the Guhila family, Kumārasiṁha made the earth possessed of a good king, having taken it away again from the possession of the enemy.[235]

The phrase, '. . . Afterwards winning fortune Kumārasiṁha made the earth possessed of a good king', indicates that Kumārasiṁha addressed himself to the people of Mewar including its chiefs—local and neighbouring. The description also points towards the role played by the *sāmantas* in restoring the throne of the Guhilas to Kumārasiṁha.

In the wake of the Caulukyan invasion, Sāmantasiṁhadeva is not likely to have received military support from the dissatisfied *sāmantas*. Kumārasiṁha, on the other hand, seems to have mastered the throne of Mewar, restored to its 'indigenous' dynasty.

A Guhila-Caulukya clash during Sāmantasiṁha's period is easily understandable in view of Caulukyan sway over the whole of Mewar in the mid-twelfth century. This is already noted from Kumārapāla's Chittaurgarh Inscription of AD 1151.[236] Their continued sway over Mewar hills till early thirteenth century is also evident from Āhaḍa copper plate grants of Caulukya Bhīma II of AD 1207.[237] It is also obvious from Vīrpur Village Inscription of Bhartṛpaṭṭābhidhāna Guhila, Amṛtapāla that the previous Guhila rulers of Vagod (Bhartṛpaṭṭābhidhāna Guhilas) acknowledged their Caulukyan overlords.[238] Thus, Sāmantasiṁha could only have a short rule in Vagod as he seems to have been defeated by the Caulukyas between AD 1179 and AD 1185. However, his short rule was succeeded by kings who came to be identified as the Guhilas of Dungarpur.

The above chapter traces the stages of state formation in Mewar on the basis of the process of territorial integration facilitated by the Guhila ruling family of Nāgdā-Āhaḍa in the period. The Guhilas of Chāṭsu evidently controlled a small area and functioned as subordinate allies of the Pratihāras of Kanauj. Godwar and Saurashtra Guhilas functioned merely as political components of Nāḍol Cāhamāna and Caulukyan states respectively. In contrast, the Guhila dynasty of Nāgdā-Āhaḍa successfully laid the foundation of a state structure in Mewar. The Mewar hills emerged as the locus of a sub-regional state by the tenth century. Political, economic, social and religious processes of state formation are amply borne out by the beginnings of political integration of both Guhila and non-Guhila chiefs into administrative structure and military apparatus. An expanding resource base, advantageous matrimonial alliances, politico-religious symbols and patronage of a locally popular sect appear to have accompanied and facilitated the process. Interestingly, as the state grew by territorial integration and incorporation of Guhila and non-Guhila chiefs, the royal family witnessed fissioning necessary to readjust under pressure in an open-ended polity. Increasing power of the Guhilas is evident from their claim of sovereignty all over Mewar. The acquisition of Chittaurgarh in the mid-thirteenth century and new politico-religious symbols identifying the Guhila dynasty as the sovereign of the whole of Mewar marked the climax of the integrative process of territorial incorporation and transformed the Guhila state of the sub-region of Mewar hills into the regional state of Mewar.

NOTES

1. Inscription of Guhila Dhanika of AD 684 from Uniyara tahsil, district Tonk, quoted in D.C. Sircar, *The Guhilas of Kiṣkindhā*, pp. 31-2.
2. *EI*, vol. XII, pp. 10-17, vv. 6-7, '. . . *abhavadvaṁśastadviparīta eṣa guhilasyāḍvārbhūto bhuvah . . . brahmakṣatrānvitoasmin samabh awadasa mein* . . .'.
3. Ibid., vv. 14-26, '. . . *bhatamjitvā gauḍakṣitipamavanim sangarhṛtām . . . śṁnṛpatimbhojaya bhantā cād au sanktāmsekasindhulaghanavi – śrī vaṁśajānvājinah*'.
4. Ibid., vv. 20-4, 33. Harṣarāja was married to Princess Silla (her lineage is not mentioned), his son Guhila married Rajjha, daughter of Paramāra Ballabharāja, and Guhila's grandson Bālāditya made another prestigious alliance with Raṭṭava, daughter of Cāhamāna King Śivarāja.
5. PRAS, WC, 1911-12, p. 53.
6. Ibid.
7. Ibid.
8. Ibid.
9. B.D. Chattopadhyaya, 'Early Memorial Stones of Rajasthan', in S. Settar, ed., *Memorial Stones*, Dharwar and Delhi, 1982, p. 144.
10. PRAS, WC, 1911-12, p. 53.
11. Ibid.
12. PRAS, WC, 1909, p. 42.

13. Ibid.
14. Ibid.
15. Ibid.
16. Ibid.
17. Ibid.
18. Stone Inscriptions of Sobhadi Vão of AD 1146 at Māṅgrol, *A Collection of Prakrit and Sanskrit Inscriptions*, Bhavnagar, n.d., pp. 158-60.
19. Ibid., vv. 4-5.
20. Ibid.
21. Ibid.
22. *RTA*, pp. 149-60.
23. *EI*, vol. VII, p. 205, 1.4, '*jitvā jagat=samastam[yo] Jagat[t]uṅga iti kṛuta[h]|| Kerala-Mālava sautan=sa-Gujjara citrakūṭa-giridurgga-sthān=baddhvā kañcisa nātha sa kīrtinārāyaṇo jagati||*'.
24. *EI*, vol. IV, p. 284, v. 30, '*dakṣiṇādigadurgga vijayamākarṇya galitā gurjjarahṛdayātka(kan)jaracitrakuṭāśā*'.
25. Pratapgarh Inscription of the Reign of Mahendrapāla II, *EI*, vol. XIV, pp. 176-88.
26. Pratapgarh Inscription, op. cit., pt. III, l.27, '*samastarājavalīpurvvamgreha mahārājādhirājaśrībhartṛipaṭṭah*'.
27. Ibid., pt. II, vv. 5-6, '*soyam rajati rājacakranīlayah śrī cāhamānanvayah govindarāja iti tatra vabhuva bhūpo*', and l. 21 '*. . . cāh amānanvaya-mahāsāmantaśrī indrarāja*'.
28. Āṭapura Inscription of Śaktikumāra of AD 977, *IA*, vol. XXXIX, pp. 186-91, v. 9, '*tatah śaktikumārobhutsutah śaktitrāyojitah bhartṛpaṭṭabhidhā śrīsraca prāpa rāṣṭramdhapayat*'.
29. Ibid.
30. Sāraṇeśvara Inscription of Allaṭa of AD 953, *IA*, vol. LVIII, pp. 161-2. Interestingly, there is no separate mention of Āhaḍa, Āghaṭa or Āṭapur in this record.
31. K.C. Jain, op. cit., p. 220.
32. See next section in this chapter: Resources of the state.
33. We have already noted in the first chapter that Āhaḍa is only 22 km south of Nāgdā. The Guhilas exercised control over the stretch of Nāgdā-Āhaḍa in the seventh century—initial stage of their rise.
34. Pratapgarh Inscription, op. cit., pt. III, l.27.
35. Āṭapura Inscription, v. 3, '*siṁghobhavattadanu tadbhṛtipi jajñe khommāṇa ityatha sutasyamahāyakobhūt khommāṇamātmajamavapa ra catrallota tasmālloka-traikatilakajani bhartṛpaṭṭah*'.
36. Ibid., v.1.
37. *EI*, vol. XXXI, pp. 237-48, ll.2-3, '*ānandapuravinirgata viprakul-ānandano mahīdeva jayati śrī-guhadattah prabhavah śrī guhilavaṁśabhyā(sya) ||*'.
38. *EI*, vol. IV, pp. 278-90, v. 30, '*dakṣiṇādigurgga vijayamākarṇya galitā gurjarahṛadyātkālaṁjara citrakūṭāśa*'.

39. *EI*, vol. V, pp. 188-97.
40. *RTA*, p. 198, see the chapter on Devapāla.
41. *URI*, vol. I, p. 124, fn. 3, '*dūrdharāmārim yu devapālam vyādhat Kabandham vyādhat*'.
42. Ibid.
43. *EI*, vol. X, pp. 20-4, v.10, '*bhāṁktāghāṭam ghaṭābhih prakatmiva madam medapāṭe bhatānām janye rājanyajanye janayati janatājam raṇam muñjarāje| śrī mane pranaste | harina iva bhiya gurjjarese vinaṣṭe tatsainyānām śaraṇyo hāririvasarane yah śaraṇam babhūva.*'
44. *RTA*, p. 248.
45. *ARRM*, Ajmer, 1920-1, p. 4.
46. *Early Chauhan Dynasties*, p. 34. Also see, *RTA*, p. 249.
47. The State, 1000-1700, p. 241. Hermann Kulke's following observations on Orissa can be compared with the political situation of the Guhila of Nāgdā-Āhaḍa during the tenth century, 'The relations with the nuclear areas of neighbouring princes, often separated by extensive forests, created no problems in this early phase. They were mainly limited to marriage relations and sporadic campaigns, which however remained in this early period without any significant long-term consequences. Permanent subjugation and annexation after a military victory were still scarcely conceivable. Considering the power potential at the disposal of the early local principalities, the neighbouring seats of the rulers were still far beyond their sphere of permanent political control.'
48. Āṭapura Inscription of Śaktikumāra, op. cit., vv. 4-5, '*rāṣṭrakūṭakulodbhūta mahālakṣmīriti priyā | abhūddyasyābhavattasyām tanayah Śrīmadallaṭah | sa bhūpati-yā yasya hūṇakṣoṇīsavaṁśaja hāriyādevī yośoyasya bhāti Harṣapurahavyam.*'
49. Ibid.
50. Ibid., vv. 6-7, '. . . *nṛpo naravāhanah cāhumānānvayodbhūtā śrī jejyanṛpatmajā*'.
51. *ARRM*, 1936, p. 2.
52. Kadmal Plates of AD 1083, op. cit., pp. 246-8, ll. 12-38.
53. Ibid., p. 244.
54. *Trade and Traders*, see the map, p. 111.
55. Kadmal Plates, op. cit., p. 246, v. 8, ' . . . *mahāvīrō vairisiṁho mahā(hī)-patiḥ || sahāyita-savāhāyēna vairi-kuṁ [ja]ramū[mu]dvasta[han]*.
56. Presence of the Paramāras of Malwa in Vagod is evident from the following inscriptions: Bhoja's Banswara Plates of AD 1021, *EI*, vol. XI, pp. 181-3; Panahera Inscription of Māṇḍalika Jayasiṁhadeva of Malwa of AD 1059, *EI*, vol. XXI, pp. 42-50. Arthuna Inscription of the time of Paramāra Cāmuṇḍarāja of AD 1078 and 1080, WC, March 1915, p. 35.
57. Bheraghat Inscriptions of Chedi year 907 (AD 1155), *EI*, vol. II, pp. 7-17, vv. 20-1, '*pṛthvīpativijayasinh iti*. . . *mālavamaṇḍalādhināthodayādityasutā surūpā śṛṅgariṇī śyāmaladevyudarcaritracintamani* . . .'.

58. Ibid., vv. 22-3, '*tasmādalhaṇadevya jāyat . . . vivāha vidhimādhāya gayakarṇanareśvarah*'.
59. Paldi Inscrption of Arisiṁha of AD 1116, *EI*, vol. XXX, pp. 8-12, v. 9.
60. *EI*, vol. II, pp. 421-4. This inscription which records an eulogy and grants made by the Caulukyan King Kumārapāla to the temple of Samādhīśa at Chittaurgarh does not mention the Guhilas.
61. *ARRM*, 1915, p. 3.
62. *ARRM*, 1931, p. 4.
63. Ibid.
64. See the last section of this chapter: Dungarpur Guhilas.
65. Ibid.
66. (i) Two Inscriptions of Tejasiṁha from Ghaghsa (near Chittaur), AD 1265, *URI*, op. cit., pp. 176-7, (ii) Chittaur Inscription of the time of Samarasiṁha of AD 1285, op. cit., (iii) Chittaur Inscriptions of AD 1287 of the reign of Samarasiṁha. PRAS, WC, 1905-6, pp. 61-2, *URI*, p. 177.
67. Achaleśvara Inscription of Samarasiṁha of AD 1285, *IA*, vol. XVI, pp. 345-55, v. 42, '*naḍūla mūlaṁkaṣabāhulakṣmīsturūṣkasainyārṇava-kumbhayonih asminsurādhīsahāsanasthe parakṣa bhumīmatha Jaitra-siṁhah*'. See also its texts by Kaviraj Shyamaldas, ed., Achaleśvara Inscription in *Vir Vinod*, vol. I, pp. 397-401 and *CPSI*, pp. 84-96.
68. Ibid., v. 42.
69. Unpublished inscriptions quoted in *URI*, vol. I, p. 166, nn. 2-3.
70. Acaleśvara Inscription, op. cit., v. 42.
71. (i) Bijolia Inscription, *EI*, vol. XXVI, pp. 105 ff. (ii) Menal Inscriptions, PRAS, WC, 1905-6, pp. 57 and 60. The Cāhamāna King Pṛthvīrāja III made grants at temples of Mahāvīra and Śiva at Bijolia and Menal respectively without referring to the Guhilas.
72. Kumbhalgarh Praśasti, 3rd slab, *EI*, vol. XXIV, p. 325, v.155.
73. We have noted that in spite of recurring intrusions by external powers into Mewar, the Guhilas of Nāgdā-Āhaḍa successfully brought about territorial integration and political consolidation of Mewar under their banner. The territorial process of regional state formation spanning over centuries coincided with the steadily rising political career of the Guhila royal family of Nāgdā-Āhaḍa. Hence, the regional state of Mewar did not owe its origin to any centre of the Gupta or Pratihāra 'imperial' power. For a general discussion, see Hermann Kulke, ed., *The State in India*, p. 235. 'But it was characteristic for the further early medieval development of the post-Gupta period that the vast majority of early medieval kingdoms did neither arise from the centres of the Gupta empire nor from its provincial capitals. They arose rather in their autonomous peripheral hinterland and in intermediate regions which had not yet been conquered but which already had come under a wide range of influences of the Gupta empire. These were therefore regions in which local princes . . . therefore regions in which local princes had the chance to establish their local rule under the

influence (or better on the model) of more advanced forms of economic and political development and to consolidate it undisturbed over many generations.'

74. *Trade and Traders*, p. 133.
75. Ibid., pp. 103 and 133; Al-Masudi speaks of Makran emerald sold in markets of Mecca.
76. Nāḍol Inscription of Śrī Rāyapāladeva, *EI*, vol. XI, pp. 37ff.
77. *Prabandhacintāmaṇi* of Merutuṅga (tr. M.A. Tawney), Calcutta, 1901, p. 121.
78. Ibid., p. 99.
79. *Tilakamañjarī Kathā of Dhanapāla*, Bombay, 1903, p. 66.
80. *Trade and Traders*, pp. 117-18.
81. Ibid.
82. Ibid.
83. Chiravā Inscription of the period of Samarasiṁha, AD 1273, *EI*, vol. XXII, pp. 285-92, vv. 15-16. It records the battle of Bhūtālā fought between Guhila King Jaitrasiṁha of Mewar and the forces of Sultan Iltutmish.
84. Elliot and Dowson, vol. III, op. cit., pp. 147-8. Ulghu, the grandson of Genghis Khan, with commanders, nobles and families stayed on and provisions for them had been made at Mughalpur in Delhi. The Mongols had crossed Sind in AD 1296. Kotwal of Delhi advised Alauddin Khalji to capture Rajput forts not only to subdue the Rajput chiefs but also to close the road of Multan against the Mongols.
85. S.C. Misra, op. cit., p. 40.
86. B.D. Chattopadhyaya, 'Markets and Merchants in Early Medieval Rajasthan', in *Social Science Probings*, vol. II, no. 4, 1985, pp. 413-40.
87. Vide *passim*, Chap. I, pp. 36-8.
88. Āṭapura Inscription of Śaktikumāra, op. cit., v.10.
89. Ekaliṅgajī Temple Inscription of the time of Guhila Naravāhana of AD 971, Bombay Branch of Royal Asiatic Society, vol. XXII, pp. 151-65. It refers to the construction of a temple of Ekaliṅga by Pāśupata *ācāryas* near Nāgdā.
90. Paldi Inscription of Guhila Arisiṁha of AD 1116, op. cit. It refers to a temple of Śiva and a Pāśupata monastery at Paldi.
91. Jagat Inscription of Sāmantasiṁhadeva, op. cit.
92. Kankroli Road Station Inscription of AD 1298-9 of the reign of Guhila Samarasiṁha in *URI*, vol. I, op. cit., p. 177. It records the grant of sixteen *drammas*, to a temple of a goddess at Dariba mines near Kankroli.
93. Chiravā Inscription of AD 1273 of the reign of Guhila Samarasiṁha, op. cit., vv. 34-40.
94. Sāraṇeśvara Temple Inscription, op. cit., v. 9, '*karnāṭamadhyaviṣayodbhavalāṭaṭakkā anyepi kecidih ye vanijo viśanti taih . . . vyabhicāraṇīyam*'.
95. Ibid., v. 10, '*drammamekam kari dadyātt urogo pūpakadvayam drammardhaviṁsakam śṛṅgī . . .*'.

96. Literally a 'balance; hence that measure of grain which is held in a balance in weighing once. In Mewar, generally 5 *sers* of a grain make a *tulā* or *takri*.
97. The term '*randhanī*' is not found in any Sanskrit lexicon. The term is apparently derived from the Sanskrit verb root *radh* meaning to cook.
98. Ibid., vv. 10-12.
99. Vide *passim*, Ch. I, see Grants of the Kiṣkindhā Guhilas.
100. R.S. Sharma, *Indian Feudalism c. 300-1200*, p. 102. Also see idem, *Urban Decay in India (c. 300-c. 1000)*, Delhi, 1987, pp. 139-40, 182.
101. R.C. Agrawala, 'Dramma in Ancient Indian Epigraphs and Literature', in *JNSI*, vol. XVII, no. 2, 1955, pp. 71-2. Also PRAS, WC, 1906, p. 59.
102. John Scott Deyell, *Living Without Silver: The Monetary History of Early Medieval North India*, Delhi, 1990, pp. 146-8.
103. Āṭapura Inscription, op. cit., v. 10, '*śrīmadāṭapura yutalayām yasya vāsa iti sampada padam*'.
104. Ibid., v. 11, '*syātam kanakādikandaragṛhodīrṇapratāpam divi khyātam . . . vibhavobhutābhiśobham subham | . . . narāh*'.
105. B.D. Chattopadhyaya, 'Urban Centres in Early Medieval India: An Overview', in Romila Thapar and Sabyasachi Bhattacharya, eds., *Situating Indian History*, Delhi, 1986, p. 32.
106. *URI*, vol. I, p. 170, Ghaghsa Inscription of AD 1261 refers to Āhaḍadurga; ibid., p. 176, Chittaur Inscription of Samarasiṁha of AD 1274 refers to Maṇḍapikā of Āhaḍa.
107. Pratapgarh Inscription, op. cit. Extent of agricultural resources from Pratapgarh locality is evident from the boundaries of the donated field Vavvūlika on the bank of river Nandya at the village of Palāśakūpikā.
108. Chiravā Inscription, op. cit., vv. 34-40.
109. Craddock et al., op. cit., p. 56.
110. Kadmal Plates, op. cit., ll. 26-32.
111. Beal, op. cit., p. 271.
112. Chittaurgarh Inscription of King Māna Morī, op. cit. This record proves that Chittaurgarh was the capital town of the Morīs.
113. Chittaurgarh Inscription of Caulukya King Kumarapala, op. cit., ll. 26-7, '*śivaṁ prapūjya ta[tap] [ma]amatprabhuh praṇamya [tāvubhau?] bhaktyā si (śi) rasā u-u-i] . . . pūjartham harpādayoh | kumārapāladevo . . . dakṣiṇapūrvvottarapaścimatah sarahpālī bhūṇāditya . . . rāj . . . dīpārtham ghāṇ akamekam sajjanopyadāt danḍanāth. . . .*?
114. Dhavagartā Inscription of Guhila Dhanika, op. cit., ll. 5-13.
115. Ghaghsa Record (near Chittaurgarh) of AD 1265 of the reign of Guhila Tejasiṁha in *URI*, vol. I, p. 170.
116. Ibid.
117. Chittaur Stone Inscription of AD 1267 in G.H. Ojha, ibid.
118. Menal Stone Inscription of AD 1168 Cāhamāna Queen Suhavadevī, PRAS, WC, 1905-6, pp. 57 and 60.

119. Bijolia Stone Inscriptions of AD 1168 and AD 1169 of the reign of Cāhamāna Someśvara, *EI*, vol. XXXVI, pp. 84-112.
120. Chittaurgarh Inscription of Samarasiṁha of AD 1274, op. cit.
121. Kankroli Road-Station Inscription of the period of Samarasimha, op. cit.
122. Acaleśvara Inscription of Samarasiṁha of AD 1285, op. cit., contains a *praśasti* of Mount Abu locality and implies Samarasiṁha's acquisition of Mount Abu, vv. 49-59, '*arbudo vijayate girir = uccaisdevasevita-kulācalaratnam yatra ṣoḍaśavikāravipākair kair = ujjhito = kṛta tapāmsī vaśiṣṭhah*'.
123. Sobhadivāo Stone Inscription, op. cit., vv. 6-8.
124. Ibid.
125. Chattopadhyaya, *Origin of the Rajputs*, p. 76.
126. Samoli Inscription, op. cit. we have already noted the possibility of weekly fairs at Araṇyakūpagiri in the first chapter.
127. Sāraṇeśvara Temple Inscription, op. cit., *passim*, pp. 66-7.
128. Pratapgarh Inscription, op. cit., *passim*, p. 94, n. 107.
129. Chittaurgarh Inscription of Samarasiṁha (AD 1274), op. cit., *passim*, p. 68.
130. Ibid.
131. Ibid.
132. Achaleśvara Inscription (AD 1285), op. cit., pp. 345-53.
133. Chittaurgarh Inscription (AD 1274), op. cit., pp. 392-6.
134. Samoli Inscription, op. cit., p. 98.
135. Udaipur Praśasti, op. cit., pp. 29-32. Sāraṇeśvara Temple Inscription, op. cit., pp. 161-2; Marble Slab Inscription of the Reign of Guhila King Śucivarman (tenth century characters)', *ARIE*, 1963-4; Āhaḍa Fragmentary Inscription of the Period of Śaktikumāra (late tenth century), PRAS, WC, 1905-6, p. 60.
136. Pratapgarh Inscription, op. cit., pp. 176-88.
137. 'Paldi Inscription', op. cit., pp. 8-12. It records grants made by Guhila Arisiṁha to the Pāśupata maṭha at the temple of Śiva at Paldi.
138. Jagat Inscriptions of Guhila Sāmantasiṁhadeva of AD 1171 and of Guhila Jayasiṁhadeva, *ARRM*, 1914-15, p. 3.
139. Chiravā Inscription, op. cit., pp. 285-92.
140. Chittaurgarh Inscription (Ghaghsa village) of Tejasiṁha of AD 1267, *URI*, vol. I, op. cit., pp. 175-6.
141. Sāraṇeśvara Temple Inscription, op. cit., v. 7, '*hūṇaśca kṛṣurajonyah sarvodevopigoṣṭikah* . . .'. The expression is 'Goṣṭhika' in the text of this inscription.
142. Udaipur Praśasti of AD 661, op. cit., pp. 29-32.
143. Sāraṇeśvara Inscription, op. cit., v. 15, '*haririh niveśitoyam ghaṭitapratimo varāheṇa*'.
144. Āhaḍa Fragmentary Inscription of the time of Śaktikumāra, PRAS, WC, 1905-6, p. 60, no. 2233.

145. Āṭapura Inscription, op. cit., v. 1, '*samvatsaraśateṣu . . . śrīnānigasvāmi devāyataṁ kārāpitam*'.
146. A Marble Stone Inscription of King Śucivarman, op. cit.
147. Sāraṇeśvara Temple Inscription, op. cit., p. 162, vv. 7-8, '*pratihāra yaśohpuṣpo . . . hūṇaśca kṛṣurājaunyah, sarvvodevopi goṣṭhikah.*'
148. Ibid.
149. Ibid., v. 8, '*hūṇaśca kṛṣurājonyah sarvadevopi goṣṭhikah kṛtamāyatanam cedamāmātye mammaṭe satī*'.
150. Āṭapura Inscription, op. cit., v. 5, '*sa bhūpati – yā yasya hūṇakṣoṇīśavaṁśaja hariyadevī.*
151. Chattopadhyaya, *Origin of the Rajputs*, pp. 77-9.
152. Sāraṇeśvara Inscription, op. cit., p. 162, v. 3.
153. Ibid., vv. 3-5.
154. Ibid., v. 8, *hūṇaśca kṛṣurājonyah sarvodevopi goṣṭhikah.*
155. Ibid., v. 7, *pratihāra yaśahpuṣpo.*
156. Kadmal Plates, op. cit., p. 248, ll. 39-40, '*dūtaka cāhamāna rajaiputra sagaṁḍā-suta rāṇādhavalah.*
157. Paldi Inscription, op. cit., p. 12, l. 15, '*atra deve goṣṭhikah saulaṁkikavaṁśīyavā rājaputra śrī ūpalarāsutaśrīsalakhaṇarā*'.
158. Chiravā Inscription, op. cit., v. 29, '*śrī bhīmasiṁhaputrah prādhānyam prāpya rājasiṁha yam*'.
159. Ibid., v. 26, '*śrīcitrakūṭasya talāṭṭikāyam śrī bhīmasiṁhana samaṁ mamāra.*'
160. Śāraṇeśvara Inscription, op. cit., v. 15, '*lekhitārau ca kāyasthau pālavellakasamjñakau*'.
161. Kadmal Plates, op. cit., p. 248, l. 38.
162. For a discussion of this important point, see Romila Thapar, 'Social Mobility in Ancient India with Special Reference to Elite Groups', in her *Ancient Indian Social History: Some Interpretations*, Delhi, 1978, p. 138.
163. B.D. Chattopadhyaya, *Aspects of Rural Settlement and Society in Early Medieval India*, Calcutta, 1990, pp. 43-4.
164. Samoli Inscription of AD 646, op. cit., ll. 8-9, '. . . *tatra jentaka mahattara śrīaraṇyavāsiṇyā devakulaṁ cakre mahājanā diṣṭa*'.
165. See Chapter IV in this book, section: Local Level Administration.
166. Chattopadhyaya, *The Making of Early Medieval India*, p. 55.
167. Thapar, 'Social Mobility in Ancient India with Special Reference to Elite Group', op. cit, p. 138.
168. Chattopadhyaya, *The Making of Early Medieval India*, p. 138.
169. Sāraṇeśvara Temple Inscription, op. cit., v. 8.
170. Aṭapura Inscription, op. cit., vv. 4-7, '*rāṣṭrakūṭakulodbhūta mahālakṣmī riti priyā . . . hūṇakṣonīvaṁśajā hariyādevī . . . cāhumānānyodbhūtā śrī jejayanṛpātmajā.*'
171. *ARRM*, 1936, op. cit.

172. Udaipur Praśasti of Aparājita, op. cit., v. 3 '*vṛtta-svachchhatay=aiva kaustubha-maṇir=jjato jagadbhūṣaṇaṁ.*'
173. Āṭapura Inscription of Śaktikumāra, op. cit., v. 10. The mention of the King Śaktikumāra settling at Āṭapura implies construction of a royal fortress at Āṭapura in the second half of tenth century. D.R. Bhandarkar also agrees that 'the place where Śaktikumāra is represented to have been settled is distinctly called Āṭapura.' See *IA*, vol. XXXIX, op. cit., p. 187.
174. Kadmal Plates, op. cit., the Guhila King Vijayasiṁha made extensive grants from resources of village Palli to a brāhmaṇa from Nāgahṛda.
175. Achaleśvara Inscription, op. cit., v. 42, '*naḍūla-mūlaṁkaṣabahul lakṣmīsturuṣka-sainyārnnava-kumbhapnihi [a] smin surādhisa-sahasana-sthe rarakṣa bhūmīm = atha jaitrasiṁhah ||*
176. Āṭapur Inscription, op. cit., v. 1.
177. Kadmal Plates, op. cit., v. 2.
178. Vide *passim*, Chap. I, pp. 38-9.
179. Aṭapura Inscription, op. cit., v. 1.
180. *Annals*, vol. I, p. 121.
181. Ekalingajī Temple Inscription, op. cit.
182. Ibid., vv. 20-1.
183. Ibid., vv. 9-11.
184. Ibid.
185. Ibid., v. 5.
186. A collection of Prakrit and Sanskrit inscriptions, op. cit., pp. 69-72.
187. Vide *passim*, Chap. I, p. 32.
188. Chittaurgarh Inscription of AD 1274, op. cit., v. 10, Bappa is called Purāṇapuruṣa.
189. Achaleśvara Inscription of AD 1285, op. cit., v. 12, '*bappakasya tanayo nayavetta sambabhūva nṛpati-guhilākhya*'.
190. Chittaurgarh Inscription, ibid., v. 13; Achaleśvara Inscription, op. cit., v. 12.
191. Chittaurgarh Inscription, ibid., vv. 10-11; Achaleśvara Inscription, ibid., vv. 10-11. When the term name Bāppā is quoted from a Sanskrit source, it should be transliterated as Bappā as per the original expression.
192. Chittaurgarh Inscription, ibid., vv. 9-10.
193. Achaleśvara Inscription, op. cit., v. 11.
194. Kadmal Plates, op. cit., pp. 245-6, ll. 1, 3-9.
195. Ibid., l. 8.
196. Ibid., l. 56.
197. Ibid., l. 10.
198. Kumbhalgarh Praśasti, 3rd slab, op. cit., vv. 143-4, '*tataśca yoga[rā]jo= bhū[nme]ḍapāṭe mahī-patihllapi rājye sthite tasmin tac-chāṣa[kha] no[cchra]yamgatā || paścād allaṭa-samtāne vairāṭo bhū[nna] reśvarah tatah śrīthaṁsapālase a vairīsimho nṛpagraṇih ||*'.

199. Rājavarṇana section, third slab of Kumbhalgarh slabs, AD 1460. Ibid., Chittaurgarh Inscription (AD 1274) and Achaleśvara Inscription of (AD 1285) Samarasiṁha, op. cit.
200. Kadmal Plates, op. cit., editorial note on geneology, p. 242.
201. Chattopadhyaya, *Political Processes and Structure*, p. 45.
202. Kadmal Plates, op. cit., p. 246, l. 10.
203. Op. cit., vv. 2-7.
204. Paldi Inscription, op. cit., v. 2.
205. B.D. Chattopadhyaya writes, 'Channels open for diffusion of such tension would not have been many. Expansion of kinship network, itself encompassed by the system of ranking . . . could only create new loci of power'. See his, *Political Processes*, p. 221.
206. G.H. Ojha, *Pratāpgarh Rājya kā Itihāsa*, p. 39.
207. Ibid.
208. Ibid.
209. *IA*, vol. VI, pp. 55-6, ll. 2-3.
210. Ibid., p. 56, ll. 7-9.
211. *IA*, vol. LVI, pp. 225-6.
212. Ibid., ll. 2-3.
213. *ARASI*, 1929-30, p. 187; *ARRM*, 1929-30, pp. 2-3.
214. Asoke Kumar Majumdar, *Chaulukyas of Gujarat: A Survey of the History and Culture of Gujarat from the Middle of the Tenth to the end of the Thirteenth Century*, Bombay, 1956, p. 74.
215. Ibid., pp. 74, 444, fn. 46.
216. Thakarda Inscription of the time of Surapāladeva, *IA*, vol. LVI, pp. 225-6.
217. Ibid., fn. 3.
218. *ARRM*, Ajmer, 1918-19, p. 2.
219. *IA*, vol. LVI, p. 225.
220. D.C. Ganguly, *History of the Paramāra Dynasty* (Hindi edition, Lucknow, n.d.).
221. Ibid., p. 120.
222. Pratipal Bhatia, *The Paramāras (AD 800-1305 Century)*, Delhi, 1970, p. 115.
223. Ibid., p. 115.
224. *DRI*, p. 45.
225. Quoted in *DRI*, p. 46.
226. Ibid., p. 46.
227. Achaleśvara Inscription, op. cit., see F. Kielhorn's edition, vv. 36-7, '*sāmaṁtasiṁha-nāma kāmādhikasarva suṁdara śarīrah || bhūpālo jani tasmādapahṛta-sāmaṁtasarvasvah khummāṇasantativiyoga vilakṣalakṣmīm senāmadṛṣṭa-viraham guhilānvayasya || rājanvatīm vasumatīmakarot kumārasiṁhastato ripu gaṇāmpahṛtyaribhūyah ||*'.
228. Kumbhalgarh Inscription, op. cit., v. 149, '*nṛpatve labdhe*'.

229. Ibid., v. 151, '*Gurjaranṛpati prasādyamisi*'.
230. Luṇavasahī Temple Inscription, *EI*, vol. VIII, p. 211, v. 38, '*sāmanta-siṁhasamitikṣitivikṣataujah śrīgūrjjarakṣitiparakṣāṇadakṣiṇāsih* | *prahlādanastadanujo danujott* | *āmāricāritramatra punarūjvalāyānc akāra*|
231. *DRI*, p. 45.
232. Ibid., p. 46.
233. Ibid.
234. Ibid., p. 49.
235. Achaleśvara Inscription, op. cit., vv. 36-7.
236. *EI*, vol. II, pp. 421-4.
237. *ARRM*, 1931, p. 4.
238. Virpur Village Inscription, op. cit., p. 225, ll. 2-5.

CHAPTER III

Mewar between the Thirteenth and Fifteenth Centuries: King, Kinsmen and Political Alliances

I have already discussed the process of territorial integration and the emergence of a regional state under the Guhila banner in the thirteenth century. However, as mentioned in the introduction, I shall extend my study of state formation in Mewar up to the fifteenth century. The purpose being not to repeat the well-known dynastic history of Mewar but to enquire into the changing political structure, the institution of Guhila kingship, its relation with royal kinsmen, the incorporation of other social groups such as the Jains in the state polity, the political links with the Bhils and social linkages with contemporary Rajput powers between the thirteenth and fifteenth centuries. As my analysis below will show, findings for the fifteenth century highlight an entirely different political structure than that of the thirteenth century the change being brought about by the political and military problems of the state of Mewar.

I

Kings and Kinship

The Thirteenth Century

An examination of the thirteenth-century records of the Guhila royal house points to the consolidation and expansion of Guhila monarchical power, which was accompanied increasingly by the concentration of power with royal kinsmen. The earliest thirteenth-century record refers to Śrī Jaitrasiṁha as *mahārājādhirāja*.[1] A Jain record from Chittaur of AD 1267 refers to Śrī Tejasiṁha as *rājabhāga vannanārāyaṇamahārāja* implying divine attributes.[2] Significantly, one of the most important of the thirteenth-century private records from Mewar, the Chiravā inscription, uses grandiose titles for the Guhila kings such as *mahīśvara* and *bhūpāla* for Padmasiṁha,[3] *ilāpati* for Tejasiṁha,[4] *nṛpati* for Mathanasiṁha,[5] *nṛpa* and *rājaña* for Jaitrasiṁha,[6] *kṣitipati* for Samarasiṁha,[7] and so on, to distinguish the Guhila kings from the rest of the Guhila royal family.[8] Both the Chittaurgarh (AD 1274) and the Achaleśvara (AD 1285) Inscriptions tracing the ancestry of the thirteenth-century Guhila kings to Bāppā, Purānapuruṣa (primeval man)[9] magnify his role in the foundation of the Guhila royal power in Mewar. The son born to him was Guhila[10] and succeeding kings are presented as follows:

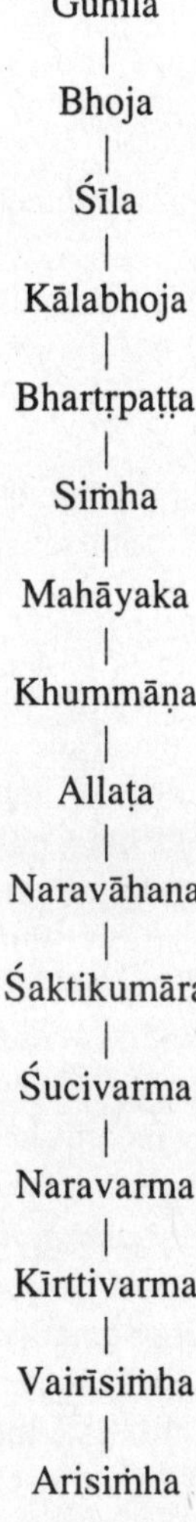

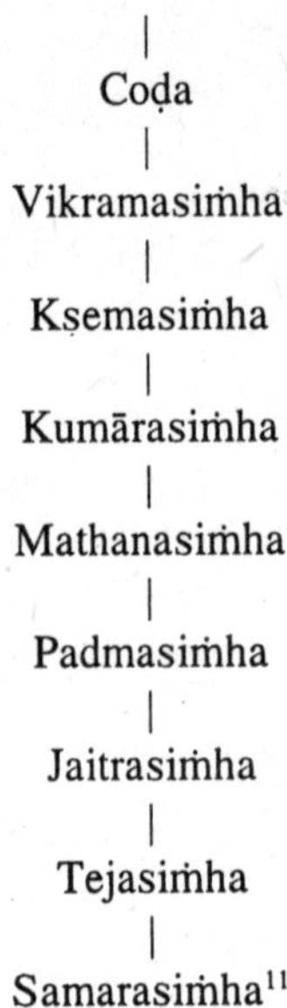

Unlike the Kadmal plates of the late eleventh century and the Paldi inscription of the early twelfth century[12] royal records of the thirteenth century neither acknowledge Mahīpāla, founder of an important junior branch in the tenth century, nor confine the royal genealogy to a few select preceding kings on the Guhila throne (see for instance, Paldi Inscription of dated AD 1116). Not only do royal records attempt to project a unified genealogy, even records of important functionaries such as those of the Ṭāmṭarāḍa family from Chiravā introduce each king as a son (*tanuja*) or younger brother of the previous ruler.[13] This recording of royal genealogies by administrative functionaries of the state reveals percolation of the royal perception of its own power to the ranks of the elite at least. However, contemporary records also points to the political importance of the royal kinsmen.

Both, royal as well as private records indicate that a political hierarchy based on rank existed. The queen mother Jayatalladevī's reference to Guhila King Samarasiṁha as *mahārājakula* (*mahārāval*),[14] seems to point to a hierarchy of *rāvals* (royal kinsmen; immediate kinsmen of the king) which was headed by King Samarasiṁha. A kāyastha family from Chittaurgarh also refers to King Samarasiṁha as *mahārājakula*.[15] Hence, both the royal and private records establish the fact that at least by the second half of the thirteenth century, Guhila kings presided over a number of *rāvals* or royal kinsmen who were recognized by their formal political status. Before moving on to a discussion of the role of kinship in the Guhila state of Mewar, one must note that besides *rāvals*, no other political title can be gleaned from contemporary records.

The presence and importance of the royal kinsmen in the political structure of the Guhila state is also evident from the royal recognition of the lineage of the Guhilas and its branches, in their official charters. Royal records which propagate legitimizing motifs for the Guhila monarch also significantly eulogize the Guhila lineage and its branches as *kuṭhāra-dhārasta brūmahe guhila vaṁśam pārośākham* (the axe-edged tree of the Guhila lineage with branches)[16] as well as '*śākhopaśākhā-kulitah suparvaguṇościtah . . . guhilasya vaṁśah* (branches and sub-branches of the Guhila royal family are full of fine qualities).[17] The same records repeatedly refer to the Guhila royal lineage as *guhila vaṁśā,*[18] *prasiddhaham gauhilyāmvaṁśā,*[19] *guhilakula,*[20] and *sanṛpatih guhilābhidhāno.*[21] These references to the royal lineage and its branches undoubtedly indicate proliferation of several branches of the royal family by the second half of the thirteenth century. Royal concern for their immediate kinsmen is also evident from royal *praśastis* of the branches and sub-branches of Guhila royal kinsmen in the organization of territorial control.

The thirteenth-century annexation of Chittaurgarh and expansion beyond Mewar further increased royal dependence on close kinsmen due to the failure of the Guhilas to enlist the support of non-Guhila chiefs (of the upper Banas plain and particularly of Chittaurgarh). Unlike tenth-century references to chiefs of non-Guhila Rajput families, thirteenth-century records do not mention non-Guhila Rajput families. At least non-Guhila Rajput families of Chittaurgarh and upper Banas plain should have been mentioned in the contemporary royal records for their continuing role in the territorial integration of the Guhila state. It is important to remember as has already been mentioned, that *sāmantas* played a significant role in the abdication of Sāmantasiṁha and in the succession of Kumārasiṁha.[22] But repeated royal references to the Guhila lineage and the conspicuous absence of references to non-Guhila chiefs point to the growing importance of royal kinsmen.[23]

However, the two royal *praśastis* of the thirteenth century maintain a conspicuous silence on the ranking system. Similarly, although the Chittaurgarh (AD 1274) and Achaleśvara (AD 1285) Inscriptions refer to the branches and sub-branches of the Guhila lineage, they do not refer to King Samarasiṁha as *mahārāval*. Also, though queen mother

Jayatalladevī's record refers to reigning king, Samarasiṁha as *mahārājakula*, it designates the preceding King Tejasiṁha (Queen Jayatalladevī's husband) as *medapāṭādhipati*.[24] This suggests that royal inscriptions were reluctant to highlight the ranking system. Thus, royal proclamation of Guhila kings as the 'sovereigns of Mewar' despite the presence of *rājakulas* cannot be taken at face value. The fact that the evidence suggests that King Samarasiṁha, who had attained extensive territorial acquisitions, was also possibly the first Guhila king to have been designated as *mahārāval* strengthens my view that by the second half of the thirteenth century, Guhila kings were increasingly depending on their close kin for the consolidation of Guhila power.

My study of the Kadmal plates and the Paldi inscription reveals a proliferation of the branches of the Guhila royal family and the creation of junior houses as well as the presence of a Guhila *mahāsāmantādhipati* at Nāgdā (early eleventh-century records). This suggests that royal kinsmen were exerting pressure for upward social mobility, some of them moving away from the paternal state without disrupting it. (See for instance, the case of King Sāmantasiṁha, who was ousted by *sāmantas*, as is evident from the Achaleśvara inscription, and was succeeded to the Guhila throne by Kumārasiṁha, his younger brother.) The criticism of the last of the *rāval* kings of Mewar, Ratnasiṁha, for his failure to protect Chittaurgarh in a major royal record of the fifteenth century[25] points to political scheming by the *rāvals* which contributed to the military defeat of the *mahārāval*. Thus, the aspirations of kinsmen for greater political power may have played a significant role in the military defeat of the Guhilas in AD 1303 by Alauddin Khalji, leading to the long absence of the Guhila monarchy in Mewar for most of the fourteenth century.

My discussion of the aspirations of royal kinsmen for upward social mobility and the political manifestations thereof in the latter half of the thirteenth century, shows that royal attempts at projecting the succession of Guhila kings in a single line of fathers and sons conceal political tensions and the presence of rival chiefs. In this context, note David P. Henige's reservations about the veracity of Guhila genealogy:

> We are asked, for instance, to believe that in the Guhila dynasty of Medapata 32 of 33 successions were of the father-to-son variety, including five ruling generations between 942 and 977 and 18 ruling generations between 942 and before 1168. This extremely narrow royal genealogy is inferred from retrospective epigraphic evidence and from the traditions recorded by Tod. And, given the propensity of the Vaṁśāvalis, Khyāts, and other chronicles that portray

succession as unremittingly from father to son one need not rely too heavily on Tod's account in this instance.[26]

Though the royal inscriptions and other sources suggest unilinear succession on the basis of descent, the actual political situation in the thirteenth century was fraught with centrifugal forces. However, I focus here on the problems that the Guhila monarchy faced in this period. At the point when the dynasty reached the zenith of its power, its chief political supporters, the royal kinsmen, were possibly its worst problems.

The long absence of Guhila rule in fourteenth-century Mewar is indicated by the absence of Guhila records (with the exception of a solitary private record referring to the reign of Rāṇā Khetā in AD 1366.)[27] Epigraphic records of the Khaljis, Tughlaqs and Songirās in Chittaurgarh[28] indicate a change in political sovereignty in the first half of the fourteenth century. At Chittaurgarh there is an intriguing absence of records between 1350 and 1400. To understand the continuities and changes during this period and later, a study of the fifteenth-century local records is indispensable for my analysis of the process of state formation in Mewar as reflected in Guhila dynastic continuity.

The Fifteenth Century

Significantly, the disruption of Guhila rule in the fourteenth century is followed by the re-emergence of Guhila kingship in the fifteenth century. This shall greatly help analyse the establishment of the institution of regional kingship and dynastic traditions in Mewar. I feel that this continuity of Guhila dynastic rule despite a break was the result of a long process of regional state formation in which the state of Mewar came to be identified with the Guhila dynasty.

The fact that the kings of the late fourteenth and the early fifteenth century were sovereigns of Mewar is significant. These kings did not acknowledge the sovereignty of any king from outside Mewar. Evidence of their sovereignty is amply borne out by royal records. Ṭhakkura Ḍālā refers to the reign of Rāṇā Khetā in AD 1366.[29] King Mokal's Chittaurgarh Inscription and his Śṛṅgirṣi Inscription, the earliest fifteenth-century royal records from Mewar, refer to an early ruler, Arisiṁha, as *kṣitipati*[30] and Hammīra (Arisiṁha's successor in royal genealogy)[31] as *bhūpati*. With the consolidation of Guhila political power, titles were magnified; King Mokal was called *mahārājādhirāja mahārāṇā śrī mṛgāṅka*; so too his successor Kumbha[32] who was also called *rāirāyā rāṇerāi mahārāṇā*.[33] Not only royal records, but those of the Jains too refer to the reigning

King Kumbha in a much more pompous tone (*śrī rāmayudhiṣṭhirādi nareśvaranukrasya rāṇā śrī kumbhakarṇa sarvovīrapatisār vabhaumasya vijayamānarājye*).[34]

Interestingly, the late fourteenth or early fifteenth-century kings of Mewar did not trace their genealogy to erstwhile Guhila kings except for lineage affiliation. They merely borrowed the legends of *bappaja vaṁśāh*[35] and *anvayo guhila narapatiḥ*[36] in the early fifteenth century. In spite of proclaiming that one of their predecessors, Hammīra (so far unlisted in Guhila genealogy), was a gem in the family of Bāppā,[37] Hammīra's kinship ties to the said family are not revealed in Mokal's records.

The evidence suggests that the early fifteenth-century kings of Mewar, who made no attempts to claim direct kinship relations with the Guhila dynasty, were possibly chiefs of local origin from Chittaurgarh. Their rise to power, associated with the fortress of Chittaur, is testified by contemporary royal records. The Kumbhalgarh Praśasti condemns Rāval Ratnasiṁha (the last Guhila king on the throne of Mewar before Alauddin's invasion of Chittaurgarh) for having failed to protect Chittaurgarh.[38] In the same record Mahārāṇā Lakṣmasiṁha is eulogized for having protected it.[39] Besides, that their political origin was different from that of the earlier Guhila dynasty is also suggested by a private record that refers to King Khetā (Kṣetrasiṁha) as a *rāṇā*[40] while one of Khetā's grandsons Mokal chooses to drop the title.[41] *Rāṇā*, being a politically subordinate title suggests that initially, the Guhila kings were mere local chiefs. Mokal later dropped the title of *rāṇā* from his records to highlight the royal status of the Guhilas.

The Guhilas were so strongly identified with the state of Mewar that no politically ascendant family aspiring to kingship, however strong and powerful, could legitimize its exercise of power without claiming direct kinship with them. Later rulers not only continued to appropriate dynastic affiliation to the Guhilas through the motifs of *nṛpati guhilābhidhāno* (kings by the name of Guhila),[42] *bappakhyah purāṇapurūṣa*[43] and *bāṣpanvatah*[44] (in the lineage of Bāppā) but gradually also began to claim direct kinship with them. Vague affiliation to Khummāṇa is hinted in a late fifteenth-century record.[45] As I have mentioned earlier, Khummāṇa is referred to as a Guhila king in the Āṭapura Inscription of AD 977,[46] which provided the very first genealogical list of the Guhilas of Mewar for the first time. Mokal, in the Chittaurgarh inscription dated AD 1429, traces Hammīra back to Arisiṁha, king of Mewar, in the family of the Guhilas.[47] Both of Mokal's records provide us with a genealogy that runs from Arisiṁha to Hammīra to Mokal via Mokal's grandfather Kṣetrasiṁha and father Lakṣasiṁha.[48] What seems to distinguish Mokal's genealogy is the lengthy *praśasti* for Hammīra[49] rather than Bāppā.

However, Mokal neither elaborates upon the ties of kinship with previous Guhila kings nor mentions their ranks. Interestingly, a Jain record, the Rāṇakpur Praśasti of AD 1439, is one of the first fifteenth-century records that refers to the reigning king, Kumbha as *rāṇā*[50] and traces the genealogy of Kumbha to *Bāppāvaṁśīya* kings and Hammīra to the thirteenth-century Guhila King Samarasiṁha[51] starting with Bāppā.[52] Thus, for the first time, fifteenth-century kings attempted to trace their descent in continuity from the earliest Guhila King Bāppā to the last of the thirteenth-century Guhila kings, Samarasiṁha. From this, a few conclusions can be drawn. First, although the genealogical list is silent about the actual relationship between Samarasiṁha and the next succeeding king, the implication is clear. Samarsiṁha might not have been succeeded by his son but possibly by one of the princes of the colateral branches. Secondly, the same list also hints at the possibility that Kumbha was the first fifteenth-century king to resume the title of *rāṇā*, for his predecessor Mokal is not mentioned as having the same title.[53]

Thirdly, this particular genealogical list provides us with four more princes in the royal family, between Arisiṁha and Hammīra—Śrī Bhuvanasiṁha, son Śrī Jayasiṁha, Lakṣmasiṁha (no kinship term appears), son Śrī Ajayasiṁha and brother Śrī Arisiṁha)[54]—indicating continuity in kinship relations. Also, we find a clue to what possibly caused Mokal's successor Kumbha to resume the use of the title of *rāṇā* and to trace direct descent without any break from previous Guhila kings of Mewar in the same genealogical list. In this context, it is significant that Sultan Alauddin is introduced between Guhila King Samarasiṁha and Prince Bhuvanasiṁha. Since the genealogical list came from the Jains, the elite perception of the sovereignty of Mewar and its political history led to the inclusion of Sultan Alauddin Khalji in its own world. Perhaps, to diminish the importance of the Khalji interregnum at Chittaurgarh and to highlight the political power of the regional kings, Kumbha chose to utilize their erstwhile title of *rāṇā* to explain their actual kinship relations with the Rāval Guhilas of Mewar.

Thus, Kumbha elaborated upon his kinship with previous Guhila rulers by claiming Rāval Khummāṇa as a direct ancestor. As already noted, Khummāṇa had always figured in the line of royal succession in the royal records between the tenth and the thirteenth centuries and Lakṣmasiṁha (titled *mahārāṇā*)[55] was said to be a scion of Khummāṇa-vaṁśa.[56] Significantly, Rāval Khummāṇa is introduced right after Rāval Guhadatta without specifying the actual relationship between the two.[57] The motif of Rāval Khummāṇa gets magnified as he is provided with an elaborate *praśasti.*[58] Rāval Khummāṇa is *nāyaka* (chief)[59] and not king as the *rājavarṇana* (description of the kings) section of the Kumbhalgarh Praśasti begins only after the account of Khummāṇa.[60] Hence, the fifteenth-century kings of Mewar gradually affiliated themselves to the erstwhile Guhila rulers by claiming direct descent from one of the ancient Guhila kings, Khummāṇa. In spite of the implication that the *nāyaka* status of Khummāṇa would hint at their junior political status in earlier days, such motifs smoothened their transitory entry into the Guhila royal family of Mewar. All the same, they never referred to themselves directly as a junior branch of the Rāval Guhilas in the fifteenth century. Even in the Purānic section (possibly composed in the post-fifteenth century) of the *Ekaliṅgamāhāṭmyam,* the *mahārāṇās* of the fifteenth century were introduced only as *aparaśākhā*[61] (*mahārāṇās* were the other branch of the Guhilas) and not as a junior branch of the Guhila family. The problem seems to have been tackled by introducing the legends of Māhap, the elder brother, and Rāhap, the younger brother, in the Purāṇic section of *Ekaliṅgamāhātmyam* in which Rāhap is said to have obtained the title of *rāṇā.*[62] Similar legends with elaborate motifs were extended to seventeenth century royal records such as the Jagannātharāya Temple Inscription of Rāṇā Jagatsiṁha,[63] *Rājapraśasti*[64] and the *Amarakāvyam.*[65]

It is significant that Kumbha introduces Mahārāṇā Lakṣmasiṁha in the royal genealogy right after the last of the *rāvals*, Ratnasiṁha.[66] Thus, claiming kinship relations with the *rāvals* was away of legitimizing power through dynastic continuities. Last, but not the least, the question of the importance of royal kinsmen in the fifteenth century remains to be answered. The royal title of *mahārāṇā* presumes the presence of *rāṇās* (kinsmen close to the king) in the political hierarchy. But there is a significant absence of royal reference to *śākhās* (branches) and *praśākhās* (sub-branches) of the royal family in fifteenth-century royal records. Unlike the thirteenth-century Guhila kings, the fifteenth-century kings of Mewar mention neither branches nor sub-branches of their family, nor do they eulogize them. Hence, royal kinsmen do not seem to have played as significant role as their thirteenth-century counterparts did in the consolidation of royal power and in controlling territory. The fact that political and social linkages of fifteenth-century Guhila kings with non-Guhila Rajput chiefs of Eastern Mewar possibly played a more important role in the exercise of Guhila power is amply demonstrated by the contemporary royal references (see following section). I feel that the shift in the importance from royal kinsmen to non-Guhila Rajput chiefs of eastern Mewar in Mewar polity the fifteenth century was due to the political-military problems of the Guhila state of Mewar that compelled the state to broaden its social base.

II

Guhila Political and Social Linkages with non-Guhila Rajputs and Other Political Groups in Mewar

The Cāhamānas in Mewar hills

The Cāhamānas continued to appear as major non-Guhila Rajput chiefs in the Mewar hills in the thirteenth century. The Kadmal Copper Plate Inscription of Mahārājādhirāja Tejasiṁha of AD 1259 records the grant of land to Brāhmaṇa Tribikrama, located in the domain of Rao Chand, Cāhamāna Rāo Sīhasu's son.[67] It is evident from this record as well as Padmasiṁha' late twelfth-century record[68] that Kadmal village and its surroundings were essentially the domain of the Cāhamānas of the Mewar hills (see Map 7). The title of *rāo* testifies to their political integration into the political structure through ranking in the *sāmanta* hierarchy. The fact that royal records continued to refer to the location of the royal land grant as the *rājya* of Cāhamāna *sāmanta* indicates the prominence of the Cāhamāna families in Kadmal near Nāgdā-Āhaḍa. The presence of the Cāhamānas in the Mewar hills core-area becomes an obvious factor in making royal land grants to brāhmaṇas in the Cāhamāna domain. Since the donee, brāhmaṇa Tribikrama, is the son of Śivaguṇa (donee in Padmasiṁha's land grant charter) the royal dynasty strengthened links with a *sāmanta* domain by patronizing the same family of brāhmaṇas through the generations.

Further down the *sāmanta* hierarchy, the presence of lower *sāmantas* such as ṭhakkuras is also attested by a late fourteenth-century inscription. The Sītalādevī temple inscription of AD 1366 from Gogunda village records the renovation of a temple and the installation of an image of Viṣṇu by Ṭhakkura Ḍālā, Ṭhakkura Ṣātala's son, in the reign of Rāṇā Kṣetrasiṁha.[69] Gogunda is a pass connecting the Nāgdā-Āhaḍa belt with the Abu-Sirohi region, traversing a part of the Bhil country. If

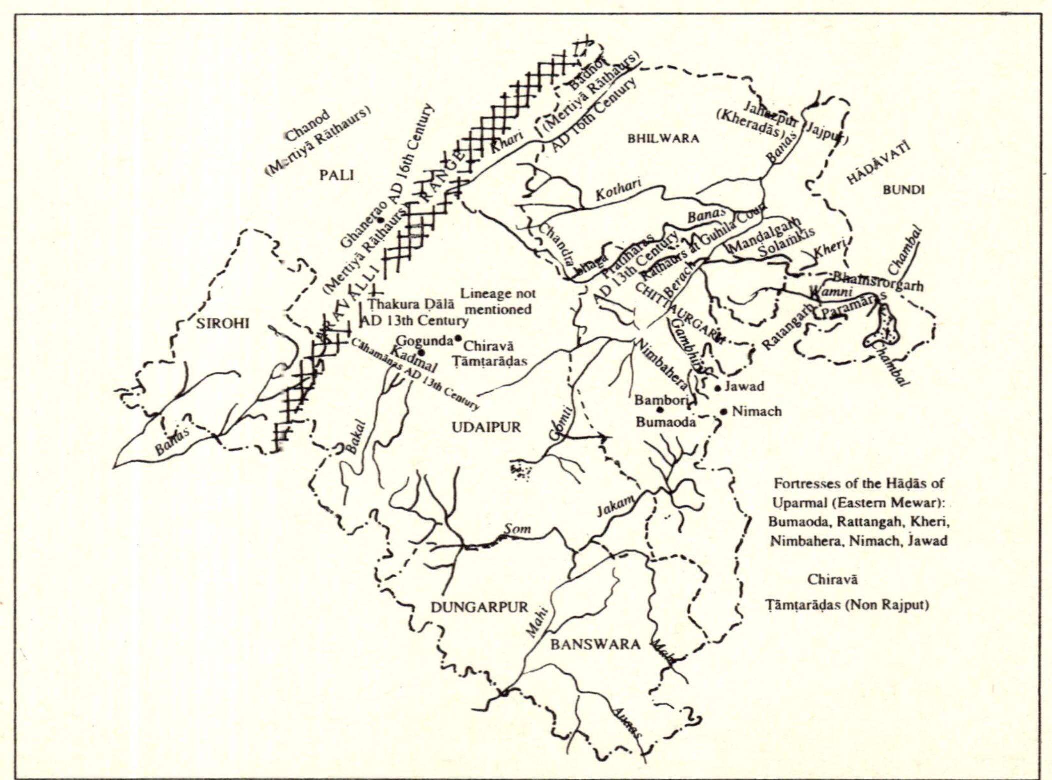

Map 7: Non-Guhila Rajput Chiefs in Guhila State: AD Thirteenth-Fifteenth Centuries.

Ṭhakkura Ḍālā was actually located at this strategic point then the possibility of a settlement with chiefs by the state cannot be ruled out. It is evident from the record that the family had been politically integrated into the *sāmanta* hierarchy in the recent past since the genealogy of the renovator of the temple is limited to the father, and no mention is made of the grandfather either. Ṣātala possibly was the first member in the family to have received the political title of *ṭhakkura*. The presence of Pratihāra chiefs at Chittaurgarh is evident from the discovery of their only record at the temple of Bhojasvāmī (Chittaurgarh) referring to Rājā Dharasiṁha, son of Rājā Pāṭā of the Pratihāra family in AD 1300.[70]

Significant changes in the Rajput components of the political structure are discerned in the fifteenth century. I feel that these were caused by the problems and the resultant preferences of the fifteenth-century state of Mewar.

The Hāḍās[71] of Uparmal or Paṭhār

Eastern Mewar; with fertile well-watered fields, thick vegetation, and trade routes to central India; appears to have been dominated by the Hāḍās in the fourteenth and fifteenth centuries. As far as the Chambal, the region belonged to Mewar throughout the medieval period, and the Hāḍās are known to have acknowledged the supremacy of the *rāṇās* of Mewar. The *annals* of the Hāḍās refer to the Guhilas as 'the lords of Medapāṭa'. However, the claim of the Hāḍās over this Uparmal region is no less legendary than that of the Guhilas over Mewar. It is significant to note the popular recognition of a small tributary of the Chambal, the Karab-kā-Khāl as the natural landmark dividing the lands of the Hāḍās from those of the Guhilas.[72] The Paṭhār resounds with the traditional tales of the Hāḍās who, in a very early period, established themselves in this region, where they are known to have erected twelve fortresses such as Bumaoda, Rattangarh, Dilwargarh, Kheri, Nimbahara, Nimach, Jawad, Jiran, etc.[73] However, the Hāḍās were so powerful in the Uparmal region that even the local tribal population such as the Bhils were aware of their supremacy over eastern Mewar. Bumaoda still reverberates with the name and chivalry of the legendary Ālu Hāḍā.[74] Hāḍā traditions also interestingly narrate the refusal by the *rāṇās* of Chittaur of a matrimonial offer of a Hāḍā princess, clearly indicating political rivalry between the Guhilas and the Hāḍās of eastern Mewar (besides hinting at the lower social status of the Hāḍās).[75] The Hāḍās claim to have defeated Rāṇā Mokal in the skirmish that followed the Guhila refusal to accept a

Hāḍā princess as a Guhila bride. A popular song commemorates the event as follows:

hāmu mokal māriyo,
lāle khetā jān,
suje ratan saṁghāriyo,
ajmal arasī rān.[76]

The song says that the bridegroom, at the spring-hunt of Arasī (Aheriā), met Mokal, and both fought to death, Rāo Sujā killed Ratan too.

Besides traditions, discovery of the inscriptional records at Menal containing the genealogy and the *praśasti* of the Hāḍās of Eastern Mewar point to Hāḍā predominance in the locality. The most important of the Hāḍā Inscriptions from Menal is dated AD 1390. It begins with a *praśasti* of the Cāhamānas, the ancestors of the Hāḍās and their presiding deity, Āśāpūraṇadevī before detailing the genealogy of the Hāḍās of Bumaoda, originating from prince Harrāj.[77] It also significantly designates Harrāj's successors as 'lords of Bumaodas'.[78] The political links between the Hāḍās of Menal (eastern Mewar) and the Guhilas can be seen in the Hāḍā claim that Hāḍā Mahādeva rescued the 'lord of Medapāṭa' (dragged Kaiṭah) from the grasp of Sultan Uni Shah.[79]

The Ekaliṅgajī Temple Dakṣiṇadvāra Praśasti of Rāṇā Rāimalla of AD 1489 narrates the military victory of Rāṇā Khetā (grandfather of Rāṇā Mokal) over the Hāḍās.

Khetāsiṁha, who was honest and intelligent, reduced the king of the East who took fines, and whose administration and taxation was very severe. He destroyed active and calm heroes who were between (him and the King of the East) and subdued the land after severe fightings in which the heads of the clan of the Hāḍā-Kshatris were cut off and their trunks wandered about.[80]

Here is a contemporary record of the Guhilas of Mewar which directly refers to the Hāḍās as the kings of east and the subsequent victory over them. In fact, references to the maladministration and unpopular taxation system of the Hāḍās of eastern Mewar appear as justifications of the Guhila military victory over the Hāḍās and their subsequent political integration into the state of Mewar. The fact is evident from the Guhila reference to eastern Mewar as Hāḍā maṇḍala.[81] The conquest of Hāḍāvatī by Mahārāṇā Kumbha (described in the Kumbhalgarh Praśasti), which evidently included the state of Bundi, would also indicate the forts held by the Hāḍās in Uparmal.[82] Apparently, Mahārāṇā Kumbha had to reassert the authority of Mewar in the land of the Hāḍās during his conquest of Vṛndāvantī (Bundi). However, the political sovereignty of the Guhilas over the Hāḍās of eastern Mewar is directly evident in an early fifteenth-century Guhila record from Singoli, eastern Mewar. The text of the Guhila inscription runs as follows: 'Samvat 1477 (AD 1421), the 2nd of Asoj, being Friday (Bhriguwar), Mahārāja Śrī Mokaljī, in order to furnish lights (Jyotiswaste) for Vijayaseni Bhavanijī (643), has granted one bigha and a half of land. Whosoever shall get aside this offering the goddess will overtake him.'[83] Thus, the annals and other evidence testify to the political incorporation of the Hāḍās of Uparmal into the state of Mewar by the early fifteenth century.

Political incorporation of the Hāḍās of Eastern Mewar is likely to have necessitated Guhila social links with the Hāḍās. In contrast to records of the tenth century, Guhila inscriptions of the fifteenth century do not mention the lineage of their queens (Baghelā and Gauḍa queens being exceptions). Possible clues are provided by bardic traditions. Bardic traditions such as *Sūryavaṁśāvalī*, *Śrī Rāṇājī rī bāt*, *Rājāvalī Bahī* and *Baḍvādevīdān Khyāt* refer to three Hāḍā queens of the Guhila kings of the period, two for Rāṇā Khetā and one for Rāṇā Kumbha[84] (Rao Bāgjī's daughter).[85] Possibly, Rāṇā Khetā's Hāḍā queens came from the Hāḍā families of eastern Mewar, for social links with the Hāḍās were politically far more important for the Guhilas to ensure control over strategic fortresses located east and north-east of Chittaurgarh.

The Solaṁkīs (Bālnotes) of Maṇḍalgarh

The annals of Mewar make it amply clear that Maṇḍalgarh, a fertile tract with mining potential, had been predominated by the Bālnotes, a branch of the Caulukyas or Solaṁkīs, in the fifteenth century.[86] The local legends attribute the building of Maṇḍalgarh to the Bālnotes and trace their ancestry to the Caulukyas of Anhilwārā. Their association with Maṇḍalgarh is so long that this tract is also popularly known as Bālnote.[87]

Their association with Maṇḍalgarh is also suggested by the fact that many other important social groups of Mewar and adjacent regions, particularly some of the Jain mercantile families, trace their descent from the Bālnotes or Solaṁkīs of Maṇḍalgarh.[88] However, more importantly, two inscriptions (unpublished) containing the genealogy of the local Solaṁkīs tracing ancestry from the Anhilwārā Caulukyas have been discovered at Kachaura, Maṇḍalgarh.[89] These inscriptional records certainly substantiate the Solaṁkī claim over the Maṇḍalgarh tract.

Actual political integration of the Solaṁkīs (Bālnotes) of Maṇḍalgarh seems to have materialized only in Rāṇā Kumbha's reign (in the latter half of the fifteenth century), for the Kumbhalgarh Praśasti refers to Kumbha's conquest of Maṇḍalgarh twice[90] and the Rāṇakpur[91] Praśasti mentions it in the list of Kumbha's conquests. However, the Solaṁkīs of Maṇḍalgarh seem to have been confined to a small tract, for unlike the reference to the Hāḍās, the Guhila inscriptions never mention the Solaṁkīs or the Bālnotes in the context of Maṇḍalgarh. Maṇḍalgarh was perhaps better controlled by the Guhilas than the Hāḍā forts. Although it is difficult to prove the social linkages of the Guhilas with the Solaṁkīs of Maṇḍalgarh, it is significant that *Baḍvādevīdān Khyāt* lists two Solaṁkī queens of the Guhila kings of the fifteenth century, one married to Mokal and the other to Rāimalla.[92] Given the strategic importance of Maṇḍalgarh, the Guhilas might have made matrimonial alliances with the Solaṁkīs of Maṇḍalgarh in the fifteenth century.

The Paramāras of Bhainsrorgarh

Being strategically situated on the banks of the Chambal and on the trade route to central India,[93] the fortress of Bhainsrorgarh (defended by a cliff with a sharp descent to the river) could act both as a second line of defence and a line of supplies and provisions to Mewar. The trading importance of Bhainsrorgarh is evident from local popular tales that associate the town with itinerant traders called banjārās.[94]

A thirteenth-century inscription discovered by Tod at Bhainsrorgarh points towards Paramāra occupation of the locality, for the land charter is executed in the Paramāra style of Malwa (Śāsan Udayāditya).[95] The predominance of the Paramāras in the Bhainsrorgarh locality in the fourteenth century is further corroborated by royal and private inscriptions in neighbouring Sontrā (Sutrawāndurga). A private record dated AD 1390 records that in the castle of Sontrā the Paramāra Udā, Kulā, Bhoonā sold their existence (indicating slavery?) along with their cattle, wives, brāhmaṇas, and *putra* Coḍa.[96] A royal record of AD 1314 registers some construction work by a scion of the ruling Paramāras of Sutrawāndurga tracing his ancestry from Dhār, Malwa.[97] But significantly, the Paramāra records from Bhainsrorgarh do not date to the period beyond the late fourteenth century (AD 1390).[98] It is also important to note that unlike Maṇḍalgarh, the fortress of Bhainsrorgarh is not even mentioned in fifteenth-century Guhila records. As it was situated close to Chittaurgarh, Guhila silence over its conquest perhaps suggests its effective incorporation and hence, the integration of the Paramāra chiefs of Bhainsrorgarh into the political structure of the Guhila state by the early fifteenth century. As far as Guhila matrimonial alliances with the Paramāras are concerned, there is once again no reference to them in contemporary official records. Bardic traditions refer to only one such alliance. *Sūryavaṁśāvalī*, *Rājāvalī Bahī* and *Baḍvādevīdān Khyāt* mention a Sānkhlī (a branch of the Paramāras) queen for Mahārāṇā Mokal.[99]

Rāṭhaurs in Mewar

Perhaps the most significant aspect of the political structure of Mewar in the fourteenth and fifteenth centuries was the growing strength of the Rāṭhaurs in the Guhila court. Sources for the study of the early period of their rise include medieval texts and bardic traditions such as *Muhaṇot Nainsi rī Khyāt*, *Jodhpur Rājya kī Khyāt*, Tod's *Annals*, etc.[100] Rāo Sīha was the founder of the ruling house of the Rāṭhaurs of Marwar.

According to tradition, one of the early Rāṭhaurs of Marwar, Rāo Raṇamal, brought the Rāṭhaurs into Mewar. Accounts seem to indicate that kinship pressures may have forced Rāo Raṇamal to settle outside his paternal state in the early fifteenth century.[101] Rāṇā Lākhā is known to have welcomed him and to have granted him an estate. Rāo Raṇamal is stated to have reciprocated by leading Rāṇā's army and bringing Ajmer under Mewar.[102] Besides, the Rāṭhaurs probably functioned as an effective check against locally entrenched non-Guhila Rajput families such as the Hāḍās of eastern Mewar. These politico-military factors seem to have greatly helped the Rāṭhaurs in quickly gaining control and in acquiriing a progressivly higher status in the royal court of Mewar in the early fifteenth century. The Rāṭhaur-Guhila alliance is likely to have been politically significant, for bardic traditions narrate at length the matrimonial alliance sought by the Rāṭhaurs with the Guhilas in the early fifteenth century.[103] Rāṇā Lākhā is known to have married a Rāṭhaur Princess Hansābī, Raṇamal's sister. The marriage took place under the understanding that a son by the Rāṭhaur princess was to succeed to the throne of Mewar, superceding the elder prince. Thus, the Guhila-Rāṭhaur marriage alliance led to the famous abdication of the throne of Mewar by its heir, Prince Cuṇḍā (Rāṇā Lākhā's eldest son), and the influx of many more Rāṭhaurs into Mewar.[104] The *Annals* understandably highlight the importance of the Rāṭhaurs for the early fifteenth century rulers of Mewar since by being pitted against old Rajput elements in the polity, including royal kinsmen, they greatly furthered the consolidation of Guhila royal power.

Hence, it was equally essential for the Rāṭhaurs in the early stage of their rise to establish close links with the Guhilas of Mewar. The fact that the traditions of Mewar do not list Rāṭhaur queens till Rāṇā Rāimalla's period except for Lākhā,[105] testifies to the fact that the rise of the Rāṭhaurs took place sometime in the fifteenth century. It is well-known that Rāo Jodha (Rāo Raṇamala's son and successor) could found the Rāṭhaur capital Jodhpur only in AD 1459.[106] More Rāṭhaurs had lived in Mewar before AD 1459. After their expulsion from Mewar in AD 1444, they acquired land in the Marwar region. For instance, Jodha obtained Sojat in AD 1455.[107] No Rāṭhaur queen is listed for Mahārāṇā Kumbha, but *Baḍvādevīdān Khyāt* lists six Rāṭhaur queens for Mahārāṇā Rāimalla as well as for Mahārāṇā Sāṅgā.[108] However, the historically known three sons of Rāimalla, Pṛthvīrāj, Jayamal and Sāṅgā are traditionally assigned to his Jhālī Queen Rājdhar Ratankanwar.[109] Although the historicity of the names of the Rāṭhaur chiefs, their daughters and their contemporaneity with the Guhila kings of Mewar are questionable, the list helps in comparing the number of Guhila queens that were Rāṭhaurs with that of those queens who were non-Raṭhaur.

Dudā, the founder of the Mertiyā Rāṭhaurs, established his seat in the locality of Mertā in the Marwar region. His son Vīramdeva and grandson Jaimal are known to have united the region under the banner of the Mertiyā Rāṭhaurs. Beginning with Mertā, they brought under their control Parbatsar, Nava, Marot, Jaitarana Kaulia, Daulatpura and held some estate in Nagaur as well.[110] Thus they made their presence felt in a larger part of Marwar. They ruled over buffer-states situated between Mewar and Marwar and it became strategically necessary for the Guhilas to establish political and social links with the Mertiyā Rāṭhaurs. On their part, the Mertiyā Rāṭhaurs who were in the process of expansion looked towards bigger powers for political and military alliances. This led to the incorporation of a number of Mertiyā Rāṭhaurs in the political structure of Mewar through service-grants. This is evident from the following list of the estates granted to Mertiyā Rāṭhaurs in the fifteenth and sixteenth centuries in Mewar.

1. *Badnor*: Mahārāṇā Udaisiṁha II had granted Badnor to Rāo Jaimal. It continued to be in possession of his son Mukundās and his successors.[111]

2. *Chanod*: Mahārāṇā Rāimalla granted Chanod to his grandson (by daughter) Pratāpsiṁha.[112]
3. *Ghanerao*: This locality was granted to Ṭhākkur Pratāpsiṁha's (Chanod) son Gopāldās by Mahārāṇā Udaisiṁha (II). It has remained in the possession of his successors.[113]

The estate of Chanod dates to the period I am discussing (the late fifteenth century) since Mahārāṇā Rāimalla granted this locality to the Mertiyā Rāṭhaurs in Mewar. Even more Mertiyā Rāṭhaur personalities figure in the political structure of Mewar in the sixteenth century. Sundardās, son of Mertiyā Kiśansiṁha (Jaimalot), was granted the estate of Dasalānā.[114] Kiśansiṁha died at the battle of Haldighati.[115] Manohardās, grandson of Jaimal and son of Viṭṭaldās, was in the service of Mahārāṇā Pratāp.[116]

Thus, Guhila links with the Mertiyā Rāṭhaurs further strengthened the political advantages that the Guhilas derived from the existence of a buffer Rajput power. In AD 1496, a daughter of Mahārāṇā Rāimalla was married to the crown prince of Mertā, Vīramdev, son of Rāo Dudā.[117] Mīrābāī, granddaughter of Rāo Dudā and daughter of Ratnasiṁha was married to Bhojarāja, son of Rāṇā Saṅgrāmsiṁha (Sāṅgā).[118] Thus by the early sixteenth century the Guhilas had established reciprocal marital exchange (Bevrā)[119] with the Mertiyā Rāṭhaurs.

Before I finish my discussion of the political and social linkages of the Guhilas with other political powers, I must mention the fort of Jajpur (modern Jahazpur) which was probably the stronghold of the Kherāḍās in the fourteenth-fifteenth centuries. Although no contemporary Kherāḍā record has been discovered, *Amarakāvyam* (seventeenth century) refers to the conquest of Kherāḍākula of Jājpur by Rāṇā Khetā.[120] It is significant that Rāṇā Kumbha claims the conquest of Yāgpur (Jājpur) since it indicates that it was a non-Guhila fortress.[121]

The Jains and the Royal Family in Mewar

The majority of western Indian merchants were Jains and the study of political links between the Jains and the Guhila dynasty between the thirteenth and the fifteenth centuries reveals the story of the induction of Jain merchants into the political structure of Mewar.[122] The state depended greatly upon this wealthy community because it was the Jain merchants who were responsible for generating more and more resources. This was especially so because the Guhilas were engaged in many wars during this period. Jains were equally interested in seeking

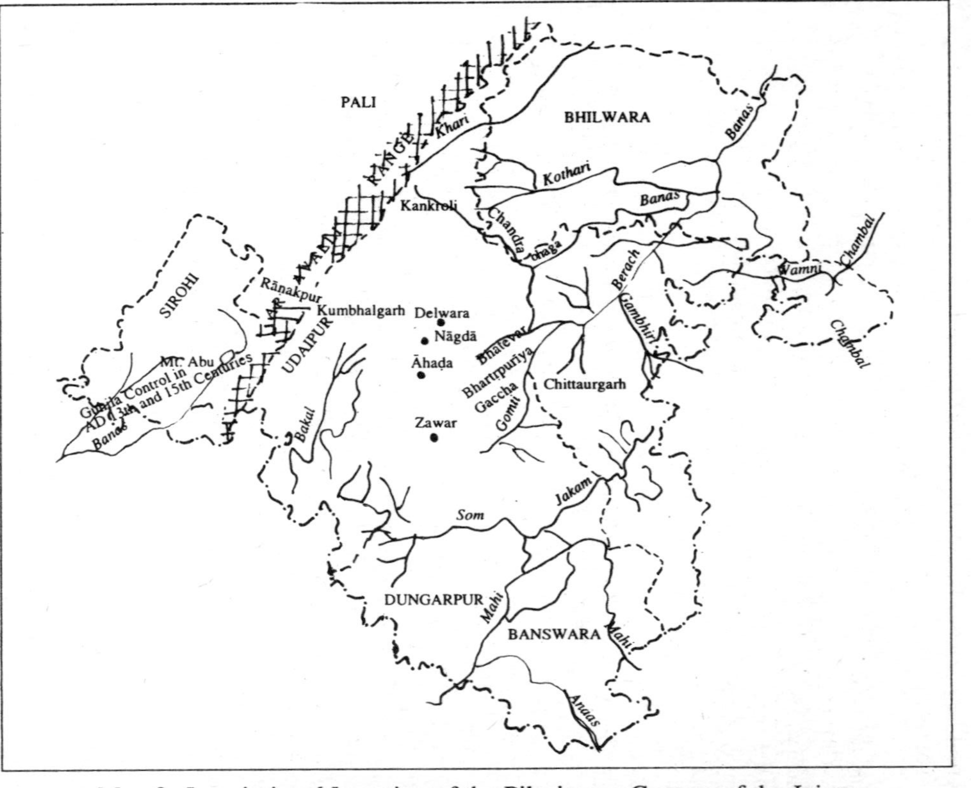

Map 8: Inscriptional Location of the Pilgrimage Centres of the Jains: AD Thirteenth-Fifteenth Centuries.

political links with the Guhilas because they sought state support to carry on with their business.[123] Thus, the state often actively contributed to further commercial activities.[124]

There is a vast corpus of inscriptional and literary sources which throw light on the elite Jain families of Mewar and the extent of their resources. A brief survey of these families and the circuit of the pilgrimage centres is necessary before the political linkages between the Jains and the Guhilas can be understood.

Chittaurgarh was the most popular Jain pilgrimage centre in Mewar. Ācārya Haribhadra Sūri, the great reformer, operated from Chittaurgarh in the eighth century.[125] His literary works indicate the popular patronage enjoyed by Haribhadra Sūri.[126] The continuing presence of Jain *ācāryas* in Chittaurgarh is evident from records and indicate increasing patronage by the Jain laity and points to the considerable influence that the *ācāryas* weilded. For instance, a Digambar Jain inscription of the reign of Guhila Jaitrasiṁha from Chittaur contains a *praśasti* of Ācārya Subhacandra, who was venerated by the Paramāras, the Cāhamānas and the Gurjara rulers.[127] Citrakūṭa became an important reference point for the Jains and a pilgrimage-cum-monastic centre.[128] The *Kharataragaccha-paṭṭāvalī* vividly describes the *ācāryas* and the training of disciples at Citrakūṭa.[129] The same text records lavish grants made by Śreṣṭhi Dhāndhal on the installation of the icons of the Jinas at Chittaurgarh on the occasion of the visit of Jinaprabodh Sūri of Kharataragaccha in AD 1277.[130] The Jain merchants, Śreṣṭhi Rālha and Śreṣṭhi Lakṣmīdhar, are known to have arranged many religious festivities here in AD 1231.[131] Many other Jain religious manuscripts such as *Daśavaitālika Pākṣika-Sūtra Pustikā* by Śrāvikā Dhānde in AD 1295,[132] *Candradūta Abhidhāna, Nighaṇṭuśeṣa, Karma Vipāka*, etc.[133] point to the presence and the considerable extent of Jain patronage at Chittaurgarh. *Kharataragaccha-bṛhadgurvāvalī* refers to the presence of Jina Vallabha and his Vasahī at Citrakūṭa.[134] Significantly, this text also refers to royal grants made from *Citrakūṭamaṇḍapikā*.[135]

Next to Chittaurgarh, Devakulapāṭaka (Delwara, 29 km from Udaipur) seems to have been an important Jain *tīrtha*, yielding several inscriptions dated between AD 1403 and 1453. These inscriptions mostly record the installation of icons of the Jinas by the *śrāvakas* and *śrāvikayas*, mostly of Prāgvaṭa lineage, at Pārśvanātha temple.[136] Many Jain *śreṣṭhis* including Rāmadeva Navalakha resided at Devakulapāṭaka.[137] Jain *śreṣṭhis*, patrons of Jain temples made lavish grants of commercial levies from the local *maṇḍapikās*. These donations indicate the control of merchants over *maṇḍapikās*.[138] It is interesting to note that Nāgdā, the famous Pāśupata centre of Mewar, was a centre of Jain pilgrimage too. Temple of the Digambara sect,[139] Aloka Pārśvanātha,[140] icons installed at the temple of Aloka Pārśvanātha by the *śvetāmbaras* of Kharataragaccha in the fifteenth century[141] and Tapagacchapaṭṭāvalī's references to Pārśvanātha temple,[142] all indicate patronage of Nāgdā by the Jains. Significantly, the Ekaliṅgajī Temple Inscription of AD 971 mentions a joint session of the Pāśupata and Jain *ācāryas* at Nāgahṛda in which Pāśupatas are claimed to have defeated the Jains in discourse.[143]

The temples of Adbhutnātha and Pārśvanātha (built in AD 1373) continued to be an important Jain *tīrtha* throughout the fifteenth century.[144] Āhaḍa and Udaipur (built in the mid-sixteenth century by Rāṇā Udaisiṁha II) also figured in the network of Jain *tīrthas*, testified by nearly one hundred and five inscriptions recording installations of icons of Jinas mostly by the merchant families of Prāgvaṭa, Śrīmāla, Upakeśa and Ukeśa (Osvāl) lineages at the temples of Śītalanātha, Vāsupūjya and Gaurī Pārśvanātha.[145]

The *Jain Pustaka Praśastis* records composition of some of the famous manuscripts such as *Śrāvakapratikramaṇasūtracūrṇī*, patronized by Mahāmātya Samuddhara (chief minister at the court of Guhila King Tejasiṁha),[146] *Daśavaikālādisūtrapatrikā*, by Jagatsiṁha (chief minister at the court of Guhila King Jatirasiṁha)[147] at Āhaḍamahādurga. The composition of these manuscripts was made possible by a grant in cash.[148] Other contemporary *tīrthas* of the Jains, Dhuleva, Zawar, Bhatevar, Rāṇakpur and Kumbhalgarh were located within the Mewar hills indicating the circulation of wealthy merchants in the very core-area of the Guhila state. A text, composed in the fourteenth century, the *Vagod Pravāsa*, refers to Dhuleva as a Jain *tīrtha*.[149] Other references also point to widespread Jain patronage. For instance, we have references to the patronage of the temple of Śāntinātha by Nānā of Prāgvaṭa lineage,[150] the construction of a new *devakulika*,[151] and patronage of *ācāryas*,[152] etc., at Zawar (the famous mining centre), to the enlargement and building of the shrines at Rāṇakpur temple complex by the wealthy merchant Dhārana Śāh,[153] to the succession ceremonies of the *ācāryas* at Kumbhalgarh,[154] to the beginning of Bhartṛpurīyagaccha at Bhatevar,[155] to the composition of the manuscripts of *Saptamāṅgacūrṇī* at village Baragrama[156] and that of *Kalpasūtra Kālikācāryakathā* at village Bauna.[157] Such scale of patronage points to the socio-economic importance of the Jains in Mewar between the thirteenth and the fifteenth centuries.

The earliest direct evidence of Guhila patronage of Jain establishments in Mewar appears in the late thirteenth century. Guhila Queen Jayatalladevī, wife of Tejasiṁha and mother of Mahārāval Samarasiṁha was a staunch Jain. The Guhila queen, at the instance of Ācārya Śrī Pradyumna Sūri of Bhartṛpurīyagaccha, got a temple of Śyām Pārśvanāth constructed in Chittaur in AD 1278.[158] The Guhila queen is likely to have patronized a local *gaccha*—Bhartṛpurīyagaccha probably being one of the most influential Jain institutes in thirteenth-century Mewar. The inscription also refers to the grants of land and *dramma* coins from the *maṇḍapikās* of Citrakūṭatalahaṭṭī, Āhaḍa, Khohar and Sajjanapura, and those of oil, ghee, etc., by the reigning king, Mahārājakula Samarasiṁha.[159] This inscription, interestingly, was not composed by any Jain *ācārya* but by the brāhmaṇas, usually employed by the royal court.[160] Such patronage attests to the importance of the Jains for the Guhila state once it acquired the most prominent centre of the Jains in Mewar—Chittaur.

Because of their vast knowledge, the Jain *ācāryas* were employed by the non-Jain members of society to compose their records. The Chiravā Inscription (AD 1273) was composed by Ācārya Ratnaprabha Sūri of the Caitragaccha.[161] The Ṭāmṭarāḍa family from Chiravā significantly mentions that Ratnaprabhasūri was revered by King Vīsaladeva (Bāghelās of Gujarat) and Tejasiṁha, the Guhila king.[162] This evidence indicates royal patronage enjoyed by the *ācāryas* of Mewar beyond the territorial boundary of the Guhila state.

The peak of Guhila patronage of the Jains was reached in Rāṇā Kumbha's reign. The Abu Inscription of Rāṇā Kumbha of AD 1449 records the Guhila order for the abolition of the pilgrimage tax, customs, *valvāhī* (armed escort), *caukīdārī* (security) and cattle taxes levied in Abu.[163] The Guhila order is politically very significant as most travellers to Abu were Jains, and because Abu was contested between Gujarat and the Devaḍās of Sirohi.[164]

The Guhila patronage of Jain *tīrthas* was parallel to the process of incorporation of the Jains into the political structure. The Jains begin to figure as important officials in Mewar by the thirteenth century. The first Jain family formally inducted into the administrative structure was from Āhaḍa. Thus, Jagatsiṁha of Āhaḍa, who had patronized *Daśavaikālikādisūtrapatrikā* appears as the *mahāmātya* (chief minister) of King Jaitrasiṁha.[165] Two more Jains figure as official favourites in the court of Jaitrasiṁha. The *Pākṣikasūtravṛtti* mentions that the writing of its manuscript was patronized by *mahan* (*mahantak*: accountant) Śrī Talhana, Śrī Karaṇa and others who had received the favours of King

Jayasiṁha (another name for Jaitrasiṁha).[166] Influential Jains continued to occupy the post of chief minister in the Guhila court in succeeding years. The ministers of Tejasiṁha (Jaitrasiṁha's successor), Jalhan, Samuddhara and Kāṅgā, were all devout Jains. In particular, minister Samuddhara seems to have been a man of great wealth and status as he figures in a number of contemporary records. He figures in a copper-plate inscription, the Ghagsa Inscription dated AD 1260,[167] and in the manuscript of the *Śrāvaka Pratikramaṇasūtracūrṇī* dated AD 1261.[168] Kāṅgā figures as *pradhāna rājā* in the administration of King Tejasiṁha.[169] It is important that he received the title of *rājaputra*.[170] This indicates absorption of the influential Jains into the political structure with a status higher than that of chiefs in the *sāmanta* hierarchy. Śreṣṭhi Dhāndhal and Śreṣṭhi Ratnā seem to have been the two most important Jain merchants in the reign of Guhila King Samarasiṁha.[171] The families of Samuddhara, Kāṅgā, Śreṣṭhis Dhāndhal, Ratnā, Rālha, etc.,[172] must have been quite influential in the Chittaurgarh belt. In the early fourteenth century, Śreṣṭhi Jījā and Punyasiṁha of Bāgherwal lineage figure as important Jain families of Chittaur.[173]

From the late fourteenth and the early fifteenth century, the family of Navalakha Rāmadeva of Ukeśa *gotra* (Osval) from Devakulapāṭaka seem to be the most important Jain family of Mewar politically. He functioned as the chief minister of Mewar in the reigns of Mahārāṇās Kṣetrasiṁha, Lakṣasiṁha and Mokal.[174] He had two sons, Sajjana and Sāraṅga. Sajjana succeeded his father to the post of chief ministership of Mewar during the reigns of Mahārāṇās Mokal and Kumbha. A Jain literary work, *Āvaśyakabṛhadvṛtti* composed in Devakulapāṭaka, refers to the reign of Rāṇā Kumbha and his chief minister, Sādhu Śrī Sajjanapāla.[175] The status of this family is evident from other contemporary sources such as *Vijñapti-Lekhā,* dated AD 1374. It mentions the event of a great *dīkṣā mahotsava* in Kareda in AD 1374, arranged by Rāmadeva.[176] *Somasaubhāgya Kāvya* refers to the visit of Somasundara Sūri at Devakulapāṭaka who was received by Mahārāṇā Lākhā, Prince Cuṇḍā and Minister Rāmadeva.[177] *Vijñapti-Lekhā* also mentions the installation of the icons of Ācāryas Merunandan and Droṇa by Rāmadeva's wife Melādevī at Devakulapāṭaka.[178] The son-in-law of Rāmadeva, Vīsal, came from the famous family of Śreṣṭhi Vatsarāj of Idar. *Somasaubhāgya Kāvya* is the source for an account of this family. It shows that a big temple named Manorathakalpadrum was built in Chittaur by this family.[179] Vīsal's wife Khimāi (Rāmadeva's daughter) and sons Dhīr and Campaka figure in the inscriptions (AD 1437) of the Jain temple at

Machind.[180] Sajjana, the elder son of Rāmadeva got a Śatruñjaya Paṭṭa (stone-slab) and some icons installed in Devakulapāṭaka in AD 1434.[181] An account of his younger brother Sāraṅga is found in an inscription (AD 1437) from the Adbhutnāthjī temple of Nāgdā.[182]

The other important office that the Jains came to occupy in Mewar was that of *bhāṇḍāgārika* (treasurer). Inscriptional references to the office begin in the fifteenth century. The Chittaur Inscription, dated AD 1448, was issued by a family of *bhāṇḍārīs* serving Mahārāṇā Kumbha. This family designates itself as in-charge of the royal treasury (*bhāṇḍārī/ bhāṇḍāgārika*). The record contains the genealogy of the family originating in Sāhakolā and registers the construction of the temple of Śāntinātha by this family.[183] The *bhāṇḍārīs* are listed as follows: Bhāṇḍārī Śrī Velaka, Bhāṇḍārī Mudharāja, Bhāṇḍārī Dhanarāja, Bhāṇḍārī Kurapāla, etc.[184] They were followers of Kharataragaccha.[185] Besides Śreṣṭhi Rāmadeva, Devakulapāṭaka had a few more contemporary Jain *śreṣṭhis* as residents. Śreṣṭhis Nimba, Kelha, Megh, Bhīm, Kaṭak, Lakṣmaṇ Siṁha, Hīsa, Dharma, etc., are the important names.[186] Hīsa and Dharma belonged to the famous Picoliyā family of Devakulapāṭaka (founder, Devapāla).[187] Inscriptional records refer to their installation projects and their patronage extended to Tapagaccha.[188]

Kumbha's court reached out to these rich Jain families through Rāmadeva Navalakha. Śreṣṭhi Saṁghapati Dhārana Śāh of the Prāgvaṭa lineage from Rāṇakpur and Saṁghapati Śreṣṭhi Guṇarāja of Chittaur were the other two important Jain personalities in the royal court of the fifteenth-century Mewar. Both of them figure in Rāṇakpur Praśasti, dated AD 1439. The *praśasti* contains a genealogy of Saṁghapati Dhārana,[189] his father, Kurapāla's charitable deeds and more importantly the construction of temple of Śrī Caturmukhayugādīśvara at the instance of Rāṇā Kumbha. Dhārana also dedicates the newly constructed temple of Śrī Caturmukha in Rāṇā Kumbha's name.[190] It is significant that Saṁghapati Guṇarāja was a favourite of the reigning king, Rāṇā Kumbha.[191] The long *praśasti* of the Guhila kings in this Jain record[192] shows that the influential Jains enjoyed extensive royal patronage. Saṁghapati Guṇarāja and other Jain personalities such as Saṁghapati Ratna (Dhārana's elder brother), son Saṁghapatis Lāṣā, Sāñja, Sona, Sālīga, Saṁghapati Dhāralde, etc., also figure as prominent men in this record.[193] Mahāvīr Prasād Praśasti refers to the family of Śreṣṭhi Guṇarāja.[194] He led the *saṁghayātrās* to Śatruñjaya and Rewantak in AD 1400 and 1405 respectively.[195] He is stated to have organized free-kitchens during famines.[196] The Rāṇakpur Praśasti refers to his leadership of a *saṁghayātrā* at the instance of Soma Sundara Sūri of the Bṛhad Tapagaccha after obtaining the necessary permission from the sultan of Gujarat.[197] The family of Rāval Śrī Lāṣaṇa of Nadlai (Godwar) figures prominently in Mewar of the late fifteenth-early sixteenth centuries. Ram Vallabh Somani misses this important family from his list of Jain families.[198] The Inscription dated AD 1500 from Ādinātha temple (Nadlai), which refers to the origin of the Guhila kings as Sūryavaṁśīya, records the *praśasti* of the *ācāryas* of Sandherāgaccha and the installation-project undertaken by the family of Rāval Lāṣaṇa.[199] The consecration of (the image of) Śrī Ādīśvara had to be performed in the Jain monastery called Sāyara which was brought to the city of Nandakulavatī (Nadlai) in samvat 964.[200] It is significant that Lāṣaṇa of Ukeśa lineage bears the title of *rāval*.[201] Thus, this record provides another instance of the incorporation of the wealthy Jains into the *sāmanta* hierarchy.

The above survey proves that a network of the local Jain families were gradually integrated into the political structure. The fact that Bhāṇḍārī Śrī Velaka's father was referred to merely as *sāhakolā*[202] suggests that this was a process of gradual absorption as titles differed from generation to generation. This led to the growth of a network of Jain families close to the royal court. A concluding note to this study of Jain-Guhila relationship is our observation that the so-called, most non-violent social group, the Jains, were actively associated with the military enterprises of the Rajputs.

Other Communities: the Ṭāmṭarāḍas and Kāyasthas

The Chiravā Inscription of the Reign of Mahārāval Samarasiṁha of AD 1273 is perhaps the most important record of a non-Rajput and a non-Jain family of Mewar which rose in status as the process of regional state formation proceeded. Besides the royal *praśasti*, this record is an eulogy and the genealogical list of the Ṭāmṭarāḍa family originating from Nāgdā. The family rendered invaluable services to the state both by functioning as *talarakṣakas* (superintendents of police) of Nāgadṛahapura (Nāgdā) and Citrakūṭa as well as captains in the army. The inscription also records the construction and restoration of the temples of Yogeśvara (Śiva) and Yogeśvarī (Pārvatī) and grants to the temples by the same family at Cirakūpa (Chiravā), a village granted to them by Guhila King Padmasiṁha.

Here I give a detailed account of the family based on this record: In the Ṭāmṭarāḍa family, there was a man named Uddhāraṇa who, being able to protect the good and punish the wicked, was made the *talarakṣa* of Nāgadṛahapura by the King Māthanasiṁha, and who had eight sons, the eldest of whom was Yogarāja, who in turn was made *talāra* in the same city by the King Padmasiṁha. His (Yogarāja's) younger brother was Ratabhū, whose son was Kelhaṇa. Kelhaṇa's son was Udayi, whose son was Karmaṇa. Yogarāja had four sons, namely Pamarāja, Mahendra, Campaka and Kṣema, of whom Pamarāja was killed fighting the army of Suratrāṇa (Sultan) near Bhūtālā, while Nāgadṛahapura was destroyed. Mahendra had three sons named Bāla (Bālaka), Alhādaṇa and Vāyaja. Bālaka's son was Peṭhaka, whose son was Sāmanta, a worshipper of Viṣṇu. While Koṭtadāka was being taken and a battle with Rāṇā Tribhuvana was being fought, Bālaka was killed fighting in front of the King Jaitrasiṁha.[203] His clever wife Bholī, being unable to bear the pains of separation of her husband, became satī. Campaka had a son named Rājasiṁha whose son was Bhacumḍa. Through the favour of the King Jaitrasiṁha, Kṣema secured the post of *talarakṣaka* of Citrakūṭa. His son named Ratna was killed along with Bhīmasiṁha in a battle fought at the foot of the fortress of Citrakūṭa. Ratna's son was Lāla and his brother was Madana. The latter proved his valour in the battlefield of Utthūnaka. Jaitramalla's son Rājasiṁha on being made a minister, paid him (Madana) much respect. Through the favour of the King Samarasiṁha, he (Madana) succeeded his father to the post of *talarakṣaka* of Citrakūṭa,[204] when he worshipped Śiva in the temple of Tribhuvananārāyaṇa built by King Bhoja. Madana's son was Mohana. Surrounded by hills and beautiful sights, the village Cirakūpa is situated near Nāgdā and was given as a gift by the King Padmasiṁha to Yogarāja serving in his army.[205] The latter built there the temples of Yogeśvara and Yogeśvarī which were restored later on by Madana who granted some land near the lake Kālelāya for the maintenance of these temples.[206] Another beautiful temple of Viṣṇu called Uddhāraṇa Svāmī had formerly been built there by Uddhāraṇa. Vāyaraka, Pāṭaka, Muṇḍa, Bhuvana, Teja, Sāmanta, Āriyāputra, Madana and their descendants were urged to preserve the grant fully.[207]

Here is a clear instance of a process in which a local family of a non-Rajput and a non-Jain, social background attained upward social mobility. Functioning as *talarakṣaka* of Nāgdā in itself is evidence of the family's prior importance in the locality of Nāgdā. The record clearly states that Uddhāraṇa was famous for 'protecting the good and punishing the wicked'. Appointments by royal authority benefited both the Ṭāmṭarāḍa family and the state. The family's career prospects grew in the service of the state as its members graduated from the post of *talarakṣaka* of Nāgdā to that of the capital town, Chittaurgarh, and as they became captains in Mewar's army. On the other hand, the state not only expanded and strengthened its base by crossing the Rajput-Brāhmaṇa-Jain barriers by integrating a locally important family of an entirely different social background through various important administrative and military appointments; but also checked the growing influence of the locally entrenched Rajput families.

The village of Cirakūpa not only took care of remunerations for their services but also expanded the social base of the state in the Nāgdā belt. During the course of the thirteenth century, the Ṭāmṭarāḍa family had undoubtedly emerged as a focal point in the local elite network.

The other influential social group in thirteenth-century Mewar seems to have been that of the kāyasthas. However, even if they had already figured as wealthy, local notables in the seventh century and as officials in the tenth century, we do not have records mentioning any kāyastha functionaries in the thirteenth century. However, their prosperity in general is evident from the discovery of a record of a kāyastha family of Chittaurgarh. A Chittaurgarh Pillar Inscription, dated AD 1287, of the reign of Samarasiṁha records the grant of few *dramma* coins to the temple of Vaidyanātha, situated on the bank of Citrāṅga lake, by Vījaḍa, son of Kāyastha Pacasīga.[208] The record is too short to throw light on Vījaḍa's ancestral home. We do not know whether he was a migrant or originally belonged to Chittaurgarh. Like the family of Vījaḍa, a few more Kāyastha families might have emerged as prosperous families in Chittaurgarh in this period. At least the family of Vījaḍa must have been part of the local elite and thus may have functioned as a link between the state and other Kāyastha families. Their status is evident from the wealth they possessed which seems to have distinguished them.

The Bhils in the State Formation of Mewar

In my discussion of the Bhil-Guhila relationship between the seventh and tenth centuries, I remarked on the political implications of Bhil legends relating to the settlement of the early Guhilas in Mewar hills indicating a possibly violent transfer of power as well as on Guhila records suggesting the peasantization[209] of core-area Bhils.[210] The long drawn out relationship between the Guhilas and the Bhils of the Oghna-Panarwa and the Undri (see Map 9) seems to have reached a significant stage in the period between the thirteenth and fifteenth centuries. The latter part of the period seems to have coincided with the incorporation of the local Bhil chiefs into the political structure of the Guhila state. The problems of integration demanded that the Bhil chiefs of the core-area be conferred with a suitable political rank. The prestigious title of *rāṇā* (status equivalent to the royal kinsmen) was conferred upon the Bhil chief of Oghna-Panarwa. This Bhil chief was one of the autochthonous chiefs.[211] The earliest documented evidence of the title of *rāṇā* for the chief of Panarwa comes from the *Sīsodiyān rī Khyāt* of the seventeenth century. Nainsī refers to Rāṇā Dayāldās Bhil, the chief of Panarwa.[212] It is equally significant that Nainsī also refers to Rāvat Narasiṁhadās, the Bhil chief of Nahesar, the area of Jura (south-west of Panarwa).[213] Since different Bhil chiefs bore different titles—*rāṇā* and *rāvat*, the possibility that these political titles were conferred on the Bhil chiefs by the state is strong. Nainsī also reports that Panarwa was the 'place' for refuge for the Bhils which belonged to the *mahārāṇā*.[214] Hence an important historical source of the seventeenth century points to traditions of close alliance between the Bhils of Panarwa and the Guhilas.

The estate of Oghna in Mewar is described as the 'sole spot in India' which enjoyed a state of natural freedom.[215] 'Attached to no state, having no foreign communication, it lived under its own head, a chief with the title of *rāṇā*, head of five thousand bows.'[216] Anthropologists like Robert Deliege seem to have taken this description literally. He observes that since many of the Bhils and Bhilālā chiefs are described as *bhumiās* or *girāsiās* (derived from *girās*, subsistence/a share of the produce of the land) in the literature, the Bhil regions did not actually .constitute the normal territories of the *rājās* but enjoyed independence even as they paid tribute.[217] However, I find such an interpretation highly questionable. It is important to note that not only the Bhils but many Rajputs of Mewar too enjoyed the status of *bhumiā* and *girāsiā*. *Girāsiā* are known to have supplied regular troops to the state while the *bhumiās* rendered local, administrative service and paid an annual quit-rent on their estates to the state.[218] The crucial issue of tribe and state does not hinge around the direct annexation of tribal territories, but their political incorporation into the state. Their incorporation not only accelerated the process of territorial integration and consolidated state power in Bhomat but also mobilized manpower for the state from within the limits of at least Oghna Panarwa and Undri (the Bhil chiefs of these regions were associated with the coronation ceremonies of the *rāṇās*).

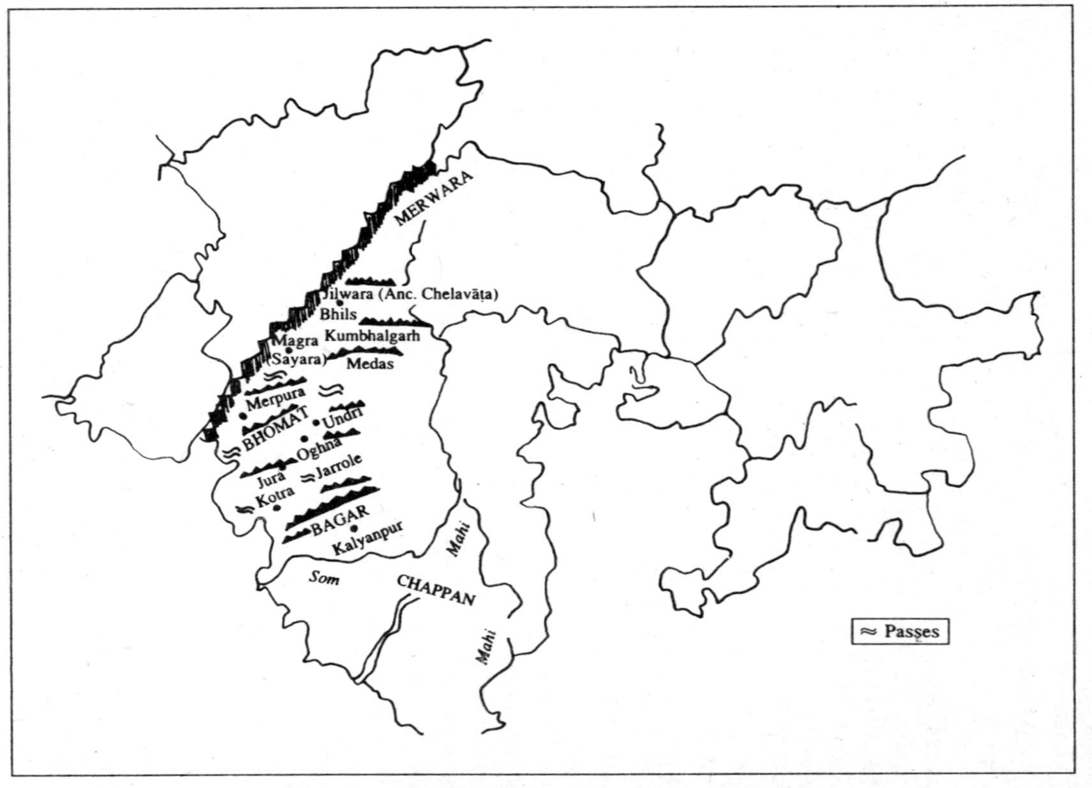

Map 9: Main Bhil Settlements in Mewar Hills.

The strategic importance of the Bhomat country for the state of Mewar has already been noted. The link routes connecting Chittaur-Malwa to the arterial route down the Palanpur gap in Gujarat-Sirohi passed through Bhomat country.[219] Hills and forests tend to restrict the capacity of governments to move humans and goods.[220] The Bhil chiefs of the core-area, once integrated, were expected to facilitate communications throughout Bhil-country because they were guarding the forests, caves, passes and hill routes. They could also function as buffers between the nucleus of the state and the rest of the Bhil population of Bhomat. The fact that local Bhils were always valuable as forest-guides is evident from names popular amongst them such as *banaputras* (the children of the forest), Māirote (born of mountain), Goind (lord of the caves) and Pāl Indra (lord of the pass).[221] Recognition of the Bhils as indispensable forest-guards can be seen in the collection of a levy called *rakhwālī* for the protection of the travellers by local, Bhil and Rajput *bhumiā* and *girāsiā* chiefs in their domination in the latter medieval period.[222] However, the beginnings of this process can certainly be dated back to the period between the thirteenth and fifteenth centuries.

The Bhil chiefs in the centre possibly established links with the *gāmetis* (village headman) of the *pāls* (villages of Bhils) in territories beyond their jurisdiction. The institution of the *gāmeti* was an old feature of the *pāls*. 'The institution, however, is indigenous to the tribe, and it carries with it a considerable amount of prestige and importance, besides financial rewards.'[223] The gradual incorporation of the Bhil *pāls* and the administrative service rendered by the Bhil *gāmetis* is evident from late medieval records of Mewar. The Dhulev *bhaṇḍār* of files and *bahīs* (registers) along with an early nineteenth-century inscription reveal some of the traditional duties of the Bhil *gāmetis* of Magra locality in Mewar. Magra is another Bhil locality in the Mewar hills, away from the Oghna-Panarwa-Undri belt. These records disclose that the ranks of *gāmeti* and *girāsiā* were once again bestowed on the former *gāmeti* and *girāsiā* of village Bilak and *pāl* Bilak enabling them to execute some of the magisterial powers and police duties.[224] Mobilization of the Bhils from Oghna-Panarwa and Undri for construction work on fortresses, roads and temporary bridges seems to have been the other important requirements.

Mobilization of miners at least from the local Bhil population continued to be an important aspect of state-tribe relationship. The following quotation from *Old World Archaeometry* gives idea of mining at Zawar:

The intensive process of mining activities specially at Zawar dated back to twelfth century. At Zawar, by the AD 12th century zinc was being produced industrially. Already in the late 14th century, production was on a considerable scale, and perhaps it is not surprising that the first direct historical reference to Zawar occurs in AD 1380 when Rana Lakshasimha was credited with founding of the mines. Production continued on a major scale for about four centuries before ending during the wars and famine which plagued Rajasthan in the early 19th century, and in the face of western competition. Ironically, the western technology was almost certainly derived from Zawar.[225]

The celebration of the worship of Zawarmātā among the Bhils is a theme of Bhil folksongs and testifies to their long association with the Zawar mines.[226] The local Bhils also seem to have continued to supply the fuel to the Zawar mines. It is evident from the discovery of charcoal retort dumps (smelting) at Zawar particularly, between the early eleventh and the seventeenth centuries.[227]

As noted in Chapter I, charcoal preparation has been one of the major economic pursuits of the majority of the Bhils engaged in non-agricultural activities. If the mahājanas were the entrepreneurs at early medieval Araṇyakūpagiri, the social group possibly involved in the organization of mining activities in fifteenth-century Zawar is likely to be the Jains. Archaeological and inscriptional evidence points to the presence of elite Jain families in Zawar in the fifteenth century. Today, remains of a number of Jain temples of the fourteenth-fifteenth century stand scattered in and around Zawar.[228] The Zawar Jain Temple Inscription of AD 1421[229] recording the building of the Śāntinātha temple at Zawar by a family of merchants attests to the long association of Jains with the Zawar mines. This association evidently had an economic basis since excavations indicate intensive mining activities at this centre of the zinc-lead concentrates, especially from the twelfth century onwards. The Jain merchants must have been involved in the entrepreneurship that went into the regular organization of mining and in the marketing of its products, both raw materials and manufactured zinc, from the local workshops. Thus, they are likely to have entered into negotiations with local Bhil chiefs to mobilize labour. Like in Araṇyakūpagiri, the presence of Jain merchants and Jain temples seem to have laid the foundation for the emergence of an exchange centre in Zawar by the beginning of the fifteenth century.

The state also depended on local Bhil chiefs for the occasional mobilization of Bhil as militia for the state. This statement can be true at least for the territories within the limits of Oghna-Panarwa and Undri.

The chief of Oghna-Panarwa has been significantly described as the 'head of five thousand bows'.[230] Traditions have preserved accounts of the Bhils fighting for both Rāṇā Hammīra in the fourteenth century and Rāṇā Pratāp in the sixteenth century.[231] The chivalry exemplified by the Bhils in the battle of Haldīghāṭī remains a popular theme in Bhil folklore.[232] The mobilization of armies by the different deities of Chittaur leading to the victory of the *mahārāṇās* of Mewar is a recurrent theme of Bhil songs.[233] These songs not only reflect the popular image of the Guhila rulers but also Bhil involvement in the Mewar army. However, such themes seem to emanate more from the ranks of Bhil chiefs.

All these contributions made by the local Bhil population towards the maintenance of the state ran parallel to the continuing process of peasantization of the Bhils in the nucleus of local Rajput states. Direct evidence of this process comes from the Mala copper plates of the thirteenth century from Vagod. Two Bhils, Nādhol and Ralhuā, figure as witnesses to the royal grants made in the village of Mala near Dungarpur.[234] In his discussion of religious attributes of the Bhils, R.S. Mann observes that the plough is an implement of occasional worship, possibly since the time the Bhils shifted to a settled agricultural economy and became dependent on agriculture.[235] The importance of agriculture is also reflected in the folk-songs of those Bhils who were settled in villages. Themes such as field preparation, the harvest and protection of crops from animals are common.[236]

However, peasantization seems to have involved very few Bhils in the core of the Guhila state. It must be remembered that the majority of Bhils had been practising hunting, gathering and shifting agriculture. The traditional economic pursuit of a majority of Bhils is reflected in one of their legends popular among the Bhils of Gujarat. Once Mahādeva took a Bhil-girl as his bride. Her brothers went to Mahādeva for the bride price. They were offered Nandī, the bull. Pārvatī (the Bhil bride in this case) told her brothers that the hump of the bull contained unlimited wealth—hinting thereby that by yoking the bull they would be prosperous. The greedy foresters killed the bull to possess the wealth immediately. This angered the goddess and she cursed the Bhils to perennial poverty.[237] The legend proves the unpopularity of agriculture among most Bhils, but the economic process of state formation (involving the horizontal spread of rural settlements) brought about a transformation in some tribal pockets in which at least a small section of the Bhils emerged as agriculturists.

In spite of Bhil participation in the functioning of the state apparatus, a paradox emerges: in the state's image of the Bhils they were a socially despised ethnic group. Though the *ṭīkā* ceremony performed by the Bhil chiefs at the royal coronations is known to have continued at a latter period,[238] there is no such mention in the official Guhila records. The official attitude is clearly expressed in a thirteenth-century record from Chittaurgarh: 'the enemies of king Allaṭa being incapable of showing their contempt towards him in the battlefield, treat Śabara women disrespectfully and they describe his actions as pleasures in each of the mountains'.[239] This official attitude possibly also point out that the fact that women were used as weapons in a clash between two political opponents and that 'disrespect' (rape?) of women was used to denigrate the opponent points to the patriarchal nature of the polity in which women had no say except as instruments of patriarchal political interests. Secondly, the Bhil residents of the village Mala have been merely designated as 'Bhils' without any such titles as *rāul*, *rāval*, etc., that designated some of the contemporary Rajput residents of the village Mala.[240] An understanding of the official image of the Bhils perhaps reveals the actual situation of the Bhils in society and highlights the problem of tribal integration in the state. In spite of a close and long Bhil-Guhila interaction, the state had to reassert itself again and again in the Bhil localities.

The problem is especially evident in the fifteenth century, probably due to the long absence of Guhila authority in Mewar for a major part of the fourteenth century. Also, the element of egalitarianism, dominant in the Bhil social structure,[241] would have generated problems for the Bhil chiefs (even those of Oghna-Panarwa and Undri) in controlling Bhils beyond their limited territorial jurisdiction. Recurrent Bhil revolts have plagued the history of Mewar. Rāṇā Hammīra is credited with victory over the Bhils of Jilwara (Merwara tract) in the Śṛṅgiṛṣi Inscription of the early fifteenth century.[242] Rāṇā Khetā is eulogized in the *Amarakāvyam* for having conquered and annexed the territories of the Bhils and the Mīnās.[243] In the fifteenth century, Mahārāṇā Kumbha fortified many passes to control the Bhils of Panarwa.[244] Every possible step was taken to fend off possible attacks by Bhils. Significantly, Tod observes that *khālisā* (royal land) in Mewar was bounded on three sides by wandering barbarous tribes.[245] In the area between the Bhil tract and the core of the state were estates of Rajput chiefs. Bhil discontent was perhaps responsible for the settlement of a Solaṁkī Rajput chief, Akṣaya Rājā, in Panarwa in the fifteenth century.[246] One of Akṣaya Rājā's successors settled in Oghna in the sixteenth century.[247] Prior to the

Solaṁkīs, a Rajput of Yadu lineage, and a Dudhiā Brāhmaṇa Udairāja, are known to have lived in the Bhil areas of Panarwa and Oghna respectively.[248] All this had a significant impact on the Bhil chiefs. The presence of Solaṁkī chiefs in Oghna-Panarwa is likely to have been responsible for the Bhil-Solaṁkī marriage in the subsequent period and the claims to Solaṁkī descent by the chiefs of Oghna-Panarwa. It is well-known that the Bhil chiefs of Oghna-Panarwa claim descent from the Solaṁkī lineage of the Rajputs.[249] Similarly, some other Bhil groups of Mewar, Magra, Kalyanpur, etc., claimed descent from different Rajput lineages.[250] The Solaṁkī Bhils of Oghna-Panarwa may be the oldest case of 'Rajputization' among the Bhils of southern Rajasthan. The Bhils claiming Rajput descent are called the Bhilālās (progeny of Rajput fathers and Bhil mothers).[251] They claim a rank superior to the Bhils. Thus the process of state formation in Mewar highlights the process of differentiation within an egalitarian tribe on coming in contact with a stratified society. Morton H. Fried makes a similar observation in the context of tribal social formation in general.[252] The Bhilālās such as the Solaṁkī-Bhils of Oghna-Panarwa demonstrate the emergence of an elite section among the Bhils as a result of their close interaction with state-society over a long period of time.

Perhaps the case of the Solaṁkī-Bhils of Oghna-Panarwa is one of the best illustrations of the social aspect of the process of state formation. It is relevant to reiterate Chattopadhyaya's observations in the context of Solaṁkī Bhils of Oghna,

> The process of caste formation remained the essence of the social processes which drew widely dispersed and originally outlying groups into a structure which allowed them in a large measure to retain their original character, except that this character was defined with reference to the structure. . . .[253]

For the Oghna Bhils of the fifteenth-century royal authority was represented by the local Solaṁkī chiefs. Therefore, for the Solaṁkī Bhils chiefs of Oghna-Panarwa of the fifteenth-century titled *rāṇā*, the following observations can be partially held true, 'Some of these tribal princes found themselves similarly involved in the process of Hinduization and rose to become tributary princes (sāmanta) in the course of further development, while others in their turn could preserve their autonomy for centuries.'[254] The study of even the core-area Bhils in Mewar demonstrates that despite their formal integration into the political structure, and beginnings of 'Rajputization', as well as their recurring revolts, we cannot definitely locate them as *sāmantas* before the fifteenth century.

III

Social Alliances and Relations with Contemporary Powers

Social relations of the Guhilas with the Cāhamānas of Suvarṇagiri (Songirā) or Jalor can be seen in the context of the Gujarat-Delhi Sultanate imbroglio. The Achaleśvara Inscription significantly states that Samarasiṁha (son of Tejasiṁha) lifted the deeply sunk Gurjara land high out of the Turuṣka sea.[255] The continuing south-western expansion of the Delhi Sultanate with its recurrent inroads into Mewar was a part of its attempt to control Gujarat is attested by the Chiravā inscription recording the battle of Bhūtālā near Nāgadrahapura (between Jaitrasiṁha and Iltutmish).[256] It is also interesting that none of the Persian sources mentions Iltutmish's ventures into Mewar indicating Iltutmish's possible failure to secure the routes to Gujarat through Mewar. The sultanate's interests in Mewar are evident from the following: Jayasiṁha Sūri's *Hammīramadamardana* referring to the burning of Medapāṭa in the context of the raids conducted by Milācchikāra Suratrāṇa, etc., in Bhāghelā King Vīradhavala's (Gujarat) reign[257] and referring to Jaitrasiṁha as *Medapāṭapṛth vīlāṭam maṇḍalam Jayatalam*,[258] the claim by Chiravā inscription that the rulers of Gurjara, Mālava, Jāṅgal (present state of Bikaner in Thar desert and northern part of Mewar)[259] could not humble his pride, similar claims by an unpublished inscription from Ghaghsa (near Chittaurgarh),[260] the Achaleśvara inscription crediting Jaitrasiṁha with victory over the army of the Turuṣkas and defence of Mewar,[261] and Jinaprabhasūri's *Tīrthakalpa* referring to Samarasiṁha's clash with Ulugh Khan, younger brother of Sultan Alauddin.[262] In response, the Guhilas attempted to create buffer zones and political allies in their immediate north. Contemporary references to Jaitrasiṁha as the 'uprooter of Naḍūla power'[263] and control over Abu-Sirohi locality for the first time in the late thirteenth century,[264] point to Guhila attempts to control their north-western frontiers. The Cāhamānas of Suvarṇagiri (Songirā) were won over as political allies in central Rajasthan through the marriage of the Songirā Princess Rupādevī, daughter of Cāhamāna Cācigadeva and sister of Cāhamāna Sāmantasiṁha, with Guhila King Tejasiṁha.[265] She was the mother of Guhila Prince Kṣetrasiṁha.[266]

The Khalji-Tughlaq interregnum in Chittaurgarh in the first half of the fourteenth century is mentioned in records dating to the reigns of Alauddin Khalji and Muhammad Tughlaq,[267] and in seventeenth-century Guhila references to the legendary Padmiṇī[268] (the Alauddin-Padmiṇī episode, more bardic lore than historic truth also testifies to the fall of the Guhilas at Chittaurgarh). However, there are references to Songirā presence at Chittaurgarh, perhaps as the subordinates of the Tughlaqs, in a record of Songirā Prince Vanavīra dated AD 1338.[269] It is strange that historians such as M.S. Ahluwalia in his *Muslim Expansion in Rajasthan: The Relations of Delhi Sultanate with Rajasthan 1206-1526*,[270] ignore contemporary evidence on the Songirās at Chittaurgarh as Nainsī too mentions the Songirās at Chittaur.[271]

The Guhila-Songirā marriage recorded in the bardic traditions of Mewar[272] highlights the importance of the Songirās for the Guhilas. Rāṇā Hammīra is stated to have married Songirā Vanavīra's sister, a Songirā Cāhamāna princess. *Baḍvādevīdān Khyāt* names a Songirā queen of the legendary Rāṇā Hammīra,[273] and Nainsī mentions a Songirā mother of Hammīra.[274] The political importance of such a marriage for the early princes of the Rāṇā branch is obvious in view of the eclipse of Guhila power at Chittaurgarh in the fourteenth century and the rise of the Songirā Cāhamānas at Chittaur, with their territorial hold over the Godwar region.[275] Political alliances of the Guhilas and the Songirās seem to have been maintained as the traditions record the marriage of a Sīsodiā (Rāṇā Guhilas) Princess Subālī with a Songirā chief Rāo Sāmantasiṁha,[276] and the induction of Songirā Prince Vanavīra into the royal services of Mewar.[277] Although none of the fifteenth-century Guhila records refers to any Guhila-Songirā matrimonial alliance, the presence of the Songirās at Chittaurgarh points towards possibilities of Guhila social linkages with the Songirā Cāhamānas.

Social linkages of the Guhilas with contemporary Rajputs such as the Bāghelās and Yādavas of Gujarat and Khīcīs of Gagraun in the fifteenth century need to be seen in view of the rise of Gujarat and Malwa as sultanates and the ensuing problems of defending the western and south-eastern frontiers. Even before the rise of the sultanate of Gujarat, there was a Guhila-Bāghelā clash at the western frontier of Mewar leading to the Guhila capture of a local fortress, Koṭṭadaka (modern Koṭra).[278]

The Bāghelās too claimed victory over Mewar in the mid-thirteenth century. A Bāghelā land grant dating back to AD 1260 refers to the Bāghelā Rāṇā Vīsaladeva of Dholka as one 'who resembled a hatchet on account of his cutting the roots of the creeper like turbulent government of the Medapāṭa country'.[279] It is equally significant that the Bāghelās acknowledged Guhila Jaitrasiṁha as *Medapāṭapṛth vīlalāṭam maṇḍalam Jayatalam.*[280] The rise of Ahmad Shah I (contemporary of Rāṇā Mokal) in Gujarat was accompanied by repeated incursions into Mewar by him and was followed by Guhila counter-claims of victory over Firuz Shah of Nagaur and Patsaha Ahmad,[281] Rāṇā Kumbha responded with a programme of territorial expansion in the north-western frontiers of Mewar to control the fortresses of Nagaur and Narena, among others[282] and tried to ally with the fugitive Ghurid princes from Malwa (necessitating a Mewar-Gujarat military alliance against Malwa). This provoked a counter alliance by Malwa with Gujarat against Mewar,[283] and necessitated close Guhila-Bāghelā and Guhila-Yādava political cooperation which led to matrimonial alliances with the Bāghelās and with the Yādavas. Mokal's Śṛṅgirṣi inscription eulogizes his Bāghelī Queen Gaurambikā at great length.[284]

Gujarat's repeated attempts at controlling the fortresses of the Abu-Sirohi belt and its protectorate, the Sultanate of Nagaur,[285] shifted Mewar's to attention its north-western frontiers. A number of inscriptional records issued by Kharataragaccha Vasahī of Abu in AD 1458,[286] an image inscription from Caturmukha Vihar of AD 1461 and the Gaumukh Inscription from Acalgarh referring to the reign of Rāṇā Kumbha, speak of the Mewar-Gujarat rivalry over Abu. Significantly Persian sources speak of repeated attempts by Gujarat to seize Kumbhalgarh and Chittaurgarh.[287] Hence, pursuing social alliances with local Rajput families of Gujarat became an important strategy against the Sultanate of Gujarat.

If Mokal had a Bāghelī queen, a Guhila Princess Ramāvatī (Kumbha's daughter) was married to Rāya Māṇḍalīka, the Yādava ruler of Junagarh. The way the Viṣṇu Temple Inscription of Ramāvatī from Zawar (AD 1497) eulogizes the Yādavas,[288] speaks of their political importance for fifteenth-century Guhilas. Even seventeenth-century sources refer to Rāṇā Kumbha's control over Junagarh (Saurashtra).[289] The Guhilas continued to strengthen their social linkages with the local Rajput powers of Gujarat at least up to the end of the fifteenth century: local bardic traditions speak of Rāṇā Rāimalla's (son and successor of Kumbha) chief queen, a princess from Idar (Banaskantha region of north-eastern Gujarat), and how Rāimalla captured Chittaurgarh from Kumbha's assassin Udayasiṁha (I) with the help of his father-in-law, the Rajput ruler of Idar.[290]

Malwa's repeated incursions into Mewar, attempted invasions of Chittaurgarh, Kumbhalgarh, Maṇḍalgarh, Hāḍāvatī and Gagraun throughout the fifteenth century,[291] and Kumbha's claim of defeating a joint army of Malwa and Gujarat[292] all led to a matrimonial alliance of the Guhilas with the Khīcīs of Gagraun. *Annals* record the marriage of

Lālbāī (Mokal's daughter) with Acaldās Khīcī.[293] Since Gagraun commanded a strategic point on the route between Malwa and Mewar, the politico-military significance of the social linkages with the Khīcīs of Gagraun cannot be underestimated for the Guhilas of the fifteenth century. Undoubtedly, the social alliances with the neighbouring Rajput powers beyond Mewar facilitated Guhila hold, however difficult and tenuous, over some of the fortresses claimed by the contemporary records.[294]

Guhila attempts at magnifying their own status *vis-à-vis* the neighbouring sultans (Qutabuddin Mahmud Beghara in Gujarat and Mahmud Khalji and Ghiyasuddin Khalji in Malwa) in their fifteenth- century charters[295] also point to Mewar's military pre-occupation with Gujarat, Malwa and Nagaur. The Guhila claim began with the liberation of Gayā from the Yavanas,[296] indicating a local *tīrtha* possibly in central Rajasthan (Nagaur),[297] Kumbha later credited the same predecessor, Lakṣasiṁha with the liberation of the *tristhalī*; the three *tīrthas* of Kashi, Prayag, and Gaya in the Gangetic plains[298] magnifying Guhila power in the eyes of the local Rajput chiefs.

Mewar was as also engaged militarily with Rajput powers that were its immediate neighbours, such as the Hāḍās of Bundi, the Rāṭhaurs of Manḍor and the Devḍā Cāhamānas of Sirohi in order to better control the fortresses strategic to its eastern, northern and north-western frontiers respectively. Conquests of Vṛndāvatī (Bundi) are mentioned twice in Kumbhalgarh Praśasti[299] while a separate reference occurs to the conquest of Hāḍāvatī (eastern Mewar extending into Bundi).[300] The first Guhila reference to possession of Vṛndāvatī appears only in the context of Kumbha's conquests.[301] In view of continuing Hāḍā resistance from Bundi, it is significant that *Baḍvādevīdān* does not mention a single Hāḍā queen for Kumbha. With the emergence of the Rāṭhaurs in Marwar in the latter half of the fifteenth century, Mewar found it difficult to control the fortresses of Manḍor and Sojat. Although the Rāṇakpur Praśasti claims Kumbha's victory over Meru Manḍor,[302] the situation had changed significantly for the Guhilas as Kumbha is later stated to have captured Mandor by killing the enemy family.[303] In contrast, Kumbha's control over the Abu-Sirohi belt does not figure in the Guhila records in such terms as that of Manḍovarpur or Vṛndāvatī. Kumbha's land grant charters appeared in Ajahari and Sirohi as early as AD 1437[304] while his inscriptions at Abu continued to appear till late fifteenth century.[305] Although local bardic traditions of Sirohi record the name of Devḍā

Cāhamāna Ḍoḍiā Narasiṁha, son of Rao Saljī, as conqueror of the fortresses of Abu, Vasantgarh and Bhula, etc.,[306] a local popular song celebrates the conquest of Abu, a Devḍā possession, and ascribes building of palaces and lakes there to Kumbha. *Ḍoḍe Rāo Sirohi dujāḍā dalasajdā par haṁsa diā Ābu girvar Śikhar uparan Kumbhe sarovar mahal kiā* (although Sirohi belonged to Rāo Ḍoḍe, it is Kumbha who gifted the swan-like mount of the Ābu with the palaces and lakes).[307] Such popular traditions reflect Guhila control of the Abu-Sirohi belt for a considerable time in the fifteenth century. Interestingly, *Baḍvādevīdān* lists a Devḍā queen each for the early kings of the Rāṇā branch like Khetā and Lākhā as well as two Devḍā queens for Rāṇā Rāimalla, Rāj Kunwar, Devḍā Rāo Gopā's daughter and Campā Kunwar, Devḍā Rāo Lākhā's daughter.[308] The social relationship with the Devḍā Cāhamānas of Sirohi became politically significant in view of the Mewar-Gujarat clash over Abu. Hence, Guhilas seem to have a better control over the Abu-Sirohi belt than the Marwar of the Rāṭhaurs or Bundi of the Hāḍās.

Last, but not the least, occasional victory over Rajput forts beyond Mewar undoubtedly brought additional resources, seized during the campaigns. Also, commercial wealth accruing from the trade routes that some of these fortresses commanded, was obviously diverted to the Guhila state of Mewar. A part of this wealth is likely to have contributed resources to the making of massive forts in Kumbha's reign.

We have tried to answer some questions related to the nature of and changes in the political structure of the Mewar state between the thirteenth and fifteenth centuries. If kinsmen dominated and participated more in the organization and control of Guhila territory in the thirteenth century, socio-political links with the non-Guhila Rajput chiefs of eastern Mewar seem to have ensured a better defence of Chittaurgarh and of the hinterland in the fifteenth century. However, the Guhilas had to reassert themselves both in eastern Mewar and in the Bhil dominion. Their social linkages with Rajput powers outside Mewar between the thirteenth and fifteenth centuries also helped them to tackle military problems and retain power. Incorporation of non-Rajput social groups such as the Jains, the Ṭāmṭarāḍa family from Nāgdā, and the Bhil chiefs, into the political structure strengthened the socio-economic and political base of the state. A long process of regional state formation culminated in a dynastic tradition in which the state of Mewar came to be identified with the Guhila royal family, as indicated by attempts of fifteenth-century kings of Mewar to legitimize their rule by claiming links with the Guhilas.

NOTES

1. A Fragmentary Inscription of AD 1213 at Ekaliṅgajī Temple, *Vir Vinod*, vol. I, p. 389.
2. Ibid., p. 396.
3. Chiravā Inscription, vv. 4 and 12.
4. Ibid., v. 7.
5. Ibid., v. 10.
6. Ibid., vv. 19 and 22.
7. Ibid., v. 8.
8. Ibid., v. 3, '*Guhilāṅgajavaṁśājahpurā kṣitipālotra babhūva Bappakah* ||'.
9. Chittaurgarh Inscription, pp. 392-6, v. 10 and Achaleśvara Inscription, pp. 345-55, v. 12.
10. Chittaurgarh Inscription, op. cit., v. 13 and Achaleśvara Inscription, op. cit., v. 12, '*bappakasya tanayo nayanetā sambabhūva nṛpatirguhil-ākhyāh yasya nāmā kalitām kila jātim bhūbhujo dadhati tat kulā jātāh* ||'.
11. Chittaurgarh Inscription, op. cit., vv. 13-58 and Achaleśvara Inscription, op. cit., vv. 12-46.
12. See section on 'Centres of the Guhila power between the tenth and the twelfth centuries beyond Mewar hills' in Chap. II.
13. Chiravā Inscription, op. cit., vv. 4-12.
14. Chittaur Inscription of Jayatalladevī of AD 1278, op. cit., l. 6. Also see D.C. Sircar, *Indian Epigraphy*, Delhi, 1965, p. 405; idem, *Indian Epigraphical Glossary*, Delhi, 1966, p. 271. *Rājakula* and *rāval* refer to kings, royal officers and members of the royal family.
15. *Vir Vinod*, vol. I, p. 401.
16. Chittaurgarh Inscription, AD 1274, op. cit., v. 8.
17. Achaleśvara Inscription, AD 1285, op. cit., v. 5.
18. Chittaurgarh Inscription, AD 1274, op. cit., v. 5.
19. Ibid., v. 13.
20. Ibid., v. 60.
21. Ibid., v. 13.
22. Achaleśvara Inscription, op. cit., vv. 36-7.
23. Although an alternative explanation can be offered that royal references to the Guhila lineage between AD 1274 and 1285 were meant to assert Guhila presence in the newly acquired territory of Chittaurgarh, repeated references to the branches and sub-branches of the Guhila lineage strongly suggest that royal kinsmen played a significant political role.
24. Chittaur Inscription of Jayatalladevī, op. cit., l. 4.
25. Kumbhalgarh Praśasti, third slab, *EI*, vol. XXIV, p. 328, v. 177.
26. David P. Henige, 'Some Phantom Dynasties of Early and Medieval India: Epigraphic Evidence and the Abhorrence of a vacuum', in *BSOAS*, vol. XXXVIII, 1975, p. 539.

27. *Shodh Patrika*, Vikram Saṁvat 2010, p. 57 (Inscription from Gogunda).
28. At least three fragmentary inscriptions dating back to Alauddin Khalji's reign—including one that is dated 1314 and refers to Alauddin Khalji as the ruler of Chittaur—have been discovered at Chittaurgarh, *ARIE*, Appendix C, no. 126, 1956. Also see *URI*, op. cit., p. 173. Two more Persian inscriptions dating back to in the reign of Muhammad bin Tughlaq have been found at Chittaurgarh, *EIAPS*, 1955-6, pp. 67-8. At least three short inscriptional records of AD 1338, including two referring to the presence of Songirā Prince Vanavīra as in-charge of fort of Muhammad follow those of Muhammad bin Tughlaq at Chittaurgarh, P.C. Nahar, ed., *Jain Abhilekha*, vol. II, Calcutta, 1927, p. 242.
29. *Shodh Patrika*, op. cit., p. 57, l. 1.
30. Mokal's Chittaurgarh Inscription dated AD 1428, *Vir Vinod*, p. 402, v. 7.
31. Śṛṅgiṛṣi Inscription, op. cit., v. 5.
32. Kumbhalgarh Praśasti, fourth slab, op. cit., v. 233.
33. Ibid.
34. Rāṇakpur Praśasti of AD 1439, *Vir Vinod*, p. 410, l. 20.
35. Mokal's Śṛṅgiṛṣi Inscription, op. cit., v. 3.
36. Mokal's Chittaurgarh Inscription, op. cit., v. 5.
37. Śṛṅgiṛṣi Inscription, op. cit., vv. 2-3.
38. Kumbhalgarh Praśasti, third slab, op. cit., v. 177.
39. Ibid., v. 177, '*atham mahārāṇā śrī lakhamsīvarnanam || khummānvaṁśā khalu lakṣmasiṁhastasmin gate durga varam rarakṣa kulasthitim kāpuruṣai na jātu dhīrāh puruṣāstyajamti*'.
40. Gogunda Inscription of Ṭhakkura Ḍālā dated AD 1366, op. cit., p. 57, l. 1.
41. Śṛṅgiṛṣi and Chittaurgarh Inscription, op. cit.
42. Kumbhalgarh Praśasti, third slab, op. cit., v. 127.
43. Ibid., v. 124.
44. Rāimalla's Ekaliṅgajī Temple Dakṣiṇadvāra Praśasti, *Vir Vinod*, vol. I, p. 419, v. 8.
45. Ibid., v. 18.
46. Āṭapura Inscription, op. cit., vv. 2-3.
47. Chittaurgarh Inscription of Mokal, op. cit., v. 7, '*vaṁśe tatrarisiṁhah kṣitipatirājña kṣatrāṅkṣtra-lakṣmī vīkṣādakṣorūpakṣamābahulajarājanīdhvaṁsbhāsvadagbhastīh || vindhyāvandhyapradeśasphuradmalakhani-vyakta ratnākaratvasphāra śrī medapāṭakṣiti valaya valadugdhapathod-candrah ||*'.
48. Śṛṅgiṛṣi Inscription, op. cit., vv. 2-13; Chittaurgarh Inscription, op. cit., vv. 7-44.
49. Mokal's Chittaurgarh Inscription, op. cit., vv. 10-13.
50. Ranakpur Praśasti, op. cit., p. 410, l. 20.
51. Ibid., p. 410, ll. 9-10.
52. Ibid., p. 410, ll. 2-10.

53. Ibid., p. 410, l. 11.
54. Ibid., p. 410, ll. 8-10.
55. Kumbhalgarh Praśasti, third slab, op. cit., v. 176.
56. Ibid., vv. 176-7, '*Atham mahārāṇā śrī lakhamsī varṇanam || khummāṇvaṁśāh khalu lakṣmasiṁha*'.
57. Ibid., v. 134, '*Iti rāulam śrī guhadattavarṇanam || atha rāula śrī khummāṇa varṇanam*'.
58. Ibid., vv. 134-6, '*Harṣādyotolayatsvaṁ nijasutagṛhiṇīsamyutam Kāñcanena pradattadyācakebhyah Kanakmiti lasatkalpavṛkṣopamānah | Kīrttim Vistārayansvām tu hinadadhisudhākṣīrahirāvadatām sa Śrī Khummāṇanāma Samabhavadavaner nāyako bhuribhāgya vilaṅghayatī sakalam mahītalam diganam vāri nidhon girivrājam khummāṇ-rājanyaśiromanesāvasau narttādbhūtakīrttinartakī Aṅgāh samprāptabhaṁgāh samrabhuvi param dattanāgāh kaliṅga vaṅga naṣṭākhīlāṁga śarattihatibhih patitaṅga striliṅgāh || Saurāṣṭra narapatitilakprasthitau digjayārtham cauḍāh samtyaktacūḍā raṇarasapatavo drāviḍa naiva gauḍāh ||*'.
59. Ibid.
60. Ibid., v. 138, '*Iti Rāulam Śrī Khummāṇa varṇanam || Atha Rājavarṇanam || Atha Śrī Rājavaṁśotra pravyaktah pracyate dhunā || cirantanapraśasto nāmanakānāmtah-vekṣanāt*'.
61. Premlata Sharma, ed., *Ekaliṅgamāhātmyam*, Delhi, 1976, p. 175, v. 62, '*Aparasyām śākhāyām Māhapa Rāhapramukha Mahīpālah*'.
62. Ibid., vv. 62-3, '*Aparasyām śākhāyam Māhapa Rāhapapramukha mahīpālāh yadvaṁśe narapatayo api Rāṇātvamprāptah san pṛthvīpatirāhapobhūpah*'.
63. *EI*, vol. XXIV, p. 66, vv. 11-13.
64. Motilal Menaria, ed., *Rājapraśasti Mahākāvyam* of Raṇachoḍa Bhaṭṭa, Udaipur, 1973, pp. 35-6, vv. 28-34.
65. Dev Kothari, ed., *Amarkāvyam of Raṇachoḍa Bhaṭṭa*, Udaipur, 1985, pp. 112-18, Chap. 5, vv. 2-33 and Chap. 6, vv. 1-10.
66. Kumbhalgarh Praśasti, third slab, op. cit., vv. 176-7.
67. Shodh Patrika, vol. V, pt. 3, p. 53, ll. 3-4, '*Cāhamāna rāo sīhasu suta rāo, cānd sakalarājye kardamvalgrāma sthiteh*'.
68. Ibid., pp. 54-5.
69. Ibid., pp. 54-5, '*Svasti Śrī Rāṇā ṣe (khe) talade rājye Samvat 1423 Varṣe āṣāḍhavadī 13 bhāunae aśvinī nakṣatre sobhana yoge ṭha. Ṣātala suta ṭha. Ḍālā jīrṇoddhara prasāda Viṣṇu mūrti pratiṣṭhitam*'.
70. Appendix to *EI*, vols. XIX-XXIII, no. 649, p. 92.
71. Hāḍās or Hāḍā Cāhamānas of Eastern Mewar claimed descent from Bhanwardhan Cāhamāna of the Cāhamāna lineage. See *Annals*, vol. III, op. cit., p. 1802.
72. Ibid., p. 1691.
73. Ibid., p. 1681.
74. Ibid., pp. 1681-2.

75. Ibid., pp. 1806-8.
76. Ibid., p. 1808.
77. Ibid., pp. 1802-4. The text of the transcription runs as follows, edited by Tod:
'By Āśāpurana (the fulfiller of our desires) the Kuladevī (tutelary goddess) of the race, by whose favour hidden treasures are revealed, and through whose power, many Chohan Kings have ruled the earth, of which race was Bhanwardhan, who in the field of strife attained the desires of victory. Of his race was the tribe of Hara, of which was Koolun, of illustrious and pure descent in both races; whose fame was fair as the rays of the moon. From him was Jypal, who obtained the fruits of the good works. . . . From him was Deva-raj, the lord of the land, ... His son was Hur-raj, whose frame was piece of fire; who, in the field of battle, conquered renown from the princes of the land (bhom-eswar), and dragged the spoils of victory from their pinnacled abodes. From him were the lords of Bumaoda, whose land yielded to them its fruits. From Deva-raj was Rit-pal, who made the rebellious bow the head, ... From him was Kelhan, the chief of his tribe, whose son Koontul resembled Dhermaraj: . . . a son was born to Koontul, fair as the offspring of the ocean. He was named Mahadeva. He was [in wisdom] fathomless as the sea, and in battle immovable. . . . The sword grasped in his extended arm dazzled the eye of his enemy, as when uplifted over the head of Uni Shah he rescued the Lord of Medpat, and dragged Kaitah from his grasp, as is Chandra from Rahoo. He trod the Sooltan's army under foot, as does the ox the corn; even as did the Danoos (demons) churn the ocean, so did Mahadeva, the field of strife seizing the gem (rutna) of victory from the son of the king and bestowing it on Kaitah, the lord of men. From the centre even to the skirts of space, did the fame of his actions extend, pure as curdled milk. He had a son, Doorjun, on whom he bestowed the title of Jiva-raj (jeoraj), who had two brothers, Soobutsal and Kumbhakama.'
78. Ibid., p. 1804.
79. Ibid. Kaitah has been identified with Rāṇā Kṣetrasiṁha (Khetā).
80. Peter Peterson, ed., Ekaliṅgajī Temple Dakṣiṇadvāra Inscription, *A Collection of Prakrit and Sanskrit Inscriptions*, Bhavanagar Archaeological Depart-ment (English translation is available only in this collection), Ekaliṅgaji Temple Dakṣiṇadvāra Inscription, *Vir Vinod*, op. cit., p. 119, v. 31, '*Hāḍāmanḍala munḍakhandanadhṛta sphūrjatkabandhoddhuram Kṛtvā Sāṅgāramātmasādvasumatīm Śrī Kṣetra Siṁhavyādhat*'.
81. Ibid.
82. Kumbhalgarh fourth slab, op. cit., vv. 259 and 263-4.
83. Ibid., pp. 1680-1. The inscription is edited and translated by Col. Tod.
84. Devilal Paliwal, ed., *Baḍvādevīdān Khyāt*, Udaipur, 1985, pp. 2 and 5.
85. Ibid., p. 5.
86. *Annals*, vol. II, pp. 1722-3.

87. Ibid. The Bālnote of Maṇḍalgarh was a branch of the Solaṁkīs who migrated to southern Rajasthan from Tonk (central Rajasthan). Regarding their settlement in Maṇḍalgarh tract, Tod narrates the following traditions: 'The first possession the founder had, was Larpoora, a town of great antiquity. He had in his service a Bhil, named Mandoo, who, while guarding the sugarcane from the wild hog, came upon one sound asleep. To ensure his arrow piercing the animal, he began to sharpen it upon a stone, and, to his astonishment, found it transmuted to gold. He repaired to his master, who returned with Mandoo, and found the stone, with the hog still asleep beside it; but no sooner had he seized upon his prize, than Baraha disappeared. With the possession of the Paris-putter, the 'philosopher's stone', he raised the walls of Mandelgurh, which was named after the fortunate Bhil. By an act of injustice to one of his subjects, he forfeited Mandelgurh to a descendant.'
88. Ibid., p. 1724.
89. Ibid., p. 1723. Unfortunately these two inscriptions discovered and read by Tod are reportedly mutilated and therefore have not been published.
90. Fourth slab, op. cit., vv. 263-4.
91. Ranakpur Praśasti, op. cit., p. 410, l.15.
92. *Baḍvādevīdān Khyāt*, op. cit., pp. 4 and 6. Solaṁkī Rāo Sātalji's grand-daughters appear as Guhila queens for Mokal and Rāimalla. Considering the long gap between Mokal's reign (early fifteenth century) and Rāimalla's reign (late fifteenth century) the historicity of the queens is doubtful.
93. *Annals*, vol. III, pp. 1687-8.
94. Ibid., p. 1691.
95. Ibid., p. 1699. 'On the Purnima (full moon) of Seoratri (the birth day of Śiva), Maha Rae'an Derae Sing Deo bestowed, in the name of Rameswar, village of Tuttagarh in poon (religious gift). These who maintain the grant, will enjoy the fruits resulting therefrom. . . . Samvat 1302 (AD 1246)'. This record justifies the popular legend of 'Universal Paramar' for the locality of Bhainsrorgarh.
96. Ibid. The inscription is edited and translated by Col. Tod.
97. Ibid.

    'Samvat 1370 (AD 1314), the 16th of Asar (Sudi ekum), he, whose renown is unequalled, the king, the lord of men, Maharaja Adheraj, Sri Alla-o-din, with his army of three thousand elephants, ten lakhs of horse, war-chariots and foot without number, conquering from Sambhur in the north, Malwa, Kurnat, Kanor'h, Jhalore, Jessulmer, Deogir, Tylung, even to the shorer of the Ocean, and Chandrapoori in the east, Victorious over all the kings of the earth, and by whom Sutrawan Doorg, with its twelve townships, have been wrested from the Pramar maunsi, by whose son, Beelaji, whose birth-place (oot-pat) is Sri Dhar, this fountain was excavated. Written and also engraved by Sydeva, the stone-cutter (sootrad-har).'
98. Ibid.

99. *Baḍvādevīdān Khyāt*, p. 4.
100. Badri Prasad Sakaria, ed., *Muhaṇot Nainsī rī Khyāt*, vol. II, Jodhpur, 1984, pp. 42-58 (henceforth, *Nainsī rī Khyāt*); *History of the Jodhpur State*, op. cit., pp. 147-8; *Annals*, vol. II, pp. 939-42.
101. Pt. Bisheshwar Nath Reu, *Glories of Marwar and the Glorious Rathors*, Jodhpur, 1943, pp. 13-14. Rao Raṇamal, the eldest son of Rāo Cūṇḍā, is known to have waived his right to the throne in favour of his brother Rāo Kanha to carry out the wish of his father. He left Marwar in AD 1408 for Mewar.
102. Ibid.
103. *Annals*, vol. I, p. 223.
104. Ibid., p. 224. Also see, Kaushik, op. cit., p. 4.
105. *Baḍvādevīdān Khyat*, pp. 3, 6.
106. Reu, op. cit., p. 17.
107. Ibid., pp. 17-18.
108. *Baḍvādevīdan Khyāt*, pp. 6-9. The list of Rāṭhaur queens for Rāimalla is as follows: Rāṭhaur Bīsā's daughter Rājkanwar, Rāṭhaur Rāṇāsing's daughter Kamkukanwar, Rāṭhaur Jodhsiṁha's daughter Vikrakanwar, Rāṭhaur Rao Dalapatsiṁha's daughter Sagatde, Rāṭhaur Rāo Māldeo's daughter Adrakanwar and Rāṭhaur Rao Bajarājjī's daughter Adrakanwar. The Rāṭhaur queens for Sāṅgā are Jodhā's daughter Barājbāī, Rāo Bhārmal's daughter Bālkanwar; Banesing's daughter Pyārkanwar, Rāo Bāgh's daughter Dhanakanwar (Rāo Sujā's granddaughter), Rāo Sur's Karmetanbāī and Lādkanwarbāī.
109. Ibid., p. 6.
110. Hukum Singh Bhati, *Rājasthān ke Mertiyā Rāṭhaur (AD 1458-1707)*, Jodhpur, 1986, p. 10.
111. Ṭhakkur Gopalsiṁha Mertiya, ed., *Jaimal Vaṁśa Prakāsh,* Ajmer, 1932, pp. 119, 126, 165.
112. Ibid., p. 109; Pt. Narottamdas Swami, ed., *Bānkīdās rī Khyāt*, Rajasthan Prachya Vidya Pratisthan, Jodhpur, 1956, p. 63.
113. *Bānkīdās rī Khyāt*, op. cit.; *Murārīdān rī Khyāt* (Hindi tr.), Rajasthan Prachya Vidya Pratisthan Granthanka (serial no.) 15657, p. 549.
114. *Murārīdān rī Khyāt*, p. 488.
115. Ibid.
116. Ibid., p. 490.
117. *Jaimal Vaṁśā Prakash*, p. 68.
118. Ibid., pp. 71-2.
119. Henri Stern, 'Power in Traditional India: Territory, Caste and Kinship in Rajasthan', in Richard D. Fox, ed., *Realm and Region in Traditional India*, Delhi, 1977, pp. 73-4.
120. *Amarakāvyam*, canto. VIII, p. 14.
121. *Rājapraśasti*, op. cit., v. 253.
122. *Trade and Traders*, pp. 240-1. The story of a merchant, the Caulukya King

Siddharāja and the Sahasraliṅga lake narrated by Merutuṅga is an indication of the royal families' concern to further relations with the merchants in early medieval western India.

123. Ibid., p. 224. Jineśvara Sūri (eleventh century) is known to have advised Jain merchants that a king could be of great service or disservice to the merchants. A merchant was advised to solicit his help by eulogizing him and paying personal homage at the court.
124. Chattopadhyaya, *Markets and Merchants*, p. 114. One of the factors responsible for the situation of partial monetization in this period was the proliferation of the varieties of demands for articles which included making preparations for the endemic wars of the period.
125. *RTA*, p. 416.
126. Ibid., p. 417.
127. Ram Vallabh Somani, Jain Inscriptions from Rajasthan, Jaipur, 1982, p. 23. Also see *ARIE*, no. B-836, 1962-3. (Henceforth, Jain Inscriptions).
128. Jinavijaya Muni, ed., Jinaprabha Suri's, *Vividhatīrthakalpa*, 'Arbudādṛ-kalpa', Shantiniketan, 1934, pp. 15-16. Citrakūṭa figures prominently in the list of *tīrthas* in the Abu and surrounding region.
129. Cited in *Jain Inscriptions*, p. 191.
130. Ibid., p. 122.
131. Ibid., p. 121.
132. Jinavijaya Sūri, ed., *Jain Pustaka Praśasti Saṁgraha*, Bombay, 1943, p. 37.
133. Cited in *Jain Inscriptions*, pp. 120-1.
134. Jinavijayamuni, ed., *Jinapāla's Kharataragacchabṛhadgurvāvalī*, Bombay, 1956, p. 12.
135. *Jain Inscriptions*, p. 124.
136. P.C. Nahar, *Jain Abhilekha*, vol. II, Calcutta, 1927, pp. 245-7, 252-3,
    (i) *Sam 1494 varṣeprāgvaṭ sā. Depāl putra Suhādsī bhāryā Suhāda de putrasā. Karana bhāryā cānu putra se Dhanadhā Hemājinapaṭṭikā Kāritā pratiṣthi Śrī tapagacchanāyaka Śrī Somasundara sūribhih.*
    (ii) *Sam 1506 verṣe sā. Soma bhā. Rudi suta sā. Samadhārena bhrātṛ phāpha sīdharakuṭumbayutena tīrtha śrī satruñjayagirinaravatār paṭṭikākāritā śrī Ratnaśekha. Sūribhih.*
    (iii) *Samvat 1493 Varṣeprasād gauṣṭhika prāgvaṭ jnātiya.*
137. For a detailed analysis of *maṇḍapikās*, their officials, and linkages with states, see Chap. IV in this book.
138. *Jain Inscriptions*, pp. 125-6. Also see, Sharda, *MK*, op. cit. pp. 333-72; Nahar, vol. II, op. cit., pp. 255-6.
139. *Jain Inscriptions*, pp. 126-7.
140. *EI*, vol. XXVI, pp. 102-12.
141. *Jain Inscriptions*, p. 127.
142. PRAS, WC, 1905, p. 38.
143. Ekalingajī Temple Inscription of AD 971, op. cit., vv. 15-20.

144. *Jain Inscriptions*, pp. 127-9.
145. Nahar, vol. II, op. cit., pp. 9-19, see for instance nos.1033-1101; Nahar, ibid., p. 11, no. 1047, '*Samvat 1399 Prāgvaṭ vaṁśe Ābada bhāryā bimbam . . . bhāvdev Sūri*'; Nahar, ibid., p. 13, no. 1063, '*Sam 1472 Varṣe Śrīmāl Saṁghe śrī Padmanandī guru Hunvād jñātīyavya Śrī Ādināth bimbam*'; Nahar, ibid., p. 16, no. 1082, '*Samvat 1506 Śrī nupakeśajñātau sā. Sāhadeva bhā. Suhavāde pu. Śāligena pitrau kumthunāth bimbam prati. Śrī Sarva sūribhih*'; Nahar, ibid., p. 19, no. 1101, '*Sam 1559 varṣe āṣāḍa nuśvāl jñāte kanoj gotre sā. seda pu. Sahasmal bhā. Suhilālde pu. ṭhākursī ṭhakur yutena Śītalnātha bimbam kāritam pra. Śrī Devagupta Sūribhih*; *Jain Pustaaka Praśasti Saṁgraha*, op. cit., pp. 116 and 219, '*Samvat 1317 varṣe Śrī madāghaṭdurge mahārājadhirāj parameśvaraparam bhaṭṭāraka umāpati varalabdhapratāp a samankṛta Śrī Tejasiṁha-devakalyāṇa vijayarājye tatpādopadmopajīvinī mahāmātya śrī Samuddhare mudrā vyāpāran paripanthayati śrīmadāghaṭvāstyavya pāṇi Rāmcandraśiṣyena Kamalcandrena pustikā vyālekhi* ||'.
146. *Jain Pustaka Praśasti Saṁgraha*, p. 126.
147. Ibid., p. 116.
148. Ibid., pp. 116 and 126. The original expression is '*mudrāvyāparan paripanthayati*'.
149. Jain Inscriptions, p. 129; Nahar, vol. I, op. cit., no. 636. Inscriptions at Rikhabhadeva's temple record visits of the pilgrims from the fourteenth century onwards.
150. *Vir Vinod*, vol. I, pp. 401-2; Somani, *Jain Inscriptions*, p. 131; also see *ARIE*, 1956-7, no. 529, pp. 73-4.
151. Somani, *Jain Inscriptions*, op. cit., p. 131.
152. Ibid.
153. Rāṇakpur Praśasti, op. cit., ll. 20-4.
154. Nahar, ed., *Jinavijayajī's Kharataragacchapaṭṭāvalī*, Calcutta, 1956, p. 56, '*Kumbhalmeru Vāstavya Kakaḍ copodagotriya Sāh Samarasiṁha Kṛtanandīmahotsavena Śrīkīrttiratnācāryena padasthāpana kṛtā tato Arbudacaloparī navaphanpārśvanāth pratiṣthā Vidhyākah* ||'.
155. Kailash Chand Jain, *Jainism in Rajasthan*, Sholapur, 1963, p. 66.
156. *Jain Pustaka Praśasti Saṁgraha*, p. 125, no. 205, '*Dhānyaśālibhadra-caritrādi pustikā Saptamāṅgcūrṇīh | granthāṅgra 101 Medapāṭe Varagrāma vāstavya śrāvak putra Samudhdhara Śrāvakbhāryāyā kuladharaputrayā sāviti śrāvikayā dhānya-śālibhadra-kṛtapuṇya maharṣi caritādipustikā svasreyonimittam lekhitā*'.
157. Ibid., pp. 38-9, ll. 1 and 17, '*Śrīmalvaṁśīya śrāvaganalekhitā Kalpasūtra Kālikācāryakathā pustikā praśastih Śrī Medapāṭamaṇḍale Vaunā grāme pustikā likhitā* ||'.
158. A Chittaur Palace Pillar Praśasti, *Vir Vinod*, p. 397, '*Śrī Bhartṛpurīyagacche śrī cuḍāmaṇi Bhartṛpure Śrī Guhilaputravihāra ādiśapratipattau śrīcitrakūṭa*

Medapāṭadhipati śrī Tejah Siṁharājye Śrījayatalladevya śrī Śyām-Pārśvanāth vasahī svaśreyase kāritā ||'.
159. Ibid.
160. Ibid., '*Oṁ! Śrī Ekaliṅgaśivasevanatatpara Śrī Hārītaraśivaṁśā Sambhutamaheśvarasitatśiṣya śrī śīvarāśi Goḍojātīyadvijadivākara Vaṁśodbhava Vyāsaratnasutajjotih Sādalatthaca Vipraddhāna-sutabhaṭṭasāda tatputradvārbhaṭṭa khīmaṭstadrabhārtṛi Bhīma sahitena ebhirmilitvā śrībhartṛpurīyagacchekārī* ||'.
161. Chiravā Inscription, op. cit., v. 48.
162. Ibid.
163. Sharda, *MK*, pp. 175-6. This inscription is engraved in the courtyard between the famous Jain temples of Vimal Shāh and Tejapāla at Mount Abu.
164. Ibid., pp. 77-81, 98 and 105-6.
165. *Jain Pustaka Praśasti Saṁgraha*, p. 116. In fact, Ram Vallabh Somani misses out on this important Jain personality in his work, *Jain Inscriptions from Rajasthan.*
166. Jain Pustaka Praśasti Saṁgraha, ibid., p. 125, '*Samvat 1309 Varṣe . . . tatpaṭṭavibhūṣana rājāśrite Jayasiṁha Vijayarājye tatpādapadmopojīvinī mahan śrītalhanapratipattau śrī śrīkaranādi-samastavyāpāran pākṣikavṛtti likhiteti*'.
167. Somani, *History of Mewar*, p. 86, *URI*, vol. I, pp. 169-70, '*Samvat 1317 varṣe mahāsudi 4 adityadine śrīmadāghaṭadurge mahārājādhirāja parameśvarabhaṭṭārakaumāpati varalabdhaprauḍa-pratāp Samalaṁkṛta Śrī Tejah Siṁha devakalyāṇa-Vijayarājye tatpādapadmopojīvinī mahāmātya śrī Samuddhare mudrā vyāparan paripanthayati śrī madāghaṭ vāstavya pan. Rāmacandraśiṣyena Kamalacandrena pustikā vyālekhi* ||'.
168. Jain Pustaka Praśasti, op. cit., pp. 125-6.
169. Chittaur Inscription dated AD 1267, *Vir Vinod*, vol. I, p. 398, *Mahārāja Śrī Tejahsiṁhadevakalyāṇa-vijayī rāja Vijayamānapradhānrāja rājaputra kāṅgā.*
170. Ibid.
171. *Jain Inscriptions*, p. 122.
172. Ibid., p. 224.
173. Ibid.
174. Ibid., p. 225.
175. *Jain Pustaka Praśasti Saṁgraha*, p. 148, '*Samvat 1492 varṣe Śrī Medapāṭadeśe Śrī Devakulapāṭakapuravare Śrī Kumbhakaraṇarājye Śrī Kharataragacche Śrī Jinacandrasūri paṭṭe Śrī Jinasāgarasūrirāja-namupadeśena Śrīukeśavaṁśīya Navalakṣaśākhāmandana sā. Śrī Rāmadeva bhāryā Sādhvīni Melāde tatputra rājmantrī dhuradhaureya Sādhu Śrī Sajjanapālastena Sā. Raṇamalla Sā. Ranadhīra sā. Raṇavira sā. Bhāṇḍā sā. Sāṇḍā sā. ranobhrama sā. Cauṇḍā sā. Karmasiṁha pramukha*

Sāraputraparivārparikālitena nija puṇyartham Śrī Āvaśyakbṛhadvṛtti dvitīyakhaṇḍam bhāṇḍāgāre likhāpitam ||'.

176. *Jain Inscriptions*, p. 225.
177. Ibid., p. 226.
178. Ibid.
179. Ibid.
180. Ibid.
181. Devakulapāṭaka Temple Inscription cited in Ram Vallabh Somani, *Jain Inscriptions*, p. 227.
182. Ibid., p. 227.
183. Śṛṅgār Chanvarī Inscription, *Vir Vinod*, vol. I, op. cit., p. 410.
184. Ibid., '*Samvat 1505 Varṣe Rāṇā Śrī Mokalanandana Rāṇā Śrīkumbhakarṇa Kośavyāpārina Sāhkolāputraratna bhāṇḍārī Śrī Velakena bhāryā Vīlhaṇadevī Jayamān bhāryāratnadeputra bhan Mudhāraj bhan Dhanarāj bhan Kurapālādiputrayutena*'.
185. Ibid.
186. *Jain Inscriptions*, p. 221.
187. Ibid., p. 222.
188. Ibid.
189. Ibid., p. 222, ll. 26-7, '*Prāgvaṭa Vaṁśāvatansa Saṁghapati Sāgarsuta Saṁghapati Kurapāla bhāryā, Kamaldeputraparamarhava Saṁghapati Dhārana*'.
190. Ibid., ll. 9-30.
191. *Vir Vinod*, vol. I, p. 410, l. 26, '*Rāṇā Śrī Kumbhakarṇa sarvovīrpatisarvabhaumasya Vijaymānarājye tasye Prasādpātrena Vinayavivekadhairaudāryaśubhakarmanirmalaśīlāddyadbhutaguṇamaṇimayābharanabhāsuragātreṇa śrī madahammadsuratrāṇadattaphuramāṇasādhu śrī guṇarājasaṁghapati*'.
192. Ibid., p. 410, ll. 1-20.
193. Ibid., p. 410, l. 28.
194. Ibid., p. 224.
195. Ibid.
196. Rāṇakpur Praśasti, op. cit., l.25.
197. Ibid., l.18, '*Śrī Madahammadsuratrāṇadatta phurmāṇa Sādhu Śrī Guṇarājasaṁghapatisāhācārya*'.
198. *Jain Inscriptions*, p. 226.
199. *Vir Vinod*, vol. I, pp. 424-5, 11.17-19. The genealogy of the family and the installation ceremony recorded by the inscription reads as follows:
'The son of Mahan Mayūra, Mahan Sādūla, belonging to the family Dudā (who was) the son of Rāval Śrī Lāṣāṇa, of the Rāyajaḍarī gotra belonging to the lineage of Ukeśa (Śrī Ukeśavaṁśe)—with their relations Karmasī, Dhārā Lākhā and other members of the family.'
200. Ibid., ll.19-20. The consecration ceremony was performed by Devasundara Sūri.

201. Ibid., l.7, '*Śrīukeśavaṁśe rāyajadarī gotre Rāul śrī Lāsạna*'.
202. Śṛṅgār Chanvarī Inscription, op. cit., ll. 2-3.
203. Chiravā Inscription, op. cit., v. 19.
204. Ibid., v. 22.
205. Ibid., vv. 34-5.
206. Ibid., v. 40.
207. Ibid., vv. 41-2.
208. *Vir Vinod*, vol. I, p. 401, ll. 1-3, '*Samvat 1344 Vaiśākha sudi 3 addya Śrīcitrakūṭe Samastamahārājakula Śrī Samarasiṁha devakalyāṇavijaya-rājye evam kāle citrāṅgataḍāgamadhya Śrī Vaidyanāthakṛtesaka rambatena —kaḍī dattam | kāyasthajñātīyam pacasīgasuta vījadena kārāpitam*'.
209. Partial deforestation leading to agricultural activities by a few of the core-area Bhils initiated the process of resource mobilization from the Bhil localities by the state.
210. See, Chap. I, vide *passim*, pp. 38-9.
211. *Annals*, vol. I, p. 262.
212. *Nainsī rī Khyāt*, vol. I, p. 41.
213. Ibid.
214. Ibid., p. 35, '*Panōro Bhīlānro Mevās Divānrā ṭhako chai*'.
215. *Annals*, vol. I, p. 262.
216. Ibid.
217. Robert Deliege, *The Bhils of Western India: Some Empirical and Theoretical Issues in Anthropology in India*, Delhi, 1985, p. 64.
218. *Annals*, vol. I, p. 191.
219. See, Chap. I, especially the map on the routes. See V.K. Jain, op. cit., p. 111.
220. Claessen and Skalnik, *The Early State*, p. 35.
221. Tod, *Tavels in Western India*, p. 39.
222. Tej Kumar Mathur, *Feudal Polity in Mewar (1750-1850)*, Jaipur, 1987, p. 138.
223. Shambhu Lal Doshi, *The Bhils: Between Societal Self-awareness and Cultural Synthesis*, 1st edn., Delhi and Jallandhar, 1971, p. 37. The institution of gāmeti seems to be internal to the social organization of the Bhils.
224. G.N. Sharma, 'Bhils in the Magra District as revealed from the records of Dhulev Bhandar' in *Proceedings of Rajasthan History Congress*, Udaipur Session, 1977, p. 65.
225. Craddock et al., eds., op. cit., p. 62.
226. Giridharlal Sharma, ed., *Rājasthānī Bhīl Geet*, 1st edn., vol. II, Udaipur, 1956, pp. 31-3.
227. Craddock, et al., eds., op. cit., p. 56.
228. Author's field trip to Zawar.
229. *Vir Vinod*, vol. I, pp. 401-2.
230. *Annals*, vol. I, p. 262.

231. Ibid., p. 269.
232. P.L. Menaria, *Bhīlon kī Lok Kathāyen*, vol. III, Delhi, 1968, pp. 23ff.
233. Giridharilal Sharma, ed., *Rājasthānī Bhīl Geet*, vol. I, p. 120 and vol. II, pp. 115-20.
234. Mala Copper Plates dated AD 1283 of the Dungarpur Guhilas, *EI*, vol. XXII, pp. 192-6, l. 35.
235. N.N. Vyas, R.S. Mann and N.D. Chaudhary, eds., *Rajasthan Bhils*, Udaipur, 1978, p. 117.
236. Giridharilal Sharma, ed., *Rājasthānī Bhīl Geet*, vol. III, pp. 15-17, 19-22.
237. P.G. Shah, 'Non-Hindu Elements in the Culture of the Bhils of Gujarat', in *Essays in Anthropology Presented to Rai Bahadur Sarat Chandra Roy*, Calcutta, n.d.; rpt., pp. 181-2.
238. Rajendra Purohit, 'Mewār ke Mahārāṇo kī Rājyābhiṣeka Paramparā', *Shodh Patrika*, Varṣa 29, no. 2, Udaipur, p. 46. Although Nainsī does not mention the *ṭīkā* ceremony (probably indicating either discontinuance of the ritual or absence of its knowledge), tribal claims regarding the performance of *ṭīkā* may signify its occasional practice or the historical memory of a ritual which played an important role in legitimizing the intrusion of the early Guhila state into Bhomat.
239. *Prakrit and Sanskrit Inscriptions*, op. cit., p. 74. Sir Monier Williams, *A Sanskrit Dictionary* (new edn.), Oxford, 1960, p. 1052. Williams defines the term Śabara, as a wild mountaineer tribe in the Deccan (in later language applied to any savage or barbarian = kirata, Pulinda, Bhilla). Since Śabara was a generic term for tribal peoples, Śabara women in case of Mewar would stand for Bhil women.
240. Mala Copper Plates, op. cit., ll. 31 and 35.
241. Surendra Kumar Navlakha, 'The Authority Structure Among the Bhumij and Bhil: A Study of Historical Causations', *The Eastern Anthropologist*, vol. 13, nos. 1-3, p. 38.
242. Śṛṅgiṛṣi, op. cit., p. 235, v. 4, '*Celākhyam Puramgrahida-riganāni Bhillānguhāgehakāni (jji) tvātānkhilānnihatya ca balātkhyātāsinā saṅgare*'.
243. Amarakāvyam, op. cit., p. 142, v. 6, '*Bhillān mallanibhānmallaihrme dacchedanabhedanaih Mīnānnādināmstanuhinānjitvā jagrāha tanmahih*'.
244. See next chapter on Military Apparatus.
245. *Annals*, vol. I, p. 166.
246. Mathur, op. cit., p. 28.
247. Ibid.
248. Ibid.
249. *Vir Vinod*, vol. I, p. 195.
250. Ibid., pp. 194-5.
251. Gahlot and Dhar, op. cit., p. 211.
252. 'On the concepts of "Tribes" and "Tribal Society"', see paper presented at a meeting of the Division, Department of Anthropology, Columbia

University: New York, 24 January 1966, Proceedings, pp. 527-50. I am grateful to Dr. Maxine Weisgrau, Columbia University, New York, for presenting this article to me.

253. Chattopadhyaya, *Political Processes and Structure*, p. 203.
254. Kulke, 'The Early and the Imperial Kingdom', in *The State in India 1000-1700*, p. 15.
255. Achaleśvara Inscription, op. cit., v. 46, '*Gurjara-mahīm = cchais = Turuṣk-ārṇavat Tejahsiṁha-saśeṣa samara, kṣonīśvara. . . .*'
256. Chiravā Inscription, op. cit., v. 16, '*Nāgadṛhapurabhaṁge samam suratrāṇ asainikairyudhvā Bhūtālāhatakūṭe Pamarājah pañcatam prāpa*'.
257. C.D. Dalal, ed., *Hammīramadamardana of Jayasiṁha Sūri*, Baroda, 1920, p. 35, '*milacchikara nandanassa nivedidam tam auli bhudena milacchi-karas*'.
258. Ibid., p. 287.
259. Chiravā Inscription, op. cit., v. 6.
260. *IA*, vol. LVII, p. 31, '*Śrī Madagurjjara Mālavaturūṣka śākambharī svarair yasya cakre na mānbhaṅgah sa svāhstho jayatu Jaitrasiṁhansipah*'.
261. Chiravā Inscription, op. cit., v. 42, '*Naḍulamūlaṁkaṣabāhulakṣmīsturuṣka sainyārva Kumbhayonih asminsurādhīśsahāsanasthe rarakṣam bhūmimatha Jaitrasiṁhah*'.
262. *IA*, vol. XXVI, pp. 194-5.
263. Achaleśvara Inscription, op. cit., v. 42.
264. Ibid., vv. 49-52, v. 58.
265. Burtra Inscription of Cāhamāna Sāmantasiṁha dated AD 1284, vol. IV, pp. 312-14, v. 5.
266. Ibid., p. 313.
267. *ARIE*, Appendix C, no. 126, 1956; *URI*, p. 173; *ARIE*, 1956, pp. 189, 198, 233; *EIAPS*, 1955-6, pp. 67-8. Also see Elliot and Dowson, vol. III, op. cit., p. 171. Ziauddin Barani in his *Tarikh-i-Ferozshahi* refers to Kotwal's advice to Alauddin in AD 1297 to conquer the forests of Ranthambhor, Chittaur, Chanderi, Mahva, Dhar, Ujjain, etc.
268. The name Padmiṇī occurs in Guhila royal source for the first time in the seventeenth century in *Rājapraśasti Mahākāvyam*, op. cit., canto 3, vv. 3-4; mentioned also in a local bardic text, *Citāi Carita* composed in AD 1526, and Malik Muhammad Jayasī's *Padmāvat* composed in AD 1540. *Padmāvatī Caritra Caupaian* and Hemaratna's *Gorā Bādal Charita* are cited in *RTA*, op. cit., p. 666; *Nainsī rī Khyāt*, vol. I, p. 14. *Ratansī Ajaisīro bhada Lakhamsīno bhāī, Padmiṇīre mamte Lakh amse nāu Ratansī Alāvadī Sulādne Kāmāyo*. Also see Elliot and Dowson, vol. III, op. cit., pp. 176-7. Amir Khusrau in *Khazainul-Futuh* narrates the sack and capture of Chittaurgarh but never alludes to Padmiṇī.
269. Nahar, vol. II, op. cit., p. 242, '*Śrī Māladevaputra Śrī Vanavīra Satkam Śīladara Mahamad adeva suhad siṁha Canumkara Satkamputra*'.

270. Delhi, 1978, pp. 103-4.
271. *Nainsī rī Khyāt*, vol. I, pp. 204-5, '*Mālde muchālo savantsīro veto gadaro hai pachālī Mālde ghana Vigad kiyā pachai sāh gaḍa citor māldenu diyovās 7 Mālde bhog kiyo Pachdi Mālde Citor kālprāpta huo*'.
272. *Annals*, vol. I, p. 219.
273. *Baḍvādevīdān Khyāt*, p. 1.
274. *Nainsī rī Khyāt*, p. 22.
275. *EI*, vol. IX, pp. 62-3. Suzerainty of the Songirā Cāhamānas over Godwar in the mid-fourteenth century is evident from the Koṭ-Solankiyā (Desuri-Nadol belt) inscription of the reign of Songirā Vanavīra dated AD 1337; *EI*, vol. IX, pp. 63-4, and from the Nadlai stone inscription of the reign of Rāṇā Vīradeva (Vanavīra's son), '*Śrī Nāḍḍulāi nagare | Cāhumānanvaya mahārājādhirāj śrī vanavīradeva sutarājāśrī raṇavīradeva vijayarājye*'.
276. *Nainsī rī Khyāt*, vol. II, p. 65.
277. *Annals*, vol. I, p. 319.
278. Chiravā Inscription, op. cit., v. 19, '*Bālakah Koṭṭaḍakagrahane śrījaitrasiṁhanṛpa puratah Tribhuvanarāṇakayuddhe jagām yuddhvā param lokom*'. Rāṇā Tribhuvana (successor to Bhīmadeva II), Bāghelā ruler of Gujarat, was evidently a contemporary of Jaitrasiṁha.
279. *IA*, vol. VI, p. 210, l. 4.
280. Jayasiṁha Sūri's, *Hammīramadamardana*, p. 287.
281. Rāṇā Mokal's Śṛṅgiṛṣi Inscription, op. cit., v. 14, Kumbhalgarh Praśasti, fourth slab, op. cit., v. 221; E.D. Bayley, *History of Gujarat*, Delhi (rpt.), 1970, p. 120. *Tabakat-i-Akbari* and *Tarikh-i- Alfi* narrate Ahmad Shah's invasion of Jilwara (Celvāṭa of Śṛṅgiṛṣi inscription, located in north-western Mewar).
282. Rāṇakpur Praśasti, op. cit., p. 410, l. 12. Nāgpura and Narānka have been identified with Nagaur and Narena respectively.
283. Day, op. cit., pp. 132-3; Bayley, op. cit., p. 148; Mangal, op. cit., p. 112, fn.12.
284. Mokal's Śṛṅgiṛṣi Inscription, op. cit., vv. 23-5 '(for her) who was illuminating to the family of Bāghelās, who had her hand renowned for charities, who was the daughter of prince . . . Nabhnama . . . who was graced with prosperity. . . . For (that) Gaurāmbikā, . . . this reservoir of water in front of that son of Vibhanda has been constructed by Mokala. . . .'
285. Bayley, op. cit., pp. 148-9; *Mirat-i-Sikandari* cited in Mangal, op. cit., p. 112, fn. 21; B. Day, ed., Nizamuddin Ahmad's *Tabakat-i-Akbari*, vol. II, Calcutta, 1927, p. 2; *Khyam Khan Rāso* cited in Tara Mangal, op. cit., p. 42, narrates the defeat of Firuz Khan of Nagaur by Rāṇā Mokal, '*Bhājī calyo Perojākhān, tānkī hau Nāgaur | Pache pāve luṭaṭo, Mokal Śrī Sirmaur*'. Also see *Annals*, vol. I, p. 331. Two Persian Inscriptions from Narena and Didwana dated AD 1437 issued in the reign of Mahahid Khan (Firuz Khan's brother) refer to Rāṇā Mokal's victory against Firuz Khan.

Also see *Epigraphia Indo-Muslimica*, 1923-4, p. 15; *Epigraphia Indo-Muslimica*, ibid., 1949-50, p. 22; Chittaurgarh Inscription of Mokal, op. cit., v. 51; Kumbhalgarh Praśasti, op. cit., v. 22; and Ekaliṅgaji Temple Dakṣiṇadvāra Praśasti, op. cit., v. 44, all claim Mokal's victory over Firuz Khan of Nagaur.

286. *Arbudacala Prācina Jain Lekha Saṁgraha* cited in Mangal, op. cit., p. 114.
287. *Tabakat-i-Akbari,* and *Mirat-i-Sikandari* cited in Mangal, op. cit., pp. 114-15, fn. 28-30.
288. *IHQ*, vol. XXXIV, no. 1, pp. 215-25, ll. 2, 4, 19, '*Śrī Citrakūṭādhipati Śrī Mahārājādhirājmahārāṇā Śrī Kumbhakarṇa putrī Śrī Jījrnprākāre Sorāthapatimahārāyam, Rāya śrī Maṇḍalika bhāryā śrī Ramāmm. bāī.śrīmatkumbhanṛpasya diggajaradātikram kīrtayam bhudheh kanyā Yādav Vaṁśāmanḍana śrī māṇḍalīka priyā || Saurāṣṭreśvara yādavanvayamaneh śrī Māṇḍalika prabhorājñī cāru Ramāvatī vitanute sam*'.
289. *Amarakāvyam*, Chap. X, p. 163, v. 23, '*Gurjaram jarjaram cakre Junāgaḍh Vikhaṇḍanah*'.
290. *Vir Vinod*, vol. I, pp. 336-7.
291. Day, op. cit., p. 140; Mangal, op. cit., pp. 61-7.
292. Sharda, *MK*, pp. 212-22. Kumbha's Kīrttistambha Praśasti, dated AD 1448, vv. 171-2; Bhandarkar's List nos. 797-8; PRAS, WC, 1903-4, p. 56; *ARRM*, 1921, p. 5; *Ekaliṅgamāhātmyam*, p. 183, v. 3, '*Rakṣorūpārimurvī bharanṛpaśamanah sukṣamī Mlecchaghāṭī jīāt Śrī Kumbhakarṇo daśavidhakṛtikṛtaśrīpatih kopi nabyah*'.
293. *Annals*, vol. I, pp. 228-9.
294. Rāṇakpur Praśasti, op. cit., l. 14, claims victory of Rāṇā Kumbha over Gāgraṇa.
295. See for instance, Kumbha's Kīrtistambha Praśasti, op. cit., vv. 171-4 and Ekaliṅgajī Temple Dakṣiṇadvāra Praśasti, op. cit., v. 54, '*Mādyān Mālavanātha mūrdhani caraṇam datvā raṇe dīdahata Kumbho śrī sāraṅgapuram sapauranikaram dharādhīśvarah*'.
296. Śṛṅgiṛṣi inscription, op. cit., v. 11, claims that Lakṣasiṁha (Lākhā, Mokal's predecessor) liberated Gaya from the burden of tax for a considerable number of years.
297. Chittaurgarh Inscription of Mokal, op. cit., vv. 38 and 41, '*Nītipritibhujārjjitāni bahuśo ratnāni yatrānādayam dāyam dāyammāyaya vyatanuta dhastāmtarāyām gayām || tīrthānām karamākalyaya vidhinā nyatrāpi yukta dhanam prauḍhagravanibadhatīrthasarasījāgraddya-śombhorūhah || Rūdhvāśeṣa padāmśakādhipakaravyaghrībhavajjīvinām dhīromumucadarjjunīmiva gayām māyāvimuktāyasah || dharmaśvāsya samastalokamahitah kāṣṭam parāmagato nih satvīkṛtadharmmarājavasate padmālayāsadmanah ||*'.
298. Kumbhalgarh Praśasti, fourth slab, op. cit., v. 207, '*Kunasapāsam*

sakalanṛpasthat yastristhal mocanatah śakebhyah. Also see Kumbhalgarh Praśasti, ibid., vv. 209-11; Ekaliṅgajī Temple Dakṣiṇadvāra Praśasti, op. cit., v. 38.

299. Kumbhalgarh Inscription, op. cit., fourth slab, vv. 259 and 263, '*Pratyārthipārthi vāparājya janmahetu Vṛndāvatīpura malidahadeśa Virahor*'.
300. Ibid., v. 264, '*Jitvā deśamanaka durgaviṣaṇam. Hāḍāvatīm helayā*'.
301. Unlike Mokal's records, Rāṇakpur Praśasti refers for the first time to Kumbha's conquest of Vṛndāvatī, op. cit.
302. Rāṇakpur Praśasti, op. cit., p. 410, l. 12.
303. Kumbhalgarh Praśasti, fourth slab, op. cit., v. 249, '*Yana Vairikulam hatvā Manḍovarapuragṛhe*'.
304. Nandiya copper-plate charter cited in Sharda, *MK,* p. 79.
305. Kīrtistambha Inscription, op. cit., v. 284, refers to Kumbha's conquest of Abu and building of the fort of Achalgarh.
306. Ojha, *History of Sirohi,* p. 194; also see *URI*, vol. I, p. 283.
307. *Vir Vinod*, vol. I, p. 332.
308. *Baḍvādevīdān Khyāt*, pp. 2, 3 and 7.

CHAPTER IV

Administrative and Military Apparatus of the State of Mewar Thirteenth to Fifteenth Centuries

The present chapter analyses the mode of the exercise of state power through the administrative and military apparatus between the thirteenth and the fifteenth centuries. The questions that I shall examine relate mainly to the structure of royal authority and the delegation of royal power in the administration. Locally influential social groups can be expected to have shared administrative and military responsibilities with the rulers. As my analysis of the evidence will show below, while the participation of wealthy Jain families in the state apparatus consisted mainly of administrative tasks, non-Guhila Rajput chiefs were predominantly engaged in the military task of maintaining a second line of defence for the state of Mewar.

I

The Administrative Apparatus

The administrative apparatus saw a series of qualitative changes involving various departments of the administration in our period. In my opinion, these changes are an indicator of the extent which the consolidation of the power of the state had reached. More significantly, there is a change in the social composition of the administrative personnel. Non-Rajput social groups—such as the Jains, the Ṭāmṭarāḍas, an important local family of Nāgdā, and others from Mount Abu—figure as prominent officials. While non-Guhila Rajput chiefs were integrated into the state polity through the system of ranking and accommodated in administrative positions between the tenth and the twelfth centuries, the state consolidated its power between the thirteenth and fifteenth centuries by integrating newly emerging non-Rajput social groups through a similar process. Further, I feel that changes in administrative personnel also reflect the growing military dimension of the state and the evolution of the 'martial identity' of the Rajputs by the thirteenth century. This was the logical culmination of the process of regional state formation that in their course of territorial expansion over a long period of time such states were bound to compete with each other over common resources at certain points of time and space. In the case of Mewar, one discerns a shift diversion of Rajput chiefs towards battle-fields from the thirteenth century onwards. Hence, the incorporation of the non-Rajput personnel into the administrative structure in the thirteenth century served the state and furthered the integrative process.

New Administrative Offices

Three offices of the administration figuring for the first time in the thirteenth-century records are those of the *pradhāna*, *mahāmātya*, and *talarakṣaka*. I shall look at each of these offices one by one.

Pradhāna: The Chittaur Inscription of the Reign of Tejasiṁha (AD 1267) is issued by the family of the *pradhāna*, Rājaputra Kāṅgā.[1] The Chiravā Inscription (AD 1273) records the death of Pradhāna Bhīmasiṁha, fighting at the foothills of Chittaurgarh.[2] The presence of the *pradhāna*, in addition to the *mahāmātya* (chief minister), suggests increasing administrative responsibilities of the state as a consequence of the growing territorial power of the centre. The expansion of the Guhila state into the upper Banas plain and the transfer of the capital to Chittaurgarh in the thirteenth century brought with it problems of consolidation. Territorial expansion and increasing administrative responsibilities might have necessitated the creation of the post of *pradhāna* to compliment that of the *mahāmātya*.

Dasharath Sharma finds it difficult to distinguish between a *mahāmātya* and a *pradhāna*.[3] However, he distinguishes the nature of their duties: '. . . the Pradhāna had probably more of military duties than the Mahāmātya who was concerned mainly with the transactions of the royal seal'.[4] Sharma quotes instances of *pradhānas* such as Bhīmasiṁha of Mewar in mid-thirteenth-century Mewar, who died fighting at the foot of Chittaur hill.[5] G.C. Sharma in the context of medieval Rajasthan defines a *pradhāna* as the premier and the military minister.[6] However, he does not explain the military functions of a *pradhāna*, simply placing him next to the ruler.[7] Somani, on the basis of two contemporary manuscripts of Mahārāṇā Kumbha's period (*Ādināth Stavan* and *Āvaśyakavṛhadvṛtti*, where the term *pradhāna* has been used for

Kumbha's Mukhyamantrī Sajjanapāla Navalakha; the term *rājamantrī* also being used for the same person) argues that the *pradhāna* and the *mukhyamantrī* or the *rājamantrī* seem to have been one and the same person.[8] At the same time he argues that since the designation of the *pradhāna* was being used in the plural in contemporary literary sources, the term *pradhāna* probably referred to ministers, and the post was probably occupied by more than one person.[9] I feel Somani's observations are misleading because he contradicts himself by claiming that it referred to both the ministers and the chief minister (*mukhyamantrī*). The parallel functioning of a *pradhāna* and a *mahāmātya* in the thirteenth century Guhila court proves the distinction between the two functionaries. The distinction between the two offices is also corroborated by *Kanhaḍade Prabandha* which mentions the *amātyas* and the *pradhāna* separately.[10] Considering the growth in the power and the functions of the office of the *pradhāna*, it is not unusual that a *pradhāna* came to combine the functions of a *rājamantrī* or *mukhyamantrī* by Rāṇā Kumbha's period in Mewar. It is significant that *mahāmātyas* and *pradhānas* figure as distinct functionaries in the royal records in the early medieval period. A copper plate grant of the Śilāhāras dated AD 1094, places Mahāmātya Śrī Nauvitaka Vāsaida, and Mahāpradhāna (translated as the great minister) Pādhīsena Śrī Mahādevaiya Prabhu in the first rank at the treasury while in the second rank *pradhāna* (translated as minister) Śrī Somanaiya Prabhu and they appear all together in the administration in the reign of Mahāmaṇḍaleśvara King Anantadeva.[11]

Mahāmātya (chief minister): The office of the *mahāmātya* too is mentioned for the first time in the thirteenth century. The office of *amātya* is evident from the pre-thirteenth century Guhila records such as those from the Sāraṇeśvara temple.[12] However, none of the Guhila records of the early medieval period ever mention a *mahāmātya* before the early thirteenth century. The evolution of the office of the *amātya* into that of the *mahāmātya* by itself is a strong indicator of the diversification of administrative duties and the growth of the state-apparatus since the office of the *mahāmātya* presumes the presence of a number of *amātyas*.

Contemporary Jain texts speak of Mahāmātya Śrī Jagatsiṁha in Guhila Jaitrasiṁha's reign[13] and of Mahāmātya Śrī Samuddhara in Guhila Tejasiṁha's reign.[14] A *mahāmātya* of the thirteenth century seems to have acquired the popular designations of *rājamantrī* or *mukhyamantrī* by the fifteenth century in Mewar. The Jain text *Āvaśyakbṛhadvṛtti* refers to Sādhu (Sāhu) Śrī Sajjanapāla Navalakha of the Ukeśa lineage (the chief minister in Rāṇā Kumbha's reign) as *rājamantrī*.[15] Rāṇā Kumbha in his *Saṅgītarāja* used the term *mukhyamantrī* for a *rājamantrī* or *mahāmātya*.[16] It has already been noted that Rājamantrī Sajjanapāla Navalakha also acquired the title of *pradhāna* as he presumably combined the duties of both a *mahāmātya* and a *pradhāna*.[17] It is also evident from the contemporary records that the post of *mukhyamantrī/mahāmātya* had become hereditary by the fifteenth century. This indicates that royal power was being increasingly delegated rather than centralized. Rājamantrī Sajjanapāla had succeeded his father Rāmadeva Navalakha to the chief ministership. Rāmadeva Navalakha is known to have functioned as the *mukhyamantrī* in the entire period of the reigns of Rāṇā Kṣetrasiṁha, Rāṇā Lakṣasiṁha and Rāṇā Mokal.[18]

A *mahāmātya/mukhyamantrī* or a *rājamantrī* was in charge of the royal seal. This seems to point to the fact that the process of state formation had reached a stage when the king was not tied to the routines of the administration of his territory any more. The term *mudrā* (seal) usually appears in association with the *mahāmātya* in contemporary sources.[19] *Śrāvaka Pratikramaṇsūtracūrṇī* testifies to the signatures of Tejasiṁha's *mahāmātya*, Śrī Samuddhara in all royal transactions, particularly in those involving cash (Śrīkaraṇādimudrāvyāpār-paripanthayati). *Kanhaḍadeprabandha* and *Pṛthvīcandracarita* of the fifteenth century mention *śrīkaraṇādhikārī* and *vyāyakaraṇādhikārī* as functionaries in the departments of income and expenditure respectively.[20] A *mahāmātya/mukhyamantrī* seems to have been in charge not merely of governmental income but of expenditure as well. 'The seal was kept in the custody of mukyamantrī who was looked upon as overall in charge of the administrative machinery.'[21] Thus all royal deeds and grants were expected to carry the *mukhyamantrī's* signature duly authorized by the royal seal.

In the same context, the Abu royal charter dated AD 1449 and issued in Kumbha's reign, has been quoted again and again by modern scholars to argue for centrifugal processes at work in the Guhila state since the charter is not duly signed by Kumbha's *mukhyamantrī*, but by a local-level functionary, Dośī Ramana.[22] Dośī Ramana is stated to have declared his subordinate status to a higher official Duṅgar Bhoja, by assuming *praṇamati nitya* as a suffix to his name.[23] On the basis of such evidence, U.N. Day observes,

The mukhyamantrī generally put his signature on charity grant-deeds, but we cannot definitely state the extent to which his signature was compulsory on such deeds. This doubt arises because we find that deeds executed by some of the *sāmantas* do not bear the signature of the mukhyamantrī. The probability is that he used to put his signature on royal grants which certainly enjoyed a higher status than others.[24]

Day's generalization that only those royal grant-deeds enjoyed higher status which were duly signed by *mukhyamantrī* is highly questionable. The record under discussion, the Abu inscription dated to AD 1449, announcing exemption of pilgrims from a number of local cesses by the state, was undoubtedly a document of immense political importance for the Guhila state, in view of the social importance (due to the concentration of the Jains) and in view of the commercial and strategic importance of Mount Abu. It is plausible that since the royal charter was issued from Abu, reasonably distant from the capital Chittaurgarh, the deed was signed by a local functionary (treated equivalent in position to a *sāmanta* by U.N. Day). It was not realistic to issue every charter for distant places from the capital, or for the *mukhyamantrī* to travel far to sign a deed. After all, the very function of local officials was to meet such administration needs. One important fact which should not be ignored is that Dośī Ramana addressed the charter to *mahan* (*mahantak*, an accountant) Duṅgar in the reign of Rāṇā Kumbhakarna (Kumbha).[25] Mahan Duṅgar was apparently a higher revenue-official, possibly associated with the commercial cesses and the toll-tax. The point is also testified by the Delwara inscription dated AD 1494 which mentions Mahan Duṅgar in connection with royal grants made from a number of local cesses.[26] Dośī Ramana followed the official rules of conduct and executed his part of the duty by signing the governmental-deed as he was locally present. Thus, practices of administrative convenience should not be misunderstood to argue for the existence of centrifugal forces.

Finally, the *amātyas/mantrīs* executed various functions. Day, discussing the office of the *mukhyamantrī* in the reign of Rāṇā Kumbha, writes: 'The mantrīs also at times addressed as amātya distributed various duties amongst themselves which included foreign affairs, home affairs.'[27]

Talarakṣa/Talarakṣaka: As I have noted earlier,[28] a Ṭāmṭarāḍa family of Nāgdā held the post of *talarakṣa* from the end of twelfth century. The Chiravā Inscription, dated AD 1273, states that Uddhāraṇa of Ṭāmṭarāḍa family was made the *talarakṣa* of Nāgadrahapura (Nāgdā) by Mathanasiṁha.[29] Yogarāja, the eldest son of Uddhāraṇa, was in turn made the *talāra* in the same city by King Padmasiṁha.[30] Kṣema, the youngest son of Yogarāja succeeded to his father's post at Citrakūṭa by the favour of King Jaitrasiṁha.[31] One of his sons Madana succeeded to the same post at Citrakūṭa through the favour of King Samarasiṁha.[32]

The post of *talarakṣa* or *talāra* was the post of a police superintendent.[33] Nāgahṛda (Nāgdā) and Citrakūṭa (Chittaurgarh, the capital town) being the two large towns of Mewar in this period, the *talarakṣas* of these settlements would have been police superintendents. The presence of police superintendents in turn assumes the existence of a full-fledged police department by the end of the thirteenth century. The fact that police officials are not mentioned in the early records does not necessarily indicate that they did not exist. However, frequent references to them in the thirteenth century may suggest the growing importance of their office. Possibly there was informal policing by the local communities in their respective localities in certain areas in earlier times. The Chiravā Inscription speaks of Uddhāraṇa of the Ṭāmṭarāḍa family who had gained a reputation for policing the locality of Nāgdā prior to his official appointment as *talarakṣa* of Nāgdā. If *talarakṣa* refers to the superintendent of police, then Uddhāraṇa was promoted to a higher rank in recognition of his service. The growing importance of the department of police in the thirteenth century was apparently caused by the growing congestion of these centres due to the ongoing process of urbanization due to large-scale commercial transactions and transits, and due to the increasing political importance of towns like Nāgdā and Citrakūṭa. The functions of a *talarakṣa* in Mewar were probably not confined to the general administration of local law and order, but might have included specific functions such as the supervision and protection of the *hiṇḍīpakas* (touring revenue officials), officers-in-charge of toll taxes, and *volāpakas* (in-charge of the militiamen accompanying merchants on their journey).[34] It is obvious that the state had to ensure the protection of those administrative and economic activities which were vital for its functioning and growth. The Chiravā Inscription points to the fact that like the post of the *mahāmātya*/the *mukhyamantrī*, the office of the *talarakṣaka* had also become hereditary by the thirteenth century.

Revenue Officials: The growth of the state's department of revenue in this period is evident from the appearance of a number of revenue officials with new designations in contemporary records. The process itself points to the growing revenue-resource base of the state as well as to better mobilization of resources. It is significant that the office of the *akṣapāṭalika* (the chief accountant) was no longer as important in Guhila records between the thirteenth and the fifteenth centuries as it had been in the tenth century. Instead, a hierarchy of revenue officials appears which I shall now discuss.

The *bhāṇḍāgārika* or *bhāṇḍārī*, treasurer, figures in the sources for the first time in the fifteenth century, and with a frequency which leaves no doubt that this category of officials occupied the highest rank in the revenue department. The rise of the *bhāṇḍārīs* as state revenue officials over the former *akṣapāṭalikas* speaks for the expansion of state control over resources and the growing need for professionals and specialists as personnel in the revenue department. None could fit the bill better than the rich local Jain merchant families who were well-educated too.

The Śṛṅgār Cāvanrī Inscription dated AD 1448 refers to the family of the *bhāṇḍārīs* of Rāṇā Kumbha in the context of the building of a temple for Śrī Śāntinātha.[35] The list of *bhāṇḍārīs* is as follows: Bhāṇḍārī Śrī Velaka, son of Sāhkolā, and Velaka's sons, Bhāṇḍārī Mudharāja, Bhāṇḍārī Dhanarāja, and Bhāṇḍārī Kurapāla.[36] The genealogical list of this family from Chittaur is also provided by Śatruñjaya Inscription dated AD 1532 and a Jain text *Śatruñjaya tīrthoddhara*.[37] The genealogical list provided by the Śṛṅgār-Cāvanrī Inscription proves that like that of many others, the office of royal treasurer was hereditary, strengthening my argument that the growing royal power was accompanied by the delegation of administrative authority to other groups. Hereditary succession ensured smooth succession of personnel irrespective of a change of rulers at the centre. Bhāṇḍārī Velaka, the chief treasurer, seems to have been assisted by his three sons. They are likely to have functioned as assistant treasurers under the supervision of the chief *bhāṇḍārī*. There also seems to have been a hierarchy of *bhāṇḍārīs* according to their areas of jurisdiction. The Abu royal charter of AD 1449 refers to four *phadyun* (a unit of currency) due to one Śrī Viśiṣṭi Bhāṇḍārī:[38] Śrī Viśiṣṭi was a local level *bhāṇḍārī* at Abu. In contrast, the term *kośvyapārina* (the official in-charge of transactions of the *kośa* or treasury) is used for the Bhāṇḍārī Śrī Velaka in the Śṛṅgār Cāvanrī Inscription.[39] Another designation, *rājavārika-bhāṇḍārī*, apparently used for a category of *bhāṇḍārīs*, figures in contemporary sources such as the *Pṛthvīcandra carita* of Māṇikyacandra Sūri (AD 1411).[40]

Dasharath Sharma suggests a slight distinction between a *bhāṇḍārī* and a *koṭhārī* in terms of the different commodities supervised by them.[41] However, he does not specify the commodities. 'All the Rajput states had a koshtapati who was responsible for treasure. The term continued till Jagat Singh of Mewar (1688-92). He was required to maintain the records of income and expenditure of the state. Soon after, due to Mughal impact the name was changed from Koshtapati to Khazanchi.'[42] However, the fifteenth-century records from Mewar refer only to *bhāṇḍārīs* and not to *koṭhārīs*.

It is evident from contemporary texts from Rajasthan such as the *Pṛthvīcandra carita*[43] that the *śrīkaraṇā* and the *vyāyagaraṇa* were important functionaries in the income and expenditure sections of the central revenue department respectively.

The Delwara Inscription dating to AD 1434 refers to 4 *ṭaṅkās* due to a *selāhathī* (official connected with the treasury and the accounts) from the local *maṇḍapikās*.[44] This record tells us about the duty of a *selāhata/ selāhathī* who was in-charge of the commercial dues from the local custom-houses.

The Delwara Inscription, dated AD 1434, and the Abu Inscription, dated AD 1449, refer to another official by the name of Mahan Bhoja, in connection with the royal grants from the local *maṇḍapikās* and the exemption of pilgrims from a number of essential levies by the state.[45] The *mahan*, an official holding a position equivalent to that of a *mahantak*, was an accountant in the department of revenue. Both the records indicate his important official status in the revenue department. Thus, it seems that accountants represented the revenue department at various important localities. It is also possible that just like the Ṭāmṭarāḍa and the Bhāṇḍārī families of Nāgahṛda and Chittaurgarh respectively, Bhoja, perhaps an influential member of the local society at Abu or Delwara (near Udaipur) and Dośī Ramana of Abu were both incorporated into the administrative apparatus.

The Sūtradhāras: The Chittaurgarh Inscription dated AD 1274 of King Samarasiṁha was engraved by Sajjana.[46] Sajjana is described as a *śilpī* (craftsman), employed by the royal court. From his name, it is difficult to ascertain his social background. The Achaleśvara Inscription dated AD 1285 was engraved by Sūtradhāra Karmasiṁha.[47] This name indicates a Rajput background. The fact that some of the kṣatriya families from Rajasthan and Uttar Pradesh were taking to non-traditional professions in the early medieval period is evident from the case of a kṣatriya *sūtradhāra* who was the son of a learned kṣatriya[48] and that of a kṣatriya *vaṇika.*[49] However, both the cases—of Sūtradhāra Karmasiṁha from Mewar and of the kṣatriya *sūtradhāra* from Jodhpur—suggest that the profession of an architect had attained the status of a skilled profession, practised by people of different social origins. Therefore the profession of an architect had not crystallized into a separate caste, at least not until the thirteenth century in Mewar.

The Chittaurgarh Stone Inscription of Rāṇā Mokal, dated AD 1428, records the names of the architects appointed by the royal court to repair the Samādhīśvara temple, and the artisans who engraved the stone inscription. The architect is described along with his genealogy. He was Mana, the son of Vījala.[50] He is referred to both as *śilpī* and as *sūtradhāra.*[51] The inscription was written on stone by Vīsala, a son of Mana, and engraved by Vīsa, also a son of Mana, the latter probably being identical with Vīsala.[52] The other important architect in the royal court during Mokal's reign was Phanā, son of Hāḍā. He is described as *sūtradhāragurunā*, the master of the *sūtradhāras*, and was fully conversant with literary works on architecture.[53] Thus, by the early fifteenth century, a few select families of artisans were being patronized by the royal court. These families not only supplied the architects for the royal constructions, but also seem to have mobilized the chief artisans from their own families.

The increasing number of towns and the numerous military, civil and religious monuments undertaken by Rāṇā Kumbha gave rise to a select band of court artisans and architects. The following is a brief inscriptional list of the prominent structures other than temples built in Kumbha's reign, that gives one an idea of the range of military architectural projects.

(1) Chittaurgarh Kīrtistambha Inscription, dated AD 1453, commemorating the construction of Kīrtistambha by Rāṇā Kumbha which includes a genealogy of the Guhila kings.[54]
(2) Chittaurgarh Kīrtistambha Inscription, dated AD 1450, recording the construction of a new gate at the Chittaurgarh fort.[55]
(3) Chittaurgarh Kīrtistambha Inscription, dated AD 1452, recording the date of the construction of the defensive ramparts around the fortresses of Chittaurgarh.[56]
(4) Chittaurgarh Kīrtistambha Inscription, dated AD 1458, recording the date of the construction of the fortress of Kumbhameru (Kumbhalgarh).[57] The extensive size of the Kumbhalgarh fort is a definite indicator of the degree of the involvement of the best artisans and architects of Mewar in royal projects in the fifteenth century.

If the architects contributed to the legitimation of the Guhila state through the building of royal monuments in this period, this select band of local architects employed by the royal court also benefited from having a career enjoying royal patronage. For instance, unlike Vījala, his son Mana bears the titles both of *śilpī* and *sūtradhāra*. Similarly unlike Hāḍā, his son Phanā bears the title of *sūtradhāraguruṇā*.

Apart from the names mentioned above, we also know of other contemporary *sūtradhāras*, such as Sūtradhāra Jaita and his sons Sūtradharas Nāpā, Puñja, Pomā, Bhūmī and Cuthī—architects of Kīrtistambha at Chittaurgarh (Kīrtistambha Inscription of AD 1453),[58] and Sūtradhara Maṇḍana, the famous architect of the Kumbhalgarh fort. That he probably designed the fort of Achalgarh, is suggested by the extent of his research-work on fort-construction in *Prāsādamaṇḍana*, a part of his famous work, *Rājavallabhamaṇḍana*. He seems to have trained some of the local junior architects and artisans in carrying out the massive programme of fortifications and re-fortifications.[59] His work *Rājavallabha* (famously known as *Rājavallabhamaṇḍana*) also contains instructions for the construction of horse and elephant stables, pointing to the growing military requirements of the state in the fifteenth century.[60] The fact that Maṇḍana too rose in career in the employment of the state is suggested by his affirming his patron in his declaration that he served King Kumbha of Medapāṭa.[61] His son, Isara, continued to be in the service of the state as he was the chief architect of the Rāmakuṇḍa and the Rāmasvāmī temples at Zawar.[62]

Revenue Administration

The increasing list of taxes in the Guhila records of the fifteenth century point to a better organization of revenue. It is also significant that the items of taxation are different from those in an earlier period.

The Land Tax (bhāga-bhoga): The largest portion of the state revenue was undoubtedly composed of the land tax, generally termed *bhāga-bhoga* in contemporary sources. *Bhāga* was the fixed land tax representing the state's share of the agricultural produce; and *bhoga*, consisted of customary presents of articles like fruit, milk, vegetables, etc., and included the provisions of lodging, bedding, etc., made for the king, his officials, and the royal army.[63]

An idea of the spatial extent and scale of land-revenue organization in Mewar can perhaps be best gleaned from an excellent contemporary source, Maṇḍan's *Rājavallabhamaṇḍana*, which describes the unit of land measurement and the system of calculation used to work out the area of various plots in detail. The tenth chapter of the *Rājavallabhamaṇḍana* is devoted to a discussion of the various methods of land measurement and the designs to facilitate the proper marking of plots.[64] A square or a rectangular plot was encircled by a rope with the help of posts. The entire encircled rope was then measured either by a hand or a stick, made of *rakta-candan* (*mahua*), or bamboo, gold, silver or copper. This measuring scale had different yardsticks for small, middle and large measurements. For instance, to measure the area of a village or town, the large yardstick was used. It is significant to note that most contemporary royal land charters contain the expression *grāmoyam svasīmāparyātam* (up to the boundaries of the village).[65] The repeated reference to this expression strongly suggests that the land of each village was being assessed meticulously. A picture of a measuring scale is inscribed on the Kīrtistambha in Chittaurgarh fort. It measures approximately 0.55 meter.[66] It is first divided into eight units, these eight units into three, and finally these three into four units each. Thus, there is a total of ninety-six divisions.[67]

Bhāga was generally calculated at the rate of one-sixth or more of produce.[68] Unfortunately, none of the contemporary inscriptional records from Mewar refers to the amount of land tax charged.[69] But an earlier reference to the imposition of *lāṭa* in the Sāraṇeśvara Inscription, dated AD 953,[70] has led to speculation among scholars like Somani that the rate of *bhāga* was high in medieval Mewar as *lāṭa* in medieval Rajasthan meant one-third or even half of the produce.[71] It is necessary to point out that Somani identifies *lāṭa* with *bhoga*,[72] which was an additional cess in kind only occasionally imposed by the state. Since Somani identifies *lāṭa* with *bhoga*, an occasional cess and not the regular land tax (*bhāga*), his observation that the rate of land tax was high in medieval Mewar is not very convincing, especially in the absence of contemporary evidence indicating high rates of tax.

The regular collection of revenue-dues is clearly evident from the Kadia Village (Udaipur) Inscription, dated AD 1443 of the reign of Kumbha as well as Ekaliṅgajī Temple Dakṣiṇadvāra Praśasti, dated AD 1488. The state revenue dues were termed the *rājakara*. The Kadia village inscription refers to the *rājakara* in the village of Śrīvajavi.[73] The Ekaliṅgajī Temple Inscription, dated AD 1488 to the reign of Rāṇā Rāimalla, in the Mewari dialect, exempts the temples, brāhmaṇas and bhāṭs of village Varṣasana from all royal taxes.[74]

None of the contemporary Guhila inscriptions mentions the *gopacara* or *gocara* (grazing tax) directly, unlike the twelfth-century inscriptional records of the Paramāras of Abu.[75] However, its prevalence in the Guhila revenue system of our period should not be entirely ruled out. James Tod reports the medieval custom of occasional payment of *kharlakhar* (supplying wood, forage, milk, flour, etc., by individuals to the royal army when the princes of Mewar were on the battlefield).[76] It is obvious that these occasional levies were temporary and find no place in the Guhila inscriptions of our period.

Commercial Revenue (maṇḍapikās and māṇḍvī tax): The Chittaurgarh Inscription of the Guhila Queen Jayatalladevī (AD 1278) records royal cash donations from a number of *maṇḍapikās* to a Jain Vasahi.[77] The list of donations is as follows: 24 *dramma* coins from the *maṇḍapikā* at Citrakūṭa-talahaṭṭī (custom house at the foothill of Chittaurgarh), 36 *dramma* coins from the Khohar *maṇḍapikā* (near Chittaurgarh) and 34 *dramma* coins from the Sajjanapura *maṇḍapikā* (near Chittaurgarh) besides other donations.[78] But the crucial problem is the nature of the precise relationship between local commercial institutions such as the *maṇḍapikās* and the royal dynasty, as the Guhilas operated from Chittaurgarh for the first time in the thirteenth century. Somani finds it difficult to define the precise nature of a *maṇḍapikā*, it is not clear whether it was an official/governmental institution or a semi-official institution.[79] Dasharath Sharma defines it as a civic institution with the *śulkādhyakṣa* (collector of the custom duties) setting up his *śulkaśālā* near the main gate of the city.[80]

Regarding the relationship between the *maṇḍapikās* and the state, B.D. Chattopadhyaya argues that although these commercial institutions might have been controlled by local merchant associations or corporate bodies, the concerned political powers ensured their regular share of the commercial revenue by retaining some control over the *maṇḍapikās*.[81] Such royal control represented the governmental mechanism of acquisition of cash and kind from the local *maṇḍapikās*.[82]

However, the thirteenth-century Guhila record of Queen Jayatalladevī donating *dramma* coins from the local *maṇḍapikās* to a Jain Vasahī, (noted above) does not specify the taxes collected at the *maṇḍapikās*. It is only in the fifteenth century that Guhila records specify all the taxes collected at the *maṇḍapikās*. This indicates more meticulous assessment by the state and hence, better resource mobilization in later times. The Delwara Inscription of Rāṇā Kumbha dated AD 1434 records royal donations of a total of 14 *ṭaṅkās* (silver coins) from the local *maṇḍapikā* and of proceeds of the sale of various items for the worship of Dharmacintāmaṇi. The list of donations is as follows: 5 *ṭaṅkās* from *māṇḍavī* (tax from *maṇḍapikā*), 4 *ṭaṅkās* from *māpā* (octroi or toll), 2 *ṭaṅkās* from *mānāheḍavāṭa* (remains unidentified by H.B. Sharda, the editor of the Inscription), 2 *ṭaṅkās* from *khārīvāṭa* (salt tax) and 1 *ṭaṅkā* from *pāṭasūtrīya* (cloth tax) at Delwara.[83] It is evident from this record that the customs-duty collected at a *maṇḍapikā* came to be known as *māṇḍavī*. In other words, everybody entering an exchange centre with goods for sale had to first pay *māṇḍavī* at the local *māṇḍapikās*. All cash donations were made from the royal share of the cash collected as taxes from the *maṇḍapikās*.

By the thirteenth century, the Guhila state controlled most of the major trade routes passing through the Mewar hills, the Abu-Sirohi route and the route through Chittaurgarh in its western, north-western and eastern frontiers respectively. It is difficult to estimate the exact amount of these amount of commercial transactions which increasingly contributed to the formation of the tax called *māpā*. The major items of local trade seem to have been salt (an item of transit-trade possibly coming from the Sambhar region of Ajmer) and cloth, both of which contributed separately to the state exchequer. This speaks for some state control over their sale. In fact, if cloth and salt were being taxed at Delwara near Udaipur then their passage all along the Abu-Sirohi route would probably have been similarly taxed. Hence, taxes such as *māpā*, *māṇḍavī*, *khārīvāṭa* and *pāṭasūtrīya* were more or less universally collected throughout the state in the fifteenth century.

The case of the security tax seems to have been different. Apparently the state levied a security tax in places of pilgrimage outside Mewar. The Abu Inscription dated AD 1449 announces exemption of such levies as *valamī* and *rāṣ(kha)valī* (tax and policing for the pilgrims visiting Jain temples at Delwara) in Arbudacala.[84]

Finally, the pilgrimage tax seems to have been another major source of state revenue. This levy is also attested to by the above Abu record, which announces exemption of from the pilgrimage (*ācandrāk*) tax.[85] The pilgrimage tax is likely to have been utilized for the upkeep of the pilgrimage centres, especially during festivals. In addition, ad hoc levies for expenditure incurred in daily or special rituals at the temples in many pilgrimage centres were a common practice. This is evident from the Delwara Inscription dated AD 1434 recording the imposition of 14 *ṭaṅkās* on travellers (entering Delwara everyday) for the worship of Śrī

Dharmacintāmaṇi at Delwara, Abu.[86] An early instance of such ad hoc impositions can best be seen in the case of the Sāraṇeśvara temple at Āhaḍa.[87] The practice extended to Jain temples by the fifteenth century indicating Guhila control over a larger commercial network.[88] More importantly, ad hoc levies for the upkeep of temple complexes probably came to be recognized as the royal share (*grāsa*) by the fifteenth century. In other words, it was looked upon as a legitimate right of the state to impose such occasional levies as its own share of resources generated in pilgrimage centres.[89]

Local Level Administration

In contrast to the earlier predominance of *pañcakulas*, records from the thirteenth to the fifteenth centuries testify to the continuing importance of rural people in village administration. It might be that the *pañcakulas* came to function at the level of bigger villages rather than at each and every rural settlement by this period. The Kadmal Copper Plate Charter of Tejasiṁha dated AD 1259 records the names of the witnesses to the royal grants as follows: Sāho Vijiyausa, Brāhmaṇa Golou Nālau, Mantrī Candu, Vaṇika Vairāu Villanu, Cāhamāṇa Vāghāranasiṁha, Meharans (Mahattaras), Vaijāu Cāvāh, Morou, Vaneu, Dhābhrā, and Kāndhāla.[90] The very fact that each of the witnesses is named speaks for their status in village Kadmal (25 km north-west of Udaipur). Secondly, the witnesses evidently represented most of the prominent social groups such as the Merchants, Brāhmaṇas, Rajputs, and Mahattaras. It is quite possible that all these witnesses were members of a village-level administrative organization. B.D. Chattopadhyaya observes: 'The existence of a village-level organization, exercising certain rights in the conduct of village affairs is attested by the consent given by mahājanas, the grāmīṇa and the janapada when a document specifying levies for a temple was drawn up.'[91] In fact, the increasing execution of the royal charters in the village in the Mewari dialect in the fifteenth century[92] should also be considered an important indicator of the incorporation of village rural level society into the state-apparatus. It appears that the state was concerned about the incorporation of rural residents as effectively as possible into the administrative-apparatus in which the elite of the local society seem to have played a significant role. However, the absence of a *pañcakulika* in the thirteenth century in Kadmal village need not necessarily indicate its absence in bigger contemporary villages in southern Rajasthan. For instance, the term *pañcaśrī* figures in a royal charter of the Guhilas of Vagod in this period. The Mala Copper Plates of Virasiṁhadeva, dated AD 1287, which record the royal grant of one and a half *halas* of land and a house with enclosures at the village of Mala (about 5 km from village Baroda, district Dungarpur) specifically mentions that the writer of the record, Vikama (Vikrama), acted under the verbal orders of the Pañcaśrī Vāvana.[93] The writer is also called a *pañca* while *pañcaśrī* is the title for Vāvana. This suggests that Vāvana was the chief of the *pañcakulika* while Vikama was one of the five members of the same local body. The village of Mala, close to the centre of power of the Guhilas of Vagod (Vāṭapadraka), seems to have emerged as a bigger settlement and to have thus become a node for surrounding rural settlements.

The political significance of such local bodies was considerable since the writing of the royal charters had to be ordered by the chief of the *pañcakulika*. Some other members of the *pañcakulika*, like Vikama, apparently a kāyastha, had to discharge their administrative duties by writing the royal record. The execution of such royal grants continued to be the responsibility of the *pañcakulikas* in major rural settlements. However, even a *pañcakulika* had to take into account local notables as is evident from the list of the chief witnesses to the announcement of the royal grants. This fact is borne out by the expression *kaḍū vīsalaśabdena sakṣiṇah* in the concluding sentence of the Mala Copper Plate.[94] It has been translated as: Kaḍū Vīsala is the one on whose authority the names of the witnesses are recorded.[95] It is significant that Kaḍū or Kaḍūā, is one of the two sects of the Kunbī tribe.[96] Thus, Kaḍūvīsala might have been the chief representative of the Kunbī population which might have formed a major portion of the local population. He is likely to have been associated with the local ruling elite and thus a linkage between Kunbī villages and the Guhila state of Vagod. The above instances, proving the importance of the local bodies in village administration also suggests decentralization of royal authority.

The Language of Administration

A study of the administrative apparatus in the context of state formation remains incomplete without a survey of the official language of communication between the state and the populace. Although Sanskrit remained the predominant language in official charters, terms from the Mewari dialect do appear in official inscriptions by the late twelfth century. By the fifteenth century, Mewar had official charters in the

Mewari dialect, particularly the sections on business transactions.[97] The use of local dialects in addition to the courtly Sanskrit in official charters is an indicator both of, the state's attempt to reach as many social groups of local society, beyond the elite strata as possible, and consequently, of the incorporation of influential local elements into the political structure. Therefore, I feel that the official charters in full-fledged Mewari dialect of the fifteenth century point to the political compulsions acting on the state which forced it to use the vernacular language and not the formal language for official communications to the public. This further strengthens my argument that the Guhila state grew due to accommodation rather than centralization.

II

The Military Apparatus

As compared to earlier, the Guhila state had to administer a larger territory with a more varied socio-cultural profile between the thirteenth and fifteenth centuries. It now also had a number of powerful neighbours surrounding its borders. It is significant that thirteenth century Guhila inscriptions refer to neighbouring powers for the first time. The other important development is the beginning of Guhila references to a number of forts (see Map 10). This was due to the transfer of the capital to Chittaurgarh which brought on the additional problem of defending the new capital town, a strategic fortress highly coveted by the neighbouring powers.

The political and military significance of the new capital is evident from such references as '*durganuttara citrakūṭa nagarasthah*' and '*śrīcitrakūṭadurge*' in the Chiravā Inscription of the Ṭāmṭarāḍa family of Nāgdā (AD 1273)[98] and '*śrī citrakūṭamahādurga*' in a Jain Inscription of Tejasiṁha's Reign from Chittaur (AD 1267).[99] To defend Chittaurgarh, a chain of fortresses seem to have been contested by the Guhilas in the thirteenth century. The foothills of Chittaurgarh seem to have been the scene of a number of battles. The location of Chittaurgarh on a major route linking northern India with central and western India made it vulnerable to attacks specially from the Delhi Sultanate in the thirteenth century. The fact is evident from the expression '*turuṣkārṇavat*' used for Tejasiṁha in the Achaleśvara Inscription.[100] Guhila references to the '*turuṣkas*' (turks) appear for the first time in thirteenth-century records. The Chiravā Inscription refers to the death of Ratna (a member of the Ṭāmṭarāḍa family) and Bhīmasiṁha (one of King Jaitrasiṁha's

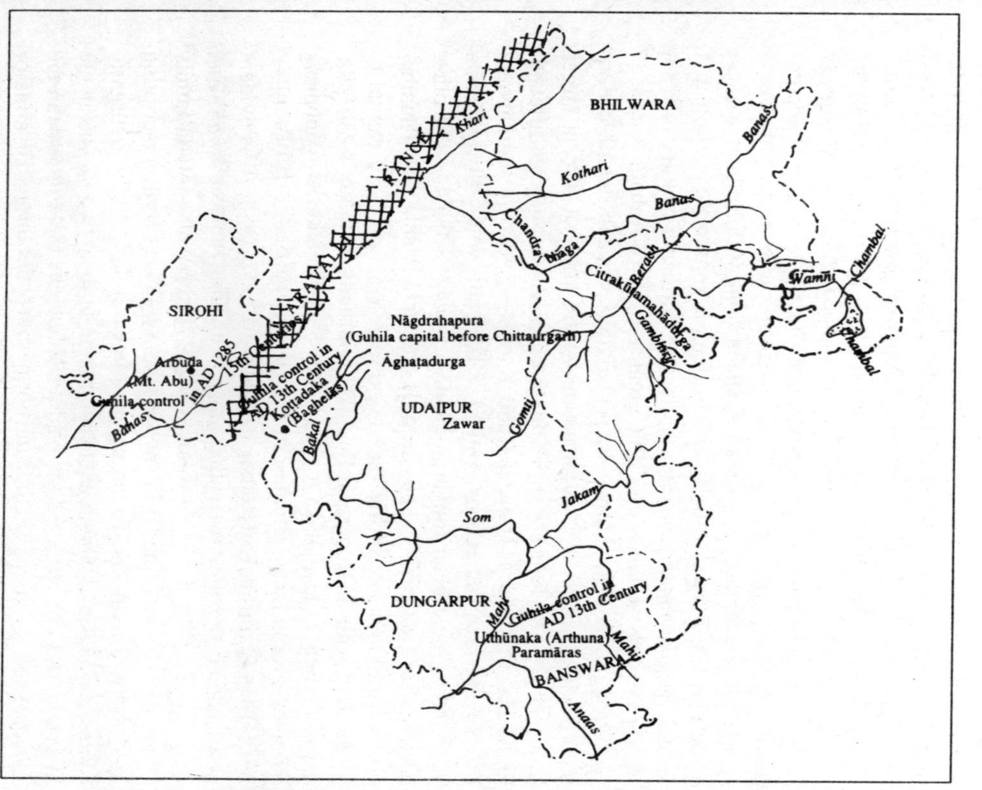

Map 10: Guhila References to the Forts: AD Thirteenth Century.

minister) in a battle at the foot (*talahaṭṭī*) of Chittaurgarh.[101] The fortress of Arthuna in Banswara and the Mewar hills from the south (which saw Paramāra attacks from Malwa in the thirteenth century) seem to have been crucial in the defence of Chittaurgarh. Madana, another member of Ṭāmṭarāḍa family, is eulogized for having proved his valour in the battlefield of Utthūnaka (Arthuna, district Banswara), while fighting with Pañcalagudikā Jaitramalla (Paramāra King Jayatuṅgideva of Malwa).[102] The fortress of Arthuna, evidently a Paramāra possession in the mid-thirteenth century, seems to have been wrested by the Guhilas from the Paramāras in this battle. This fortress must have been coveted by the Guhilas for a long time, probably ever since they took over Chittaurgarh.

The former capital, the fortress of Āhaḍa along with Nāgdā continued to defend the Mewar hills in the thirteenth century. The Jain text, *Śrāvakapratikramaṇacūrṇisūtra*, of the late thirteenth century refers to Āhaḍa as '*Āghaṭamahādurga*' (the great fortress of Āghaṭa/Āhaḍa).[103] The stronghold of Nāgadṛahapura is also figures in a thirteenth-century record which refers to its destruction by the army of the Suratrāṇa, Iltutmish.[104] The four sons of Yogarāja the *talarakṣaka* of Nāgdā—Pamarāja, Mahendra, Campaka and Kṣema—fought in the battle of Bhūtālā in which Pamarāja was killed.[105] The battle with Sultan Iltutmish is stated to have been fought at Bhūtālā (village Untala, 19 km from Nāgdā, near Udaipur).[106] Thus the hills of Nāgdā-Āhaḍa were no longer obstacles to invaders of Mewar.

To deal with the recurrent Caulukyan inroads from the south-west, the settlement of Koṭṭadaka was captured.[107] Koṭṭadaka, or Kotra in the Bhomat region, was situated at the periphery of the Bhil country bordering Gujarat. Koṭṭadaka is likely to have been a Caulukyan possession in the mid-thirteenth century. With King Jaitrasiṁha's capture of Koṭṭadaka in his fight against Rāṇā Tribhuvana (successor of Bhīmadeva II in Gujarat),[108] the Guhilas secured a front line fortress against the Caulukyas. To defend the Mewar hills from the Caulukyan forces, it was equally important to control the Godwar region. Jaitrasiṁha is known to have uprooted the Nāḍol Cāhamāṇas (*Naḍūlamulaṁkaṣa-bāhulakṣmī*).[109] Having secured the northern frontier through the fortress of Nāḍol, the Guhilas further blocked the Caulukya passage into Mewar from the north-west by conquering the hill fortress of Abu, a Caulukya possession. Samarasiṁha in the Achalgarh Inscription is eulogized as *arbudo bijayate girirūccairdevaṣu vitakulācalaratnam*.[110] The Guhila acquisition of Abu by the late thirteenth century secured the north-western boundary of Mewar. Abu controlled the trade-route of the Abu-

Palanpur gap, strategic for the movement of troops from Marwar, north-western India and Gujarat.

Most military personnel continued to be the local Rajput chiefs in the thirteenth century. It is significant that the Kumbhalgarh Inscription, dated AD 1460, describes Rāval Samarasiṁha, the last Guhila king of the thirteenth century, as the 'jewel of all the *sāmanta*s'.[111] In view of the intensification military activities in the thirteenth century, the military significance of all the local *sāmantas* seems to have been the most important political reason for reference to the *sāmantas* in royal *praśastis*. The Achaleśvara Inscription too, hints at the military support coming from the *sāmantas* in the wake of the Caulukyan invasion in the reign of Guhila Sāmantasiṁhadeva, and at their role in his abdication of the throne and the succession of his younger brother, Kumārasiṁha's, following Sāmantasiṁhadeva's clash with the local *sāmantas*.[112] It seems true to some extent that the increasing militarization of the Guhila state in this period was one of the chief causes of the induction of non-Rajput social groups into the administrative apparatus as more and more Rajput chiefs were contributing to and were occupied with the building of a strong military apparatus in the thirteenth century. In fact, at times even non-Rajput social groups such as the Jains joined the Rajputs in the battlefields from the fifteenth century onwards.

The territorial integration of Merwara (a hilly, forested tract in north-western Mewar) and the incorporation of its tribal population of the Medas (Mers), possibly took place in phases between the late fourteenth and the fifteenth centuries. The capture of the fortress of Celvāṭa (Jilwara, Merwara tract), which attributed to Rāṇā Hammīra,[113] and of the hilly fortresses of Vardhana (Badnor, Merwara) and Beratgarh (Merwara), which is attributed to Rāṇā Lākhā,[114] seems to have begun the process of the annexation of Merwara. The annals of Mewar also credit Rāṇā Khetā with the subjugation of the mountaineers (Mers) of Merwara and their stronghold Beratgarh followed by the construction of the fortress of Badnor.[115] Control of the local fortresses of Merwara was essential to strengthen the royal grip over this newly acquired territory and its resources. Merwara was immensely important for the Guhila state. It was essential to command the fortresses of Merwara and to defend Mewar against the Sultanates of Nagaur and Gujarat. The fortresses of Merwara were to function as the frontier and could also function as a safe-retreat for the ruling family in the eventuality of the fall of Chittaurgarh since Merwara is defended naturally by hills and forests. Also, the fortresses of Merwara could effectively function as a launching ground for Guhila inroads into Nagaur, Ajmer and Śākambharī regions. In fact, Rāṇā Mokal's repeated references to the defeats of Firuz Shah (the sultan of Nagaur)[116] indicate some Guhila control over the northern frontiers, facilitated by the fortresses of the Merwara tract.

Similarly, the claims to conquest of fortresses in eastern Mewar attributed to Rāṇā Khetā in the local annals of Mewar might be indications of early Guhila attempts to control local Hāḍā fortresses. Eastern Mewar is referred to as 'Hāḍāvatī' in contemporary Guhila records. The fortresses of Maṇḍalgarh, Bambaoda, etc., could function as a second line of defence for Chittaurgarh, specially against inroads from the north-eastern and Malwa fronts as well as from the Bundi-Kota region. They could also function as hinterland fortresses for Chittaurgarh in case the latter was seized. It is significant that Mokal is eulogized for having won victory over the best of the forts, the Citrakūṭa (*rājahaṁsai-rāgamyastaddurggam citrakūṭo jayati*).[117]

Rāṇā Kumbha and the Building of Forts and Fortifications: Augmentation of the military apparatus reached its zenith under Mahārāṇā Kumbha. Traditions narrate that Kumbha built thirty-two of the eighty-four fortresses constructed for the defence of Mewar.[118] 'He triumphed over the enemies of his race, fortified his country with strongholds, embellished it with temples, and with superstructure of her fame laid the foundations of his own.'[119] To defend Mewar, Kumbha took three steps. The first step was to either annexe or re-assert Guhila control over forts strategic to the defence of Chittaurgarh. The next step was to construct new fortresses and to fortify old ones in the captured areas which were strategic to Mewar. The third step was to fortify the existing fortresses in the core area (see Map 11). This enabled the fifteenth-century Guhila state to defend the newly integrated areas as well as the core and to secure the state's territorial frontiers. To enhance the existing military capacity, Kumbha also added structures to the leading fortresses of Mewar. Finally, to project Mewar as a military power and to muster additional resources, Kumbha embarked upon a career of military expansion. But this programme of expansion is likely to have been undertaken in the second half of his reign, for the first three steps of defence listed earlier formed the essential basis of his military career. Hence, the following discussion will unfold in three sections: the first section lists and discusses the forts captured/fortified by Kumbha which were strategic to Mewar. The second section will deal with the forts and military structures constructed entirely/fortified by Kumbha and the third

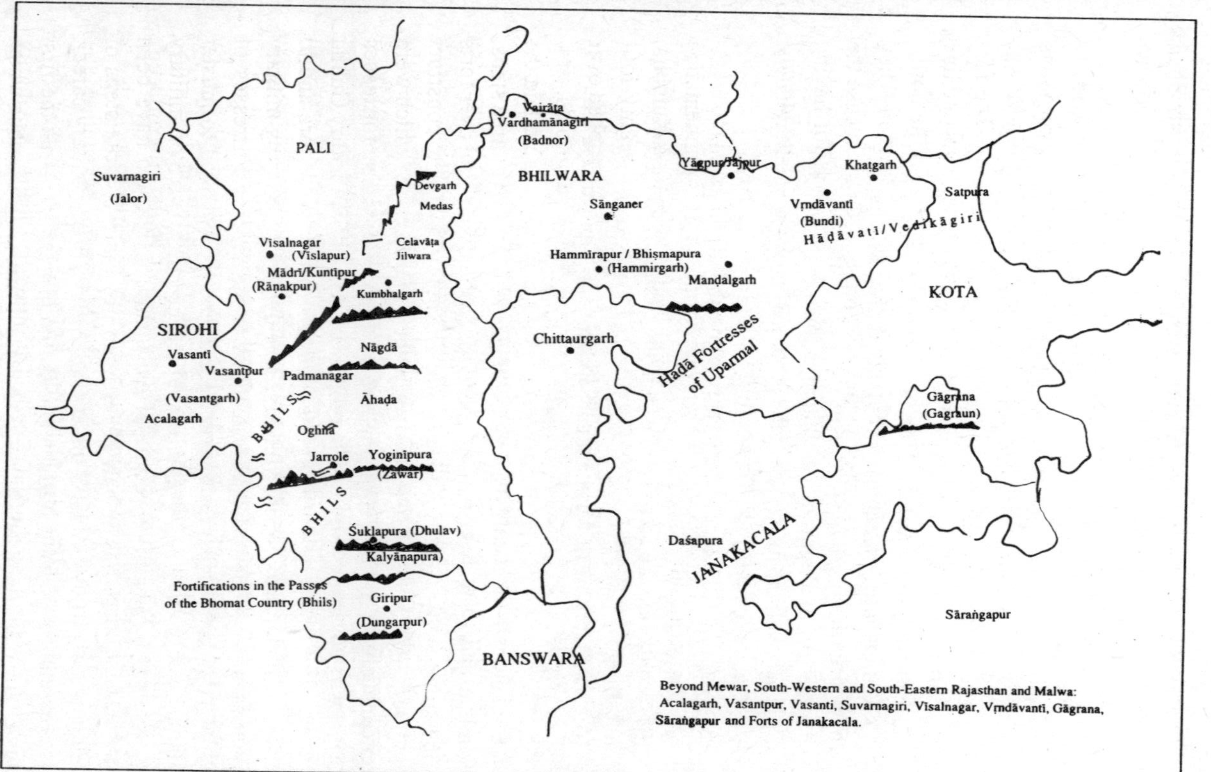

Map 11: Mahārāṇā Kumbha and his Forts: AD Fifteenth Century.

with his claims regarding the conquest of forts external to Mewar.

Forts captured by Kumbha in the upper Banas plain, Vagod, Hāḍāvatī, Jhalawar and Godwar, etc., were:

(1) Maṇḍalgarh: southern Bhilwara district (upper Banas plains).[120]
(2) Giripur: Dungarpur, district Dungarpur (Vagod).[121]
(3) Yāgpur[122] (also called Jajpur in the Ekaliṅgajī Temple Dakṣiṇa-dvāra Praśasti)[123]: Jahāzpur in north-eastern part of district Bhilwara (upper Banas plain).
(4) Vardhamānagiri: Badnor in north-western part of district Bhilwara (a part of the Merwara country).[124]
(5) Campāvatī: Chapaneri in southern Ajmer district.[125]
(6) Gārgarāṭa[126] (also called Gāgaraṇa in the Rāṇakpur Praśasti[127]): the fort of Gagraun near Jhalawar town in district Kota.
(7) Hāḍāvatī: the fortresses of the eastern Mewar such as Bambaoda, etc., and the Bundi-Kota belt.[128]
(8) Ṣaṭpura: Khāṭkar or Khāṭu. This is possibly Khāṭgarh in the north-east of Bundi.[129]
(9) Vṛndāvatī: the fortress of Bundi, the capital of Hāḍāvatī (district Bundi).[130]
(10) Vīsalampurī or Vīsalanagar: Bisalpur in Godwar belt, district Pali.[131]

Evidences from Kumbha's epigraphical records amply prove that Kumbha had to reassert Guhila suzerainty in Hāḍāvatī by capturing Maṇḍalgarh and the surrounding Hāḍā fortresses. As noted in an earlier section,[132] the Guhilas had left Maṇḍalgarh to the Solaṁkīs and the remaining fortresses in the hands of local Hāḍā chiefs. I have also argued that it was not for the Guhilas to annexe the Hāḍā fortresses of eastern Mewar. But it was militarily essential to create a chain of fortresses in eastern Mewar, and Kumbha not only secured Maṇḍalgarh in the upper Banas plain, but also tried to win control over the bigger fortresses of greater Hāḍāvatī such as Vṛndāvatī (Bundi), the capital-town of the Hāḍās, Khāṭgarh, and other fortresses in the Bundi region.

However, the fortresses of Maṇḍalgarh and Hāḍāvatī could only defend Chittaurgarh in the immediate north and the north-east. To defend Chittaurgarh from an increasingly hostile Malwa in the south-east, it was essential to hold the formidable fort of Gagraun, strategically situated on a hill overlooking the Kali Sindh. The strategic location of Gagraun makes it clear that it held the key to Malwa for Mewar. Attempts to control Gagraun reveal the realities of Guhila power. It seems that not only was Guhila control over the second line of defence in eastern Mewar tenuous, but the actual hold over Chittaurgarh was also questionable since the fortresses of eastern Mewar fell to invaders. Hence, by extending the line of defence towards Malwa, attempts were made to devise a possible mechanism of securing Chittaurgarh. It is significant that a much smaller power, the Khīcīs of Gagrauṇ were indispensable for the Guhilas.

The fort of Giripur (Dungarpur) could guard the passes to Mewar from an invading Gujarat army—it was militarily indispensable for the defence of Mewar. It was the capital-town of the Guhilas of Vagod (Dungarpur-Banswara districts). Besides Vagod, it was important to annexe Mount Abu so as to control trade routes. The Sirohi and Mount Abu belt commanded routes to Godwar, Jalor (Suvarṇagiri) and Marwar. Increasing hostilities from the Sultanates of Gujarat and Jalor created a compelling necessity to build new Guhila bastions and to gain control to the existing fortresses in the region of Mount Abut and Sirohi. Thus was captured Padmanagar; the fortress of Vasantpur or Vasantgarh, an early medieval stronghold of the Paramāras of Abu. It had probably come under the control of the Devḍā Cāhamāṇas by the fifteenth century. The Kīrtistambha Inscription states that Kumbha repopulated Vasantapur (the reference is probably to garrisoning) and built seven lakes near it in the vicinity of Anhalkuṇḍa of Vaśiṣṭa (probably to increase the water supply for the army) in Sirohi.[133] To convert the Sirohi region into a military garrison, Kumbha built two more fortresses, Vasanti near the present town of Sirohi, and Achalgarh near Mount Abu. 'He fortified the passes between the western frontier of Mewar and Abu and erected the fort of Vasanti near Sirohi.'[134]

Achalgarh: The fort of Achalgarh was constructed in AD 1452. It is situated on a peak and seems to have been built over the ruined fortress of the ancient Paramāras of Abu (Candrāvatī). 'The upper fortress is attributed to Kumbha, but he probably only repaired this, the D'onjon of Achalgarh, which with the interior works, is of the most remote antiquity. There are the ruins of a granary, the Bhantar of Kumbha Rana.'[135] The D'onjon of a fortress is its highest 'keep' (the last post). If it falls to the enemy, the fort is surrendered to the enemy and the campaign is completely lost for the defending power. The Kīrtistambha Inscription testifies to the construction of a huge tank, Rāmakuṇḍa, and four more tanks as reservoirs by Kumbha near the temple of Kumbhasvāmī in Achalgarh.[136] The long association of Mahārāṇā Kumbha with the fort of Achalgarh is indicated by the presence of a statue of Mahārāṇā Kumbha on horse-back with the statues of the other two Mahārāṇās. A bigger statue of the *purohit* of Kumbha is located on the descent from Achalgarh to Dilwara.[137] The evidence that I have cited here as well as Kumbha's Abu Inscriptions[138] testify to the annexation of the region of Abu-Sirohi by Kumbha.

Kumbha and the Merwara: The seizure of the fort of Vardhamānagiri (Badnor) has been attributed to Rāṇā Lākhā.[139] The references to its recapture by Rāṇā Kumbha speak of the difficulty of holding a Meda stronghold. To ensure that it was retained by the Guhilas, Kumbha is known to have built a new fortress at Vairāṭa near Badnor.[140] The fortresses of Badnor and Vairāṭa were to be utilized to integrate Merwara as well as to create a second line of defence for the newly constructed second capital-town of Kumbhalgarh in Merwara. These fortresses played an important role in engaging an invading army from the region of central Rajasthan and from the Delhi Sultanate. They are likely to have been entrusted to a band of comparatively trusted chiefs. In the absence of direct contemporary evidence, it is difficult to comment upon the posting of the actual chiefs at Badnor and Vairāṭa in the reign of Kumbha. However, it is likely that the charge of both these strongholds was conferred upon those chiefs who were new entrants to the Guhila court. This strategy of posting new Rajput chiefs in such sensitive peripheral areas would have ensured less trouble for the state because the new Rajput elements could become politically dominant only through their linkages with the royal family. It is important that a contemporary official record refers to Kumbha's Gauḍa queen, the mother of Rāṇā Rāimalla.[141] Social linkages with the Bāghelās and Gauḍas seem to have assumed political significance in the fifteenth century. It is also evident from the *Baḍvādevīdān Khyāt* that Rajput lineages like the Gauḍas and Tomars were becoming prominent for the first time in Guhila polity during Kumbha's reign. *Baḍvādevīdān* lists a Gauḍa and a Tomar queen for Rāṇā Kumbha.[142] It is not unlikely that some Gauḍa and Tomar chiefs (the queens' kinsmen) might have been appointed to take charge of the forts of Badnor and Vairāṭa. Although these references in the *Khyāts* may also reflect the fact that the Rajput chiefly families of the Gauḍas and Tomars in Mewar claimed social prestige later on by tracing matrimonial links with the legendary Kumbha; the absence of their strongholds in fifteenth-century Mewar strengthens our assumption that the Rajput chiefs other than the Hāḍās, Rāṭhaurs, Solaṁkīs or Paramāras (local Rajput chiefs) are likely to have been appointed to control the fortresses of Merwara. Moreover, contemporary references to the Gauḍa queen indicate the presence of her kinsmen. However, the subsequent history of Badnor proves that the military *paṭṭās* (service deeds) were not necessarily hereditary in nature. Mahārāṇā Sāṅgā (early sixteenth century) is known to have conferred the charge of Badnor on Duṅgarsiṁha Cāhamāṇa, a famous official in the *mahārāṇā's* army. His sons and nephews all lost their lives in the siege of Ahmadnagar. Muhanot Nainsī confirms this fact.[143] The case of Badnor suggests that the court never made the office of a fort in-charge a hereditary post in such militarily and politically sensitive areas as the Merwara tract.

Kumbhalgarh: The greatest Guhila achievement in Merwara was the construction of the Kumbhalgarh fort by Rāṇā Kumbha. The text *Saṅgītarāja* refers to the fort of Kumbhalgarh variously as Agastipura, Kāmeśvarigīri, Mahiṣmeru and Mahiṣcala.[144] The Kīrtistambha Inscription eulogizes the fort.[145] The fort was designed and built by Kumbha's famous architect Maṇḍana. The construction began in AD 1443 and was completed in AD 1458.[146] It is situated at the top of a hill 914 m high and is at a distance of 64 km from Udaipur. The location of this fortress, overlooking the Godwar region on its north-west and commanding the Merwara belt, made it more difficult to approach than Chittaurgarh because of its steep hilly terrain and the surrounding forests. The winding road leads over deep ravines through forests. About thirteen Arāvalli peaks surround it and made it impregnable.[147]

Local annals emphasize the association of Kumbhalgarh with the Meda tribe at an early stage of its construction. Local legends claim that before these mountain ranges were conquered by Kumbha, they had belonged to a Meda ruler. The vanquished Meda is said to have offered himself as a voluntary sacrifice for the foundations of the fortress. The story goes that a shrine at the bottom of the fort lies over the head of the Meda (the vanquished king of Medas) and another on the highest terrace of the fort over the body of the vanquished Meda king.[148] It is relevant to mention the Medas here for they too seem to have influenced the construction plans of military structures at Kumbhalgarh which I shall discuss here. The purpose of erecting this fortress was to ensure the personal security of the royal family (apart from its obvious military significance), as is evident from the following description of its series of defensive walls and gateways. 'In the distance, wall after wall appears. Seven great gates stand sentinel at the approaches, and seven ramparts, one within the other, with crenellated walls, strengthened by rounded bastions and immense watch towers, make this fort strong and impregnable with seven formidable gate ways.'[149] It is known that the fort could support three thousand troops with provisions for a year and provide drinking water through small tanks spread over the whole fort.[150] Such vast security arrangements at this fort, which served as a royal residence too, raise interesting questions regarding the actual strength of the Guhila kings' power even at their capital Chittaurgarh. Kumbhalgarh was the standby capital if Chittaurgarh fell.

However, one must not ignore the importance of the personal security of the royal family. Assassinations of Guhila rulers including Mokal and Kumbha[151] reveal the vulnerability of the rulers to attack on their person. Rāṇā Kumbha realized that intrigue and conspiracies at the royal court left the royal family insecure at Chittaurgarh. Both the location and the inhospitable terrain of Kumbhalgarh offered Kumbha a refuge. Hence, he undertook the programme of building the massive bastions and gates here. The presence of the recalcitrant Medas, evident from the Guhila recapture of their strongholds near Kumbhalgarh, also necessitated constructions of safety walls at Kumbhalgarh.

Kumbhalgarh was further defended by yet another inner fort, Kāṭārgarh, on a conical hillock.[152] It is well-known that 'the highest monument of Kumbha's military and constructive genius . . . is the wonderful fortress of Kumbhalgarh or Kumbhalmer, second to none in strategic importance. . . . It was to this impregnable fortress that the Maharanas of Mewar always turned their eyes, when Udaipur became unsafe and Chittaur untenable'.[153] Finally, the association of Kuntīpur with Rāṇā Kumbha[154] indicates that he built another small fortress near Kumbhalgarh at Rāṇakpur. Kuntīpur of *Saṅgītarāja* is identified with Rāṇakpur.[155]

In addition, Kumbha is known to have built the fortress of Mechan to defend Shera *nallah* and the fortress of Devgarh to contain the Medas.[156] Devgarh is situated to the north-west of Kumbhalgarh on the bank of river Khari, bordering the districts of Pali, Ajmer and Bhilwara.

The forts of Yāgpur/Jājpur (Jahāzpur in the north-eastern part of Bhilwara district) and Campāvatī in the north-eastern part of upper Banas plain were militarily important in guarding the northern frontier, as were the forts of Badnor and Vairāṭa in the Merwara tract, and as a second line of defence (an outlying chain of fortresses parallel to main fortresses) to Maṇḍalgarh and other Hāḍā forts in eastern Mewar. The *Amarakāvyam* ascribes the conquest of Jahāzpur to Rāṇā Khetā and also mentions that it was a stronghold of the Kherāḍā Rajputs.[157] However, fifteenth-century Guhila inscriptions cited earlier show that Jahāzpur was captured by Kumbha probably for the first time in the fifteenth century, even though traditions and seventeenth-century official sources indicate that Guhila attempts to control Jahāzpur began in the pre-Kumbha period. The fort of Campāvatī, north of Jahāzpur, is likely to have functioned as a complimentary stronghold defending Jahāzpur.

Kumbha and the Bhomat: Similar to his policy in the Merwara, was Kumbha's military policy of defending strategic forts in central Mewar and at the western borders of the Mewar hills against the Bhils. Sporadic and recurrent Bhil revolts characterized the fourteenth-fifteenth century history of Mewar. Popular traditions credit Kumbha with the building of fortresses to contain the Bhils of Bhomat. 'He built various other forts to overawe Bhumia Bhils of Jarole and Panora. . . .'[158] The association of some of the fortresses of Mewar with Kumbha in the *Saṅgītarāja* proves the point. These include Kalyāṇapur (ancient Kiṣkindhā/Kiṣkindhipur), Maṇipur (Ratanpur near Koṭḍa), Mahādamhamātṛkāpur (Yoginīpura/Zawar) and Śuklapura (Dhavalapura/Dhuleva near Zawar mines).[159] As evident from the map (Rāṇā Kumbha's fortresses) these four fortresses are situated almost in a straight line east of Jarole and Panarwa. This chain of fortresses stands as a guard not only against the Bhils of Jarole and Panarwa but also seems to have been militarily significant in controlling a major part of the Bhomat and the Chhappan—the Bhil countries in the south-west and the southern parts of Mewar respectively.

Kumbha and the Capital Town, Chittaurgarh: The chain of forts discussed here remains incomplete without a discussion of the capital, Chittaurgarh. Unlike Gwalior which is praised for its strength and invincibility in contemporary Persian works such as the *Tarikh-i-Mubarakshahi* and Al-Bada'uni's *Muntakhab-i-Tawarikh*;[160] Chittaurgarh is not referred to in such glowing terms in contemporary Persian works. However, indirect references to its military might and to the military support it enjoyed from its hinterland and from the surrounding forts can be gleaned from one of the contemporary Persian texts. For instance, the *Tarikh-i-Firozshahi* of Ziauddin Barni, gives the following account of Alauddin's return from Chittaurgarh after his first siege: 'The Sultan now returned from the conquest of Chitor, where his army had suffered great loss in prosecuting the siege during the rainy season . . . the Sultan had just returned from Chitor, and had had no time to refil and recruit his army after his great losses in the siege. . . .'[161] The hilly terrain and its natural fortifications undoubtedly played a very significant role in defending the fort and had the advantage of functioning as a natural watch-tower for the surrounding landscape.[162] If Bhīṣmapura (identified as Hammīrapura) of *Saṅgītarāja*[163] can be identified with Hammīragarh of the southern Bhilwara ditrict, it would not be inaccurate to suggest that Kumbha had either built or fortified an old fort on the banks of the Banas with a view to defend the capital town of Chittaurgarh.

Pre-Kumbha Guhila fortifications at Chittaurgarh are evident from the surviving fragments of the palace attributed to Rāval Cūṇḍā, the eldest son of Rāṇā Lākhā (the late fourteenth to the early fifteenth centuries), which include a watch tower, standing at the north-western corner of a building.[164] Tillotson points out that such architectural patterns of the fifteenth-century palaces at Chittaur are a continuation of a long-established tradition.[165] Contemporary records amply testify to the programme of defence undertaken by Mahārāṇā Kumbha at the fortress of Chittaurgarh. The Kīrtistambha Inscription states that in AD 1450 Kumbha built a new bastion with battlements at Kumbhalgarh.[166] The same record ascribes the erection of the following gates to Kumbha: Rāmpol (pol or *pratolī* means gateway), Hanumānpol, Bhairavapol, Lakṣmīpol, Cāmuṇḍāpol, Tārāpol and Rājapol.[167] The last four pols are now popularly known as Lakṣmaṇpol, Jarolpol, Gaṇeśpol and Pādalpol.[168] The Kīrtistambha Inscription also mentions that he built the main road up the hill for the smooth passage of carriages.[169] Kumbha also took steps to ensure a regular supply of water to the fort by getting the Rāmakuṇḍa and several stepped wells and reservoirs constructed. These would be of great importance militarily during a seige.

The location and architectural features of Kumbha's palace give one an idea of the importance of Kumbha's contributions to making this fortress a military focal point of the Guhila state and in ensuring the security of the royal family. Kumbha's palace was situated on the western side of the fort, approached through the two gateways from the east, Baḍīpol and Tripoliā.[170] These gates lead to a *darikhānā* or *sabhā*, a low hypostyle hall which seems to conceal the main entrance to a private apartment in the southern façade.[171] A small doorway in the back of the *sabhā* gives access to a flight of stairs which leads one into the body of the palace. The north-western corner of the palace is flanked by two towers. The towers have three storeys, each a single square chamber. The central block consisted of two rectangular chambers, and a roof terrace. In front of the whole apartment is a small *chowk* (courtyard) and the entrance to the apartment is from this *chowk.*[172] The interior arrangement of this set of towers points to its military purpose. They definitely functioned as the watch-towers.

Having ensured Mewar of a strong chain of fortresses, Rāṇā Kumbha claimed victory over the following forts of neighbouring polities: Mahoragapura of the *Saṅgītarāja*[173] or Nāgapur of the Kīrtistambha Praśasti,[174] referring to the fort of Nagaur (central Rajasthan) under the suzerainty of the Sultanate of Gujarat; Vedikāgiri of the *Saṅgītarāja*[175] or Hāḍāvatī of the Kumbhalgarh Praśasti[176] referring to the fortresses of Bundi-Kota region east of Maṇḍalpur in the possession of the Hāḍās; Śrīpur of the *Saṅgītarāja,*[177] referring to Śrīnagar near Ajmer, possibly a Rāṭhaur possession in the fifteenth century; Saṅgmatī of the *Saṅgītarāja,*[178] tentatively identified with Sāṅgāner near Jaipur (the Delhi Sultanate (Saiyyaids) may have claimed suzerainty over this part (north-eastern) of Rajasthan which was emerging as a domain of the Kacchawāhās); the Suvarṇagiri of the *Saṅgītarāja,*[179] the reference being to the fort of Jalor (Hassan Khan Pathan held Jalor in this period under the suzerainty of the Sultanate of Gujarat); Ajaymeru of the Rāṇakpur Praśasti,[180] referring to the fort of Ajmer, a Rāṭhaur possession; Sāraṅgapura of the Rāṇakpur Praśasti[181] or Khalji or Kuraṇgagiri of the *Saṅgītarāja,*[182] referring to the fort of Sāraṅgpur in Malwa, south-east of Jhalawar, Manḍovarapur of the Kumbhalgarh Praśasti,[183] referring to the Rāṭhaur fort of Manḍor near Jodhpur; Janakacala of the Kumbhalgarh Praśasti,[184] the reference being to the Khalji forts of Malwa; Mallanārāyaṇapur of the Rāṇakpur Praśasti,[185] referring to the fort of Mālarāṇa near Sawai Madhopur (likely to be in the possession of a local Rajput chief); Raṇastambha of the Kumbhalgarh Praśasti,[186] a reference to the fort of Raṇathambhor near Sawai Madhopur (being close to Mallanārāyaṇapur, Raṇastambha is likely to have been under the same Rajput power); Chatsu, referring to the fort of Chatsu near Jaipur (possibly a Kacchawāhā stronghold);[187] Khāṭu of the Rāṇakpur Praśasti,[188] referring to the fort of Khāṭu near Jaipur, a Rāṭhaur possession; Amardakagiri of the *Saṅgītarāja,*[189] a reference to the fort of Amradādrī or Amber, the political-seat of the Kacchawāhās.

Such massive campaigns undoubtedly reflect a diversion of resources from the localities of the above forts to the Guhila state in the fifteenth century. It is significant that the world of the Guhilas in the fifteenth century was dominated by the forts, indicating Guhila dependence on them for strategic and the economic reasons. The resources diverted from the neighbouring forts undoubtedly went into the making of massive fortresses and temple-complexes, particularly in the reign of Rāṇā Kumbha.

The Role of the Horse in the Military Apparatus of Mewar: Fifteenth-century sources from Mewar clearly point to the presence of horses and elephants in the royal army. The *Rājavallabhamaṇḍana* provides details of the constructions of horse and elephant stables separately in the campus of the forts.[190] The *Rāimalla Rāsa*, a bardic account of Mahārāṇā Rāimalla (Kumbha's son and successor) provides a long list of chiefs and their horses in the army of the *rāṇā* in the fight against Zaffar Khan, the Khalji governor of Malwa. The famous battle of Maṇḍalgarh against the Khaljis is also recorded by the Ekaliṅgajī Temple Dakṣiṇadvāra Praśasti.[191] Significantly, the *Rāimalla Rāsa* also refers to the control and distribution of horses on the eve of battle. It is stated that Mahārāṇā Rāimalla himself distributed horses (indicating royal control over the best horses of Arabic breed) to all the chiefs on the eve of the battle with the Khaljis.[192]

One of the bardic texts from Rajasthan, the *Bagḍāvat Devnārāyaṇa Mahāgāthā* narrates the tale of a Gurjara community from central Rajasthan claiming Cāhamāṇa lineage and tracing their history from Cāhamāṇa Vīsaldevrāo's reign (early thirteenth century) and throws significant light on the breeding of horses by the Bagḍāvats. It is significant that centres in Mewar such as Rupaheli, Badnaur, Bagor, Asind, etc., are repeatedly mentioned in this ballad.[193] The Arabic text, *Zafar-ul-Walih-Bi-Muzaffar-Walih*, narrates an interesting anecdote—merchants complained to Sultan Mahmud I of Gujarat regarding the seizure of their horses by the king of Abu (Mount Abu) in AD 1458-9.[194] The seizure of horses by a king testifies to the military importance of horses.[195]

In this chapter I have discussed the important changes in the administrative and the military apparatus of the Guhila state between the thirteenth and the fifteenth centuries. The changes essentially relate to the growing importance of various administrative offices and a significant change in administrative personnel. Unlike early medieval times, this period saw increasing royal control over the *maṇḍapikās*, and over commerce and taxation pointing to strongly the growth of state power by the thirteenth century through the incorporation of more and more locally influential social groups into the administrative apparatus. While Rajput chiefs had been important politically in the early medieval period, members of non-Rajput social groups such as the wealthy and the influential Jains and the Ṭāmṭarāḍa family of Nāgdā emerged as important administrative functionaries between the thirteenth and the fifteenth centuries. The change in the nature of the administrative personnel reminds us of Henri Stern's observations about the royal court of the Rajput where departments of royal administration were generally managed by high dignitaries of non-Rajput castes such as the brāhmaṇas, the osvāls and the kāyasthas.[196]

As the political structure changed in the fifteenth century, so did the Rajput components of the military apparatus. While the Paramāras, Hūṇas, Rāṣṭrakūṭas and Cāhamāṇas had been important social groups from the tenth to the twelfth centuries, the newly emerging Rajput chiefs such as the Hāḍās, Kherāḍās, Gauḍas, Tomars, Solaṁkīs, Sāṅkhlās, etc., made up the military leadership in the fifteenth century. The increasing Guhila hold over a chain of forts and fortresses beyond the Mewar hills and Chittaurgarh in this period in contrast to early medieval times points to an extended line of defence in the fifteenth century. Similarly, the Guhila state fortified old bastions or built new ones in the tribal areas of the Bhomat (Bhils) and the Merwara (Medas) in the fifteenth century to defend the extended core-areas and the northern frontiers respectively. The massive programme of construction of gateways and additional bastions at Kumbhalgarh and Chittaurgarh ensured the personal security of the royal family amidst court-intrigue and conspiracies, giving the two forts a political importance which gave them a status beyond mere military structures. To sum up, this study of the administrative and military apparatus of the state of Mewar between the thirteenth and the fifteenth centuries reveals that the state apparatus grew in strength by sharing, accommodating and delegating governmental power to different locally important social groups rather than by centralizing state-power.

NOTES

1. Chittaur Inscription of the Reign of Tejasiṁha, op. cit., p. 398, l. 1, *Śrī Tejasiṁhadevakalyaṇa Vijayī rājā Vijayamāna Pradhānarājā Rājputrakāṅgāputraparonārī Sāho.*
2. Chiravā Inscription, op. cit., v. 26. Besides the official sources of Mewar, contemporary literary texts such as the *Kharataragacchabṛhadgurvāvalī* mention the office of *pradhāna*. For instance, Rāja Pradhāna Jagaddeva Pratihāra led the armies of Bhīmadeva II (Caulukya) against Sapadalakṣa and Malwa, op. cit., p. 34.

3. *RTA*, p. 705. 'Chitor records familiarize us with two ministerial titles Mahāmātya and Pradhāna. How they differed is not exactly clear.'
4. Ibid.
5. Ibid.
6. G.C. Sharma, *Administrative System of the Rajputs,* Delhi, 1979, p. 15.
7. Ibid., p. 16.
8. *MK*, pp. 158-9.
9. Ibid., p. 159.
10. *Early Chauhan Dynasties*, p. 245. Meena Sogani and R.M. Khandelwal make a pertinent observation that perhaps best describes the post of *pradhāna* in the context of medieval Rajasthan: 'According to the administrative traditions of Rajputana, the pradhan was next to the ruler. He exercised a number of civil, financial, judicial and military powers. The vast powers of the pradhan carried with them enormous responsibilities of the office. A pradhan in order to successfully perform his duties was expected to be an accomplished courtier, besides having a thorough understanding of the various branches of administration', in *State Level Personnel Administration in India: A Case Study of Rajasthan*, Jaipur, 1987, p. 2.
11. *IA*, vol. IX, p. 35, ll. 65-8.
12. See, Chap. II, the section on Administrative Apparatus.
13. *Daśavaikālikādisūtrapatrikā*, in *Jaina Pustaka Praśasti Saṁgraha*, p. 116.
14. Ibid., *Śrāvaka Pratikramaṇasūtracūrṇī*, p. 126.
15. Ibid., p. 148.
16. Premlata Sharma, ed., *Kumbhapraṇita Saṅgītarāja*, Delhi, 1963, p. 23, '*rājāsa syādvivādī ṛpuriva vivadan mukhyamantrīva tasmin samvādī samvadan yonuvadati khalu tam sonuvādī svaroasmin*'.
17. Cf. C.D. Dalal, ed., *Lekhapaddhati*, Baroda, 1925, p. 2. *Lekhapaddhati*, a contemporary text from Gujarat, discusses the office of the *mahāmātya* and not that of the *pradhāna*.
18. *Jain Inscriptions*, p. 225.
19. A thirteenth-century Jain text, Tarunaprabhasūri's *Samyaktva tathā Śrāvana bār vrata* refers to the authority of *mantrī* over the royal-seal. Cited in *MK*, op. cit., p. 159. '*Mantrī nā āvoi taun māhārī sarvādhipatya mudrā le ā vi*'.
20. *Early Chauhan Dynasties*, p. 245; *Lekhapaddhati* also begins the list of the governmental departments—*karaṇas*—with *śrīkaraṇa* (income) and *vyāyagarana* (expenditure), op. cit., p. 1.
21. Upendra Nath Day, *Mewar under Mahārāṇā Kumbha*, Delhi, 1978, p. 130.
22. *MK*, pp. 159-60, 393, l. 18. Also see Sharda, *MK*, pp. 175-6.
23. Ibid.
24. Ibid., pp. 130-1.
25. Abu royal charter dated AD 1449, op. cit., pp. 175-6, l. 6, '*Gaḍapotyāru rāṇi kumbhakarṇī mahan dugar bhojā jogyam mayā udharī jiko jyātri āvi tihirū sarvamu*'.

26. *MK*, p. 393, ll. 6-13.
27. U.N. Day, op. cit., p. 131.
28. See Chap. III, the section on Socio-Political Linkages with non-Rajput Social Groups.
29. Chiravā Inscription, op. cit., v. 10, '*yam duṣtaśiṣṭaśik ṣanrakṣanadakṣatvā-tastalārakṣam | śrī māthanasiṁhanṛpatiścakāra nāgadrahadrange*'.
30. Ibid., v. 12.
31. Ibid., v. 22.
32. Ibid., v. 30.
33. *Lekhapaddhati* refers to the *talāras*, the *deśatalāras* and the *grāmatalāras*, translated as *kotwāls*, police superintendents and *foujdārs* respectively, op. cit., p. 8.
34. Ibid., pp. 8 and 101.
35. *Vir Vinod*, vol. I, p. 410.
36. Ibid., p. 410, ll. 1-2.
37. Cited in *MK*, p. 163.
38. Abu royal charter, op. cit., pp. 175-6, ll. 13-14.
39. Śṛṅgār Cāvarī, op. cit., p. 410, ll. 2-3.
40. Ibid.; also see *Early Chauhan Dynasties*, p. 245. *Kaṇhadadeprabandha* lists *koṭhārī* (*koṣṭhagārika*) instead of *bhāṇḍārī*, in the sense of the chief treasurer.
41. *RTA*, p. 705. 'Kothari was an officer with duties similar to those of bhāṇḍāgārika or bhāṇḍārī, the only distinction between the two perhaps being that they stored two different sorts of commodities'; ibid., fn. 1, '*bhāṇ dām koṭhārī jeu, purāi varau rālaguṇi teu*'.
42. G.C. Sharma, op. cit., p. 20. Also see *URI*, vol. II, p. 645.
43. *MK*, p. 163.
44. Ibid., p. 370, l. 10.
45. Abu royal charter, op. cit., pp. 175-6, l. 12.
46. Chittaurgarh Inscription dated AD 1274, op. cit., p. 396, last verse, '*Sajjaneva samutkīrṇa praśasti śilpīnāmuna*'.
47. Achaleśvara Inscription, op. cit., v. 62, '*utkīrṇa Karmasiṁhana sūtra-dhāreṇa*'.
48. Mandlika Tal Inscription from Jodhpur dated AD 956, *EI*, vol. XXXIV, pp. 77ff.
49. An inscription of the period of the Gurjara-Pratihāras from Doab, Uttar Pradesh, of the tenth century, *EI*, vol. XIX, pp. 52-4.
50. Chittaurgarh Stone Inscription of Rāṇā Mokāl, op. cit., v. 4. According to Shyamaldas's text, he was the son of Vidyādhara, *Vir Vinod*, vol. I, Appendix: Lekhasaṁgraha.
51. Chittaurgarh Stone Inscription of Mokala, ibid., v. 4 of the last 5 verses, '*vī [jalasya] sutah śilpī manākhyaḥ sūtradhārakaḥ* ||'.
52. Ibid. '*Manākhyah sūtradhārakah | tasyātmajana vīsena praśastimut-kṛtā || 4 || rucirakṣaramutkīrṇa praśastiriya mujvala, lilekha vīsalah śilpī samadhīśaprasādattah || 5 ||*'.

53. Ibid., v. 29, '*utkīrṇasi* [*khi*] *lasūtradhāragurunā seyam praśasti śubha likhyate* [*na*] *phanābhidhena* [*su*] *dhiya hāḍātmajenamuna* [*l**]*sāhitya-dikaś*[*ilpī*] *śāstravilāsatapa thoḍina sādhuna śrī nārāyaṇa sevakena nṛpateh śrī mokalasyajnāya* ||'.
54. D.R. Bhandarkar, List no. 813 (Appendix to *EI*, vols. XIX-XXIII). Also see PRAS, WC, 1903-4, p. 56.
55. Ibid., List no. 802, G.H. Ojha, *Rājasthān kā Itihāsa*, vol. II, pp. 622-6, n. 5.
56. Ibid., List no. 806.
57. Ibid., List no. 820, Ojha, *Rājasthān kā Itihāsa*, vol. II, p. 623, fn.1.
58. Kīrtistambha Inscription, PRAS, WC, op. cit., p. 56.
59. See the section on Military Apparatus.
60. *Prāsādamaṇḍana and Rājavallabhamaṇḍanam*, Calcutta Sanskrit Series no. 32, Calcutta, 1948, Chap. 9, pp. 97-8, vv. 24-9.
61. Ibid., Chap. 14, p. 127, v. 43, '*śrī medapāṭe mopakumbhakarnastād amghpirājīvaparagasevī sa maṇḍanakhyobhuvī su tradhāroste noddhṛto bhūpati vallabhoayam*'.
62. Ramābāī's Zawar Stone Inscription dated AD 1490, op. cit., p. 225, ll. 39-40, '*kṣetrakasūtradhārasya putro maṇḍana ātmavan* || *sūtradhāra maṇḍanasuta isara e kāmāthanuviracitam devīdāsa pratikāritā* ||'.
63. Dasharath Sharma opines that *bhoga*, a technical word, went almost invariably with the *bhāga*. See *RTA*, p. 325.
64. Rājavallabhamaṇḍana, op. cit., pp. 100-3, vv. 2, 3, 7 and 18, '*vyāsena dairghye-guṇite yadaikyam tat konākṣetrasya phalam pradiṣtam* | *pinde-tadaikyam punareva tadyam khatasya bhitteścayanādisilhih* || *kare karāghne ca karāpramānam karaṁgulinām guṇāmeva sankhyā* | *syādaṁgulrirangulataditaiśca labdham phalam jainvibhajitena* || *vṛttakṣetre paridhiguṇitavyāspadah phalam tat kṣunnam vedairupari paritāh kandaksyaiva jalam* | *golasyaivam tadapi ca phalam pṛṣṭhajam vyāsanighnamsaḍabhirbhaktam bhavati niyatam golagarbhe ghanākhyam ṣaṣṭo vibhāgopi* [*ca?*] *dairghyaksya tasaiva ṣaḍbhāgayuto vidheyah* | *bahupramāṇam kathitamkalāstre kṣetre tathānyāni vicārya kuryāt* ||'.
65. See for instance, charters to the brāhmaṇas, in Chap. V. Also see Mala Copper Plates of Guhila Vīrasiṁhadeva dated AD 1287, op. cit. It records the specific boundaries both of the plot as well as of the house donated to a brāhmaṇa in village Mala. ll.10-12 '*mālāgrāme bhūmīhal sārda-vahalaikasya bhūmih* | *gṛham* | *agrevāṭaka pache vāḍakakhala sahitametata śāsanodakapūrvam dharmeṇa sampradattam*'.
66. *MK*, p. 161.
67. Ibid.
68. Dasharath Sharma, *Lectures on Rajput History and Culture*, Delhi, 1970, p. 117.
69. Dasharath Sharma finds it difficult to arrive at the actual figures of land tax in the Pratihāra Empire. See *RTA*, p. 324.

70. Sāraṇeśvara Inscription, op. cit., p. 162, v. 9, '*drammamekam karī daddyatturago rūpa kadvayam drammārdhaviṁśakam śṛṅgī lāṭahaṭṭe tulāḍhakau*'.
71. *MK*, p. 170.
72. Ibid.
73. Kadia Village Inscription, Sharda, *MK*, op. cit., pp. 173-4, no. 5; *ARRM*, 1932, p. 4, no. 6; *MK*, op. cit., p. 389, v. 26, '*tasmai dadau hāṭaka paṭṭavāsah svestarthadeharānvita gadalekam | śrīvājāvī gramamāpārasimāṁsamkalpe tam rājakaraiḥ praṇitam*'.
74. Ekaliṅgajī Temple Dakṣiṇadvāra Praśasti, op. cit., p. 424, the concluding part is in Mewari dialect, '*deva brāhmaṇa bhāṭa nājkā varṣasana grāma pūrvajane apanidedhi tina samasta rājakara mukarar kidhā*'.
75. Hathal Copper Plate Inscription of the Reign of Paramāra Dharavarsha, dated AD 1180, *CII*, vol. VII, pt. 2, pp. 245-7, ll. 10-12.
76. *Annals*, vol. I, p. 118.
77. Chittaurgarh Inscription of AD 1278, op. cit., p. 397.
78. Ibid., p. 397, ll. 9-12. Also see Chap. III: the section on the Guhilas and the Jains.
79. *MK*, p. 174.
80. *RTA*, p. 353.
81. *The Making of Early Medieval India*, p. 94.
82. To quote B.D. Chattopadhyaya from *The Making of Early Medieval India*, p. 116:

    'It would appear from the social composition of those who regulated mārgādāya and maṇḍapikādāya that some form of commercial revenue farming was gradually coming into existence. This was true not only of early medieval Rajasthan but of other regions as well. The autonomous character of such bodies is suggested by the phenomenon that local merchant associations or other corporate bodies could impose levies on local communities and on the items of exchange. To some extent this may have been so, but the phenomenon surely needs a more satisfactory explanation, and in a political situation where 'bureaucracy' lacked a distinctly identifiable character, one way of looking at it would be to consider it a mechanism of control over the acquisition of cash and kind and over their redistribution, assuring at the same time the concerned political powers of a regular return in the form of a share. Of course, this would not apply to ad hoc levies intended as contributions to religious institutions, but then terms such as mārgādāya or maṇḍapikās cannot be conceived in terms of ad hoc levies alone.'
83. Sharda, *MK*, p. 170. The text of the inscription is also published in Ācārya Vijayadharmasūri's booklet, *Devakulapāṭak*. However, Sharda does not identify the tax on the item or the institution called *mānāheḍavāṭa*.
84. Abu royal charter, op. cit., pp. 175-6, ll. 2-9, '*mahārāṇā śrī kumbhakaraṇ vijayrājye śrī arbudacale delvārā grāme vimal vasahī śrī ādināth, tejavasahī*

śrī neminātha tathā bīje śrāvya (va) ke dehāre dāna muṇḍika valamī rāṣavalī. . . jyātri āvi. . . iko koi māṅgva nā lahi' (Mewari) dialect). The expression '*dānavolāpānādi viṣaye*' in *Lekhapaddhati* has been translated as a tax collected by officer-in-charge who led *volāpaka* men accompanying merchants in their journeys for the safety of their goods. See *Lekhapaddhati*, p. 8; also see glossary.

85. Ibid., '*jiko jyātrī āvi tihirū sarvāmu kābu jyātrā samāndhi ācandrāk lāgī pāyak iko koi māṅgvā nā lahi*' (Mewari dialect).
86. Delwara Inscription of AD 1434, op. cit., ll. 15-16, '*evam karai ṭaṅkā 14 śrī dharmacintāmaṇipūjā nimitta sā sāraṅgī samastasadhi lāgukidhu*' (Mewari dialect).
87. Sāraṇeśvara Temple Inscription dated to AD 953, op. cit., vv. 12-18.
88. See Chap. III, the section on The Guhilas and the Jains.
89. Devakulapāṭaka Temple Inscription dated to AD 1434, op. cit., p. 227, ll. 17-18, '*ee grāsu jiko lopoi tehārhim rāṇāśrī hammīra rāṇā śrīṣeta rāṇā śrīlāṣa ra. mokal rāṇā śrī kumbharnāṇī ana chāi*' (Mewari dialect).
90. *Shodh Patrika*, vol. V, pt. 3, op. cit., p. 53, ll. 7-10.
91. *Aspects of Rural Settlements and Rural Society*, p. 77. The author makes this observation in the context of early medieval villages in south-eastern Marwar (Rajasthan).
92. See the following section on the Administration and the Language.
93. Mala Copper Plates, op. cit., p. 196, ll. 38-9, '*pañcaśrī vāvanaśabdena śāsanamidam pañcavīkamenā likhitam*'.
94. Ibid., p. 196, l. 39.
95. Ibid., p. 196.
96. Ibid., p. 196, fn. 5.
97. See for instance, Kumbha's Abu Inscription dated to AD 1449 and Ekaliṅgajī Temple Dakṣiṇdvāra Praśasti, op. cit., the last paragraph describing the royal gifts is in Mewari.
98. Chiravā Inscription, op. cit., vv. 30 and 40.
99. Jain Inscription from Chittaur dated AD 1267, op. cit., p. 396, l. 1.
100. Achaleśvara Inscription, op. cit., v. 46.
101. Chiravā Inscription, op. cit., v. 26.
102. Ibid., vv. 27-8.
103. *Jain Pustaka Praśasti Saṁgraha,* p. 126.
104. Chiravā Inscription, op. cit., vv. 15-16.
105. Ibid.
106. Ibid.
107. Ibid., v. 19.
108. Ibid.
109. Achaleśvara Inscription, op. cit., v. 42.
110. Ibid., v. 49.
111. Third slab, op. cit., vv. 160, 162, '*rāval samarasiṁhavarṇanam* || *durge*

śrīcitrakūṭe, [vila]sati [nṛ]patau sarvasāmanta cūḍāratnapraddy otitāmcakravabhaditi matiṭṭ akpatham samprayāti'.

112. Achaleśvara Inscription, op. cit., vv. 36-7, '*Sāmantasiṁhanāma kāmadhikasarva-sundaraśarīrah bhūpālojani tasmādaprtaśāmanta-sarvasvah || khummāṇsantativiyogavilaksalakṣmīm senāmdṛṣṭavirahām guhilānvayasya || rājavantīm vasumatīmkarotkumārasiṁhastato ripugana napahṛtya bhūyah'.*
113. Śṛṅgiṛṣi Inscription, op. cit., v. 4.
114. Kumbhalgarh fourth slab, op. cit., v. 212.
115. *Annals*, vol. I, p. 221.
116. Chittaurgarh Inscription of Mokal, op. cit., v. 51; Śṛṅgiṛṣi Inscription of Mokal, op. cit., v. 14.
117. Chittaurgarh Inscription, ibid., v. 69.
118. *Vir Vinod*, vol. I, p. 334. Also see *Annals*, vol. I, p. 289.
119. *Annals*, vol. I, ibid., p. 290.
120. Kumbhalgarh Praśasti, fourth Slab, op. cit., vv. 263-4.
121. Ibid., v. 266.
122. Ibid., v. 253; Ekaliṅgajī Temple Dakṣiṇadvāra Praśasti, op. cit., v. 43.
123. Ibid., v. 253.
124. Kumbhalgarh Praśasti, op. cit., v. 254.
125. Ibid., v. 258.
126. Ibid., v. 259.
127. Op. cit., l. 12.
128. Kumbhalgarh Praśasti, fourth slab, op. cit., v. 264.
129. Ibid.
130. Ibid.
131. Ibid., vv. 264-5.
132. See Chap. III, the section on Linkages with the Hāḍā chiefs and the Solaṁkīs of Maṇḍalgarh.
133. Kīrtistambha Inscription, op. cit., vv. 8-9.
134. *Annals*, vol. I, p. 289.
135. Tod, *Travels in Western India*, p. 94.
136. Kīrtistambha Inscription, op. cit., vv. 12-13.
137. Sharda, *MK*, p. 123.
138. See, Chap. III, the section on Kumbha and the Devḍā Cāhamāṇas of Sirohi.
139. Kumbhalgarh Praśasti, fourth slab, op. cit., v. 212, '*medānārādbhalla-sādulla sattadebharīdhīradhvānavidh vastadhairyān kāram, kāram yo grahidurgatija dagdhārāti vardhanākhyam girindram*'.
140. Kumbhalgarh Praśasti, fourth slab, op. cit., v. 254.
141. Ekaliṅgajī Temple Dakṣiṇadvāra Praśaṣti, op. cit., Mewari part, ll. 16 and 19, '*śrī kumbhakarṇarā putra gauḍarājanya vaṁśabharaṇa rānī śrī puvāḍare garbharatna aśva, kalpanīkalpadrum mahārāya śrī rāimalla rājye*'.
142. *Baḍvādevīdān Khyāt*, p. 5.

143. Cited in *Mahārāṇā Sāṅgā*, p. 80.
144. *Saṅgītarāja*, Appendix IV, p. 680, sub-page: ṇa.
145. Kīrtistambha Inscription, op. cit., vv. 126-46.
146. Sharda, *MK*, p. 128.
147. Prabhakar V. Begde, *Forts and Palaces of India*, Delhi, 1982, p. 107.
148. Ibid.
149. Ibid., pp. 107-8.
150. Ibid., p. 108.
151. *Vir Vinod*, vol. I, pp. 315 and 334.
152. James Tod writes, 'It would be vain to attempt describing the intricacies of approach to this far-famed abode . . . [a] massive wall, with numerous towns and pierced battlements . . . the eye ranges over the sandy deserts and the chaotic mass of mountains which are on all sides, covered with the cactus, which luxuriates amidst the rocks of the Aravalli'. See *Annals*, vol. I, p. 670.
153. Sharda, *MK*, pp. 125 and 127.
154. *Saṅgītarāja*, p. 680, sub-page: ṇa.
155. Ibid.
156. *Annals*, vol. I, p. 289.
157. *Amarākāvyam*, op. cit., p. 141, vv. 2 and 4, *rājyam cakre kṣetrasiṁho raṇakarmaṇi karmathaḥ | nirmame nirmalayaśo sarvā sarvasahā vaśe. rudhvā jājpuram sanyairjaghān sa tadiśvaram | lālākhyam kṣetrasiṁhendraḥ kherāḍ-kulagulāhat ||*
158. *Annals*, vol. I, p. 289.
159. *Saṅgītarāja*, p. 680, sub-page: ṇa.
160. B.D. Mishra, *The Forts and Fortresses of Gwalior and its Hinterland*, Delhi, 1993, pp. 73-4.
161. Elliot and Dowson, vol. III, op. cit., p. 189.
162. Mishra, op. cit., p. 11. Prabhakar V. Begde also observes, 'The fort is defended by a formidable crenellated curtain wall. The fort was approached from three sides, north, east and west' along difficult paths with gates at intervals over the ascent, op. cit., p. 104.
163. *Saṅgītarāja*, op. cit., p. 680, sub-page: ṇa.
164. G.H.R. Tillotson, *Rajput Palaces: The Development of an Architectural Style, 1450-1750*, London, 1987, p. 41.
165. Ibid.
166. Kīrtistambha Inscription, op. cit., vv. 26, 184 and 187.
167. Ibid., vv. 184 and 187.
168. Sharda, *MK*, op. cit., p. 138.
169. Kīrtistambha Inscription, op. cit., vv. 34-5.
170. Tillotson, op. cit., p. 41.
171. Ibid., pp. 40-1.
172. Ibid., p. 44.

173. *Saṅgītarāja*, p. 680, sub-page: ṇa.
174. Kīrtistambha Inscription, op. cit., vv. 20-2.
175. Ibid., p. 680, sub-page: ṇa.
176. Kumbhalgarh Praśasti, op. cit., v. 264.
177. *Saṅgītarāja*, p. 680, sub-page: ṇa.
178. Ibid., p. 680, sub-page: ṇa.
179. Ibid.
180. Rāṇakpur Praśasti, op. cit., p. 410, l. 12.
181. Ibid.
182. *Saṅgītarāja*, p. 680, sub-page: ṇa.
183. Kumbhalgarh Praśasti, op. cit., v. 249.
184. Ibid., v. 256.
185. Rāṇakpur Praśasti, op. cit., p. 410, l. 12.
186. Kumbhalgarh Praśasti, op. cit., v. 261.
187. Rāṇakpur Praśasti, op. cit., p. 410, l. 13.
188. Ibid.
189. *Saṅgītarāja*, p. 680, sub-page: ṇa.
190. Rājavallabhmaṇḍana, op. cit., pp. 97-8, for instance see vv. 24-9, '*turaṅga mānām gṛhavāmbhāge śālā catuhṣaṣṭikara vidheyā śatārdat madhyamikā ca dairgheya konīyasī tairdaśabhirvihīna || tejohānimanī hayā vidadhate pūrvāparāsyam nṛnām te yāmyottarotomukhā hi satatam kīrttiyarśo dhānyakam rāgābdhyaṁgula-kaistu vājīvijayosītya tathā bhairavah saptadhā || iti aśvaśālā || siṁhadvāram pūrvamānena kāryam svātam madhye | taḍhakau rakṣaṇārthamtullau vāpi sārdhāi || bhāge dakṣiṇavamake ca karīnām śālā haredvāritah nagainirgadito mando nandaih karairucchritah || iti gajaśālā*'.
191. Ekaliṅgajī Temple Dakṣiṇadvāra Praśasti, op. cit., vv. 77-8.
192. *Vir Vinod*, vol. I, pp. 339-41.
193. Usha Kasturia, *Rājasthānī Virāgāthatmak Pavāḍe: Samrachana Evam*, Delhi, 1989, pp. 45-6; Also see, Lakshmikumari Chundawat, ed., *Bagḍāvat Devanārāyaṇa Mahāgāthā*, Jaipur, 1993.
194. M.F. Lokhandwala, ed., *Zafar-ul-Walih-Bi-Muzaffar-Walih of Abdullah Muhammad Al-Ulughkhani Hajji*, tr. Al-Makki Al-Asafi Addbir, Gaekwad Oriental Series, no. 152, Baroda, 1970, p. 30.
195. Norman P. Ziegler in his study of the Rāṭhaur state discusses linkages between the Rāṭhaur land grants to the different Rajput chiefs and the maintenance required for the horses. These *paṭṭa* grants were being extensively used in the time of Rāo Gaṅgo to enforce the obligations of the service to the state and to recruit the new Rajputs into the military services. See his 'Evolution of the Rathor State of Marvar: Horses, Structural Change and Warfare', in Karine Schomer et al., eds., *The Idea of Rajasthan: Explorations in Regional Identity*, vol. II, op. cit., p. 199.
196. Stern, op. cit., p. 67.

CHAPTER V

Strategies of Legitimization of the Guhila State: The Religious Dimension

Any study of state formation will remain incomplete without an enquiry into the aspect of legitimization of state power. Early medieval states derived validation of authority from diverse sources. At the core of the legitimization was the relationship between a sacred authority and a temporal power, which for early Indian monarchical organization continued to be defined by the relationship between the brāhmaṇa and kṣatriya. In the early medieval period the temple had emerged as the nucleus of a sacred space and various sects, with their institutional locii in monasteries and temples, developed close links with royalty. Royal power drew upon these for ideological and symbolic support in diverse ways. I begin here with a discussion of the pattern of the land-grants made to brāhmaṇas, as well as brāhmaṇa presence in the royal court followed by an analysis of the origin myths of the Guhilas, and finally, a survey of the religious situation in early medieval Mewar, with particular emphasis on the royal patronage of the cult centre of Ekaliṅga and the Pāśupata sect associated with it. I will highlight the process through which the Guhila monarchy affiliated itself to the central cult of Ekaliṅga in Mewar and drew legitimacy from it and how the protagonists of Ekaliṅga successfully integrated the various local religious traditions and local *tīrthas* to shape the traditions of Mewar. However, before I begin with my discussion of the strategies of legitimization in Mewar, I shall look at the historiography about the ideological apparatus of legitimization.

I

General Historiographical Survey of Ideological Legitimization of the State

Recent literature on legitimization provides some excellent studies on the interdependence of the sacred and the temporal. While Sibesh Bhattacharya discusses the power of the brāhmaṇas *vis-à-vis* the kṣatriyas with the rise of *mahājanapadas* leading to a growth in the political power of royal priests in validating the growing state power,[1] Louis Dumont and J.C. Heesterman highlight the dependence of the priest on the king for subsistence so that the brāhmaṇa trades his transcendant authority to legitimize temporal power in return for material benefit.[2] In a more specific study, Romila Thapar, while discussing social mobility amongst elite groups in early India, remarks that the rise of local ruling families to political power was possibly faster in the post-Gupta period when memories of their low caste origins could be expunged.[3] Hence, genealogists grew in status with the multiplication of small regional kingdoms during the period. Consequently, the increasing political importance of brāhmaṇas can be traced to their increasing involvement with the court.[4] 'By the medieval period the office of purohita is not only frequently hereditary but has also been politicized.'[5] B.D. Chattopadhyaya, in his analysis of the origin of the Rajputs, highlights the significance of the changes in the genealogical claims of leading Rajput families.[6] The fabrication of genealogies clearly reflects upward mobility.

If land-grants to brāhmaṇas ensured the territorial spread of state-society,[7] the *bhakti* ideology, by integrating local cults and *tīrthas* into the expansive Purāṇic fold, made the temple the institutional focus that effectively linked temporal power with the sacred domain in the early medieval period. Such an alliance could be achieved through two possible mechanisms. The king could seek to appropriate the sacred domain through a process of identification with the divinity enshrined in the temple (a practice initiated by the Pallavas and augmented by the Colas, similar to the Devarāja cult of South-East Asia). The second way was to surrender temporal power to the divinity (like the dedication of the kingdom of Orissa to the cult of Jagannātha by the imperial Gaṅgas).[8]

Hermann Kulke has provided a detailed framework to analyse royal patronage of tribal deities in the early stages of state formation[9] and the patronage of a supra-local cult centre in the later stages of state formation in Orissa.[10] Modes of legitimization through cult centres underwent change through different stages of state formation. Orissa in the early medieval period witnessed royal patronage of local or regional cults, this was moulded by the deep influence of *bhakti* movements which had strong local and regional roots, becoming the genuinely popular religion. Religious legitimization of the state has ranged from princely patronage of tribal deities by upcoming monarch to the construction of imperial temples by the rulers of regional kingdoms. During the medieval period, royal religious policy shifted its emphasis to patronage of places of pilgrimage, their cults and of sectarian leaders.[11] The 'imperial' temples popularized mythical accounts of founder-kings of the 'hoary past' and gave legendary accounts of former imperial royal donors as well as descriptions of more recent historical local kings.[12] The political purpose served by such mechanisms was the legitimization of the state. For instance, comparison between Hindu temple cults and the cults of autochthonous local deities certainly induced people to draw comparisons between the status of their earlier tribal chiefs and that of the new 'Hindu' *rājā.*

However, tribal groups were not the only components of the political structure of early medieval states. There were big and small *sāmantas* controlling nuclear and peripheral areas beyond the core. The transition from a sub-regional to a regional state meant integration of these areas and incorporation of local *sāmantas* into the state polity. In other words, having surveyed the process of horizontal legitimization, we enter into the arena of vertical legitimization as the state attains the status of a regional power. Kulke observes that the Hindu *rājās* achieved integration of 'dangerous feudal forces' by three ritual means. Rulers patronized *tīrthas* of regional and supra-regional importance within their respective states. Secondly, brāhmaṇas were systematically settled throughout the territorial expanse. Thirdly, construction of grand new temples was undertaken. Kulke points out that the lack of scholarly attention to these great temples is surprising, for they were built in various regional states precisely in the period of the 'heyday of political feudalism'.[13] Kulke has shown that the Gaṅga state in Orissa, ably combined both vertical and horizontal legitimation through their patronage of the sub-regional autochthonous Jagannātha cult. From the early thirteenth century onwards, Jagannātha had come to acquire the status of the 'king of the Orissan Empire' (Oḍisa-*rājya-rājā*)[14] under whose overlordship (*sāmrājya*) the Gajapati king ruled as his deputy (*rāvutā*) and son (*putra*).[15]

An excellent survey of the linkage between the monarchy and cult centres in the state of tribal Bastar was made by the anthropologist Surajit Sinha. He points out that many of the local chiefs including Rāj Gonds of Bhopal-patnam are perhaps of earlier origin than the Kākatīya state of Bastar.[16] Wilfred Grigson feels that 'before Annamdeo's arrival there was a nominal suzerainty of Warangal over most of Bastar, the authority resting with local chiefs, or in the hands of old tribal organization that was a marked feature of the medieval kings of the eastern Central

Provinces and some of the Chotanagpur and the Orissa estates'.[17] In this context the cult of the royal goddess Danteśvarī or Maṇikeśvarī (Māoli) became central to the legitimation process of state formation in tribal Bastar.[18]

States and cult centres in south India have received considerable attention. Research includes studies of religious cults and institutions of the Deccan, of temple cities in Tamilnadu in the Cola period, of Kālāmukha and Kāpālika monasteries in Karnataka in the Cālukya period, and of the Sthalapurāṇa *Cidambaramāhātmyam* among others. R.N. Nandi's approach towards the study of cults and religious institutions in Deccan works under the broad rubric of the 'feudal' state in early medieval period. The kings, governors and their officials with their vast resources, patronized local temples and their sects or, in some cases, some particular sect, such as the Kālāmukhas of Karnataka, Tamilnadu, and Andhra Pradesh in order to legitimize increasing extractions in cash, kind and labour.[19] In a work of a similar genre but highlighting the validation of monarchical power, Keshavan Veluthat cites the case of the Pallavas, who chose to identify themselves with divine or Purāṇic figures, with the consecration of kings in the temples.[20] David N. Lorenzen in his detailed study of the Śaivite Kālāmukhas and Kāpālikas of early medieval Deccan for the first time highlights the socio-religious importance and popularity of these sects, that eventually attracted royal patronage.[21]

R. Champakalakshmi observes changing royal patronage to the temple cities of the medieval south. The city of Kuḍāmukku witnessed a general decline of Cola temples, but new centres of religious importance emerged in the post-Cola Vijayanagara-Nayaka periods. A distinct shift is noted in royal patronage from Śaiva to Vaiṣṇava religious institutions.[22] For instance, new temples of Rāmasvāmī and Cakrapāṇi dotted the landscape of Kuḍāmukku.[23] Similar royal patronage to the Śaṅkarācārya *maṭha* and the Vīra Śaiva *maṭha* in the city of Kumbhakonam is recorded from the Vijayanagara period onwards.[24] Champakalakshmi further contributes towards the study of state and cult in her review-essay of Burton Stein's *Peasant State and Society* in which she points out the utilization of the cult of Śivaliṅga by the early Colas in legitimizing their power.[25]

Hermann Kulke in his recent study of *Cidambaramāhātmyam*, analyses the political significance of the legend of Hiraṇyavarman and the career of the Cola King Kulottunga I. Kulke observes that we meet with a historical figure in Hiraṇyavarman whose legendary story alludes to a historical situation.[26] Hence, analysis of *māhātmyams* (*Sthala Purāṇas*) such as *Ekaliṅgamāhātmya* of Mewar becomes essential for the study of process of legitimization of royal authority.

Finally, the linkage between state and cult was not the domain of Purāṇic sects alone but also permeated the history of 'heterodox' sects. This is especially true of Jainism in early Karnataka. R.B.P. Singh's detailed research on the growth of Jain monasticism in early medieval Karnataka refers to a number of contemporary records which point to close links between Jaina *ācāryas* and the members of the ruling elite in Karnataka.[27] The Kadambas, Gaṅgas, western Cālukyas, Rāṣṭrakūṭas, later western Cālukyas, and Hoysalas championed the cause of Jainism in Karnataka during the fifth to twelfth centuries.

II

The Role of Brāhmaṇas

In its earlier stages the Guhila state's power seems to have been legitimized by brāhmaṇas. Seventh-century Guhila land grant charters to brāhmaṇas, particularly to those migrating from Ujjain, are in line with the dominant pattern of legitimation of the local states. This period did not see royal patronage of any particular religious sect. Guhila King Bhetti turned the village of Ubbaraka into an *agrahāra* grant in favour of Brāhmaṇa Bhaṭṭināga of Candratrāya *gotra* and Vājasaneya *cāraṇa* for the religious merit of Mahārāja Bappādatti (the king's father) in AD 679-80.[28] King Bābhaṭa granted two plots in the village of Mitrāpallikā in Maṇḍalacchaka to five brāhmaṇa brothers, viz., Gopāditya, Gopādya, Debhāṭa, Debhāṭa Dhondhā and Gopasvāmin, sons of Gopā of Kurāgiri in AD 688-9.[29] The fact that three out of five Kiṣkindhā Guhila records were royal land grant charters to brāhmaṇas in the seventh century itself is an indicator of the political role of the migrating brāhmaṇas. These land grants were made for the performance of such *yajñas* as *balī*, *cārū*, *sattra*, *vaiśvadeva*, *agnihotra*, etc., by the donee.[30] The grants consisted of a village (the name of which is lost) in Purāpaṭṭa *viṣaya*.[31]

The brāhmaṇas had already appeared at the royal court by the tenth century. They furnished the Guhila kings with a long genealogy, introduced brāhmaṇa status and brought in the theme of Guhila origin from Ānandapura (Gujarat) for the first time.[32] The motif of Anandapur might allude to the presence of the Nāgar brāhmaṇas (originating from Ānandapura) in the Guhila court of the tenth century.

If the Pāśupatas legitimized increasing Guhila power in the emerging Guhila state of Mewar, in the eleventh century, brāhmaṇas validated

Guhila power in areas of territorial expansion. Unālācārya (son of Ācārya Sāhīya and belonging to the Vatsa *gotra* and Mādhyandina *cāraṇa*) from Nāgahṛda was settled in the village of Pali (modern town of Pali in Godwar) with substantial land granted by King Vijayasiṁha.[33] This instance points to legitimization by sending brāhmaṇas from the core-area of the state to the new areas that had come under the state's control.

Although the Ekaliṅga cult was an important source of legitimization in the twelfth century, the royal family continued making land grants to brāhmaṇas in the core-area. A land grant charter of King Padmasiṁha, dating to AD 1194, records the grant of land in the domain (estate) of Cāhamāna Rāo Mokaja in Kadmal village to a Brāhmaṇa Śivaguṇa, son of Ārādhara, as a source of livelihood.[34] According to the record the piece of land was located in the midst of an *araghaṭṭa* named Gājana.[35] The village of Kadmal is situated 40 km north-west of Udaipur. It is significant to note that the grant was made in a domain predominated by Cāhamāna chiefs. Royal links with the same brāhmaṇa family were further strengthened as it continued to receive royal land grants in the same locality. The Kadmal Copper Plate Inscription of Tejasiṁha, dated AD 1259 records land grant to Trivikrama, Brāhmaṇa Śivaguṇa's son. The land was located in the domain of Cāhamāna Rāo Cānd in Kadmal village.[36] The record also states that the land was also situated in the midst of an *araghaṭṭa* called Gājan and that it was granted as *vṛtti* (livelihood).[37] The fact that this area of Cāhamāna dominance was well integrated with the state by this period is evident from the fact that the Guhila kings did not have to seek permission from Cāhamāna chiefs to make such royal land grants. This shows the growing power of the Guhila state in successive stages of state formation. More importantly, one notes the role played by brāhmaṇa donees in legitimizing the Guhila state especially in localities dominated by the non-Guhila Rajput chiefs.

Another way in which brāhmaṇas contributed to the process of legitimization of the state was by composing Guhila Praśastis and providing legitimizing motifs. For instance, in the reign of Samarasiṁha, the Chittaurgarh Palace Inscription, dated AD 1278 (recording royal grants to Bhartṛpurīyagaccha and the building of Śyām Pārśvanāth Vasahī by the queen-mother Jayatalladevī) was composed by a number of brāhmaṇas. Two families were involved in this task and they give their genealogies in this record. It was composed by Brāhmaṇa Sāḍhala of Goḍa *gotra* and Divākara lineage,[38] and by two brāhmaṇa brothers, Khīmaṭa and Bhīma, the sons of Bhaṭṭasāḍa and the grandsons of Vipra Delhana.[39]

The famous Chittaurgarh Praśasti, dated AD 1274, and the Achaleśvara

Praśasti dated AD 1285 introduce the legends of Bappā Hārītarāśi-Ekaliṅga in Mewar, legitimizing Guhila power at Citrakūṭa and in the whole of Mewar were composed by Vedaśarmā of Nāgarjñāti (Nāgar *gotra*).[40] Since both the Chittaurgarh and Achaleśvara Praśastis stand apart as the two most outstanding royal charters of the Guhilas in the thirteenth century, Nāgar brāhmaṇas too seem to have received royal patronage in the second half of the thirteenth century. If it were the Pāśupata *ācāryas* who popularized the legitimizing motifs of Bāppā-Hārītarāśi-Ekaliṅga, it was Nāgar Brāhmaṇa Vedaśarmā who officially propagated this motif. Since Vedaśarmā describes himself as a favourite of Śrī Samādhīśa (the cult of Śiva in a royal temple in Chittaurgarh fort),[41] he seems to have been a local resident of Chittaurgarh, and not a migrant. The Daśapura brāhmaṇas seem to have dominated the Guhila court in the fifteenth century. The Chittaurgarh Stone Inscription dating to AD 1428 can be considered as one of the earliest royal *praśastis* of the *rāṇās*. It was composed by Ekanātha, son of Bhaṭṭa Viṣṇu, of the Daśapur clan.[42] Daśapura is the ancient Mandasaur (in Malwa), close to the Chittaurgarh region. The Śṛṅgirṣi Inscription of Mokal was composed by one Yogīśvara who bore the epithets *vāṇīvilāsa* and *kavirāja*.[43] Clearly he enjoyed a status and position of esteem at the court of Mokal.

These two epigraphic records of Mokal's reign throw light on the groups of local brāhmaṇas in Mewar. The Chittaurgarh Inscription which records the construction (repairs and embellishments?) of the temple of Samādhīśvara at Citrakūṭa also registers the royal grant of the whole village of Dhanapura for the maintenance of the temple.[44] The grant of village Dhanapura for the upkeep of the royal temple of god Samādhīśvara in effect benefited the priests of the temple. And since Samādhīśvara did not exactly qualify as a Pāśupata *tīrtha*, the non-Pāśupata brāhmaṇa priests must have presided there.

The mention of Rāṇā Mokal's personal preceptor, Trilocana, in the Śṛṅgirṣi Inscription is significant. His permission was sought by Mokal to consecrate the reservoir built for the spiritual merit of his late Bāghelā Queen Gaurāmbikā.[45] Guru Trilocana is likely to have been connected with the Samādhīśvara temple. The king was probably inspired by his preceptor to provide funds for the renovation of the temple. Mokal is described as a devotee of Samādhīśvara.[46] Besides, this record specifies that the construction site of the reservoir was in a hilly terrain called Śṛṅgirṣi and in this context, the inscription provides a *praśasti* for this sage Śṛṅgirṣi as well.[47]

Mahārāṇā Kumbha was the patron of a number of brāhmaṇa families.

These families were undoubtedly locally established brāhmaṇa families. Significantly, the earliest land grant made by Mahārāṇā Kumbha to a brāhmaṇa was outside Mewar. The village Cūrī in Ajahari *parganā* (district Sirohi) was granted by Rāṇā Kumbha to brāhmaṇa Devaprabhā.[48] This grant of a whole village to a local brāhmaṇa during the early period of Kumbha's programme for territorial expansion in the Sirohi region was part of an attempt to legitimize Guhila power through brāhmaṇical approval in the newly annexed Sirohi region where the Devaḍā Cāhamānas were fast emerging as a local Rajput power. Moreover, as Sirohi controlled the trade routes between Marwar and Gujarat via Mount Abu, it was essential to hold the region to divert resources towards Mewar. The many rich Jain merchants in Dilwara, Mount Abu, and other towns had caused an appreciation in the revenue-potentialities of this region increasingly over the period. It has already been noted that Mahārāṇā Kumbha exempted the pilgrims (who were mostly Jain pilgrims) from payment of a number of taxes.[49]

It was equally important for Kumbha to renew Guhila links with the brāhmaṇas in the core-areas of Guhila state. The Kadiya (Udaipur district) inscription dating to AD 1443 records the construction of a temple of Kṛṣṇa in the reign of Rāṇā Kumbha in Kadiya village by Tillabhaṭṭa of Bhāradvāj *gotra*, a favourite of Kumbha.[50] The very fact that the inscription mentions that Tillabhaṭṭa was a favourite of Rāṇā Kumbha highlights the extent of Guhila patronage of brāhmaṇas of varied background in the fifteenth century. In all likelihood, village Kadiya in the Āhaḍa belt (Udaipur) had emerged as a centre of the Kṛṣṇa-cult. The resources required for the construction of the Kṛṣṇa temple also seem to have come from the state. Kacchar Copper Plate Grant (a village in Kumbhalgarh *parganā*), dated AD 1453, records the grant of Kacchar village to Brāhmaṇa Godhā Gohad by Rāṇā Kumbha.[51] Land grants in the tribal tract of Merwara (Meda tribe) were essential for several political and economic reasons. Such royal grants in the Aravallian regions are likely to have continued the process of bringing cultivable land under agriculture within the spatial limits of the villages, generating more resources for the local economy as well as beginning the peasantization of some of the members of the local Meda tribe.

It is equally important to note the language of the royal land grant charters of Kadia and Kacchar villages. These were composed in the local dialect, the Mewari. This contrasts with the use of Sanskrit in contemporary royal *praśastis* and points to royal attempts at effective implementation of religious land grants at the respective centres which meant that the state was forced to recognize the vernacular as a language of administration.

Rāṇā Lakṣmasiṁha made the following gifts to the brāhmaṇas: (i) the village of Piṣpalikā to a learned brāhmaṇa named Jhotiṅga with all due ceremonies;[52] (ii) a village containing the five temples (*pañca-devālaya*) to the west of mount Citrakūṭa to Dhaneśvara Bhaṭṭa,[53] and; (iii) a gift of one lakh gold coins to the brāhmaṇas.[54]

King Rāimalla too, made the following gifts of villages to the brāhmaṇas: (i) being pleased with the poet named Maheśa, he granted him the village of Ratnakhetā which produced jewels (*ratnas*);[55] (ii) the village of Prahaṇa was granted to Gopālabhaṭṭa as *dakṣiṇā*-village (gift);[56] and (iii) the villages of Thūra (with lakes full of lotuses, fruitful trees, rows of rice-fields irrigated by water, a fine rosary of Mudgas and fields of sweet sugar canes) to his guru, Gopālabhaṭṭa.[57] Rāimalla issued an injunction to the public as well as to future Guhila kings that none, even in distress, was to use anything produced from lands donated to the brāhmaṇas by the Guhila kings.[58] It is significant that this record, essentially a royal *praśasti*, also provides a lengthy *praśasti* for a family of brāhmaṇas of Bhṛgu clan, associated with the court of Rāimalla.[59] It is for the first time in the history of Mewar that we have such a long *praśasti* for brāhmaṇas in a royal document. The trend undoubtedly points to the increasingly important role of the brāhmaṇas in the late fifteenth-century Guhila court as they provided a new (and more pompous) which was derived from a more exalted origin of the Guhilas status, Sūryavaṁśa, at a time when the Guhila state emerged as one of the biggest regional powers in western India.

III

Legitimization through Origin Myths

Since the creation of origin myths by brāhmaṇas for their Guhila patrons, I shall now analyse the origin myths of the Guhilas. A chronological study of the evolution and shifts in the Guhila origin myths helps one situate the Guhilas in the history of Mewar. Shifts in the Guhila origin myths reveal stages of state formation, and hence helps one understand the political career of the Guhilas, their territorial domains, their rise to power, and finally the emergence of the Nāgdā-Āhaḍa Guhila dynasty as a formidable regional power in western India.

The Guhilas of Dhavagartā known from the Dabok Inscription of

AD 644 claim only a simple family name, Guhila. There is no mention of any claims for an exalted origin of Guhila Dhanika in this private record of a local kāyastha family. Nor does Guhila Dhanika bear any grandiose political title. Instead, this inscription refers to the contemporary Morī King Śrī Dhavalappadeva as *parambhaṭṭāraka mahārajādhirāja-parameśvara.*[60] This clearly indicates a difference in the political status of the two. The area of control of Guhila Dhanika was obviously limited, given the occupation of other nuclear regions of Mewar by the Guhilas of Nāgdā-Āhaḍa and Kiṣkindhā and by the Morīs of Chittaurgarh in the seventh century. Guhila Dhanika was a local chief controlling the area around the village of Dhavagartā,[61] which included smaller rural settlements. The inscription suggests that Guhila Dhanika functioned as a subordinate ally of the Morī sovereign; he was merely a local chief and had not attained monarchical status in this period. Reference to his lineage or family name simply as Guhila, without elaboration, proves that the Guhilas of Dhavagartā in the seventh century did not have a very high political status.

Significantly, the Guhilas of Nāgdā-Āhaḍa, initially known from the Samoli Inscription dating to AD 646, and the Udaipur Praśasti, dated AD 661, do not refer to their overlords nor bear any politically subordinate title. Yet they refer to themselves only as Guhilānvaya (belonging to the lineage of the Guhila).[62] Although silence about an overlord may indicate a comparatively independent position, it has already been reiterated that the title of *rāval* for the legendary Bāppā indicates a politically subordinate status for the Nāgdā-Āhaḍa Guhilas in the seventh-eighth centuries, since their territorial control was confined to the central parts of Mewar hills, and the hill and forest tract of the Nāgdā-Āhaḍa belt. Resources were largely rural-centred and attempts had been initiated to mobilize natural resources and bring land in the tribal tracts of the core area under cultivation. In the forest and hills of the core-area, resources were restricted in this early period. Yet it is significant that the Guhilas of Nāgdā-Āhaḍa emphasized upon their lineage identity and eulogized it as a 'glorious one' in their seventh-century official record.[63] Such attempts definitely reflect a concern to proclaim themselves 'royal' and distinct from the rest of society. In the absence of a reference to origins, however, we can only infer that these were the beginnings of the process of state formation.

The Guhilas of Kiṣkindhā, known from their five inscriptional records (four official charters and one private record), also do not claim any high-sounding ancestry. Similar to the contemporary Nāgdā-Āhaḍa

Guhilas, they refer to their family as *guhilaputrānvaye*[64] or simply *kiṣkindhipurāt guhila-narādhipa-vaṁśe*.[65] Their limited political status is clearly testified by titles such as *avāpta-aśeṣamahāśabda*, *samādhigata-pañcamahāśabda* and *samupārjitapañcamahāśabda*,[66] usually used by subordinate rulers. They were evidently controlling a limited territorial unit in the southern Mewar hills, bordering the district of Dungarpur. Although they enjoyed a considerable rural base, resources were still limited in view of the hilly and forested nature of Kiṣkindhā. Thus, all three Guhila ruling families in the seventh-eighth centuries are likely to have functioned as *sāmantas* of the Morīs of Chittaurgarh, even as the Kiṣkindhā Guhilas project their royal status through association of *narādhipa* (king) with their lineage-identity Guhilavaṁśa.[67] Similarly, the Guhilas of Chāṭsu, known from their Nāgar Inscription dating to AD 684 and controlling a limited locality in Tonk district which was under the formal sway of the Morīs, also referred to themselves as Guhila and nothing more.[68]

The rise of the Nāgdā-Āhaḍa Guhilas to significant political heights is clearly reflected in the new claims made about the origins of their lineage in their official records of the tenth and the eleventh century. In contrast to the simple reference to their lineage as *Guhilānvaya* in the seventh century, the Āṭapura Inscription, dated AD 977, tries to exalt the social status of the Guhilas by speaking of the progenitor Guhadatta as a brāhmaṇa belonging to a family of Ānandapura (*ānandapura vinirgata viprakulānandanoh-mahīdeva, jayati śrī guhadattah prabhavah guhila vaṁśasya*).[69] Ānandapura is identified with present Vadnagar in Idar, north-eastern Gujarat. The Kadmal Plate dating to AD 1083 also repeats the same claim.[70] Around the same time, a long genealogical list of the Nāgdā-Āhaḍa Guhilas also appears for the first time in the Āṭapura record listing all Guhila kings from Guhadatta to Śaktikumāra.[71] Thus we find that the Nāgdā-Āhaḍa Guhilas made claims to a brāhmaṇa origin for the first time in the tenth century. The process of legitimization had begun to work. Guhilānvaya was no longer an adequate label, especially with control over more territory (as is testified to by the disappearance of the Kiṣkindhā Guhilas after the eighth century). The Nāgdā-Āhaḍa Guhilas had evidently integrated the southern part of the Mewar hills into their kingdom by the ninth century. Not only had their power been enhanced territorially, but organizationally too the Nāgdā-Āhaḍa dynasty had consolidated its political hold. If Pratihāras and Hūṇa Rajputs had been inducted into the emerging political structure from outside the state, important local and neighbouring ruling families such as the Rāṣṭrakūṭas of Hastikuṇḍī (Godwar), the Paramāras, and the Caulukyas had also been integrated into the polity by the tenth century.[72] Political links were cemented by matrimonial alliances.[73] It is significant to note that Guhila King Bhartṛpaṭṭa II bears the title of *mahārājādhirāja* (king of kings) in the Pratapgarh record of the reign of Pratihāra Mahendrapāla II.[74] Also, a contemporary Rāṣṭrakūṭa record from Hastikuṇḍī refers to the reigning Guhila king of Nāgdā-Āhaḍa as the 'lord of the Gurjaras' and to Āghaṭa (the Guhila capital of Āṭapura), as 'the pride of Medapāṭa'.[75] It was no small military achievement that Guhila Allaṭa had decisively defeated Pratihāra Devapāla (Kanauj).[76] Thus the Nāgdā-Āhaḍa Guhilas not only figured in the records of the contemporary Rajput powers for the first time in the tenth century, they were also perceived as the 'lord' of Medapāṭa (the entire region of Mewar) and Gurjaras.

If the Nāgdā-Āhaḍa Guhilas claimed brāhmaṇa origin in the tenth-eleventh centuries, the Guhilas of Chāṭsu claimed *brahmakṣatrānvita* (*brahma-kṣatra*) origin and retained their family name, Guhilavaṁśa in the ninth century.[77] The Guhilas of Chāṭsu had emerged as a significant political ally of the Pratihāras of Kanauj in eastern Rajasthan by this period. Their recent political and military growth, extended territorial control and social links with some of the contemporary leading Rajput lineages like the Paramāras and the Cāhamānas, explain their claim to *brahma-kṣatra* origin.

In contrast, the Guhilas of Māṅgrol (Kathiawar), Unsṭrā (district Jodhpur) and Nāḍol (Godwar) referred to themselves simply as Guhila as late as the twelfth century. The Guhilas of Unsṭrā[78] and Nāḍol[79] were small local chiefs controlling very limited pockets and resources, whereas the Guhilas of Māṅgrol had risen in their political career in Saurashtra in the dominion of the Caulukyan state. Their political subordination to the Caulukyas of Gujarat is clearly evident in Guhila Mūlaka's title, *saurāṣṭranāyaka*. Therefore, the Guhilas of Māṅgrol, in spite of their considerable political power in Saurashtra in the twelfth century, were never the focus of a local state but an integral part of Caulukyan polity.

In view of the above study it is necessary to review the opinion of D.R. Bhandarkar about Nāgar brāhmaṇa origins of the Guhilas of Mewar (Nāgdā-Āhaḍa).[80] This view fails to explain the discrepancy between the *Guhilānvaya* status of the seventh century and the *brahma-kṣatra* status of the thirteenth century,[81] and the Sūryavaṁśa status of the sixteenth century for the same family of Guhilas.[82] The claim to brāhmaṇa origin made by the Guhilas for the first time in the tenth century should be considered as legitimization of the emerging sub-regional state in the Mewar hills. The motif of Ānandapura may suggest the presence of Nāgar brāhmaṇas at the Guhila court in the tenth century. Hence, the claims to brāhmaṇa origin took place only at one point of time. The theme of migration facilitated the predominance of the Guhilas in an area occupied by Bhils and by non-Guhila Rajput chiefs.[83]

The thirteenth century marks a decisive stage. The Guhilas now transferred their capital from Nāgdā-Āhaḍa to Chittaurgarh. They claimed *brahma-kṣatra* status for the first time in the thirteenth century (instead of a brāhmaṇa origin as in the tenth-eleventh centuries). Along with the new origin-status came the new motifs of Bappā-Hārītarāśi-Ekaliṅga-Medapāṭa. If Bappā is called a brāhmaṇa in the Chittaurgarh Inscription dating to AD 1274 ('May the city of Nāgahṛda be victorious . . . coming from which brāhmaṇa Bappā'. . .),[84] Bappā is credited with the new status of *brahma-kṣatra* in the Achaleśvara Inscription.

> From Hārīta, resembling the creator, Bappaka, so the tale goes, obtained royal splendour in the guise of an anklet, after he had bestowed on the sage priestly (splendour) under the guise of devotion. Even now these princes who are born in his race, are shining intensely on the surface of the earth, verily, like the regal duties in bodily form.[85]

Both the phrases that Bappaka 'obtained regal splendour' from Hārīta and Bappaka 'had bestowed on the sage priestly (splendour)' clearly indicate that Bāppā exchanged his brāhmaṇahood (priestly splendour) with sage Hārīta for kṣatriyahood (regal splendour). Thus was legitimized the kṣatriya role of the Guhila. The transition from brāhmaṇa origin to prestigious *brahma-kṣatra* is obviously reflective of greater power as sovereigns of Mewar. Although they acquired Chittaurgarh, the political landmark of Mewar, mere fresh territorial possessions could not legitimize the new Guhila political status. It was equally necessary to claim a new social status befitting their newly achieved political and military status. It is the kṣatriya status that legitimizes territorial and military achievements. Hence, the necessity of *brahma-kṣatra* title in the thirteenth century. Guhila claims to *brahma-kṣatra* status at this stage reminds us of the Pallavas of Kanchipuram and the Karṇāṭas of Mithila who also claimed *brahma-kṣatra* status at the height of their political career. B.D. Chattopadhyaya observes,

> when one looks at the different stages in which the genealogies were being formulated, it further appears that for the majority of the newly emerging royal lines, 'Brahmā-Kṣatra' was a transitional status, which once acquired was not

however, entirely given up and explanations continued to be given for the supposedly authentic transition from Brāhmaṇa to Kṣatriya status. . . . It may also well be that the "Brahmā-Kṣatra" was a relatively open status as can be gathered from its wide currency in India in this period, which was seized upon by the new royal families before they could formulate a claim to pure Kṣatriya origin.[86]

Jaiswal has also pointed out that 'the category of Brahma-Kṣatra' seems to have a multiple origin.[87]

The Guhila hold over Chittaurgarh had to be legitimized more elaborately because the Nāgdā-Āhaḍa Guhilas never actually conquered the mighty fortress before Jaitrasiṁha's period. Moreover, the conquest of Chittaurgarh implied Guhila sovereignty all over Mewar. From the legends of 'Śrī Bappaka in Nāgahṛda',[88] were created the legends of 'Bappā, Hārītarāśi and Ekaliṅga in Medapāṭa and Citrakūṭa' in the thirteenth century. It was officially claimed that Bāppā, the progenitor of the lineage obtained regality over Mewar through the grace of the Pāśupata Ācārya, Hārītarāśi.[89] Eventually, it is Bappā, the *brahma-kṣatra*, and not Guhadatta, who is claimed as the progenitor of the Guhila dynasty and founder of Guhila royal power in Mewar. Guhadatta appears as Bappā's son in both the Chittaurgarh and the Achaleśvara Inscriptions.[90]

Brahma-kṣatra status for the Guhilas in the thirteenth century served two essential political functions. Having settled at Chittaurgarh, the Guhilas confronted the Rajput chiefs of eastern Mewar (the Solaṁkīs of Maṇḍalgarh, the Cāhamānas of the former Śākambharī house at Bijolia, Menal, etc., the Paramāras of Abu, and the Sonagirā-Cāhamānas in the Godwar region) for the first time in their history. It was necessary to claim a social status higher or at least equal to these immediately neighbouring kṣatriya elites to facilitate matrimonial alliances. Secondly, by the early thirteenth century, they had begun to militarily confront such neighbouring powers as the Paramāras of Malwa and the Bāghelās of Gujarat as well as the Delhi Sultans. Rāval Samarsiṁha's increasing military career could be further politically supported by the recently proclaimed prestigious social origin that facilitated mobilization for military purpose. The Guhilas had undoubtedly transformed themselves from the rulers of Nāgdā-Āhaḍa to the kings of Mewar.

The fifteenth century marked a leap towards full-fledged kṣatriya status for the Guhilas. The Śṛṅgirṣi Inscription of Rāṇā Mokal proclaims Rāṇā Khetā as a jewel of the kṣatriya race. '. . . his (Hammīra's) son Kṣetra (who was) an ornamental jewel of the Kṣatriya race, the destructive fire to (his) enemies, and worthy well to take up responsibility, went to the abode of gods'.[91] This shows that claiming *brahma-kṣatra* status was politically a transitional phase in the stages of state formation. Kṣatriya status was proclaimed by the Guhilas at that stage of state formation when the Guhilas had emerged not only as a leading western Indian power but when they had already forged matrimonial links with those contemporary Rajput powers who claimed kṣatriya status too. For instance, we recall that the Guhilas themselves had referred to the Hāḍās of eastern Mewar as the *kṣatrīs* of the east.[92] Moreover, claims to the status of *kṣatriyavaṁśamaṇḍanamaṇi* facilitated military support from the local Rajput powers that helped transforming the fifteenth-century Guhilas into a major political power. Later on, Mughal sources such as the *Akbar Nama* and *Tuzuk-i-Baburi* mention the military career of Rāṇā Sāṅgā.[93] By the fifteenth century the Guhilas were not only considered a regional power but also perceived as a front-ranking western Indian power.

Just as kṣatriya status evolved from *brahma-kṣatra*, similarly the motif of Bappa of the thirteenth century, the legendary founder of Guhila royal power in Mewar, got transformed into *Bappavaṁśa/Bappajavaṁśa* by the fifteenth century. By the fifteenth century, the royal family changed its family name from Guhilavaṁśa to *Bappajavaṁśa*. The Śṛṅgirṣi inscription refers to the Guhila kings belonging to *Bappajavaṁśa* (lineage of Bappā).[94] The fact that the new Guhila claim was accepted widely is evident from a contemporary Jain record, the Rāṇakpur Praśasti. This begins the genealogical list with Bappā, the king of Mewar (*Śrīmedapāṭa-rājādhirāja Śrī Bappā*)[95] and refers to Śrī Guhila as Bappā's son.[96]

At the turn of the fifteenth century the Guhilas made claims to an even more exalted origin than that suggested by kṣatriya status—they claimed Sūryavaṁśa origin. A Jain record, the Nadlai Adinath Temple Inscription dating to AD 1500, refers to the lineage of the Guhilas as *Sūryavaṁśīyamahārajādhirāja Śri Śilādityavaṁśe*.[97] The ruling dynasty must have started claiming Sūryavaṁśa status, enhancing their status further by claiming the ancestry of the Ādityas (solar lineage) before the end of the fifteenth century.

However, in the latter half of the fifteenth century, some important adjustments took place in the legends about Guhila origins. The Kumbhalgarh Praśasti repeats the Bappā-Hārītarāśi-Ekaliṅga-Medapāṭa legends (*Bappā Hārītarāśi Ekaliṅgaprasāda*).[98] Here Bāppā is called *purāṇapuruṣah*, the original progenitor or founder of the Guhila dynasty.[99] The kings are stated to be named after Bappā's son Guhadatta (*sa nṛpatiḥ guhilābhidhāno*). Thus, the inscription continues to refer to Rāval Śrī Guhadatta as Bappā's son.[100]

By the early sixteenth century Guhadatta's role as progenitor of the Guhila royal family had been internalized. The Jain Nadlai inscription lists Guhadatta as the progenitor of the royal dynasty of Mewar while Rāula Śrī Bappaka follows as Guhila's son.[101] In fact, standardization of the tradition of Guhadatta as progenitor and Rāval Bappa as founder seem to have begun by the early sixteenth century, and most of the seventeenth century official sources conformed to this pattern with further enhancement of the Sūryavaṁśa status to Īkṣavāku ancestry (Rāmacandra's lineage).[102]

IV

Cults, both, of local goddesses and of Śiva had become popular in the seventh century in Mewar. The Dabok Inscription, dated AD 644, attests to the patronage of the cults of Maheśvara (Śiva) and Ghaṭṭavāsinī (the goddess residing in the pot) by a local kāyastha family through land and cash grants in Dhavagartā locality near Chittaurgarh.[103] At this stage it is important to note that the process of identification of a local goddess, Ghaṭṭavāsinī with Durgā, the mother goddess, had already taken place in the seventh century in the upper Banas plain. The direct identification is evident in the inscriptional reference to *Ghaṭṭavāsinī nāmna Durgādevyā* (Durgādevī by the name of Ghaṭṭavāsinī).[104] Such identification follows appropriation of Ghaṭṭavāsinī by the brāhmaṇa priests and installation of this deity in a temple.[105] The record also pays obeisance to goddess Caṇḍikā (Durgā).[106] The cult of Śiva was also patronized by the ruling elite in upper Banas plain in this period. One of the predecessors of King Māna Morī of Chittaur is called Maheśvara (Śiva) in his Manosarovar Inscription.[107] An inscription from eighth-century Chittaurgarh records the erection of the temple of Kukkureśvara Mahādeva by King Kukkureśvara.[108] Such royal patronage points to the popularity of the cult of Śiva in early medieval Chittaurgarh. An ancient temple of Kālikā belonging to the seventh-eighth centuries has also been discovered in the fortress of Chittaur.[109]

The cult of Śiva appears to have been equally popular in the hilly-forest-tribal locality of Kiṣkindhā. The Guhila King Bhāvihita describes himself as a *paramamāheśvara* (a devout worshipper of Śiva).[110] The earliest direct evidence of royal patronage to the Śaiva sects comes from the Kiṣkindhā locality. The Kalyanpur Fragmentary Inscription of

King Padda (early eighth century) records the construction of a temple of Śiva by Guhila Kadachi's queen Voṇṇa who was assisted in the pious work by her preceptor, a Śaiva, called Kuṭukkācārya.[111] Royal patronage is likely to have followed popular patronage of local Śaiva temples. A Śaiva temple of the seventh-eighth century exists in Kalyanpur where a Caturmukha Śivaliṅga is presently worshipped.[112]

Interestingly, in contrast, Mewar hills, the core-area of the Nāgdā-Āhaḍa Guhilas, have no inscriptional records referring to any temple of Śiva, let alone presence of any Śaiva sect in the seventh century. An earlier record of the Nāgdā-Āhaḍa Guhilas, the Samoli Inscription of the reign of King Śilāditya, registers the construction of the temple of goddess Araṇyavāsinī by a migrating community of mahājanas at Araṇyakūpagiri.[113] But unlike the contemporary Dhavagartā tradition, the Samoli record does not refer to Araṇyavāsinī as a form of Durgā. Nevertheless, Araṇyavāsinī (the goddess who dwells in the forest), presumably the goddess initially associated with the tribal Bhils, was installed in a newly constructed temple. The construction of the temple of Araṇyavāsinī points to the penetration of the state-society into the tribal pockets. The Samoli record, which contains a *praśasti* of the Guhila King Śilāditya,[114] also supported the royal cause in the Bhil dominion. Popularity of the cult of Viṣṇu amongst the members of the ruling elite in the Nāgdā-Āhaḍa state is evident from the construction of a temple of Viṣṇu. Udaipur Praśasti of the reign of King Aparājita is a private record belonging to his Commander-in-Chief Mahārāja Varāhasiṁha. It records the construction and patronage of a temple of Viṣṇu by Varāhasiṁha's wife, Yaśomati.[115] Thus, unlike the upper Banas plain and the southern Mewar hills, the Nāgdā-Āhaḍa belt of Mewar hills shows evidence of the popularity of the cult of local goddess Araṇyavāsinī in the tribal pockets and of the cult of Viṣṇu in the core-areas of the Nāgdā-Āhaḍa state.

An important development takes place in the Mewar hills by the tenth century. The Guhila state of Nāgdā-Āhaḍa had emerged as an important political power. Now appeared the most crucial mechanism for legitimization—royal affiliation to a local cult centre. Unlike the seventh century, the cult of Śiva figures on a significant scale in Nāgdā-Āhaḍa Guhila records of the tenth century. The Pāśupatas, one of the major contemporary Śaiva sects, also appear for the first time in the same royal records. This indicates that not only had the Pāśupatas (who always had a strong institutional base outside Mewar)[116] established the cult of Śiva successfully, but had themselves grown into a locally popular and influential religious sect. However, the Guhilas of Nāgdā-Āhaḍa did not seem to have felt any urgent need to seek legitimization before the tenth century. This point is supported by the fact that the royal temple of Ekaliṅgajī (Śiva) at the Pāśupata centre of Nāgdā was constructed for the first time only in AD 971.[117] On the other hand, the Pāśupatas seem to have emerged as an important religious community in the Mewar hills before the mid-tenth century.

The increasing interdependence of the sacred and the temporal is as gradual as any other process of state formation. A number of royal temples of the cult of Śiva came to be constructed only from the tenth century onwards, and one can speculate that the Pāśupatas were looking for royal support. It is significant that the Pāśupatas claim victory over the Jains in the Ekaliṅgajī Temple Inscription dating to AD 971 (the very first record from Mewar mentioning the Pāśupatas).[118] This may allude to their attempts at establishing their superiority over the Jains to strengthen bonds with the royal court. The process culminated in the construction of the royal temple of god Ekaliṅga at Nāgdā in AD 971 in the Reign of Guhila King Naravāhana (see Map 12). The temple is stated to have been constructed at the instruction of such Pāśupata *ācāryas* as Supujitarāśi, Viṁścitarāśi, etc.[119] The Ekaliṅgajī Temple Inscription dating to AD 971, is also the first epigraphical record in southern Rajasthan which contains the Kāyāvarohaṇa episode, the origin story of the Lakulīśa-Pāśupata sect,[120] which described Śiva as incarnating himself at Kāyāvarohaṇa in Bhṛgukaccha. The incarnation evidently refers to Lakulīśa, the founder of the Lakulīśa-Pāśupata doctrine of Śaivism. He was followed by his disciples Kuśika and others. This inscription, which eulogizes the reigning King Naravāhana, significantly states that Śrī Bappaka of Guhila *gotra* established himself at Nāgahṛda.[121] The inscription seems to establish the following facts: first, that Nāgahṛda (Nāgdā) had emerged as a centre of the Pāśupatas, second, that the Pāśupata sect had come to enjoy the patronage of the Guhilas of Nāgdā-Āhaḍa and third, that the royal patronage of the Pāśupata sect and the consequent legitimization of the Guhila power seem to have begun on a significant scale by the tenth century. Therefore the process can be expected to have picked up momentum in the following period, in which the Guhila state integrated Mewar into a single regional power. Besides, Bappā, the legendary founder of the state of Mewar, not only figures for the first time in the official records of the period but also figures in association with Nāgahṛda, the Pāśupata centre. Also, Guhadatta of the tenth-eleventh- century records is neither associated with Nāgahṛda nor

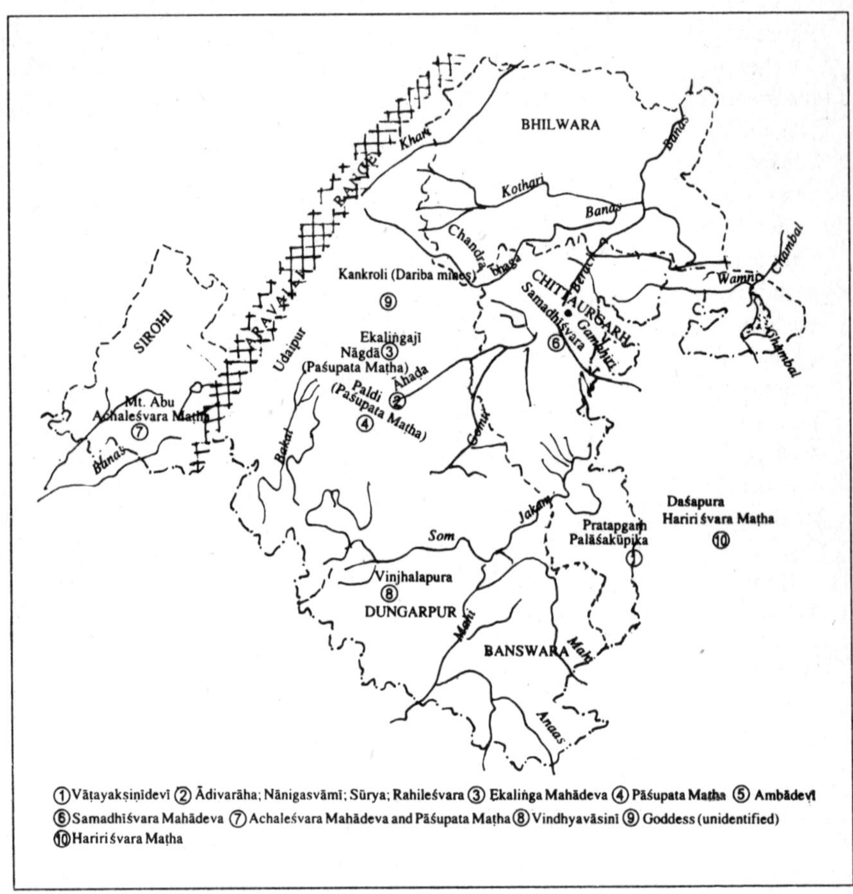

Map 12: Inscriptional Location of the Temples in the Guhila Territory: AD Tenth-Thirteenth Centuries.

the Pāśupata *ācāryas*. The inscription also points to the fact that, neither Bappā nor any Pāśupata *ācārya* was in any capacity associated with the sovereignty of Mewar at this stage. There is no mention of Mewar in the Ekaliṅgajī temple inscription, but there is a significant reference to the Pāśupata centre, Nāgahṛda and its eulogy. We also see how the Pāśupatas began to link their seat of power, Nāgahṛda, with a legendary figure of royal stature Śrī Bappaka, to claim royal patronage.

Therefore, in all likelihood the legend of 'Bappaka in Nāgahṛda' was the creation of the Pāśupata sect to highlight the ancient association of Nāgahṛda, the Pāśupata centre, with a mythical king of the past. In this connection it may be noted that the early medieval inscriptions of *sāmanta* ruler Aṁśuvarmā of Nepal also use the expression *bappā* as meaning father.[122] The ruler was undoubtedly associated with the Paśupatināth temple and the Pāśupata *ācāryas.* A mythical king with local roots can certainly be popularized, and *bappā* is a generic term. *Bāppā* was not the actual name of any Guhila prince of the Nāgdā-Āhaḍa house. Bappā appears for the first time in the Ekaliṅgajī Temple Inscription. *Bappā* literally means father or father-like figure. Since Nāgahṛda (Nāgdā) was also the first capital of the Guhilas, any mythical king of the past who was said to have flourished at Nāgahṛda was obviously going to be identified with an ancient Guhila king of the region. The very mention of Bappaka in an official record at this juncture would assume that the legend of 'Bappaka in Nāgahṛda' must have become popular among the different communities of the area. This spelled out the role of the Pāśupata sect in legitimizing the state which I shall examine in greater detail in the next section.

IV

Legitimization of the State through Patronage of Local Religious Cults

Legends were being created by the Pāśupatas to legitimize the rule of their patrons. Since Nāgahṛda had come to acquire the status of a religious landmark in the region, it was equally important for the Guhilas to associate themselves with it and its protagonists, the Pāśupatas. Thus, with the legend of 'Bappaka in Nāgahṛda', the Guhilas began their affiliation to Ekaliṅga and the Pāśupatas. Affiliation to a religious landmark was seen as the most appropriate mechanism to legitimize royal power. As the pilgrimage flow to Nāgahṛda continued to increase over the period, the Pāśupata *ācāryas* began to popularize appropriate legends. That part of the popular annals which depicts Bāppā Rāval, the Guhila king of ancient Nāgdā, as the disciple of Ekaliṅgajī was elaborated.

The influence of the Pāśupatas in the tenth century is further corroborated by a stone inscription of Naravāhana (AD 971) at the temple of Nātha (near Ekaliṅgajī temple): 'They [Guhilas] sought the protection of Śaṅkara, lord of Pārvatī . . . who favoured Bhṛgukaccha. . . . There came Kuśika and other munis, who possessing knowledge and pure bodies took delight in bhasma (ashes) and put on the barks of trees and crowns of Jaṭā (braided hair).'[123] In this record the Guhilas are mentioned in direct association with the Pāśupatas. The story of the Lakulīśa-Pāśupata in fact begins at Bhṛgukaccha.

With the royal patronage of an Ekaliṅga temple, there began the period of the construction of temples of Śiva by the Guhila rulers. For instance, a marble slab inscription of King Śucivarman (tenth century) records the construction of the temple of Rahileśvara (another name of Śucivarman) at Āhaḍa.[124] The patronage of other Pāśupata *maṭhas* at Paldi near Udaipur[125] and at Achalgarh in Mount Abu[126] by the Guhilas is attested to in inscriptional records. The Paldi Inscription of the early twelfth century also contains the story of the origin of the Lakulīśa sect and a list of their chief *ācāryas*.[127] Some of the Pāśupata *ācāryas* from Paldi *maṭha* are listed as follows: Khaṇḍeśvara, Janakarāśi, Trilocanarāśi, Vasantarāśi, Valkala and Śivaśakti.[128] A number of images of Lakulīśa have been reported from Bijolia and Menal localities of the upper Banas plain.[129] Notable among these are the Hājareśvara and Undeśvara temples at Bijolia. Both the temples have a number of images of Śiva with a *lākuṭa* or club in the left hand.[130] Two four-armed Lakulīśa images, dated around the eighth-ninth centuries,[131] and a standing statue of Lakulīśa[132] have been reported from Chittaur, while a number of statues of Śiva fashioned in the form of Urddhavaretas have been discovered at ancient Kiṣkindhā.[133] On the other hand, a number of seated four-armed Lakulīśa figures have been found in Kota and Jhalawar districts of Hadoti region, the south-east of Mewar.[134] Since most of these sculptures have been dated between the eighth and the twelfth centuries,[135] the Guhilas are likely to have patronized some sculptural activity.

The profusion of Lakulīśa images and Pāśupata motifs at Ekaliṅgajī temple undoubtedly indicate that the construction took place under the instructions of the Pāśupata *ācāryas*. This reminds us of Devangana Desai's observations on the Lakṣmaṇa temple at Khajuraho (a Vaiṣṇava shrine). 'Its systematically planned architecture and sculptural scheme indicates the role of a competent architect (sūtradhāra) and also a religious ācārya learned in the Pañcarātra Vaiṣṇava tradition who must have guided the architect.'[136]

To legitimize Guhila hold on Chittaur, the motif of Pāśupata sage Hārītarāśi was adopted in the thirteenth century. The popular traditions of Mewar regarding the bestowal of the kingship of Mewar or Citrakūṭa on Bāppā (the legendary founder of Mewar state), by Pāśupata sage Hārītarāśi (a devout worshipper of god Ekaliṅga), is officially claimed by the Nāgdā-Āhaḍa Guhilas for the first time in the thirteenth century. Both the Achaleśvara and Chittaurgarh inscriptions of Rāval Samarasiṁha in the late thirteenth century claim that Hārītarāśi, the preceptor of Bāppā, was the bestower of the regal fortunes of *Medapāṭa deśa*, by the favour of god Ekaliṅga. To quote the Achaleśvara Inscription, '[the region] which has excelled paradise itself . . . bears the name of Śrī Medapāṭa. Here is a large town named Nāgahṛda where Hārītarāśi . . . performed penance. . . . Hārīta who became united with Śiva, . . . granted regal fortunes to the famous Bāppā in return for services rendered'.[137] Similarly, the Chittaurgarh inscription reads as follows:

> May the city of Nāgahṛda be victorious. . . coming from which Brāhmaṇa Bappa . . . worshipped the two lotus-like feet of Hārītarāśi Muni. . . . Hārītarāśi gave Bappa five golden anklets which he has got as wonderful fruit of the favour of the lotus-like feet of Ekaliṅga. . . . Bappa now acquired royal fortune by the great favour of Hārītarāśi.[138]

Thus the boon of Nāgdā to Bappā, the Pāśupata sage Hārītarāśi and god Ekaliṅga legitimized the hold of the Nāgdā-Āhaḍa Guhilas over all of Mewar when they acquired Chittaurgarh and integrated the upper Banas plain with the Mewar hills. The hold over Chittaurgarh had to be legitimized because the Nāgdā-Āhaḍa Guhilas had not held Chittaur at the beginning of their career. It is evident from inscriptions that Chittaur belonged to the Morīs when the Guhilas began their career in the seventh century.[139] The Nāgdā-Āhaḍa Guhilas had been their subordinate allies in the seventh-eighth centuries. Hence, the need for legitimization for the Guhilas obviously arose in the thirteenth century with the acquisition of Chittaurgarh and their consequent sovereignty over all of Mewar. From the legends of 'Śrī Bappaka in Nāgahṛda', were created the legends of Bappa, Hārītarāśi and Ekaliṅga in Mewar. The expansion of the legends associating Bāppā with sovereignty over Mewar, is likely to have begun in the post-tenth-century period. The Paldi Inscription

(AD 1116) was already claiming the Guhila Arisiṁha as the 'king of the glory of Medapāṭa'.[140] Their military success in this period set the stage for the Guhila claim to this title. However, Chittaurgarh was still elusive, a feat achieved only in the thirteenth century.

It is assumed that the priests of the Ekaliṅga temple, the Pāśupata *ācāryas*, would narrate temple legends to pilgrims. These would then spread through the villages of Mewar. The temple town of Ekaliṅga and the Pāśupata centre of Nāgahṛda had evolved as the 'source of the highest legitimation of royal authority'.[141] Kulke notes that:

> The political significance of the temple towns was in no way limited to their being occasionally also 'royal towns'. Far more important was their role as cosmic centres and sources of the highest legitimation of royal authority. Very soon the founder kings were included in the temple legends in which they were elevated to mythical heroes of the hoary past.[142]

I have already pointed out that in the case of Mewar, the founder King Bappā was not the actual founder of the Guhila dynasty but the creation of legitimizing agents. The legend about him seems to have been born in the temple town of Nāgahṛda (Ekaliṅgajī). Bāppā does not figure as 'the founder king' before the thirteenth century, unlike in Orissa where founder kings were included in temple legends right from the beginning. Thus, in the thirteenth century, it is Bappā and not Guhadatta who is claimed as the founder of the Guhila dynasty.[143]

In a period when the Ekaliṅgajī temple at Nāgdā was emerging as a regional *tīrtha* in Mewar, the spread of the cult of Śakti was equally pervasive in contemporary Mewar. It is to this that I shall now turn. Local traders made land-grants to the temple of Vaṭayakṣiṇīdevī (goddess residing in the Banyan tree) in the village of Ghonṭavarṣikā belonging to the Harirṣiśvara *maṭha* of Daśapura.[144] The temple of Yogeśvara (Śiva) at Cīrakūpa near Nāgdā-Ekaliṅgajī built by Yogeśvara, the *talarakṣaka* of Nāgdā (Ṭāmṭarāḍa family).[145] Jagat situated in south-east of Udaipur district (52 km from Udaipur) bordering Chittaurgarh, had emerged as a dominant *tīrtha* of Ambikā (Durgā) in this period. The popularity of Ambikā is borne out by Guhila royal grants to her temple. Jagat Inscriptions of Guhila King Sāmantasiṁhadeva dating to AD 1171-2 and of Guhila king Jayasiṁhadeva dating to AD 1249 record the grant of *suvarṇakalaśas* to the temple of Ambikā at Jagat.[146] It is significant that the cult of Vindhyavāsinī figures for the first time in records of the thirteenth century. An inscription of the time of Rāval Sīhadadeva of Dungarpur-Guhila family, dated to the late thirteenth century, records the construction of the temple of Vindhyavāsinī by one Vijayā, at Vinjhalapura in Dungarpur district.[147] Interestingly, popular patronage of local goddesses continued in the mining centres and hilly terrain. The Kankroli (near Dariba mines) Road-Station Inscription of the reign of Rāval Samarasiṁha (AD 1298-9) records the grant of few *dramma* coins to a temple of the local goddess.[148]

Thus recorded references to the local goddesses Araṇyavāsinī,[149] Ghaṭṭavāsinī,[150] Vaṭayakṣiṇī,[151] and Vindhyavāsinī[152] spanning the period from the seventh to the thirteenth centuries in Mewar indicate an overall process of change: incorporation of cults, integration of localities and hence local goddesses into the pantheon some of these supra-local deities. Chattopadhyaya points out, '[these cults] do not all develop into major cults, but some do. They function towards the integration of other local cults and become one of the recognizable symbols of the region. The religious and ideological expressions of a region in their varied forms thus become enmeshed in the web of its polity, economy and society'.[153] The incorporation of local goddesses and the patronage of their cults marks the building of an ideological framework to support the process of state formation in Mewar. This is clearly indicated by the *Ekaliṅgamāhātmyam* with Vindhyavāsinī along with her associates Jayā and Vijayā, predominating its early part,[154] followed in the second part by references to the royal patronage of Ekaliṅga and the Pāśupata *ācāryas*. The second stage in the construction of the ideological framework corresponds to the installation of Ekaliṅga by Vindhyavāsinī at Nāgdā and the spread of the cult of Śiva.[155] The third and the final stage seems to relate to the direct appropriation of the cult of Ekaliṅga by the Guhila dynasty.

The process of religious legitimization of state formation in Mewar seems to have culminated in the fifteenth century, when Guhila affiliation to the central deity, Ekaliṅga was sought directly, by passing the medium of Pāśupata Ācārya Hārītarāśi. The process finds its expression in the title of *Ekaliṅganijasevaka* (the personal servant of Ekaliṅga). The Kumbhalgarh Slab Inscription (AD 1460) calls the reigning king, Mahārāṇā Kumbha, *Yasyaikaliṅganijasevaka* (Ekaliṅga's personal servant).[156] The same title is attributed to Mahārāṇā Kumbha in the Kumbha Praśasti section of the *Ekaliṅgamāhātmyam*, which describes the relationship between the king of Mewar and god Ekaliṅga as that of servant and master.[157] In the 'Kṣīreśvara Māhātmyam' section of the *Ekaliṅgamāhātmyam*, Śiva (Kṣīreśvara) is also *kṣetrapāla* (lord of the land of the region).[158]

The major local cult that was next only to Ekaliṅga in *Ekaliṅgamāhātmyam* as well as contemporary Guhila records is that of goddess Vindhyavāsinī. A temple of Vindhyavāsinī was well-established by the fifteenth century, as is indicated by the Kumbhalgarh slabs which describe the temple and eulogize the goddess.[159] The fact that Vindhyavāsinī represented the goddess traditions (popularity of cults of different goddesses in early medieval and medieval Mewar has been discussed earlier) of Mewar is evident from her predominance over Ekaliṅga in the early portions of *Ekaliṅgamāhātmyam*. The centrality of the cult of Vindhyavāsinī in Mewar can be perceived in the fact that in spite of the absence of a mother goddess in the central pantheon in the literature of the Lakulīśa-Pāśupata sect,[160] Vindhyavāsinī remains identified with Pārvatī in the *Ekaliṅgamāhātmyam*.[161] We realize that śāstric injunctions and theoretical compulsions did not always correspond to the reality of historical processes. Pārvatī is not worshipped along with Ekaliṅga in the same temple.

The temple of Vindhyavāsinī figuring in the *Ekaliṅgamāhātmyam* probably refers to an ancient temple of Vindhyavāsā (popularly known as Vanavāsinī) on the slope of the Trikūṭa hills to the north of the rampart of the Ekaliṅgajī temple. Description of Vindhyavāsinī in *Ekaliṅgamāhātmyam* relates more to the popular aspects of Durgā (killer of demons and title of Caṇḍikā) rather than to a typical local goddess. Vindhyavāsinī figures along with Ekaliṅga in an Ekaliṅga Temple Inscription of the sixteenth century (AD 1534-5) in which Pāśupata Ācārya Śrī Naroharinā figures as the chief *ācārya* of the temple, engaged in an expansion of the *maṭha*.[162] Significantly, the record also refers to the legendary Pāśupata Ācārya Hārītarāśi.[163] Thus, the integration of the goddesses of Mewar into the central pantheon was accomplished by the Pāśupatas. Incidentally, the sixteenth-century Ekaliṅga Temple Inscription also shows that at least till the mid-sixteenth-century Ekaliṅga temple was a Pāśupata institution.

In *Ekaliṅgamāhātmyam*, Vindhyavāsinī installs Ekaliṅga in Nāgahṛda and instructs Bappā to worship him.[164] Hārītarāśi who is said to have worshipped both Vindhyavāsinī and Ekaliṅga, is instructed by Vindhyavāsinī to invoke Ekaliṅga.[165] Being invoked, Ekaliṅga confers the state of Mewar on Bappā and the abode of Kailāśa on Hārītarāśi.[166] Vindhyavāsinī is eulogized again and again in the *Māhātmyam* and the *bīja mantra* is imparted to the initiators (according to *tāntrik* system).[167] The *tīrtha* of Vindhyavāsinī is known to be situated in the north of the Cakrapuṣkariṇī *tīrtha* (Viṣṇu and Lakṣmī).[168] She is stated to bless the devotees of Ekaliṅga.[169] As expected, her *tīrtha* is said to be in the forests (*vāṭikā gahraṇye vane*).[170] Here, the best of the sages worship her after taking the ritual dip (*tatra snātvā munivaro vindhyavāsām prapūjya ca*).[171] An entire chapter is devoted in the *Māhātmyam* to her royal worship on a grand scale (*rājopcarānkhilān*).[172] It is significant to note that the 'weapons and accessories' of the goddess are also worshipped.[173] Vindhyavāsinī is worshipped on the third day, next to Ekaliṅga, in the fourteen days' annual festival of Mewar, the Caitrayātrā (annual *yātrā* to Ekaliṅgajī temple).[174]

It also appears that it is through Vindhyavāsinī that other local cults of mother goddesses were integrated in the greater pantheon in the fifteenth century. Jayā and Vijayā, the two associates of Pārvatī, are identified with the Banas and Gambhira rivers respectively.[175] These could signify the local goddesses of the geographical expanse between Banas and Gambhira which were then identified with Pārvatī's (Vindhyavāsinī in case of Mewar) associates. The assumption is plausible in view of the absence of the local cults of Ghaṭṭavāsinī[176] or Vaṭayakṣiṇīdevī,[177] in the list of deities worshipped during Caitrayātrā.[178] Even today, the annual fairs of Kārṇīmātā in Kunwariya and Bāmīmātā (in Deogarh and Kotra tahsils respectively in Udaipur district), and Ghaṭarānīmātājī (in Jahāzpur tahsil, Bhilwara district) are important festivals in Mewar.[179] Ghaṭarānīmātājī reminds one of goddess Ghaṭṭavāsinī of the Dabok Inscription (AD 644).[180]

The identification of the cult of local goddesses with goddesses connected with Pārvatī in Mewar is also evident from the famous festival of Gaṇagaur. *Gaṇa* refers to Pārvatī (also known as Gaurī). Though over time, the meaning of Gaṇagaur has become limited to Pārvatī this may not have been the case earlier. The festival of Gaṇagaur is celebrated especially in Udaipur, Nathadwara and Gogunda.[181] A procession of the image of Gaṇagaurmātā is taken out for four days in Udaipur. At lake Pichhola, the Gaṇagaurmātā is worshipped. The convoy of Gaṇagaur is followed by that of Ekaliṅgajī. In earlier times, Ekaliṅgajī is said to have been followed by the *mahārāṇā* and his *sāmantas*.[182] There are various traditions regarding the origin of Gaṇagaur. But one of the earliest traditions identifies Gaurī with a maiden of the land. Gaurī in the disguise of a girl, tells her friends that the 'country' (Mewar) is her father's place. Similarly, another tradition also identifies Gaṇagaur with a maiden of Udaipur (Vīramdās's daughter).[183] Thus the traditions attempt to trace the roots of Pārvatī in Mewar, which, significantly, is the land of a number of important cults of local goddesses. It is important that in Udaipur, the

Gaṇagaur procession is taken out in the name of Ambāmātā as well. Inscriptions have already testified to the popularity of Ambāmātā in early medieval Mewar.[184] Gaṇagaur in Mewar is not only a state festival but is also a widely popular festival—*īsar pūjun pārvatī jī rāṇyān pūje rāj men māhen pūjun evat men.*[185]

Perhaps the most obvious indicator of Bhil devotion to Vindhyavāsinī, is the celebration of Gaṇagaur by the Bhils, specially recorded in the case of Gogunda.[186] Each Bhil girl performs a dance with a clay image of Gaṇagaur, dressed like a Bhil maiden, placed on her head.[187] Some other aspects of the goddess-worship of the Bhils also suggest that Vindhyavāsinī was venerated by the Bhils. Gaṇagaur is also celebrated by the Gerasias, the other important tribe in southern Rajasthan. The popularity of the cult of Śiva and Pārvatī among the Bhils is also evident from their traditions and legends. It has already been noted that Bhil folklore narrates the marriage of Mahādeva with a Bhil bride.[188] She evidently becomes Pārvatī, the consort of Śiva.[189] The tradition highlights the popularity of the cult of Śiva among the Bhils. The *Māhātmyam* specifies the assimilation of militant Bhils through *Śivabhakti.*[190] Such specific mention definitely indicates the importance of the political integration of the Bhils into the state of Mewar. Acceptance of the cult of Śiva and its growing popularity among the Bhils in the medieval period may be linked with the centrality of Vindhyavāsinī along with Ekaliṅga in state formation.

It is significant to note that today each Bhil clan has one *mātā*, each with a different name such as Dhāral, Ambar, Lemāsh, Māliyā, Kārel, etc.[191] However, more significantly, it should be noted that all of them have the same attributes and appear to be manifestations of one *mātā.*[192] Bhavānī or Durgā continued to be identified with the local goddesses in Mewar in medieval times. Tradition attests to the construction of a magnificent temple of Bhavānī known as Vijayasenī-Bhavānī.[193] Another contemporary medieval temple of Bhavānī is to be found at Sitoor in the Hāḍā dominion, eastern Mewar. The goddess is popularly known as Sitoor-ki-Bhavānī.[194]

The Pāśupatas were instrumental in the creation of goddess Rāṣṭrasenā. She figures for the first time in the *Māhātmyam.* There is no mention of her in contemporary epigraphical records. Literally, '*rāṣṭrasenā*' means the 'army of the state'. She is stated to have been created out of the body of Vindhyavāsinī and as having war-like characteristics.[195] From the early fourteenth century onwards, Mewar was invaded again and again by the rulers of Delhi, Gujarat and Malwa.

Inscriptional and literary sources of the period, including the Arabic accounts of Gujarat, illustrate the military career of Mahārāṇā Kumbha (AD 1433-68).[196] The continuous military campaigns and invasions necessitated the creation of an ideology supporting a military culture. This was provided by the Pāśupatas in the form of goddess Rāṣṭrasenā. The *Ekaliṅgamāhātmyam* records a custom of the worship of warlike goddesses.[197] This suggested that it is possible that the Pāśupatas adopted a local war-goddess. The success in foiling repeated military attacks helped establish the popularity of Rāṣṭrasenā. Guhila military successes in defence as well as territorial expansion ensured her popularity. Thus, through the spread of the cult of Rāṣṭrasenā, the loyalty of the people could be ensured in periods of military venture. As the literal meaning of her name indicates, loyalty to Rāṣṭrasenā would have helped in the military mobilization of men for the military, especially in mobilizing tribal militias. The case of the cult of Rāṣṭrasenā may be compared with the cult of Raṇacaṇḍī (goddess of war) of the Dimasa state in Cachar (Assam). In the case of the Dimasa state, the original titulary deity, Kācāi Kāṭī, was transformed into Raṇacaṇḍī.[198] To quote J.B. Bhattacharjee,

> the hymns and verses were made available by the Brahmins for her worship. As Dimasas were then locked in prolonged wars with the Ahoms and the Jaintias and had to reckon with Mughal invasions, the 'Goddess of War' could easily command loyalty. Further the deity was projected as fierce. . . . The success in foiling the repeated Ahom onslaughts strengthened the belief that Ranachandi was the protectress of the tribe and worshipping her would ensure victory in war.[199]

An entire chapter of the *Māhātmyam* is devoted to the worship of Rāṣṭrasenā.[200] When Ekaliṅga is invoked in a crisis to protect the state, Ekaliṅga instructs Rāṣṭrasenā to militarily and politically help restore Citrakūṭa to the Guhilas.[201] Today, a temple of Rāṣṭrasenā (Rāṭhāsenā) stands near that of Vindhyavāsinī and Ekaliṅgajī.[202] Besides Vindhyavāsinī, Cāmuṇḍā, Kālikā, Ambikā and the goddesses of villages and hills were also integrated into the pantheon.[203] But they do not figure in the central pantheon.[204] Next to Ekaliṅga and Vindhyavāsinī, Gaṇeśa, Takṣaka (Takṣakesam Maheśvaram), Kumāra (Kārtikeya), Bhāskara (Sūrya), Bhairava (malignant form of Śiva), Durgā, Dharmeśvar (another form of Śiva), Viṣṇu, Lakṣmīnārāyaṇa and Kāmeśa (Kāmadeva?) are worshipped during Catirayātrā.[205]

I will now discuss the use of the local *tīrthas* to legitimize the state.

The Indrasarasi (lake of Indra) at Ekaliṅga temple, Nāgahṛda, obviously tops the list of the *tīrthas.*[206] It legitimizes the supremacy of Pāśupata sect in the region. Śaivite *tīrthas*, such as Dhāreśvara,[207] Kṣīreśvara in the land of rivers Chandrabhāgā and Gomatī (Bhilwara and Udaipur districts),[208] Gautameśvara (Godwar region, Pali district, north of Mewar hills),[209] Takṣaka Maheśvara,[210] Kuṭilakuṇḍa[211] and Kedārakuṇḍa[212] make up the list of regional *tīrthas*. The list of the *tīrthas* in *Ekaliṅga-māhātmyam* testifies to the spread of the cult of Śiva.

Patronage for the Pāśupatas was sought again and again through a threat that whenever Ekaliṅga was neglected, Mewar would be attacked by the *mlecchas,*[213] and relief can only come when help is sought through Hārīta's disciples.[214] The *Māhātmyam* hails the Pāśupata system as the best way to achieve spiritual liberation—the ultimate goal of man.[215] At the same time the *tīrtha* of Vindhyavāsinī at Karaja Kuṇḍa and that of Lakṣmī-Nārāyaṇa also figure in the list for obvious reasons.[216] Thus were integrated all the local deities into the pantheon of Ekaliṅga.[217]

The final stage of legitimization was sought through the office of the personal servant of the god, Ekaliṅga. The first official appearance of the title *Ekaliṅganijasevaka* takes place in the fifteenth century.[218] As the Guhila king became Ekaliṅga's deputy, the deity assumed kingly attributes and the king underwent some sort of deification.[219]

> The Mahādevas . . . were increasingly transformed into imperial Lords by fitting them out with all symbols of an earthly mahārāja and by assimilating their temple rites increasingly to the palace rites. For, the greater the ostentation of the Mahādeva and his divine court, all the more legitimate was the splendour and power of his earthly representatives and his royal court. This development contributed decisively to the legitimation of the mahārāja who, while not really deified, was brought, nevertheless, nearer to the divinity.[220]

The rituals of Ekaliṅga were performed on a royal scale.[221] The *abhiṣeka* of Ekaliṅga seems to have had something in common with that of the king. While Ekaliṅga is bathed in *pañcamṛtam* (*dadhī, kṣīram, sīta, madhu* and *ghṛtam*),[222] the king is bathed in *pañcagabya* (clarified oil, milk, curd, honey and sugar) during his *abhiṣeka* (coronation).[223] The king is first given *bhasmīsnāna* (bath in ashes) during the ritual of *abhiṣeka*. It reminds us of the Pāśupata ritual of bathing in ashes.[224] However, the aim seems to be to stress that the Guhila king is a deputy of Ekaliṅgajī. The king is permitted to rule only with the permission of Ekaliṅgajī. The fact is amply demonstrated by the coronation ceremony. After the Bhils perform the *ṭīkā* ceremony it is the turn of the chief priest of the Ekaliṅgajī temple to put the *tilak*,[225] to garland the king, and confer on him a stole and other articles.[226] At the end of the long coronation ceremony, the *rāṇā* pays a visit to the Ekaliṅgajī temple. The *rāṇā*, dressed as the priest, performs the worship of Ekaliṅgajī.[227] The chief priest of the temple, on behalf of Ekaliṅgajī, presents to the *rāṇā* a sword, royal umbrella, *caurī* and other insignia of royalty.[228] The king then donates a huge amount in the name of Ekaliṅgajī and also a sum to the priest.[229] After the ceremony at the temple, the king takes leave of Ekaliṅgajī and returns to the royal palace.[230]

Once the political centre of the state shifted from Nāgdā-Āhaḍa to Chittaurgarh the Śaiva centres became even more important. Chittaurgarh had a popular Śaiva *tīrtha* at Samādhīśvara, close to the royal funerary station and an ancient Kuṇḍa called Gaumukh. There is no reference to Samādhīśvara Mahādeva in pre-thirteenth-century Guhila records. As expected, references to Samādhīśvara Mahādeva begin to figure in Guhila records from the thirteenth century onwards only. In other words, once the Guhilas established themselves at Chittaurgarh, relationship was extended to the local, popular Śaiva *tīrtha* of Samādhīśvara. The relationship is revealed gradually. In the beginning, the royal dynasty claimed indirect links with Samādhīśvara Mahādeva of Chittaurgarh. The popularity of the cult among the local elite is attested to by the royal records. Royal priest and court-bard Vedaśarmā declares himself to be a favourite of Ekaliṅga as well as Śrī Samādhīśa in Achaleśvara Inscription, dated to AD 1285.[231] A similar situation continues to prevail till the early fifteenth century when royal artisan Vīsala declares himself a favourite of Samādhīśa and prays for the eternal existence of the temple of Śrī Samādhīśmaheśvara in the Chittaurgarh (Samādhīśvara temple) Inscription of Mokal.[232] The situation changes significantly in the latter half of the fifteenth century when the royal family claims a direct relationship with Samādhīśvara indicating the popularity and influence of this *tīrtha*. Rāṇā Kumbha claims to be a worshipper of Samādhīśvara of Citrakūṭa,[233] so does Mokal in the Purāṇic section of the *Ekaliṅgamāhātmyam*.[234]

All the same, Ekaliṅga continued to be the highest source of legitimization, and large-scale land grants were made to the temple at the end of our period of study. The Ekaliṅgajī Temple Dakṣiṇadvāra Praśasti records the grant of a number of villages to it in the fourteenth and the fifteenth centuries (see Map 13). The list runs as follows: Siṁhavallīpura by Hammīra,[235] Pānavādapura and Khetanaranātha by Kṣetrasiṁha,[236] Chiravā by Lakṣasiṁha, Vādhanavādam and Rāmagrāma

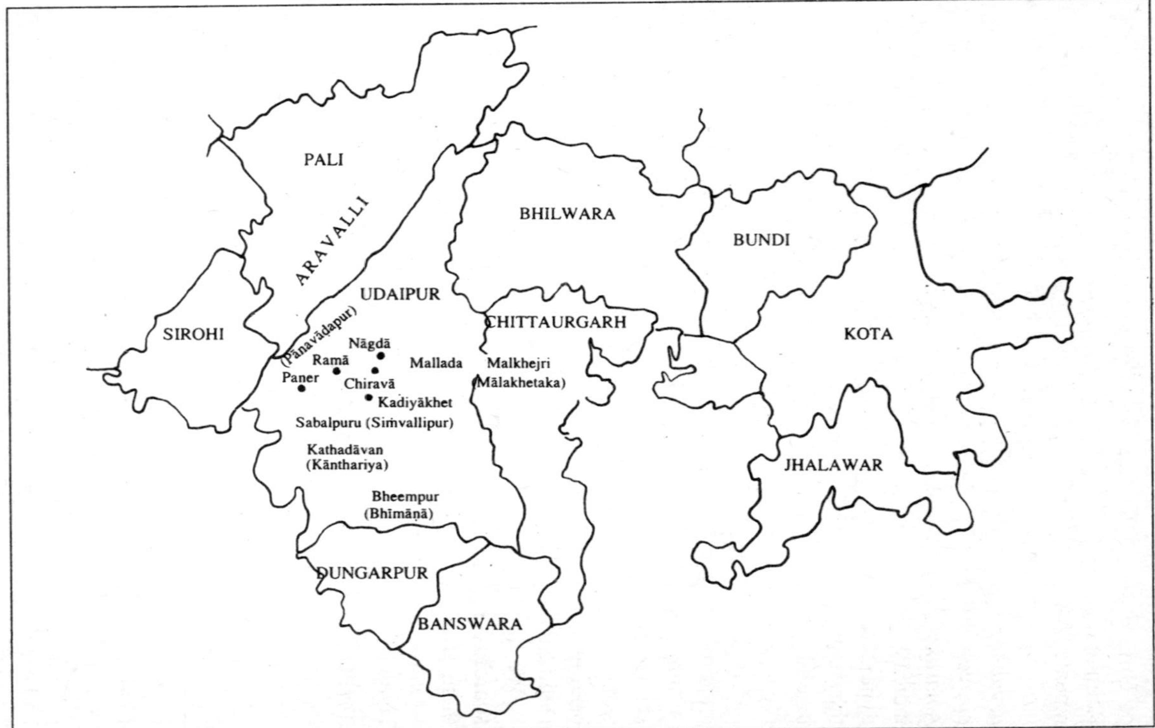

Map 13: Guhila Grant of Villages to the Temple of Ekaliṅgajī: AD Late Fourteenth-Fifteenth Centuries.

by Mokal,[237] Nāgahṛda (renewing or granting additional resources), Kaṭhadāvana, Mālakakhetakā and Bhīmāna by Kumbha for the worship of Umā-Maheśa (in addition to Ekaliṅga[238]) and Ratnakhetā by Rāimalla.[239] This list of villages donated by the royalty is, significantly, repeated in the Mewari (dialect) part of this record: '*rāi kedār, hammīra huo, tina śrī ekaliṅga caturmukha mūrti dhāravī, si heta grāma devabhogārtha cadavyum, seto . . . pānavād grāma . . . lākhansena, tini ciravogrām. . . .*'[240] The same list of royal land grants is attested by *Amarakāvyam.*[241] Such an extensive network of royally donated villages indicates the renewal of a symbiotic relationship between the Guhila dynasty and Ekaliṅga, particularly in the reign of the *rāṇās* (post-thirteenth century). This record of Rāimalla repeats the well-known legends of 'Bāppā at Nāgahṛda' and the bestowal of the kingdom of Medapāṭa on Bāppā by Hārītarāśi (of the temple of Trikūṭagiri, a devotee of Śrī Ekaliṅga).[242] Such reiteration of the age-old legitimizing motifs undoubtedly helped stabilize the political situation for Rāṇā Rāimalla. A similar link between the cult of Ekaliṅga and royal power is also echoed by the *Ekaliṅga-māhātmyam* which refers to the renewal of the worship and patronage of the Ekaliṅga temple by Rāimalla after the brief interregnum of Udaisiṁha I (assasin of Kumbha) and his ally the Delhi Sultan.[243]

We have seen that the sacred domain emanated from a variety of sources in Mewar. The Guhila state patronized brāhmaṇas who provided them with respectable origin in the early phase of state formation. Brāhmaṇas composed and officially propagated legitimizing motifs in legends and *praśastis* in the later phases and continued to legitimize Guhila power beyond Mewar in tribal centres and in non-Guhila Rajput localities. In the peak period of state formation in Mewar, between the tenth and the thirteenth centuries, Guhila power drew validation from what was considered the highest source of legitimization, the cult of Ekaliṅga of Nāgdā and the Pāśupata *ācāryas.* The Guhila title *Ekaliṅga-nijasevaka* in the fifteenth century links Guhila political power directly to the central cult of Ekaliṅga. The surrender of sovereign power to Ekaliṅga, the *de jure* ruler of Mewar, legitimized the rule of the fifteenth-century Guhilas in Mewar and hence facilitated massive mobilization for the army of the Guhila state. A general survey of monarchical myths and royal links with cult centres in Orissa, Bastar and south India in the context of state formation in the early medieval and medieval periods confirms these observations.

NOTES

1. *IHR*, vol. X, nos. 1-2, 1983-4, pp. 3-20.
2. Louis Dumont, 'The Conception of Kingship in Ancient India', in *Religion, Politics and History in India: Collected Papers in Indian Sociology*, Paris-The Hague, 1970, p. 65; J.C. Heesterman, 'Power and Authority in Indian Tradition', in R.J. Moore, ed., *Tradition and Politics in South Asia*, Delhi, 1979, p. 82. Also see J.C. Heesterman, 'Power, Priesthood and Authority', in his *The Inner Conflict of Tradition: Essays in Indian Ritual, Kingship and Society*, Chicago and London, 1985, pp. 111 and 141.
3. Thapar, 'Social Mobility in Ancient India with Special Reference to Elite Groups', in her *Ancient Indian Social History: Some Interpretations*, p. 133.
4. Ibid.
5. Ibid., p. 136.
6. Chattopadhyaya, 'Origin of the Rajputs', pp. 66-70.
7. Chattopadhyaya, 'Political Processes and Structure', p. 198.
8. Ibid., p. 199.
9. Kulke, 'Royal Temple Policy and the Structure of Medieval Hindu Kingdom', in A. Eschmann, H. Kulke and G.C. Tripathi, eds., *The Cult of Jagannatha and the Regional Tradition of Orissa*, pp. 129-30.
10. Kulke, 'King Anaṅgabhīma III, the Veritable Founder of the Gajapati Kingship and of the Jagannātha Trinity at Puri', in his *Kings and Cults*, pp. 17-32.
11. Kulke, 'Preface', in *Kings and Cults*, p. ix.
12. Ibid., pp. 9-10.
13. Idem, 'Royal Temple Policy and the Structure of Medieval Hindu Kingdom', in A. Eschmann, H. Kulke and G.C. Tripathi, eds., *The Cult of Jagannatha and the Regional Tradition of Orissa*, p. 132.
14. Kulke, 'King Anaṅgabhīma III, the Veritable Founder, pp. 21-2. Here, the concept of empire has been used by the Gajapati dynasty as a symbol of their sovereignty over the entire region of Orissa.
15. Kulke, 'Early Royal Patronage of the Jagannātha Cult', in *Kings and Cults*, pp. 150-5.
16. Surajit Sinha, 'State Formation and Rajput Myth in Central India', *Man in India*, vol. 42, no. 1, 1962, pp. 68-9.
17. Wilfred Grigson, *The Maria Gonds of Bastar*, London, 1949. Also see Verrier Elwin, *The Muria and Their Ghotul*, Bombay, 1947, p. 183.
18. Surajit Sinha writes, 'The most striking feature about the Bastar State is the completeness of interaction between the cults of the tribals and those of the Raja. The cult of the royal goddess Danteswari, Manikeswari or Maoli has spread over wide areas in Bastar, although when she is worshipped by the local tribal priests, the rituals become necessarily simple with local non-Sanskritic connotations. On the occasion of the Dussehra

festival it is customary for all these village priests to bring the emblems of their gods and goddesses, and to assemble these around the emblem of the royal goddess Danteswari at Jagdalpur', 'State Formation and Rajput Myth in Central India', p. 69.

19. R.N. Nandi, *Religious Institutions and Cults in Deccan*, Delhi, 1973, pp. 14-16; R.N. Nandi, *Social Roots of Religion in Ancient India*, Calcutta, 1986, p. 100.
20. Kesavan Veluthat, 'Royalty and Divinity: Legitimization of Monarchical Power in the South', in *PIHC*, 39th Session, Hyderabad, 1978, pp. 241-9.
21. David N. Lorenzen, *The Kāpālikas and Kālāmukhas: Two Lost Śaivite Sects*, Delhi, 1991, 2nd edn., pp. 129-60.
22. R. Champakalakshmi, 'Growth of Urban Centres in South India: Kuḍāmukku-Pālaiyarai, the Twin-city of the Colas', in *Studies in History*, vol. I, no. 1, 1979, p. 13.
23. Ibid.
24. Ibid., p. 14.
25. R. Champakalakshmi, 'Peasant State and Society in Medieval South India', a review article in *IESHR*, vol. XVIII, pts.3-4 (1981), p. 420. 'The early Chola temples, on the other hand, systematically used the liṅga mainly due to its assimilative character as the only convenient aniconic form which could incorporate in canonical temples, local and popular cult practices centering round the Kandu or pillar and tree, thus providing a constantly widening orbit for bringing in divergent socio-economic and ethnic groups into Śaiva worship.'
26. Kulke, *Kings and Cults*, pp. 194-5.
27. R.B.P. Singh, *Jainism in Early Medieval Karnataka, c.* AD *500-1200*, Delhi, 1975; p. 109. 'The Jaina epigraphs as well as the literary texts from Karnataka reveal that some of the Jaina teachers acted as preceptors or instructors to Kings, princes, and feudal lords who ruled over different parts of Karnataka. Pujyapada, Jainasena, Gunabhadra, Ajitasena-bhattaraka and Vadighangala Bhatta were some of the prominent Jaina teachers who took active interest in the day-to-day activities of the royal courts'.
28. Dhulev Plate of Maharaja Bhetti, op. cit., vv. 2-4.
29. Dungarpur Plates of Bābhaṭa, op. cit., vv. 12-19.
30. For instance see Dungarpur Plates of Bābhaṭa, ibid., p. 174, l. 15.
31. Ibid., ll. 13-14.
32. Āṭapura Inscription, op. cit., vv. 1-10.
33. Kadmal Plates dated to AD 1083, op. cit., vv. 27-33.
34. *Shodh Patrika*, Vikram Samvat 2010, op. cit., pp. 54-5. '*mahārājādhirāja śrī padmasyamāndevah rāo cāhuān rāo vāhaḍasuta rāo mokajasya sakala rājye ārādhara suta brāho śivaguṇa hasteudaka pūravakam | śāvilarabhumyamkardamval grāme vṛttisam juktā pradattam*'.
35. Ibid.

36. Ibid.
37. Ibid.
38. Chittaurgarh Palace Inscription of AD 1274, op. cit., p. 397, ll. 13-14, '*gaḍajātīyadvijadivākara vaṁśodbhavavyāsaratna-sutajjyotih sāḍala*'.
39. Ibid., ll. 14-15, '*tathā ca vipra delhaṇasutabhaṭṭa sāḍā tatputrā dvārabhaṭṭa khīmaṭastadbhrātṛ bhīma sahitena ebhirlikhitvā*'.
40. See Achaleśvara Inscription, op. cit., v. 60, '*yokārśid-ekaliṅga-tribhuvana vidita śrī samādhīścakrasvāmī-prāsād vrinde priyapaṭu tanayo vedaśarmā praśastih || ten=aiṣāpi vyadhāyi sphuṭaguṇaviśadā nāgarjñātibhājā vipreṇāśeṣa vidvajjana hṛdayaharā citrakūṭasthitena*'.
41. Ibid.
42. Chittaurgarh Stone Inscription of AD 1428, op. cit., last additional five verses, v. 1, '*śrī maddaśapurajñātiḥ bhaṭṭa viṣṇostanudabhavaḥ nāmnāi-kanāthanāmāyāmlikhat kṛtimujvalam ||*'.
43. Śṛṅgirṣi Inscription, op. cit., v. 28.
44. Chittaurgarh Inscription of Mokal, op. cit., vv. 72-3.
45. Śṛṅgirṣi Inscription, op. cit., v. 29.
46. Kumbhalgarh Praśasti, fourth slab, op. cit., v. 222, '*nṛpaḥ samādhīśvara-siddhatejaḥ samādhībhājām paramam rahasyam || arādhya tasyalaya-muddhas śrīcitrakūṭe maṇitornamkam ||*'.
47. Ibid., vv. 19-21, 24.
48. Nathulal Vyas, ed., *Shodh Patrika*, vol. 7, no. 1, Udaipur, 1955, p. 65, '*svasti rāṇā śrī kumbha ādeśata || deva prabhā jogyam ajaharī parganan cūrīyā sīmābdum samvat 1496 varṣe*'.
49. See, Chap. III, the section on Jains and the Guhilas.
50. Sharda, *MK*, no. 5, pp. 173-4.
51. *Shodh Patrika*, vol. 7, op. cit., pp. 65-6, '*svāsti rāṇā śrī kumbha ādeśatu karī kācchār grāma dāve godhā gohad jogya sāsane datta samvat 1510 varṣe āṣāḍha pūrve*'.
52. Ekaliṅgajī Temple Dakṣiṇadvāra Praśasti, op. cit., v. 39.
53. Ibid.
54. Ibid., v. 40.
55. Ibid., v. 67.
56. Ibid., v. 82.
57. Ibid., v. 87.
58. Ibid., vv. 83-6.
59. Ibid., vv. 127-33.
'There was a brāhmaṇa named Śrī Somanātha on this earth in the family of Bhagvān Bhṛgu known throughout the world, devoted like a wasp to the lotus-like feet of Śaṅkara, performing sacrifices in every vasanta. His son Narahari, who was like the Sun to the grave of the lotus-like science of Aṇvikṣikā, was Hari incarnate, and being the illustrious abode of the four vedas, was a Brahmā on earth. Like Manu from the Sun, Sūrya from Kāśyapa, Bhṛgu was Brahmā, the Moon from the ocean, Śrī Keśava, of

incalculate fame, a lion to all Narahari. His son Atri who was the abode of virtues, was above all the wise and the learned, was possessed of prodigious intelligence feasting upon the essence of the Mīmāṁsas, was a genius in the poetic art, lived as a leader of the Brāhmaṇas of the Daśapura caste, and was highly esteemed by the lord Kumbha, the Sun of the large forest of the lotuses of the line of Guhila Maheśa son of Atri, who is in the court of Rājamalla, bravely conducts himself against those who contest with him as a mad elephant does against trees. Maheśvara, son of Atri, whose style of composition is acknowledged by these verses in the high way of poetic composition, who is the poet of king Rājmalla, and who is a man of good parts and knowledge, added this eulogistic poem to the collection already existing poem full of heroic sentiments and placed in the five temple which is beautiful in its new arrangement. May this eulogy which is like another creeper of the fame of lord Rājamalla, made by me wishing his rule to last as long as the earth bears the beauty of the crest-jewel, of Ahindra (Śeṣa) as long as Śrīkaṇṭha (Śaṅkara) bears on his head Tuṣāra-tṛṣā (the moon), as long as Hari bears the (sign of) Śrī Vatsa on his chest, and as long as the ocean contains water, prosper in all its splendour.

60. Dabok Inscription, op. cit., p. 123, l. 1.
61. Ibid., l. 2.
62. Udaipur Praśasti, op. cit., v. 3.
63. Ibid.
64. Grants of Bhāvihita, op. cit., p. 172, l. 2.
65. Grants of Bābhaṭa, op. cit., p. 174, l. 1.
66. Ibid., l. 9.
67. Ibid., l. 1.
68. Sircar, *The Guhilas of Kiṣkindhā*, pp. 31-2.
69. Āṭapura Inscription, op. cit., v. 1.
70. Kadmal Plate, op. cit., vv. 1-2.
71. Āṭapura Inscription, op. cit., vv. 1-9.
72. Ibid., vv. 3-8. Also see Sāraṇeśvara Inscription dated AD 942, for the Hūṇa and Pratihāra functionaries, op. cit., vv. 6-7.
73. Āṭapura Inscription, ibid., vv. 3-8.
74. Pratapgarh Inscription, op. cit., pt. III, p. 187, l. 28.
75. *EI*, vol. X, pp. 20-4.
76. *URI*, op. cit., p. 124, fn. 3.
77. Chāṭsu Inscription of Guhila Bālāditya, op. cit., v. 6.
78. Memorial Stone Inscription dated to AD 1179-80, op. cit.
79. Nāḍol Cāhamāna Inscription dated to AD 1137-8, op. cit.
80. D.R. Bhandarkar, 'Foreign Elements in the Hindu Population', *IA*, vol. XL, p. 35.
81. Achaleśvara Inscription, op. cit., v. 11.
82. Nādlāi Ādināth Temple Inscription dated to AD 1500, op. cit., v. 13..
83. Romila Thapar generalizes the importance of the theme of migration that

facilitated the establishment of new dynasties. See, 'Origin Myths and the Early Indian Historical Tradition', in her *Ancient Indian Social History*, p. 321. 'The theme of migration, often disguised as exile, sets the geographical dimensions of the social group and can be used to establish rights and priority of a particular group over a particular region. This assumes significance in periods when new groups are moving in as entrepreneurs in either previously occupied areas or in newly opened up lands. Those who succeeded in establishing new dynasties would either have to link themselves genealogically with the descent groups, who were already associated with the area or else would have to introduce the idea of migration.'

84. Chittaurgarh Inscription dated to AD 1274, op. cit., v. 8.
85. Achaleśvara Inscription, op. cit., v. 11. F. Kielhorn transliterates this verse as '*hārītāt=kila Bappako smhri-valaya-vyājena lebhe mahaḥ kṣātraṁ dhātṛnibhād=vitīrya munaye brāhmyaṁ sva-sevāccha lāt ete s dy=āpi mahībhujah kṣiti-tale tad-vaṁśa-saṁbhātayah śobhaṁte sūtarām=upātta-vapushah kṣātra hi dharmmāiva ||11||*'
86. 'Origin of the Rajputs', p. 69.
87. Suvira Jaiswal, 'Status in early Indian Social History: Trends and Possibilities', *IHR*, vol. VI, 1979-80, p. 32.
88. Ekaliṅgajī Temple Inscription dated to AD 971, op. cit., v. 5.
89. Chittaurgarh Inscriptions, op. cit., vv. 9-11; Achaleśvara Inscription, op. cit., vv. 10-11.
90. Chittaurgarh Inscription dated to AD 1274, op. cit., vv. 12-13.
91. Śṛṅgiṛṣi Inscription, op. cit., v. 5 '*kṣetram kṣatriyavaṁśamaṇḍanamaṇim pratyarthikalanalam*'.
92. See, Chap. III, the section on Political and Social Links with the Hāḍās.
93. H.M. Elliot and John Dowson, vol. IV, op. cit., pp. 259-61.
94. Śṛṅgiṛṣi Inscription, op. cit., v. 2; Ekaliṅga Temple Dakṣiṇadvāra Praśasti refers to Bāṣpanva, op. cit., v. 8.
95. Rāṇakpur Praśasti, op. cit., p. 409, l. 2.
96. Ibid.
97. Nadlai Adinath Temple Inscription, op. cit., p. 425, l. 13.
98. Fourth slab, op. cit., v. 123.
99. Ibid., v. 124.
100. Ibid., v. 127.
101. Ibid.
102. See Chap. VI.
103. Dabok Inscription, op. cit., p. 123, ll. 1-5 and 12.
104. Ibid., l. 2.
105. B.D. Chattopadhyaya, '"Reappearance" of the Goddess or the Brāhmaṇical Mode of Appropriation: Some Early Epigraphic Evidence bearing on

Goddess Cults', G.-D. Sontheimer Memorial Symposium, *An Integrated View of Indian Culture* (unpublished Symposium Paper), Delhi, 1994, pp. 2-3.

106. Dabok Inscription, op. cit., p. 123, l. 1.
107. Inscription of Mori King Māna of Chittaur, op. cit., pp. 625-6.
108. *RTA*, p. 240.
109. Author's field-trip to Chittaurgarh.
110. Grant of Bhāvihita, op. cit., v. 1.
111. Kalyanpur Fragmentary Inscription of King Padda, op. cit., v. 4.
112. Rajshekhar Vyās, *Mevār kī Kalā aur Sthāpatva*, Jaipur, 1988, p. 77.
113. Samoli Inscription, op. cit., p. 98, ll. 8-10.
114. Ibid., ll. 4-5.
115. Udaipur Praśasti of Aparājita, op. cit., vv. 6-8.
116. Contemporary Pāśupata *maṭhas* such as Caṇḍikāśram at Ujjain (*IA*, vol. XI, pp. 220-3), Sītaleśvara Mahādeva at Chandrabhaga, Jhalarapatan originating in the seventh century (A. Cunningham, *Report of a Tour in the Punjab and Rajasthan*, Archaeological Survey of India, 1983-4, Calcutta, pp. 125-31), etc., speak for the establishment of the Pāśupatas in early medieval Rajasthan.
117. Ekaliṅgajī Temple Inscription of the Reign of Naravāhana, op. cit.
118. Ibid., v. 17.
119. Ibid., v. 21.
120. Ibid., vv. 9-11.
121. Ibid., v. 5.
122. D.R. Regmi, ed., Inscription nos. LXXVI-LXXVII, in *Inscriptions of Ancient Nepal*, vol. II, Delhi, 1983, pp. 48-9.
123. 'A stone inscription in the temple of Hastamātā, Udaipur (dated in the eighth decade of tenth century)', in *A Collection of Prakrit and Sanskrit Inscriptions*, op. cit., p. 73, l. 5.
124. *ARIE*, 1963-4, see Chap. Rajasthan, p. 103.
125. Paldi Inscription, op. cit., vv. 11-14.
126. Achaleśvara Temple Inscription, op. cit., vv. 55-7.
127. Paldi Inscription, op. cit., vv. 11-14.
128. Ibid.
129. PRAS, WC, 1905, pp. 54-9.
130. Ibid.
131. R.C. Agrawala, 'Two Standing Lakulīśa Sculptures from Rajasthan', *Journal of Oriental Institute*, vol. XIV, nos. 1-4, Baroda, 1965, pp. 388ff.
132. Ibid.
133. Ibid.
134. Ibid.
135. PRAS, WC, 1905, pp. 54-9.
136. Devangana Desai, 'The Patronage of the Lakshmana Temple at Khajuraho',

in Barbara S. Miller, ed., *The Powers of Art: Patronage in Indian Culture*, Delhi, 1992, p. 83.

137. Achaleśvara Temple Inscription, op. cit., vv. 7-10.
138. Chittaur Inscription of Rāval Samarasiṁhadeva (AD 1281), vv. 8-11.
139. *Annals*, vol. I, see Manosarovar Inscription in the Appendix (old edition).
140. Paldi Inscription, op. cit., vv. 8-9.
141. Kulke, 'The Early and Imperial Kingdom: A Processual Model of Integrative State Formation in Early Medieval India', in his *State in India AD 1000-1700*, op. cit., p. 29.
142. Ibid.
143. Achaleśvara Inscription and Chittaur Inscription, v. 12, and vv. 10-13, respectively.
144. Pratapgarh Inscription, op. cit., pt. IV, v. 12, ll. 7-9.
145. Chiravā Inscription, op. cit., v. 2.
146. *ARRM*, 1915, p. 3. Also see Rajshekhar Vyas, op. cit., pp. 85-8; R.C. Agrawala, 'Early Sculptural Art of Mewar', in D.L. Paliwal, ed., *Mewar Through the Ages*, p. 15. The temple of Ambikā at Jagat is traced back to the tenth century. The Mahiṣamardinī Durgā stands out as one of the best of all temple sculptures here. The other outstanding image is that of Nārāyaṇī-Vaiṣṇavī in the posture of a Cāmuṇḍā. On the exterior wall of Sabhāmaṇḍapa, there is an exquisite fiture of Śubhahaṁtrī Durgā and the temple abounds in beautiful images of Sarasvati, Godhāsana, Gaurī, Cāmuṇḍā, etc. Some of the motifs used here are supposed to betray *tāntrik* traditions so much so that Jagat has also earned the epithet of 'Khajuraho of Rajasthan'.
147. *ARRM*, op. cit., p. 3.
148. *URI*, p. 177.
149. Samoli Inscription, op. cit., l. 9.
150. Dabok Inscription, op. cit., l. 4.
151. Pratapgarh Inscription, op. cit., pt. IV, v. 12, l. 7.
152. *ARRM*, op. cit.
153. *The Making of Early Medieval India*, p. 34.
154. *Ekaliṅgamāhātmyam*, Chaps. 5-6.
155. Ibid., Chaps. 6-19.
156. Kumbhalgarh Praśasti, fourth slab, v. 239.
157. *Ekaliṅgamāhātmyam*, p. 99, v. 23, '*ekaliṅgasamīpe sa rājā bhṛtya ivaparah*'.
158. Ibid., p. 59.
159. Kumbhalgarh Praśasti, first slab, op. cit., vv. 20-2.
160. Haripada Chakroborti, *Pāśupata Sūtram*, Calcutta, 1970, p. 17.
161. *Ekaliṅgamāhātmyam*, Chaps. V-VI.
162. Nathulal Bhagirath Vyas, ed., Ekaliṅga Matha Praśasti (AD 1535), *Shodh Patrika*, vol. IX, no. 1, Udaipur, Vikram Samvat 2014, p. 28, '*ākaśavāsī pāśupatācārya śrī naroharinā kāritoyam maṭhīvistārah*'.
163. Ibid.

164. *Ekaliṅgamāhātmyam*, p. 9, v. 15.
165. Ibid., p. 27, vv. 39 and 41.
166. Ibid., p. 30, vv. 6 and 7.
167. Ibid., p. 154, vv. 19 and 24.
168. Ibid., p. 143, vv. 20 and 23.
169. Ibid., vv. 23-4.
170. Ibid., v. 24.
171. Ibid., v. 31.
172. Ibid., p. 155, v. 37.
173. Ibid., v. 34.
174. Ibid., p. 163, vv. 56-7, '*tṛtīyāyam vindhyavāsinī pūjayet bhaktimuktidam | a gamoktena vidhinā ṣoḍaṣairūpacārakaih*'.
175. Ibid., p. 9, vv. 17-19.
176. Dabok Inscription, op. cit., vv. 1-2.
177. Ibid.
178. *Ekaliṅgamāhātmyam*, Chap. 32.
179. *Rajasthan District Gazetteers: Chittorgarh (1977), Bhilwara (1975), Udaipur (1981)*. See list of fairs.
180. Dabok Inscription, op. cit., vv. 1-2.
181. Mahendra Bhanawat, *Rājasthān kī Gaṇagaur*, Udaipur, 1977, pp. 12-20.
182. Ibid., p. 13.
183. Ibid., pp. 4-5.
184. Jagat Inscriptions dating to AD 1171-2, op. cit.
185. Ibid., pp. 9-10.
186. Ibid., p. 20.
187. Ibid., pp. 25-6.
188. Shah, op. cit., p. 181.
189. Ibid.
190. J.K. Doshi, *Social Structure and Cultural Change in a Bhil Village*, Delhi, 1974, p. 108.
191. Ibid.
192. *Ekaliṅgamāhātmyam*, p. 144, vv. 45-6, '*bhillaiśca vividha-kārairbṛtam paramadhārmikaih śiva bhaktirtairvīrair bhutāhimsā-divarjitaih*'.
193. Kalyan Kumar Ganguly, *Cultural History of Rajasthan*, Delhi, 1983, p. 168.
194. *Annals*, vol. II, p. 539.
195. *Ekaliṅgamāhātmyam*, op. cit., p. 33, vv. 15-16.
196. See Chap. III, the section on Relations with the Contemporary Powers. Also see Sharda, *MK*, pp. 77-114.
197. *Ekaliṅgamāhātmyam*, p. 34, v. 19, '*pūjayettam rāṣtrasenām tadrūpam ca strīyām tathā brāhmaṇapi sampūjya devī pṛttayai viśiṣṭha*'.
198. J.B. Bhattacharjee, 'Dimasa State Formation in Cachar', in Surajit Sinha, ed., *Tribal Politics*, p. 181.
199. Ibid.

200. *Ekaliṅgamāhātmyam*, p. 145, vv. 1 and 4.
201. Ibid., p. 134, vv. 55-7.
202. *District Census Handbook*, Udaipur, 1981, p. xxviii.
203. *Ekaliṅgamāhātmyam*, p. 35, v. 23, '*cāmuṇḍā vindhyavāsinī kālikāthambiketi ca | grāmanāmnī kvācitiddevī tīrthaparvatagotrajā ||*'.
204. Ibid., pp. 160-5. These goddesses do not figure in the list of deities worshipped during Caitrayātrā.
205. Ibid., pp. 162-5, vv. 50-90.
206. *Ekaliṅgamāhātmyam*, p. 144, v. 40.
207. Ibid., p. 9, vv. 25-7.
208. Ibid., Chap. 15.
209. Ibid., p. 70, v. 123.
210. Ibid., p. 142, vv. 9-10.
211. Ibid., pp. 141-2, v. 308.
212. Ibid., p. 144, vv. 33-9.
213. Ibid., p. 134, v. 59.
214. Ibid., p. 133, v. 49, '*hārītasya ca śiṣya te vinayenābhi baddyaca*'.
215. Ibid., p. 160, v. 14, '*vratam pāśupatam nāmā śivalokagatipradam*'.
216. Ibid., p. 143, vv. 18 and 20.
217. Ibid., p. 7, v. 10, '*yādṛśam yasya devasya rūpamāyudhavāhanam | tadṛśam dārṣadīm mūrtīm prāpya pūjya bhaviṣyatha ||*'.
218. Kumbhalgarh Praśasti, fourth slab, op. cit., v. 239.
219. Kulke, 'The Early and Imperial Kingdom', p. 27.
220. Ibid.
221. *Ekaliṅgamāhātmyam*, Chaps. 23-5 and 32.
222. Ibid., p. 117, v. 8.
223. Rajendranath Purohit, op. cit., p. 43.
224. J.N. Banerji, 'Lakulīśa—the founder of the systematizer of Pāśupata order', *PIHC*, Jaipur, 1951, pp. 33-7; B.P. Majumdar, 'Lakulīśa Pāśupatas and their Temples in Medieval India', in *Journal of the Bihar Research Society*, vol. XXXIX, 1953, pp. 1-9.
225. Rajendra Purohit, op. cit., p. 46. The fact that the Bhils have the foremost right to put *ṭīkā* at the coronation ceremony also highlights the political importance of the Bhils, signifying transfer of power and legitimization.
226. Ibid.
227. Ibid., p. 48.
228. Ibid., p. 49.
229. Ibid.
230. *Annals*, vol. I, p. 600. About the priests of Ekaliṅgajī, Tod also writes, 'the Ranas of Mewar as the Deewans or Vice-regents of Śiva, when they visit the temple, supercede the high priest in his duties, and perform the ceremonies, which the reigning prince does, with particular correctness and grace'.

231. Achaleśvara Inscription, op. cit., v. 60, '*yokārśīd ekaliṅga atribhuvana-vidita śrī samādhīśa cakrasvāmī prāsāda vṛṁde priyapaṭutanayo vedaśarmmā praśastih*'.
232. Mokal's Chittaurgarh Inscription, op. cit., vv. 3 and 5 of last part, '*atipraśas tairalikhatpraśastimvarnairavarṇena bahih kṛtairyah || śrīmatsamādhīśamaheśvara syaprasādata sau cirajīvanostu || rūcirākṣaramutkārṇa praśastiriyamujvata || lilekha vīsalah śilpī samādhīśaprasādatah*'.
233. Kumbhalgarh Praśasti, fourth slab, op. cit., v. 222, '*nṛpah samādhīśvara-siddhatejah samadhībhājam paramam rahasyam || ārādhya tasyalayamidd-dhara śrīcitrakūṭe maṇitoronāmkain*'.
234. *Ekaliṅgamāhātmyam*, p. 181, v. 111.
235. Ekāliṅgajī Temple Dakṣiṇadvāra Praśasti, op. cit., v. 26.
236. Ibid., v. 32.
237. Ibid., v. 46, '*grāmam vādhanavādam rāmagrāmam ca mokalo nṛpatiḥ || śivabhūtagāmśulkam śivabhogārtham samarpāyāmas*'.
238. Ibid., v. 48.
239. Ibid., v. 67.
240. Ibid., the concluding part of this inscription is in Mewari dialect.
241. Amarakāvyam, p. 143, v. 13; p. 145, v. 24; p. 150, v. 20; p. 169, v. 52.
242. Ekāliṅgajī Temple Dakṣiṇadvāra Praśasti, op. cit., vv. 11-17.
243. *Ekaliṅgamāhātmyam*, Chap. 30.

APPENDIX 1: ORIGIN MYTHS BASED ON LEGENDS (I): MEDIEVAL TRIBAL POLITICS IN ORISSA, BIHAR, BENGAL AND ASSAM

State	Sources	Status Claimed	Origin Myth
ORISSA			
1. State of Bonai; possibly Bhuiyan or Bond or Binjhal tribal and chiefs	Oral Traditions at Court[1] Late Royal Chronicle[2]	Kadam Vaṁśī Rajput	Originating in Ceylon, the founder of this dynasty was left under a Kadam tree and was brought up by a peacock.
2. State of Mayurbhanj; Bhanja tribal chiefs	Royal Chronicles[3]		Sūryavaṁśa Vaśiṣṭha gotra.
3. State of Keonjhar: Bhanja royal family, rulers sponsored by the Pabudi Bhuiyan, Saonti, Rajkuli Bhuiyan and Konth tribes	Local Annals[4]		Child prince Jyotibhanj of the Bhanja royal family was stolen from the royal palace by some members of the Bhuiyan tribe of Keonjhar to redress their grievances. The boy-prince was brought up by the Bhuiyans as their king.
BIHAR			
State of Chhotanagpur: Nāgvaṁśī royal family. Important tribal partners in state formation of Chhotanagpur are the Mundas	Royal chronicles Veni Ram's *Nāg-vaṁśāvalī*[5]	Kṣatriya Nāgvaṁśī	Founder Puṇḍarīka Nāga disguised as a brāhmaṇa and married to a brāhmaṇa wife.

(contd.)

APPENDIX 1 (contd.)

State	Sources	Status Claimed	Origin Myth
WEST BENGAL			
State of Malabhūm: sixteenth century to end of eighteenth century AD (spread over a major portion of present-day Bankura district) Malla Royal family	Royal chronicles[6]	Rajput Kṣatriya	Ādi Malla, founder of the Malla dynasty, son of a Rajput Kṣatriya *rājā*, brought up by a brāhmaṇa in a forest. The boy-prince in alliance with an aboriginal prince, carved out a principality in the forest territory.
Bāgdis, a low-caste community from eastern Malbhum	Bāgdi chronicles	Bāgdi origins of the Malla kings[7]	First Bāgdi child of Śiva and Pārvatī.
ASSAM			
Ahom state: AD 1228-1800; Ahom royal family	Royal Ahom chronicles[8]	Divine origins of the first Tai kingdom	First Tai kingdom came from heaven to bring fallow land under cultivation and stateless people under a stable ruler (this points to the superiority of Tai agriculturists over their non-Tai neighbours practising Jhum cultivation.
Dimāsā state of Herambyarājya;	Royal chronicles[9]	Divine origin	First Dimāsā king Nirbhoya

(contd.)

APPENDIX 1 (contd.)

State	Sources	Status Claimed	Origin Myth
(north Cachar hills and parts of Nowgong district in Assam, Dayung-Dhansiri valley in Nagaland and Jiri frontier area in Manipur) Dimāsā royal family descending from Bodo lineage of Tibeto-Burmese origin.	Local legends[10]		Nārāyaṇa discovered his divine origin through his *dharmādiguru*, a brāhmaṇa. First Dimāsā king Nirbhoy Nārāyaṇa was blessed by war goddess Raṇacaṇḍī, which made him invincibe in battles.
	Brāhmaṇical tradition[11]		The son of Hiḍimbā and Bhīma (Pāṇḍava brother) Mahābhārata—Ghatotkac was the ancestor of Nārāyaṇa, the first Dimāsā ruler, the genealogy beginning with Bhīma.

APPENDIX 2: EVOLUTION OF AND SHIFT IN ORIGIN MYTHS OF NON-GUHILA RAJPUTS

Dynasties	Sources	Status Claimed	Origin Myth
Gurjaras of Nandīpurī	Seventh century AD	Subordinate allies, suggested by such titles as *mahāsāmanta*, etc.	Descent from Mahārāja Karṇa[12]

(contd.)

APPENDIX 2 (contd.)

Dynasties	Sources	Status Claimed	Origin Myth
Pratihāras of Mandor	*c.* Mid-eighth century	–	Descent from kṣatriyas, implying *brahma-kṣatra* status. Also claim links with Lakṣmaṇa who acted as the Pratihāra (door keeper) of Rāma[13]
–do–	*c.* Late eighth century	–	–do– (Name of the brāhmaṇa wife dropped)[14]
Pratihāras of Rajasthan and Kanauj	*c.* Ninth century	Sovereign power	Descent from the Sun, implying Sūryavaṁśī origin through Lakṣmaṇa[15]
–do–	*c.* Tenth century	Mentioned as the overlords of the Cāhamānas	Raghuvaṁśī[16]
Gurjara-Pratihāras of Rajor (Alwar)	*c.* Late tenth century	Subordinate allies of the Pratihāras of Rajasthan and Kanauj[17]	–
Cāhamānas of Nāḍol (Godwar; Marwar)	*c.* Early twelfth century	–	Descent from Indra through a person who was born out of Indra's eyes[18]
Cāhamānas of Śākambharī	*c.* Mid-tenth century	Subrodinate allies of the Pratihāras[19]	–
–do–	*c.* Late twelfth century	Sovereign Power	Brāhmaṇical descent, Vipraśrī Vatsagotra[20]

(contd.)

APPENDIX 2 (contd.)

Dynasties	Sources	Status Claimed	Origin Myth
–do–	*c.* Late twelfth century	–do–	Descent from Sun-god, described as the right eye of Viṣṇu[21]
–do–	AD 1191-3	–do–	Descent from the Sun and the Ikṣavākus of the *kṛta* age.[22]

APPENDIX 3: ORIGIN MYTHS OF GUHILA DYNASTIES AND CHIEFLY FAMILIES

Locality	Period	Family Name	Political Status	Nature of Claim about the Origin of family
1. Guhilas of Kiṣkindhā	Seventh century	Guhilaputrān-vaya	Subordinate allies, suggested by such titles as *sāmanta*, *samadhigata-pañca mahaśābda*, *mahārāja*, etc.	–
2. Guhilas of Chatsu	Middle of the tenth century	Guhilavaṁśa[23]	Subordinate allies of the Morīs and Pratihāras	Brahma-Kṣatrānvita
3. Guhilas of Mewar	AD 661	Guhilānvaya[24]	Although they bear no subordinate political title, they possibly functioned as	–

(contd.)

APPENDIX 3 (contd.)

Locality	Period	Family Name	Political Status	Nature of Claim about the Origin of family
			subordinate allies of the Morīs	
–do–	AD 977[25]		Sovereign in Mewar hills	Founder of the family, Guhadatta is described as '*ānandapura vinirgata viprakulā-nandanoḥ mahīdevaḥ*' implying descent from a brāhmaṇa family of Ānandapura (Vadnagar in north-eastern Gujarat)
–do–	AD 1083[26]	Guhilavaṁśa	–do–	–
–do–	AD 1285[27]		Sovereign in Mewar	Brahma-kṣatra
–do–	AD 1428[28]		–do–	
–do–	AD 1500[29]	Guhila	–do–	Sūryavaṁśa
–do–	AD 1680[30]		–do–	Sūryavaṁśa and Ikṣvākuvaṁśa
4. Guhilas of Maṅgrol (Saurashtra)	AD 1146	Guhilānvaya	Functionary of the Caulukyas title of	–

(contd.)

APPENDIX 3 (contd.)

Locality	Period	Family Name	Political Status	Nature of Claim about the Origin of family
			'*Surāṣṭra-nāyaka*'	
5. Guhilas of Unsṭrā Jodhpur (Marwar)	AD 1179-80		Small, local chiefs	–
6. Guhilas of Nāḍol (Godwar)	AD 1138		Local chief at Nāḍol in the Nāḍol Cāhamāna state	–

NOTES

1. C.E.B. Cobdan-Ramsay, *Orissa Feudatory States*, Calcutta, 1910 and *Report on Tour in Bonai*, Government of Bengal, 1863-4.
2. L.K. Mahapatra, 'Ex-princely States of Orissa: Mayurbhanj, Keonjhar and Bonai', in Surajit Sinha, ed., *Tribal Politics*, p. 13.
3. Ibid., pp. 16-18.
4. Ibid., p. 19.
5. K. Suresh Singh, 'The Chhotanagpur Raj: Mythology, Structure and Ramification', in Surajit Sinha, ed., *Tribal Politics*, pp. 52-64.
6. Hitesranjan Sanyal, 'Mallabhum', in Surajit Sinha, ed., *Tribal Politics*, pp. 73-7.
7. Ibid., p. 79.
8. Amalendu Guha, 'The Ahom Political System', op. cit., pp. 153-5.
9. J.B. Bhattacharjee, 'Dimasa State Formation in Cachar', op. cit., p. 180.
10. Ibid., pp. 181-2.
11. Ibid., pp. 182-3.
12. *IA*, vol. XIII, pp. 70ff; *EI*, vol. XXIII, pp. 147ff.
13. *EI*, vol. XVIII, pp. 97-8.
14. *JRAS*, 1895, pp. 519-20.
15. *EI*, vol. XVIII, p. 110.
16. *IA*, vol. XLII, p. 58.

17. *EI*, vol. III, pp. 263-7.
18. Ibid., vol. XI, p. 304.
19. *IA*, vol. XLII, pp. 57ff.
20. *EI*, vol. XXVI, pp. 84ff.
21. Ibid., vol. XXIX, p. 179.
22. 'Pṛthvīrājavijaya of Jayanaka', quoted in V.S. Pathak, *Ancient Historians of India: A Study in Historical Biographies*, Bombay, 1966, pp. 98-136.
23. Chāṭsu Inscription of Guhila Bālāditya, op. cit., vv. 6-7.
24. Udaipur Praśasti of Guhila Aparājita, op. cit., vv. 1-2.
25. Āṭapura Inscription of Śaktikumāra, op. cit., v. 1.
26. Kadmal Plates of Vijayasiṁha, op. cit., v. 2.
27. Achaleśvara Inscription, op. cit., vv. 10-12.
28. Śṛṇgirṣi Inscription, op. cit., v. 5.
29. Nādlāi Adinath Temple Inscription, op. cit., l. 13.
30. *Rājapraśasti Mahākāvyam*, canto 1, vv. 28-9.

CHAPTER VI

Perceptions of the Guhila State: Literary Representations

This chapter consists of four sections. The first or the introductory section briefly discusses the sources and their reliability—the methodological issues. The second section probes the self-perception of the state based on: (a) the royal inscriptions from the thirteenth to the fifteenth centuries, (b) the *Ekaliṅgamāhātmyam* (*Sthala Purāṇa*), (c) the royal inscription of the seventeenth century; the *Rājapraśasti*, and (d) a text, the *Amarakāvyam* of the seventeenth century. The third section discusses the perception of the influential, non-Rajput social groups engaged in the functioning of the state: the Ṭāmṭarāḍas and the Jains, between the thirteenth and the fifteenth centuries. I then probe popular perceptions of the Guhila state, represented by bardic literature such as Cāraṇ Girdhar Āsiā's *Sagat Rāso* and Muhaṇot *Nainsī rī Khyāt*, and Col. James Tod's *Annals and Antiquities of Rajasthan*. The chapter will be appended with the genealogical lists from the *Nainsī rī Khyāt*, the *Sūryavaṁśāvalī* and *Rājābalī Bahī*.

The Sources

Methodologically, our sources would be utilized to analyse the contemporary political situation. Royal inscriptional records between the thirteenth and the fifteenth centuries situate the Guhila rulers in the context of their contemporary political and territorial achievements and problems. My analysis here will deal with Guhila attempts at projecting particular images in specific situations. Both, Raṇachoḍa Bhaṭṭa's *Rājapraśasti Mahākāvyam* and *Amarakāvyam,* reflect royal Guhila perception in the seventeenth century. Raṇachoḍa Bhaṭṭa, patronized by the royal court, was obviously presenting exaggerated accounts of the Guhila kings of Mewar to the elite in the royal court and to a similar audience beyond Mewar in contemporary Rajasthan.

The Jain sources between the thirteenth and the fifteenth centuries are one of our best historical sources as they are the least mediated. They are composed by Jain *ācāryas* and reflect their perception of the Guhila state.

Muhṇot Nainsī, a seventeenth-century official and an historian in the royal court of Marwar wrote about the Guhila state in Marwari while the *cāraṇ* poet from Mewar, Girdhar Āsiā, composed *Sagat Rāso* in Mewari. Unlike the *bhāṭs* who are essentially genealogists, the *cāraṇs* are specialists in compositions and recitations of family traditions and histories. They are the primary preservers and transmitters of family tales.[1] They are rewarded just like the *bhāṭs* with grants of land called *śāsan* held in perpetuity.[2] If *Nainsī rī Khyāt* was meant for a larger audience beyond the royal court in the Rajasthan of the seventeenth century, *Sagat Rāso*, although patronized by the court of Mewar, was also directed at a popular audience in Mewar in the same period. What emerges out of a juxtaposition of *khyāt*, *cāraṇ* traditions and the royal-accounts, dating to the seventeenth century is the presence of both parallels as well as contrasts in the two traditions.

Finally, we have the account of Col. James Tod, an official of the East India Company, who learnt Sanskrit and Mewari dialects from a local Jain *ācārya*. He travelled widely through Mewar, met various Rajput chiefs and collected local bardic traditions. His presentation of Rajput traditions therefore seems to be doubly mediated, as the local annals that he collected were interpreted by Tod. My purpose here is to compare and contrast nineteenth-century perception of the Guhila state with those of the seventeenth century to assess whether changes occurred in popular perceptions or whether the general perception of the Guhila state had become standardized. My analysis can also be tested against some current popular idioms and songs from Mewar.

II

Self-perception of the Guhila State

My discussion of the royal perception of the state of Mewar begins with the late thirteenth century as the Guhilas attained regional statehood through integrative processes in this period. The Guhila state of Nāgdā-Āhaḍa, which had graduated from a local state (seventh century) to a sub-regional state of Mewar hills (between the tenth and thirteenth centuries) and finally to the regional state of Mewar (late thirteenth century) projected a magnified self-image for the first time in the late thirteenth century. I have already discussed the legitimizing motifs of Bappā-Hārītarāśi-Ekaliṅga-Medapāṭa that legalized the exercise of power by a local dynasty over the whole of Mewar. I feel that it is equally important to discuss the self-perception of the Guhila state, as distinct from the problems of legitimization.

In view of the territorial expansion and consequent political integration in the late thirteenth century, the Guhila dynasty claimed local roots to popularize its image. The Guhilas drew legitimization from the Pāśupata sect and the cult of Ekaliṅga through the legendary King Bāppā. Actually the aim was to utilize these legends to signify the long association of the Guhilas with a locally popular sect as well as with the regional cult. The legendary Bāppā who seems to have attained popularity by the thirteenth century was appropriated as the founder of the Guhila dynasty.[3] Similarly, sage Hārītarāśi, and the regional *tīrtha* at Nāgdā with its Ekaliṅga cult[4] had been appropriated to project ancient linkages with popular local religious motifs and landmarks.

Having succeeded to the throne of Mewar in the late fourteenth century, a chiefly family from Chittaurgarh was faced with two essentially political problems: it had to go through a process of identifying itself with the Guhila dynasty and it had to tackle with the recurrent inroads from the neighbouring sultanates of Malwa and Gujarat as well as engage in constant territorial expansion of the Guhila state. Hence, the fifteenth-century kings of Mewar made every attempt to match up to Guhila glory and traditions. Hammīra, a legendary prince (alluding to an early scion of the family) was claimed to be the conqueror of the enemies on all sides.[5] Hammīra is said to have possessed all the kingly attributes, and was eulogized as the best of the kṣatriyas.[6] The fact that the existence of Hammīra was a mere legend and that he never sat on the throne of Mewar is evident from the fantastic legends woven around him.[7] The possibility of Hammīra having alluded to an early prince of the Rāṇā branch of the Guhilas[8] has already been discussed and the situations described pertain to the early phase of the ascendancy of the Rāṇā Guhilas. Political exigencies demanded the projection of a self-image that was enhanced by a founder of the royal house who was as legendary as Bappā. Such an image was necessary not only to highlight their political and military power but also to claim kinship connections with the Guhila dynasty. However, an interesting phenomenon accompanied the creation of the legend of Hammīra in the fifteenth century. The importance of the legendary Bāppā seems to have been transferred to Hammīra. The saga of Prince Hammīra was elaborated throughout the fifteenth century because it was Hammīra and not Bappā who was to expand the rule of the chiefly family that had succeeded the original Guhilas.

The self-image of the state was important at the beginning of the military career of the fifteenth-century Guhilas and even more so at the peak of this career. Rāṇā Mokal began eulogizing Hammīra in the early part of the fifteenth century,[9] and Rāṇā Kumbha further elaborated upon Hammīra's attributes.[10] Enhancing the self-image of the ruling lineage for political consolidation was the need of the hour.

With Hammīra began Mewar's battles with the Sultans and the fifteenth-century Guhilas projected themselves as the 'saviours' of the region who rescued it from the yoke of *mlecchas*.[11] Thus, it is important to enquire into the antecedents of the title of Hammīra. Interestingly, the word *hammīra*, *hamīma* or *hamvīra* appears to be a corruption of the Arabic word amīr (commander) derived from the root amīr (commander).[12] It is evident from coins and Sanskrit inscriptions that sultans like Mu'izzuddin (Muhammad bin Sam) and even sultans of Delhi like Balban were given the title of Śrī Hammīra.[13] Hence, the status of *amīr* or *hammīra* seems to have been internalized by Rajput society, and Rajput princes were given the title Hammīra from the thirteenth century. The use of the title Hammīra by Cāhamāna Hammīra of Ranathambhor in the late thirteenth to early fourteenth centuries and by Guhila Hammīra of Mewar, as well as the status attached to the legendary Hammīra by the fifteenth-century Guhilas, both testify to the percolation of the courtly standards of the Delhi Sultanate into Rajasthan.

The process of image-building also demanded that the fifteenth-century kings claimed that their rule over Mewar had been comparatively more ancient than it actually was. Hence, Prince Arisiṁha, Hammīra's father, was proclaimed 'lord of Medapāṭa' in the early fifteenth century[14] and occupied a significant position in the royal genealogy at the end of the fifteenth century.[15] In fact, Arisiṁha too was not a historical entity like some other early princes of this family seems to have been a legendary figure.[16]

The problem of repeated incursions from the neighbouring sultanates and the maintenance of the self-image of the state seems to have been tackled by the Guhila state in the early period through motifs of 'liberator of the holy *tīrthas*'. In the first half of the fifteenth century, the Guhilas claimed that they were the 'liberators' of the holy *tīrtha* of Gaya from the yoke of the Yavanas,

May the famous line of that prince Lakṣa ever rejoice (in this world) by whom Gaya was freed from the burden of tax for a considerable number of years, by paying lofty horses and heaps of gold to the lord of Gaya, and for which (whose) ancestors gone to the upper world, gratified as they are, even now confer (on him) genuine benedictions.[17]

It is significant that the role of the 'saviour' of the *tīrthas* is only confined to Gaya in the early part of the fifteenth century. Such claims limited to specific times perhaps reflect the actual results of early incursions from Nagaur and Gujarat in which the losses for Mewar might have been substantial.

By the second half of the fifteenth century, the royal claim of having liberated Gaya gets magnified to become the claim of having liberated the holy *tristhalī*—the *tīrthas* of Gaya, Prayag and Kashi in the Gangetic plains. The Guhilas were obviously using a sacred motif to enhance their credibility in the face of external threats. It is worth noting that the more it got involved in the military campaigns against the sultanates of Malwa and Gujarat, the more the state dwelt on this theme. Such claims were aimed at winning popular appeal. The scale on which Rāṇā Kumbha undertook his campaigns called for massive mobilization. Without claiming to be the 'liberator of the *tīrthas*' it was difficult for the state to wage war especially against Malwa and Gujarat. The fact that mobilization was the need of the hour is also corroborated by the creation of the goddess Rāṣṭrasenā in more or less the same period.[18] A definite indicator that the state had to reorient its self-image to undertake campaigns against Malwa and Gujarat, is also evident from the high-sounding titles of Kumbha as the conqueror of Malwa and its sultan (*śrī kumbho mālavambhodhīnāthmanthalumahidharah* and *mahamma damahipateh*),[19] as lord of Gujarat and as the conqueror of Malwa and its sultan (*sphurjodgurjaramanḍaleśvaramsau kārāgṛhe vivāsat* and *rāṇāpahṛtakunjarairmitagurjaradhīśvara*).[20] Till the end of our period, Rāṇā Lākhā (one of Rāṇā Kumbha's predecessors) continued to be credited with the liberation of Gaya in the royal records.[21]

Victory over the 'Śakas' (the Khaljis) was a central theme: Rāimalla was proclaimed the 'lord of Gyāsaśaka' (Giyasuddin Khalji of Malwa) pervading Citrakūṭa.[22] In their *praśasti*, not only did the Guhilas of the fifteenth century eulogize their victories over the sultans by singling out their names but also always appended the term *śaka* to such defeated kings. This would have further enhanced their image as protectors of the brāhmaṇical sacred centres and hence those of local society.[23] Such an image proclaimed the Guhilas as the 'uprooter of Delhi power',[24] and victory over Malwa was equated with victory over the Yavanas.[25]

It is significant that by the end of our period the scope of the royal perception of the state of Mewar extends beyond western India and the Yavanas. It takes the Guhilas to the realm of conquests of distant countries like Kashmir, Karnataka and Andhra. Rāṇā Rāimalla is described as the 'Sun of Gurjara-maṇḍala' and the conqueror of Kashmir, Karnataka and Andhra.[26] Thus, by the end of the fifteenth century, the Guhilas attempted to project an exaggerated military image for themselves. A chronological study of such claims from the thirteenth to the fifteenth century shows the various stages by which a self-image is built. Starting with the region of Medapāṭa, the claims graduated to military conquest of both the Yavanas and regions from for flung parts of the Indian subcontinent.

Finally, to enhance their political image, their epithets were further elaborated by the second half of fifteenth century. The epithets used graduated from the simple Kṣitiśa and Bhūpati[27] to Mahārājādhirāja Rāirāyā Rānerāya Mahārāṇā for Kumbha (Śrī Kumbhakarṇa).[28] It is significant to note such changes in royal epithets in the same record, the Kumbhalgarh Praśasti projected the gradual rise of the dynasty to power, its zenith being Kumbha's period. However, one of the most significant developments at the end of our period is the reiteration of the old popular motifs of Bappā-Hārītarāśi-Ekaliṅga[29] to assert their claim of belonging to the Guhila dynasty and hence to win popular mandate for their sovereignty over Mewar.

The process of building this self-image by the royal house continues beyond our period of study. The Purāṇic section of the *Ekaliṅga-māhātmyam*, believed to have been composed immediately after this period, introduced new royal motifs. Here, two mythical figures, Māhap and Rāhap, figure for the first time. The legends about Māhap and Rāhap pertain to the problems of identification with the Guhila dynasty. Rāhap, who is stated to have belonged to another branch of the Guhilas, is said to have become the king after obtaining the title of *rāṇā*.[30] Quite clearly this implies that the *rāṇās* invented new myths to project their legitimacy over the throne that had belonged to the erstwhile Rāval Guhilas. By assigning Rāhap to the Sīsodiā, a distinction from the Rāval Guhilas is also maintained.[31] The problems of identifying themselves with the erstwhile Guhila rulers while simultaneously maintaining their own distinct identity as a separate family of the Guhilas probably became acute in view of a series of assassinations of the *rāṇā* kings in the fifteenth century.[32] In an open-ended polity, where any chiefly family could uphold its claim to the Guhila throne, political assassinations reveal the vulnerability of the royal family. Hence, it became necessary for the royal family at the end of the fifteenth, or in the early sixteenth century, to elaborate upon its military origin through the legend of Rāhap obtaining the kingdom by acquiring of the title of *rāṇā*. Arisiṁha, Hammīra, etc., are replaced by some more mythical kings such as Narapati, Gajapati, Chatrapati, etc.,[33] as descendants of Rāhap.

The claim to Ādityavaṁśa (Sūryavaṁśa) is further modified in the *Ekaliṅgamāhātmyam* by referring to the Guhila kings as the descendants of Brāhmaṇa Vijayāditya of Nāgarvaṁśa and Vaijavāpa *gotra* hailing from Ānandapura.[34] Perhaps it was an attempt to reiterate kinship links with the Rāval Guhilas who had claimed *brahma-kṣatra* status at the end of their career in the late thirteenth century. Moreover, by assigning each chapter of the *Sthala Purāṇa* including that of the royal genealogy (*Rājavarṇana*) to the *Vāyu Purāṇa*,[35] religious sanctity was lent to the entire story of the foundation of the Guhila state. However, once again the foundation story of the Guhila state revolving around Bappā-Hārītarāśi-Ekaliṅga was repeated in the *Sthala Purāṇa* to draw popularity from the regional cult of Ekaliṅga.

With the emergence of the Mughal Empire in the second half of the sixteenth century, the political situation certainly changed for Mewar. From a position of political pre-eminence in the early sixteenth century, Mewar seems to have found it difficult to adjust itself to its new status of a vassal state of the Mughals. That the change in the political situation was drastic is evident from the Mughal accounts themselves. In his *Tuzuk-i-Baburi*, Babur describes Rāṇā Sāṅgā as follows:

> Although there were many small and inconsiderable Rais and Rajas in the hills and woody country, yet there were the chief and the only ones of importance. Afghans, Bahrah to Behar, Sultan Muhammad Muzaffar in Gujarat, Bahmanis in Dekhin, Sultan Muhmud in Malwa and Nuzrat Shah in kingdom of Bengal. . . . The most powerful of the Pagan princes, in point of territory and army, is the Raja of Bijanagar (Vijaynagar). Another is Rana Sanka, who has attained his prasasti, high eminence, only in these later times, by his own valour and his sword. His original principality was Chitur. During the confusion that prevailed among the princes of the kingdom of Mandu, he seized a number of provinces which had depended on Mandu such as Rantpur (Ranthambhor), Sabangpur, Bhilsan and Chanderi.[36]

The fact that an empire-builder from Central Asia considered his contemporary Guhila king a powerful Rajput chief testifies to the politico-military power enjoyed by Mewar.

In contrast, in his *Akbar Nama*, Abul Fazal portrays a different picture for Mewar. He looks on Udaisiṁha II as merely an arrogant Rajput chief with substantial territorial control who prided himself on his past only:

> It has already been mentioned that the Rana's arrogance was swollen by the fact of the glory of his line of ancestors who were in ancient times were rulers of India. The strength of his position, the extent of his territory, and the large number of his Rajputs who would sacrifice life for honour, cast a veil over his vision. He did not perceive the marvels of the Shahinshah's fortune, and abandoned obedience and went astray.[37]

Mewar did not any longer enjoy the same strategic predominance in the latter half of the sixteenth century that it did in the time of the Delhi Sultanate. The very fact that the Mughals reached Malwa to contain the recalcitrant chiefs via Dholpur and Gwalior[38] and that Mughal forces reached Gujarat without forcing passage through Mewar,[39] indicates the reduced strategic importance of Mewar. Finally, the recently founded Rajput states of Rajasthan, especially the Rāṭhaur states of Jodhpur (Marwar) and Bikaner and the Kacchawāhā state of Jaipur had begun to legitimize their power and political predominance in western India through their Mughal connections.[40] Economically too, Mewar declined in the sixteenth century.[41] There then appeared new understandings of the Guhila state as it struggled to retain pre-eminence amongst Rajput states.

The clash between Rāṇā Pratāp and Akbar was not particularly important as Mewar was not strategically important for the Mughals in the late sixteenth century. It is evident from Abul Fazal's *Akbar Nama* that Akbar seems to have taken Chittaurgarh to control the recalcitrant Rajput chiefs.[42] But the magnitude of Rāṇā Pratāp's struggles against Akbar in Rajput bardic lore[43] point clearly to attempts to magnify the Rajput image in a situation of confrontation with a far greater power—the Mughals—and the consequently, diminished military image of the Guhila state. Long poems were composed by *cāraṇ* poets of sixteenth century Mewar to highlight Rāṇā Pratāp's resistance to Akbar. For instance, a poem of three hundred lines, composed by Sārdu Mālā, his contemporary, eulogizes Rāṇā Pratāp's victory over the Mughal army at the battle of Khamnor.[44] It is significant that Sārdu Mālā refers to Akbar only as *dilī deśa nareśa* (king of Delhi).[45] The clash continued to be perceived in epic terms in the royal records of the seventeenth century. Both *Rājapraśasti* and *Amarakāvyam* eulogize Pratāp as the epitome of pride and power who never bowed down to *Dillīpati*.[46]

It is well known that in his *Annals*, Col. Tod too has immortalized the Bhil-Pratāp alliance against Akbar.[47] It is significant that a popular theme in Bhil songs continues to be the Rāṇā fighting the king of the east and the ultimately winning with the help of the deities of Mewar.[48] Although the theme is supposed to refer to the coming of the Britishers into Rajasthan from the east, the theme is known to have been older than the nineteenth century. Since the Mughals were situated to the east of Rajasthan, the theme might have originated in the days of the Pratāp-Akbar clash.

Hence, by the seventeenth century, the claim of Sūryavaṁśa origins gets further magnified into that of Īkṣvāku, the lineage of the epic hero, Rāmacandra by the seventeenth century. Raṇachoḍa declares that since King Bāṣpa is Sūryavaṁśī, the account of Rāṇā Rājasiṁha (the Guhila king contemporary to Raṇachoḍa Bhaṭṭa) would be preceded by that of Sūryavaṁśa.[49] Thus the motif of Sūryavaṁśa of the early sixteenth century is further consolidated by connecting the Guhilas to the Īkṣvāku lineage of Rāmacandra. The Guhila genealogical account is compared with that of the Sūryavaṁśa in *Rāmāyaṇa*.[50] Then begins a detailed genealogical account of the Īkṣvāku lineage originating with Caturmukha Brahmā, the god of the universal creation and ending with Rāṇā Rājasiṁha via the line of the Āditya kings.[51] King Vijaya is stated to have received heavenly instruction that he should give up the title of '*rājā*' and to adopt the title of '*āditya*' for the generations to come.[52] Vijaya was followed by Padmāditya, Śivāditya, Haradatta, Sujāsāditya, Sumukhāditya, Somadatta, Śilāditya, Keśavāditya, Nāgāditya, Bhogāditya, Devāditya, Āśāditya, Kālabhojāditya, and Grahāditya. The sons of the last prince came to be known as 'Gahalot'. The eldest of the Gahalots was Bāṣpa, the able one born out of Pārvatī's tear-drop.[53]

Borrowing from the late fifteenth and the early sixteenth century traditions, Raṇachoḍa Bhaṭṭa in the *Rājapraśasti* declares the *Ekaliṅgamāhātmyam* to be the sixth chapter of the Medapāṭa Khaṇḍa of the *Vāyu Purāṇa*.[54] The foundation story of the Guhila state of Bāṣpa (Bāppā)-Hārīta-Ekaliṅga-Pārvatī-Medapāṭa is borrowed from the *Ekaliṅgamāhātmyam* without much elaboration. Here the story of Pārvatī's lamentation and the declaration that her tear-drop would be born as King Bāṣpa is repeated. It was claimed that Bāṣpa would acquire the kingdom and later on heavenly abode by worshipping the lord of the earth (Jagannātha) at Nāgahṛda *tīrtha*. Pārvatī is stated to have cursed one of her lesser associates (named Caṇḍa) to become Hārīta in Medapāṭa. It was stated that he too would attain heavenly abode by worshipping Śiva.[55] The loss of politico-military status became worse with Aurangzeb's inroads into Mewar, and Mughal attempts at direct annexation of the Rajput states in the seventeenth century.

These attempts to compensate for the loss of their political status may perhaps partly explain why the seventeenth-century court of Mewar produced two of the most important and longest royal records. In fact, the *Rājapraśasti* is the first royal record from Mewar that claims Bāppā's victory over the ancient Morīs of Chittaurgarh. Bāṣpa (Bāppā), having received immense strength from Hārīta, attained the *praśasti* meant for sage Agastya.[56] This is followed by narration of the legend of Bāṣpa's military conquest over his contemporary Morīs of Chittaur. Being supported by other kings, Cakravartī King Bāṣpa is stated to have defeated King Manu of the Morī family, and to have acquired Citrakūṭa as his capital. Subsequently, King Bāṣpa adopted the title of *rāval*, Raṇachoḍa Bhaṭṭa offers a new and very significant analysis of the formation of this title. It is stated that *rā* stands for *rājyatipūrṇatva* (sovereignty), *va* for *varatva* (greatness) and *la* for *lakṣmīmatva* (wealth).[57] This shows how a political title was magnified to glorify the Guhila dynasty rather than reveal the historical facts. Rāval Bāṣpa is followed by Khummāṇa, Govinda, Mahendra, Ālu, Siṁhavarma, Śaktikumār, Śālivāhana, Naravāhana, Ambāprāsāda, Kīrttivarmā, Naravarmā, Narapati, Uttama, Bhairava, Puñjarāja, Karṇāditya, Bhavasiṁha, Gotrasiṁha, Haṁsarāja, Śubhayogarāja, Tejasiṁha, and Samarasiṁha.[58] Interestingly, it is for the first time Rāval Samarasiṁha is stated to have been the husband of Pṛthvīrāja Chauhān's sister Pṛthā. He is said to have attained heavenly abode in a battle against Sahabuddin Ghori while assisting the ruler of Delhi, Pṛthvīrājā.[59] It can be seen that neither the above names of Guhila kings nor Samarasiṁha's marriage to Cāhamāna Princess Pṛthā can be historically corroborated by the contemporary official records. They are instead borrowed from bardic literature. Raṇachoḍa Bhaṭṭa does mention in this context that he quotes Rāsa literature (he seems to mean *Pṛthvīrājā Rāso* by this).[60] Incorporations from bardic literature reflect royal attempts to appropriate the popular imagination and emphasize Guhila social links with another ancient Rajput dynasty.

The legend of Māhap and Rāhap, borrowed from the *Ekaliṅga-māhātmyam*, was later elaborated. It was the *rāṇā* branch that ruled Mewar in the seventeenth century. According to tradition, Samarasiṁha was succeeded by Karṇa, the twenty-sixth Rāval. Karṇa was succeeded by sons Māhap and Rāhap. The eldest son, Māhap became the king of

Dungarpur. Rāhap, the younger one who was also the more daring of the two, defeated Mokālsī of Manḍor and brought him to the feet of Rāval Karṇa. Karṇa is stated to have deprived Mokālsī of his title *rāṇā* and conferred the same on his favourite Rāhap. Thus, just like the title *rāval*, the history of the title of *rāṇā* is shrouded in the glory of military achievements.

Ideological support was sought by bringing in the Paliwal brāhmaṇa, Śaraśalya, who is stated to have blessed Rāhap with the kingdom of Citrakūṭa. Here, an attempt is made to draw parallels with the legendary Bappā Rāval, the first of the Rāval kings who received the kingdom of Citrakūṭa from Ekaliṅga through the mediation of sage Hārītarāśi. Hence, mere affiliation to the Guhila dynasty does not seem to be sufficient in the seventeenth century to claim control over Chittaurgarh. The recurrent fall of Chittaurgarh to the Mughal army after *c.* 1550 seems to have had repercussions on the hold of the *rāṇās* over Chittaurgarh. Hence, a popular appeal similar to the legends of Bappā-Hārītarāśi, was made through the myths of Rāhap, the founder of the *rāṇā* branch and Śaraśalya, the Paliwal brāhmaṇa. Clearly the Paliwal brāhmaṇas (originating from Pali, Godwar) enjoyed patronage in the royal court of Mewar in the seventeenth century. Rāhap was called Sīsodiā as he hailed from the town of Sīsodā (again borrowed from *Ekaliṅgamāhātmyam*). As he acquired the title of *rāṇā*, all his successors came to bear the same title. It is further asserted that Rāṇā Rāhap was a Nārāyaṇa. Similar to the etymological formation of *rāval*, the title of *rāṇā* was formed by the first two letters of his two epithets, 'Rājendra' (the great king) and 'Nārāyaṇa' (the universal god of preservation).[61] Thus the actualities of the political structure were sought to be shrouded in a mystical garb to create a new perception of the Guhila state in the seventeenth century.

Interestingly, the importance of the bardic traditions seems to have increased by the seventeenth century. It appears that even affiliation to the Ādityas and the Ikṣvākus was not sufficient to ensure the popular image of the state. The motifs of Ādityas and Īkṣvāku were meant to enhance their social status amongst the Rajput states of western India. Yet they must surely have lost esteem in the eyes of the populace at large. How far could the epic and the Purāṇic motifs appeal to the popular mind? Incorporation of a popular tale of Guhāditya's birth in the context of Gujarat in the *Amarakāvyam* seems to indicate that the epic motifs were not sufficient to appeal to the popular imagination.

Having introduced a royal genealogical list similar to *Rājapraśasti* (*Śrī Amarakāvyam Vaṁśāvalīgrantho yamasyati*),[62] *Amarakāvyam* takes the birth-story of Guhāditya to a popular realm. The history of the Guhila family and its arrival in Mewar begins with the coming of Kamlāvatī, queen of Śilāditya, and her daughter-in-law (widow of Śilāditya's son) to Mewar during the Arab invasion of their kingdom. The daughter-in-law was expecting her first child. They decided to stay on in Mewar as Śilāditya was killed in battle. Śilāditya's daughter-in-law (who belonged to the Rāṭhaur lineage) gave birth to her posthumous son, entrusted him to a brāhmaṇī named Lakhmāvatī, and became satī. Lakhmāvatī's husband was Vijayāditya Śarmā. He named the baby boy, Keśavāditya and identified his *gotra* as Vaijavāpāyan. The brāhmaṇī brought up Keśavāditya as his son. Thus Keśavāditya came to combine the best qualities of a brāhmaṇa and a kṣatriya. He settled down in a village of olden times called Ānandīpura near Citrakūṭa (presently known as Ārṇodā in Chittaur district) and founded his own kingdom at Ānandīpura. Being endowed with magical power, he turned the statues of Vindhyavāsinī and Rāṣṭrasenī, deities of the hills, into gold. He ruled for one hundred and nine years, five months and nine days. Keśavāditya was followed by the Kings Nāgāditya, Bhogāditya, Devāditya, Āśāditya, Kālabhojāditya and Grahāditya. This ruling family came to be known as Guhila after King Grahāditya. The list of the fourteen Āditya kings ends with Grahāditya and the account of the Rāvals (*vaṁśyāmo rāvala atha*) begins.[63]

The story of invasion by the Arabs, satī, Keśavāditya, a refugee and the Āditya progenitor of the royal Guhila family certainly drew sympathy. The other significant point in the above description is the location of Ānandīpura near Citrakūṭa. It has already been noted that the Guhilas did claim migration from Ānandapura as early as the tenth century. But Ānandapura has actually been located in north-east Gujarat (Vadnagar). Neither does any early medieval royal record from Mewar ever claim that Ānandapura lay near Chittaurgarh. The purpose of identifying present Ārṇodā of Chittaurgarh district with Ānandīpura in the seventeenth century was to align the Guhilas with the political landmark of Citrakūṭa as far back as possible.

The text borrows the story of Bappa (not introduced as Bāṣpa in *Amarakāvyam*) from *Ekaliṅgamāhātmyam* and *Rājapraśasti* as far as his birth from Pārvatī's tear-drop is concerned. It introduces the popular story of Bappā's marriage to twenty-six local princesses in frolic (the game of swinging). The marriage is stated to have been officially solemnized. Young Bappā is depicted as a shepherd. Here again the story of Bappā meeting Hārīta and pleasing Ekaliṅga through his services is repeated. Here again one witnesses an incorporation of legends from thirteenth-century royal *praśastis*, *Ekaliṅgamāhātmyam* and folk-lores of Mewar. Bappā is stated to have worshipped both Ekaliṅga and Vindhyavāsinī and is said to have became a disciple of Hārīta. According to tradition, Bappā was blessed with the kingdom of Mewar and the lordship of Citrakūṭa by sage Hārīta, who was favoured both by Ekaliṅga and Vindhyavāsinī.[64] Thereafter, Bappā built a temple of Ekaliṅga, the patron deity and made arrangements for its worship according to the Pāśupata traditions. In the battlefield, he killed the Morī King Matūrāja and snatched the fort of Chittaur and the kingdom from him. Bappā installed Samādhīśvara in Citrakūṭa. He came to bear the title of *rāval* since he is said to have excelled in the possession of kingdom (*rājya*), greatness (*varatva*) and prosperity (*Lakṣmī*) (just like the *Rājapraśasti* claims).

This account of Bappā in the *Amarakāvyam* proves that the legendary figure of Bappā which remained popular as late as the seventeenth century continued to be appropriated by the Guhila state by making Bāppā out to be a pan-Indian king. To ensure control over Chittaurgarh, Bāppā was shown to have been militarily superior to the ancient Morīs of Chittaurgarh. Finally, to create a political aura Bappā was made to extend his kingdom from Mewar till Bay of Bengal to the east and till the river Indus to the west. Mewar was said to have included Central Asia and Kashmir as well. This can be seen as an attempt to project Bappā Rāval as a Cakravartī, king of all of India. This supports my suggestion that the exalted status of the Mughal emperors and thus the importance of their original home, Central Asia, influenced Guhila perspectives even though they tried hard to conceal it. While *Rājapraśasti* emphasized social links with the ancient Cāhamānas, *Amarakāvyam* highlighted their connections with the Rāṭhaurs. Depicting Bappā's queen as a Rāṭhaur princess indicates that the Guhilas acknowledged the socio-political importance of the Rāṭhaurs in the seventeenth century. I have already pointed that the Rāṭhaurs enjoyed an advantageous socio-political status through their connections with the Mughals. Rāṭhaur pre-eminence in the sixteenth-seventeenth centuries is evident from Guhila claims regarding the existence of a matrimonial alliance between the Kānya-kubja Rāṭhaurs and the legendary Bappā Rāval.

The story of the two brothers, Māhap and Rāhap is narrated with further elaboration: Rāhap, the younger brother, is depicted as more courageous and a successful military general who even marched towards Delhi.[65] Māhap is portrayed in dark colours intentionally so that Rāhap, the younger brother can become the ruler legitimately. This justifies the supersession of the *rāvals* by the *rāṇas*. A very interesting anecdote is narrated regarding Rāhap's rise to power. This story reflects the political structure of Mewar in which the Bhils too are mentioned.[66] The politically subordinate position of the Bhils in the Guhila state of Mewar is clearly evident in the story.

III

The Guhila State perceived through other Social Groups

Having discussed the royal perception it becomes essential to examine the perspective of the Jains and other social groups who participated in the functioning of the Guhila state of Mewar. I begin my discussion here with the Jain perception of the Guhila state. In this context, it is important to find out in which period the Jains began to recognize the Guhilas as the rulers of Mewar.

The Jains

Since Chittaurgarh had been held by a number of political powers before the Guhilas, the time of the earliest Jain references to the Guhilas as kings of Citrakūṭa/Medapāṭa becomes important. On the other hand, impressions of the Jains were valuable for the royal family because they helped forge political links with the wealthiest of the local communities, the Jains.

It is significant that pre-thirteenth-century Jain inscriptional records of Mewar do not mention Guhila kings. This is important in view of the fact that the bulk of the pre-thirteenth-century Jain inscriptions came from the Āhaḍa-Udaipur locality which was the core area of the Guhila royal family. The first three inscriptions listed from Sītalnāth temple of Udaipur[67] are such instances. It is the thirteenth-century Jain inscriptions which refer to Guhila rulers for the first time. These inscriptions belong to the most elite Jain families.

The earliest significant inscriptional reference to the Guhilas as kings comes from a Jain Inscription of AD 1267. It refers to the reign of king Tejasiṁha, who is known to have been the first Guhila king to have made Chittaurgarh the capital.[68] King Tejasiṁha also figures in a short Jain Inscription of AD 1260 from Ghaghsa, Chittaurgarh.[69]

The Jain texts of the thirteenth century similarly acknowledge the rule of the Guhila rulers. The Jain manuscript *Daśavaikālikādisūtra-patrikā*, patronized by Mahāmātya Śrī Jagatsiṁha, prime minister of King Jatirasiṁha was composed in the fortress of Āhaḍa/Āghaṭa. It refers to the Guhila King Jaitrasiṁhadeva as *mahārājādhirāja*.[70] The *Pākṣikasūtravṛtti* of Yaśodevasūri, patronized by two Jain personalities of king Jaitrasiṁha's court refers to his reign as '*saṁvat 1309 varse ... tatpaṭṭāvibhūṣana rājāśrite jayāsiṁhavijayarājye*.[71] Vijayāsiṁha-suri's *Śrāvakapratikramaṇasūtracūrṇī* refers to the Guhila King Tejasiṁha by the titles of *mahārajādhirājaparameśvaraparam-bhaṭṭārakaumāpativaralabdhaprauḍapratāpasamālaṅkṛta*'.[72] The *Kharataragacchālaṅkār* section of *Kharataragachhabṛhadgurvāvalī* refers to the reign of Guhila King Samarasiṁha in the context of celebration of great festivals, the congregation of a large number of people from various backgrounds and the installation of the idol of Śrī Nemīnātha. This is an important reference as the description pertained to Śrī Citrakūṭa Vihāra.[73]

However, it is important that the Guhila claim to power through the legends of Bappā-Hārītarāśi-Ekaliṅga find no mention in the thirteenth-century Jain records. Nor do they acknowledge the long genealogical traditions claimed by contemporary Guhila kings. The contrasts indicate the fact that even though the Guhila dynasty had adopted the legitimizing motifs of Bappā-Hārītarāśi-Ekaliṅga in the recent past, the Jains, particularly from Chittaurgarh, had not accepted so new a legitimizing tradition.

The very first fifteenth century Jain Inscription from Zawar (AD 1421), refers to the reigning Guhila king modestly, *Rājādhirāja Śrī Mokala-devavijayarājye*.[74] However, the importance of the record lies in the fact that it came from a local Jain merchant family of the Prāgvaṭa lineage. Sāh Nānā was a rich and influential local merchant.[75] The next batch of Jain inscriptional records come from the reign of Mahārāṇā Kumbha-karṇa. It is significant that the Jains refer to the detailed genealogies of the Guhila kings for the first time during Kumbha's reign. Such a development in the fifteenth century after a time lag speaks for the late acceptance of the claims of the royal Guhila family by most of the elite Jain families. Hence, internalization as well as acknowledgement of the Guhila genealogy seems to have come late.

Perhaps the best instance of Jain tribute to the Guhilas in the period is the Rāṇakpur Praśasti of AD 1439. In fact it is one of the earliest fifteenth-century records from Mewar that give a detailed genealogy of the Guhilas after their own version. It is the first Jain record to specify the Guhilas as the rulers of Medapāṭa and to acknowledge the founder of Guhila power, Bappā. This very development is indicative of a gradual process of incorporation of the Jains into the political structure. The longer the association, the deeper was the percolation of Guhila claims into the Jain community. Bappā not only gets mentioned for the first time in this Jain record but Guhila kings are also acknowledged as the descendants of Bappavaṁśa.[76] There is also an elaborate *praśasti* for Mahārāṇā Kumbha in which he is referred to as Śrī Kumbhakarṇa, an epic figure from *Mahābhārata* and is also compared with the epic heroes, Rāma and Yudhiṣṭhira.[77] It is significant that this record comes from a Jain merchant family, Dhārana Sāh of Sirohi,[78] and not from the Jain state officials. The record contains a genealogy and a *praśasti* of the Guhilas.[79] It is significant that the Jains standardized the title of Kumbhakarṇa for Rāṇā Kumbha, comparing the Guhila sovereign with an epic figure. Śṛṅgār Chavanrī (Chittaurgarh fort) inscription of AD 1448 also refers to the reign of Rāṇā Kumbha as that of Śrī Kumbhakarṇa and also gives his genealogy.[80] This fact is equally evident from Jain Inscription of AD 1437 from the temple of Śāntinātha.[81] Rāṇā Kumbha figures as Kumbhakarṇa in the text, *Śrī Āvaśyakbṛhadvatti* too.[82] However, it is important to remember that the Guhilas could not erase the knowledge from the memory of the Jains of the actual political history of Chittaurgarh in the early fifteenth century. The inclusion of Sultan Alauddin in the genealogy of the kings of Mewar points to the Jain remembrance of the former hegemony of the Delhi Sultanate over the Guhila state of Mewar.[83]

The last of the Jain records under discussion, the Nadlai Inscription from the Temple of Adinath of AD 1500, is perhaps our most important document for it is the earliest source to speak of the Sūryavaṁśa origin of the Guhilas. It is clear that the Jains were one of the first non-Rajput social groups to acknowledge the latest claim of the Guhila kings to Sūryavaṁśa.[84] The record not only mentions the Sūryavaṁśa status but also traces the ancestory of the Guhila kings to King 'Śilāditya'.[85] Bappa is readjusted as Guhadatta's son, keeping the 'Guhila nomenclature' of the royal family intact.[86] Therefore, the royal claims to Sūryavaṁśa and Ādityavaṁśa can actually be traced back to the late fifteenth-early sixteenth centuries, when such royal claims seem to have been internalized at least by the Jains.

The Ṭāmṭarāḍas

The Ṭāmṭarāḍa family from Nāgdā was possibly one of the first important non-Rajput social groups of Mewar to acknowledge the genealogical origins of the Guhila kings. Unlike the Jains, not only did they identify the Guhila kings as members of the Guhilavaṁśa but also accepted Bappā as the first king of the same dynasty.[87] The Ṭāmṭarāḍas, unlike the Jains of Chittaurgarh, came from the core area of the Guhila state, Nāgdā. Due to their long-standing familiarity with the Guhila dynasty, they easily accepted the Guhila kings as the sovereigns of Mewar as well as the royal claims of Bappā being the ancient founder king of the Guhilas. This familiarity can probably explain the contrast between the representations of the Guhila kings by the Ṭāmṭarāḍas and those by the Jains in the thirteenth century. Due to the late entry of the Guhila kings into Chittaurgarh, the Jains were reluctant to acknowledge them at the outset. Since the Ṭāmṭarāḍas came to Chittaurgarh almost with the Guhilas, acquisition of Chittaurgarh by the Guhilas was easier to accept for the Ṭāmṭarāḍas who therefore acknowledged this local dynasty that was seven-hundred year old by the thirteenth century.

IV

Popular Perceptions of the Guhila State

I shall now discuss the essential points of two seventeenth-century texts, *Nainsī rī Khyāt*, a historical account of Rajasthan, and Cāraṇ Girdhar Āsiā's *Sagat Rāso*, both parts of the bardic tradition in order to understand the popular perception of the Guhila state. As this literature was composed in the vernacular, it may be considered a part of popular tradition. It is interesting to compare royal accounts and the *khyāt* and *cāraṇ* traditions of the seventeenth century.

Muhaṇot Nainsī, a seventeenth-century official and a historian from the royal court of Marwar, wrote *Sīsodiān rī Khyāt* (a part of *Nainsī rī Khyāt*), a historical account of the Guhila state. Nainsī is known popularly as the Abul Fazal of Rajasthan. His account of historical Rajasthan, is considered authentic. He is known to have consulted both the official records and the local bardic traditions while writing his account. His *Sīsodīyān rī Khyāt* provides us with some idea regarding the extent of the acceptance of the royal perception in the rest of Rajasthan. Nainsī repeats the legends of Bāppā Rāval-Hārītarāśi-Ekaliṅga-Medapāṭa, while assigning Dita-brāhmaṇa (Āditya brāhmaṇa) origin to the Guhila kings of the seventeenth century. Nainsī narrates that Bāppā Rāval served Hārītarikhī (Hārītarāśi) for twelve long years while the latter served both Śrī Ekaliṅgajī and goddess Rāṭhāsenā. Hārītarikhī complained to Rāṭhāsenā for having ignored his disciple Bāppā and prayed for a kingdom for Bāppā. Rāṭhāsenā asked him to serve Śrī Mahādeva since acquisition of a kingdom was not possible without his favour.[88] Hārītarikhī soon devoted himself to the service of Mahādeva. Since both Mahādeva and Rāṭhāsenā were pleased with him, they granted the state of Mewar to Bāppā. Bāppā was blessed.[89] Hārītarikhī further instructed Bāppā to win Chittaur from its king Morī.[90]

Thus, both the thirteenth-century official motifs of Bappā-Hārītarāśi-Ekaliṅga-Medapāṭa and the seventeenth-century royal claims that Bappā, the conqueror of Māna Morī and Chittaurgarh, had traversed the gap from Mewar to the Marwar of the contemporary times. The Guhila version seems to have been received well by the elite in Marwar and was presented to a larger audience as the *khyāt* which was composed in the Marwari language.

Similarly, the Guhila claim of Āditya (Sūryavaṁśī) origin is repeated in *Sīsodīyān rī Khyāt.* The genealogical list begins with Brahmā followed by the names of the fifty-eight kings of Vaijavāpān *gotra* and the titles of Śarmā[91] followed by the names of fifty-five Āditya kings with Grahāditya (Guhadatta), third in the list.[92] After giving an account of the mythological King Parīkṣit, it ends with Bāppā Rāval's descendants, the Sīsodiā kings (*rāṇās*), of the seventeenth century. It is important that Nainsī designated the Guhila kings as the 'Āditya brāhmaṇas' highlighting the thirteenth-century Guhila claim of *brahma-kṣatra* origin. However, the only contrast between Nainsī's story of Bāppā Rāval and that of the seventeenth-century Guhila record is the shift that seems to have taken place in the importance of goddess Rāṭhāsenā *vis-à-vis* goddess Vindhyavāsinī. The role assigned to Vindhyavāsinī in the *Ekaliṅgamāhātmyam* and the seventeenth-century Guhila records in conferring royal power on Bāppā Rāval along with Ekaliṅga had shifted to Rāṭhāsenā (Rāṣṭrasenā of *Ekaliṅgamāhātmyam*) indicating both the military significance of the story of the foundation of the Guhila state of Mewar as well as the popularity of the militant goddess rather than the benign Vindhyavāsinī.

It is important that Nainsī collected some of the songs on Bāppā, Khummāṇa, Allaṭa, Hārītarāśi and the Morīs of Chittaur since it points to the popularity that these legendary kings of the Guhila dynasty had come to enjoy in medieval Rajasthan. I cite here a few poems with their translations to further emphasize my argument.

Kavitta Rāval Bāppā ro

rāo buharāi bar, rāo ghar pāṇī ānai
rāo karais manjaṇo, rāo mojariyān tānnai,
rāo pāna graha rahai, rāo panarai nita jagai,
aāo tega gahi pulai, rāo lula pāvai lāgai gaja caḍa ratha caḍa turiya caḍa, rāo na.
ko māndanta rāṇā, citavai cyāra cakkaha taṇā, sahu rāo bāpā saraṇā || 1 ||

Translation: At the gate of Rāval Bāppā some kings used to sweep, while others carried water, washed utensils, helped him wear shoes, served betle-leaves, watched all night, carried arms and other things for Rāval and touched his feet in obeisance. The kings who rode on elephants, horses and chariots never dared to challenge Rāval Bāppā in battle. Kings from all the four directions desired the protection of Rāval Bāppā.

Rāval Khūmāṇa Bāpāro-tinaro
(Bāppā's son Rāval: His Kavitta)

binai lakhkha pāyakka, lakhkha mattā tokhāraḥ,
sahansa eka chatrapati, huye gahamaha darabāraha
khavre sena kharabanḍa, dhūṇa līdhī dhara dhāraha
paramārān dala pahaṭa, dīdha prasaṇā pāhāraha
pañcāsa lakhkha mālavāpatī, mevaḍe soho gānjiyo,
khūmāṇ rāo bāpai tanaii, siddharāo || 1 ||

Translation: There are two lakh infantry soldiers and one lakh good horses in the army of Rāval Khūmāṇa. One thousand kings adorn his court. He has conquered the earth speedily with the help of his army and sword. He conquered his enemies by destroying the Paramāras. He routed fifty lakh soldiers of the lord of Mālavā. Thus, Rāval Bāppā's son Khūmāṇa also defeated brave Siddharāo.

Kavita Rāval Ālū-Mehandāra ro
(Allaṭa Mahendra)

tīna lakhkha tokhār, hasat so tīna tayāsī,
pañca lakhkha payakka, karai olog mevīsī |
āur nayar neresa, māl mānḍa ugrāvai,

ghar baiṭhā ḍar hunt, bheṭa gujjaraha paṭhavai.
āṭha hī pohar ālū bhaye, tayan nīnd koye na karai,
gahlot ganjī dal cālatān, avar rāya odrak marai || 3 ||

Translation: There are three lakh horses, three hundred and eighty-three elephants and five lakh infantry soldiers in the army of Rāval Ālū. Tribal peoples in his service eulogize him. The king of the town of Ahore, receives tributes from the lord of Manḍava and the lord of the Gurjaras is so scared that he sends tributes voluntarily. The enemies do not get sleep due to the fear of Ālū. The rest of the kings die of fear when the elephants of the Guhilas charge.

Kavitta Rāval Bāpā

ādi mūla utpati, brahma piṇa khatrī jānān
ānandapura singāra, nayar āhor bakhāṇān
dala samūh rāo rāṇ, milai manḍalīka mahābhaḍ,
milai sahai bhūpatī, gurū gahlot naresai
ekalla malla dhu jyūn acala, kahai
ekaliṅgadeva āhūṭhmān rājpāṭa rāj bāpaī ki yau,
iṇ a par dīyo || 1 ||
chapan koḍa sovranna, rikhī hārīta samappai
saindehī śraga gayau, rāya-rāyām uthappai |
antarīkha le amṛta, siddha piṇa āgho kīnho,
bhayo hāth das deha, sastra vajra mai sis dinhau |
āvadhdha aṅga laggai nahīn, ādi deva ima varadīyau,
guhadita-taṇai bhairava bhanai, medapāṭa in a par līyau || 2 ||
hara hārīta pasāya, sāt-bīsān vara taraṇī
maṅgalvara aneka, caita vada pañcam paraṇi
citrakoṭa kailāsa, āp vasa pargaha kidhau,
morī dala māreva, rājā rāyām gura līdhau ||
bārah lākh bohotar sahasa, haya gaya dala paidal vanai,
nita mūḍo mītho ūparai, bhunjai bāpā tanai || 3 ||

Translation: The lineage of Bāpā Rāval owes its origin to brāhmaṇa, now known as kṣatriyas. This lineage is the pride of Anandapura. This town is famously known as Āhore. Many kings, *rāṇās*, *manḍalikā* and *mahābhaṭa bhūpatis* accept Rāval Bāpā as their preceptor. Rāval Bāpā ruled his kingdom like a pole star. Ekaliṅga Mahādeva being happy with Rāval Bāpā gifted him the incorrigible kingdom of Medapāṭa.

Hārītaṛṣi gave fiftysix crore of gold coins to Bāpā. Before Hārīta left for his heavenly abode, he gifted Bāpā with a *bajra*-like weapon and the power of enlarging his body up to ten hands. Bāpā became gifted with Ādideva Mahādeva's nectar that made him immune to weapons. Poet Bhairava says that it was thus that Guhāditya's son Bāpā received the kingdom of Mevār. Rāval Bāpā married one hundred and forty young women on the fifth Tuesday in the month of Chaitra with the blessings of Mahādeva and Hārītarṣi.

The mentor of the kings, Rāval Bāpā exterminated the lineage of the Mauryas and took over their kingdom. Bāpā made Kailash-like Chittaur his own abode. Bāpā built-up an army of twelve lakh and seventy two thousand consisting of infantry, elephants and horses. A huge amount of salt (one *mūḍhā*) was daily spent in Bāpā's kitchen.[93]

Having discussed Nainsī's account, I now move on to a discussion of *Sagat Rāso* which was composed by *cāraṇ* poet Girdhar Āsiā in AD 1673. It is an account of Śaktisiṁha, younger brother of Rāṇā Pratāp and the Saktāvats, who fought against the Mughals. It is important to note that *cāraṇ* Āsiā was patronized by Rāṇā Rājasiṁha.

Cāraṇ Girdhar Āsiā too designates the Guhila as Sūryavaṁśī who are claimed to be perfectly trained to carry out the duties of *kṣatratva* (warriorhood). He elaborates upon their kṣatriya status. The Guhilas are eulogized as creators of an excellent model of *kṣatratva* on earth to be followed by the rest of the world.[94] The Sīsodiās, powerful and charitable, are placed at the head of the twenty-four branches of the Guhilas.[95] It is significant that the seventeenth-century *cāraṇ* poet continues to use the motif of King Hammīra, which had assumed significance for the royal house as early as the fifteenth century. Hence, Āsiā repeats that Mahārāṇā Hammīra of the house of Mewar is a powerful *Hindupati* (lord of the Hindus). Hammīra is described as having enhanced the glory of the twenty-four branches of the Sīsodiās and as being the one who saved Chittaur.[96] In addition, Hammīra's lineage is described as simply 'the House of Mewar' (Mewāḍa gharānā).[97]

What is interesting in this *cāraṇ* account is the continuation of the fifteenth-century royal attempts at magnifying the Guhila leadership of the local community *vis-à-vis* the sultans. Hammīra was given such popular titles as 'the general of the Hindus who increased the glory of the Mewar house', 'Kedār Rāi for uprooting the scandals', 'Prayag-Rāja' washing the sins of the sinners, 'Viśiṣtha Vārāṇasī', for liberating the killers, and 'Gaṅgā and Maheśa' for the alcoholics, etc. Rāṇā Hammīra, the chief of the Hindus, rules on the land of Mewar.[98] In that lineage of the famous Hammīra was born Rāṇā Khetā. He was so powerful that he drove away Sultan Amisah by inflicting a defeat in the battlefield.[99] If Mokala adorned Gaṅgā and Maheśa on his head (accepted Gaṅgā and Maheśa as his ideal),[100] Kumbha came to be known as lord

Kṛṣṇa's incarnation and endowed with supernatural qualities. He bore wounds on the battlefields but led his army to victory and captured eighty-four forts.[101] Saṅgrāmsiṁha remained unrelenting in war, defeated and captured two Sultans as lord of Chittaur, and brought Chanderi under the sway of Chittaur through sheer military superiority.[102]

TOD'S *ANNALS* OF MEWAR

We conclude this section with a brief note on the Guhila state as perceived by Col. James Tod, an officer of the East India Company, who travelled extensively in Rajasthan in the early nineteenth century. He repeats the story of Guhadatta, the posthumous son of the last Maitraka king of Valabhī Śilāditya, and brāhmaṇī Kamlāvatī of Birnagar (Nāgar *gotra*) bringing him up as a Rajput prince. Since this version of the origin of the Guhila dynasty reflects the royal perspective of the seventeenth century, the early part of Tod's work certainly points to the continuity and percolation of the royal perspective to the ranks of the local elite. The rest of Tod's version can be briefly summed up as follows:

Guhadatta, although brought up as a brāhmaṇa, associated with the Rajput boys, hunted wild animals, and at the age of eleven became uncontrollable. In the words of the legends, 'How should they hide the ray of the Sun?'[103] At this period Idar (north-east Gujarat) was governed by a Bhil chief, Māṇḍalīka. The young Guhadatta frequented the forests in the company of the Bhils and soon became a favourite with the *banaputras* (Bhils), who gave Idar to him with all its hills and forests.

One day, the Bhils having determined in sport to elect a king, chose Guhadatta. One of the young Bhils cut his finger and applied the blood as the *ṭīkā* of sovereignty to his forehead. What was done in sport was confirmed by the old forest chief. What followed this was Guhadatta's treacherous act of slaying his benefactor, the old Bhil chief, as he seized power. The Bhils, tired of alien rule, assailed Nāgāditya, the eighth Guhila prince, and deprived him of his life and Idar. The infant Bāppā, son of Nāgāditya, three years old, was taken to the fortress of Bhander, where he was protected by a Bhil of Yadu descent. This is followed by the account of Bāppā and his marriage to the Solaṁkī princess of Nāgdā and his subsequent flight into the interior hills of Nāgdā valley.

> The companions of his flight were two Bhils: one of Undri, in the valley of the present capital, the other of Solaṁkī descent, from Oghna Panarwa, in the western wilds. Their names, Baleo and Dewa, have been handed down with Bāppā's, and the former had the honour of drawing the *tika* of sovereignty with his own

blood on the forehead of the prince, on the occasion of taking the crown from the Morī. It is pleasing to trace, through a series of ages, the knowledge of a custom still 'honoured in the observance'. The descendants of Baleo of Oghna and the Undri Bhil still claim the privilege of performing the *tika* on the inauguration of the descendants of Bappa.[104]

In the wilds of Nāgdā where the Trikūṭa hills rose, was the abode of Mahādeva and brāhmaṇas who performed the *yajñas*.[105] In this retreat the early years of Bāppā, the sheperd, were passed. What follows is the all too familiar account of Bāppā, and Hārītarāśi, who initiated the former in the rites of Śiva. 'By the hands of the sage, who became his spiritual guide, and bestowed on his pupil the title of "Regent" (Diwan) of Ekaliṅgajī.'[106] Bāppā received a lance, bow, quiver, and arrows, a shield and a sword from goddess Bhavānī and a double-edged sword from the famous sage, Gorakhnāth.[107] With this, was opened door leading to the throne of Chittaur and fortunes was opened. Then follows an account of Bāppā's career in Māna Morī's service, as he led the local *sāmantas* against a foreign foe, as the campaigns were extended to Gazni. Bāppā is said to have won the esteem of the chiefs who transferred their services and homage to him, and thus Morī was ousted.[108] Hence, Bāppā became the *mor* (crown) of the land and obtained by universal consent the title of 'the Sun of the Hindus' (*Hinduā Sūraj*), 'the precepts of princes' (*Rāja Guru*), and 'the Universal Lord' (*Chakravartīn*),[109] Bāppā's progeny continued to rule as powerful chiefs in Saurashtra after him as late as Akbar's reign.[110]

The essential difference between the seventeenth-century royal perspective and Tod's version lies in the appropriation of popular motifs such as 'shepherd' for the legendary Bāppā. The legend of the extension of Bāppā's expedition to Gazni and the story of his having received weapons from Bhavānī and Gorakhnāth certainly mystified the status of Bāppā in the eyes of the local society.

Similar magnification of Bāppā's image can be perceived from another local version of Bāppā's expeditions to West Asia. Tod reports having collected an old volume of historical anecdotes, belonging to the chief of Delwara, which states that Bāppā became an ascetic at the foot of Menī, where he was buried alive after having overcome all the kings of the west, in Ispahan, Kandahar, Kashmir, Irak, Iran, Turan, and Kafiristan; all of whose daughters he married and by whom he had one hundred and thirty sons, called the Naushahra Pathans.[111] 'His Hindu children were ninety-eight in number, and were called *Agni-upasi Sūryavaṁśī*, or sunborn fire-worshippers'.[112]

The story of Bāppā's campaign, victories and social links with Central and West Asia is likely to have been influenced by Mughal chronicles. Since the ancestors of the Mughals who were the emperors of the entire subcontinent came from Central Asia attributing a similar background to the first Guhila king of Mewar undoubtedly enhanced his prestige. Propagation of such a magnified image of Bāppā in nineteenth-century Rajasthan certainly contributed to the process of making of historical traditions of Mewar.

Before concluding, I shall recapitulate the essential points of the perspectives of the major social groups that I have discussed earlier. The royal perspective was discussed in the context of political developments between the thirteenth and the seventeenth centuries. The Guhila state had to relate to a larger society in the second half of the thirteenth century as it came to exercise power over the whole of Mewar from Chittaurgarh, the ancient political landmark of Mewar. Hence, the state constructed and appropriated some of the local popular myths such as those of the Bāppā-Hārītarāśi-Ekaliṅga-Medapāṭa to popularize its political image. What Bāppā did for the thirteenth-century Guhilas, Hammīra did for the fifteenth-century Guhilas. What is significant is that if the Guhilas redeemed their image by magnifying their status by claiming victories over the *śakādhipatis* (referring to the sultans of Nagaur, Gujarat and Malwa) and by claiming to have liberated the holy *tīrthas* of Gaya, Kashi and Prayaga, they also appropriated the title of Hammīra for one of their early ancestors, a title so popular amongst the sultans of Delhi. Hence, motifs used by the Delhi Sultanate continued to influence the Guhila self-image so that the adoption of the title of Hammīra within Rajput society was actually an attempt to deal with the problem of redeeming their image which was pitted against a powerful adversary. The confrontations with the Mughal emperors and consequent political crises between the sixteenth and the seventeenth centuries led to further attempts at magnifying of the Guhila status from kṣatriya-Sūryavaṁśī in the early sixteenth century to Ikṣvāku lineage in the seventeenth century.

If the Ṭāmṭarāḍas acknowledged Bāppā as the progenitor of Guhilavaṁśa, the Jains at Chittaurgarh accepted the Guhila merely as their kings, without elaborate claims. Only in the fifteenth century did the Jains acknowledged Bāppā as the progenitor of the Guhila dynasty even as Alauddin Khalji continued to be included in the royal genealogy.

The bardic traditions of the *Khyāts*, *Rāsos* and Tod's *Annals* between the seventeenth and the nineteenth centuries repeat many a royal motif and perhaps reflect the percolation and standardization of the royal claims. The story of Bāppā receiving the state of Mewar along with the various stories of the granting of Citrakūṭa by Ekaliṅga, the titular deity of Mewar through the mediation of Pāśupata sage Hārītarāśi, favour of Ekaliṅga's consort, Bhavānī, and the story of the takeover of crown from Māna Morī as well as the projection of Bāppā as the best of the Sūryavaṁśī-Kṣatriyas and as the leader of the community (*Hinduā-Sūraj*)—all came to be an integral part of the historical traditions of Mewar. If the current folksongs and idioms are any indication of the popularity of such royal figures as Bāppā and Kumbha,[113] then the contribution of the royal *bhaṭṭas*, the *cāraṇ* poets, historian Nainsī and Col. James Tod, amongst others, was great in the making of such traditions.

NOTES

1. Norman Ziegler, 'Marwari Historical Chronicles: Sources for the Social and Cultural History of Rajasthan', *IESHR*, vol. 13, 1976, p. 221.
2. Ibid., p. 223.
3. Chittaurgarh Inscription dated to AD 1274, op. cit., vv. 10-13 and Achaleśvara Inscription dated to AD 1285, op. cit., v. 12.
4. Ibid.
5. Śṛṅgiṛṣi Inscription, op. cit., vv. 2-5 and Chittaurgarh Inscription dated to AD 1429, op. cit., vv. 13-18.
6. Śṛṅgiṛṣi Inscription, ibid., v. 5.
7. *Annals*, vol. I, pp. 217-21.
8. See, Chap. III the section on king and kinsmen in the fifteenth century.
9. Śṛṅgiṛṣi Inscription, op. cit., vv. 2-5 and Chittaurgarh Inscription dated to AD 1429, op. cit., vv. 13-18.
10. Kumbhalgarh Praśasti, fourth slab, op. cit., vv. 185-90, '*mahārāṇā śrī hammīravarṇanam raṇoraṅgodhīra vīraśrīvarene rāṇe hammīrabhūpateh*'.
11. For a recent analysis of the descriptions of the Muslims in the inscriptions of early medieval/medieval periods see Brajadulal Chattopadhyaya, *Representing the Other? Sanskrit Sources and the Muslims, Eighth to Fourteenth Century*, Delhi, 1998, p. 26.

    'The more appropriate perspective from which to view the inscriptions would therefore be legitimational rather than overtly political. It is important to note this difference . . . legitimation, rather than any handy political explanation, will clarify much better the way to rulers in general—and not necessarily rulers belonging to any particular community—continued to be portrayed in the texts in "indigenous" languages. If there are political references to other communities—there often are in early medieval/

medieval sources—then they, I feel, have to be understood in terms of the overall context of legitimation in which gift and patronage were what were relevant.' See also, Cynthia Talbot, 'Inscribing the other, inscribing the self: Hindu-Muslim Identities in pre-colonial India', in *Comparative Studies in Society and History*, vol. 37, pt. 4, 1995, pp. 692-722. For a study of perceptions towards outsiders in an earlier period, see Romila Thapar, 'The Image of the Barbarian in early India', in *Comparative Studies in Society and History*, vol. 13, 1971, pp. 408-36; Aloka Parasher, *Mlecchas in Early India: A Study in Attitudes towards Outsiders up to* AD *600*, Delhi, 1991; Romila Thapar, 'Tyranny of Labels', in *Social Scientists*, vol. 24, nos. 9-10 (Sept.-Oct. 1996), pp. 3-23.

12. D.C. Sircar, *Glossary of Indian Epigraphy*, p. 341.
13. Pushpa Prasad, *Sanskrit Inscriptions of Delhi Sultanate:* AD *1191-1526*, Delhi, 1990, p. 17.
14. Chittaurgarh Inscription dated to AD 1429, op. cit., v. 7.
15. Kumbhalgarh Praśasti, fourth slab, op. cit., vv. 182-4; Rāṇā Rāimalla's Ekaliṅgajī Temple Dakṣiṇadvāra Praśasti, op. cit., v. 20.
16. *Annals*, vol. I, p. 218.
17. Śṛṅgirṣi Inscription, op. cit., v. 11.
18. See, Chap.V, section pp. 220-1.
19. Chittaur Kirtistambha Inscription dated AD 1460, in Sharda, *MK*, p. 213, op. cit., pt. II, v. 17.
20. Ibid., pt. I, v. 23; pt. II, v. 173.
21. Ekaliṅgajī Temple Dakṣiṇadvāra Praśasti, op. cit., vv. 28 and 38, '*nṛpatitanuh kṣetrasiṁhah kṣitiśah || gayātīrtham vāyarthikṛtakathāpurāṇa smṛtipāṭham śakaiḥ kruralokaiḥ karakatakaniryantranamdhāt*'.
22. Ibid., v. 68, '*tanvānam tamulam mahāsihatibhih śrī citrakūṭe galadgarvam gyāśakeśvaram vyārcayat śrī rājmallo nṛpah*'.
23. Brajadulal Chattopadhyaya, *Representing the other*, p. 88. 'And destruction did not imply political subjugation alone, it has to mean the destruction of the social order informed by use of motifs that belong to the brāhmaṇīcal discourse, in greater splendour than before.'
24. Ibid., v. 80, '*māṇḍyanmaṇḍapacanadbhudharaharirḍhillī dṛdhon mulan apraudāham-kṛtiriddha sindhu dharaṇipāthodhimanthā calah*'.
25. Ibid., vv. 77-8. '. . . *śrī rājmalla-drutam gyāskṣonipateh kṣanannipatita mānonnatāmaūlayah || kherāvaḍatrūn vidārya yavanaskandhān vabhidyāsibhiranddadanmālavajānbalādupaharan bhindanśca vaṁśānidvipām || kīrtermaṇḍalamuñcakairvyārcayat śrī rājmallo nṛpah ||*'.
26. Ibid., v. 80, '*sphurjjadagurjjara candramaṇḍalaravih kāśmīrakaṃsācyutah karṇāṭandhakadhūrjjatirvijayate śrī rājmallo nṛpah ||*'.
27. Chittaurgarh Inscription dated to AD 1429, op. cit., vv. 37 and 49.
28. Kumbhalgarh Praśasti, fourth slab, op. cit., v. 233.
29. Ekaliṅgajī Temple Dakṣiṇadvāra Praśasti dated to AD 1488, op. cit., vv. 11-17.

30. *Ekaliṅgamāhātmyam*, p. 175, v. 63, '*rāṇātvam prāptaḥ san pṛthvīpati rāhapo bhūpaḥ*'.
31. Ibid., v. 65.
32. See, Chap. IV, the section on Military Apparatus, p. 180.
33. Ibid., v. 63.
34. Ibid., p. 171, vv. 1-2.
35. Ibid., Chap. 26.
36. H.M. Elliot and John Dowson, eds., op. cit., vol. IV, pp. 259-61.
37. *Akbar Nama*, vol. III, p. 244.
38. Ibid., vol. II, pp. 341-2.
39. Ibid., pp. 607-15.
40. Susanne Rudolph and Lloyd I. Rudolph, *Essays on Rajputana: History, Culture and Administration,* Delhi, 1984, pp. 44-5.
41. Ibid.
42. *Akbar Nama*, vol. III, p. 244.
43. *Annals*, vol. I, pp. 264-78.
44. Devilal Paliwal, ed., *Jhulnā Mahārāṇā Pratāp Singhjī Rā,* in *Mahārāṇā Pratāp Smṛti Grantha*, Sahitya Sansthan, Udaipur, 1969, pt. II, pp. 55-67.
45. Ibid., p. 58, v. 5.
46. *Rājapraśasti*, op. cit., fourth canto, vv. 21-50; *Amarakāvyam*, op. cit., canto, 16, pp. 55-67.
47. *Annals*, vol. I, pp. 266-76.
48. Giridharlal Sharma, *Bhilon ke Geet*, vol. II, pp. 115-20, '*dev to sāne laḍāī laḍe hāi re pūrbiā rājā nava lākhe dev to dhūlo uḍāve re pūrbiā rājā bhuriā vālī fauje re pūrbiā rājā mevāḍ no rājā jiti gio re pūrbiā rājā devatā hele āāo re pūrbiā rājā*'.
49. *Rājapraśasti*, op. cit., first canto, v. 29.
50. Ibid., v. 28.
51. Ibid.
52. Ibid., second canto, third slab, pp. 21-7, vv. 3-38.
53. Ibid., fourth slab, pp. 29-30, vv. 2-9.
54. Rājapraśasti, op. cit., p. 18, v. 19.
55. Ibid., v. 24.
56. Ibid., vv. 15-17.
57. Ibid., v. 19.
58. Ibid., vv. 20-4.
59. Ibid., vv. 20-7.
60. Ibid., v. 27.
61. Ibid., vv. 28-34.
62. *Amarakāvyam*, p. 299, last line of the text.
63. Ibid., second canto, pp. 77-84.
64. Ibid., third canto, p. 93, v. 43, '*bhūmaṇḍate kṣitipālakaḥ syaḥ śrī medapāṭaviṣaye sthirarājyakārī/śrīcitrakūṭa patirūccatamastava syāt kīrttiśca sānttiralam vitatdharitryam* ||'.

65. Ibid., canto, vv. 1-23.
66. Ibid., vv. 10-15. Rāhap witnessed a fight between a hare and lion in the forests of Sīsodā. He wondered about the strength of the hare. A local magician advised Rāhap to eat the whole of that wonderful hare and to not share it with others nor leave any part of it. Rāhap killed the hare and cooked it in his kitchen. But he is stated to have partially forgotten the magician's advice. He ate some of its meat and distributed the rest of it amongst the Rajputs such as Khakharos, Chandanos and others. The Bhils ate up its bones. It is clearly claimed that Rāhap acceded to the throne of Mewar at Chittaur because of this episode. The Rajputs who shared the meat as well as the Bhils got established in Mewar too. It is said that the Bhils and the kṣatriyas (Rajputs) cannot abandon Mewar simply because they shared in this feast. The above episode clearly demonstrates the fact that in the process of their rise to power, the fifteenth-century Guhilas acknowledged the locally powerful political powers including the Bhils. The distinction between the eating of the flesh and the bones reflects the subordinate social and political situation of the Bhils in a Rajput state.
67. Nahar, vol. II, op. cit., pp. 9-10.
68. *Vir Vinod*, vol. I, p. 396. The record reads, '*śrī tejasiṁhadeva kalyāṇvijayī rājā vijaymāna pradhānarājā-rājaputrā kāṅgāputrā paranārī sāho*'.
69. *URI*, pp. 169-70. Also see Somani, *History of Mewar*, p. 86.
70. *Jain Pustaka Praśasti Saṁgraha*, p. 116, '*saṁvat 1284 varṣe śrī-madāghaṭadurge . . . mahārājādhirāja śrī jaitrasiṁhadeva kalyāṇi vijayrājye*'.
71. Ibid., p. 125.
72. Ibid.
73. *Kharataragaccha-bṛhadgurvāvalī*, op. cit., 1956, p. 56, '*pauṣ sudi 9, śrī citrakūṭe vihāraḥ | . . . phālgun vadī 5, śrī samarasiṁha mahārāja-rāmrājyepakda rājlok sakalanāgarikaṭoke savistāraḥ praveśakmahotsavaḥ kāritāḥ*'.
74. Jain Inscription from Zawar, op. cit., l. 1.
75. See, Chap. III, the section on Political Linkages with the Jains.
76. Rāṇakpur Praśasti, op. cit., p. 410, ll. 2 and 10.
77. Ibid., ll. 12-18.
78. See, Chap. III, the section: The Jains and Royal Family in Mewar, p. 181.
79. Ibid., ll. 2-18. '*śrīmedapāṭarājādhirāja śrī bāppā, śrī guhila, bhoja, śīla, kālabhoja, bhartṛbhaṭa, siṁha, mahāyaka, rājñīsutayutasvasuvarṇa-tulātolaka-śrīkhummana, śrīmadallaṭa, naravāhana, śaktikumāra, śuci varma, kīrttivarma, yogorājā, vairāṭa, vaṁśapāla, vairisiṁha, vīrasiṁha, śrī arisiṁha, coḍasiṁha, vikramasiṁha, kumārasiṁha, māthanasiṁha, padmasiṁha, jaitrasiṁha, tejasvīsiṁha, samarasiṁha, cāhumāna śrī kītūkanṛpaśrī allāvadīnasuratrāṇajaitra bappa vaṁśa śrī bhuvanasiṁha, suta śrī jayāsiṁha, mālāveśagogadevajaitra lakṣmasiṁha, putrā śrī ajayasiṁha, bhartṛ, śrī arisiṁha, śrī hammīra, śrī khetasiṁha, śrī laksan*

kayanarendra, nandansuvarṇtulādidāna-puṇya nandana śrī mokalamahīpati . . . rāṇā śrī kumbhakarṇa'.

80. *Vir Vinod*, vol. I, p. 410, '*rāṇā śrī lākhāputrarāṇāśrīmokalanandanaraśrī kumbhakarṇa*'.
81. *MK*, pp. 371-2, '*śrī medapāṭadeśe śrī devakulapāṭaka puravare nareśvara śrī mokalaputra śrī kumbhakarṇa bhūpati vijayārāje*'.
82. *Jain Pustaka Praśasti Saṁgraha*, op. cit., p. 148, '*śrī medapāṭe deśe śrīdevakulapāṭakapuravare śrī kumbhakarṇarājyeśrī ukeśavaṁśīyanijapuṇyartham śrī-āvaśyakbṛhadvattilikhāpitam*'.
83. Rāṇakpur Praśasti, op. cit., ll. 11-18, '*kulakānanapañcānansya sāraṅgapurānagapura merumaṇḍoramaṇḍalakara bundī khāṭucāṭasu mahādurgalīlā mlecchapālavyālacakravāla prabalaparākramakrāntā-dhittimaṇḍala gurjarātra suratrāṇa datta t hindusuratrāṇa virudasya kīrttidharmaprājāpālana śrī rāmayudhiṣṭhirādinareśvarānukarasya rāṇāśrī kumbhakarṇa sarvovipatisarvabhaumasya vijayamānarājye*'.
84. Nadlai Inscription of the reign of Rāṇā Rāimalla, op. cit., ll. 12-13, '*atheha śrīmedapāṭadeśe | śrī sūryavaṁśa mahārājādhirāj*'.
85. Ibid., l. 13, *śrī śilādityavaṁśe śrī guhadatta.*
86. Ibid., pp. 424-5, '*rāula śrī bappaka śrī khummāṇadimahārājanvaye | rāṇā hamīra śrī khetasiṁha śrī lākhāmsiṁhaputra śrī mokalmṛgāṅkavaṁśoddypta karakapratāp asamudramahāmaṇḍalakhaṇḍala-atulamahābalarāṇāśrīkumbhakarṇaputrarāṇā, śrī rāimallavijayamānaprājyarājye | tatputramahākumāraśrī pṛthvīrājānuśāsanāta*'.
87. Chiravā Inscription, op. cit., v. 3, '*guhilāṅgajavaṁśajah pura kṣitipālotra babhūka bāppāka-prathamah paripanthipārthīvadhvajīnidhvaṅsan layah* ||'.
88. *Nainsī rī Khyāt*, vol. I, p. 11, '*tarāi devī kahayo-śrī mahādevjī prasana karo | rāj mahādevjī rī sevā binā pāijāu nā chhāi*'.
89. Ibid., '*rāj tahāro avicala rahasi*'.
90. Ibid., pp. 11-12, '*tarāi rikhīśvar kahayo-thāhara pag sun mevādrī rāj kadai jāi nahīn | nau bāpā nun kahayo – saman kar nau citoḍa upar jā. morī āge rāj karau chau su mār nau rāj citoḍa ro uḍo līyo. sāmant 50 kahau chau. bāpā nu huvo bāpāu morī mār nau citoḍa ro rāj līyo*'.
91. Ibid., p. 9.
92. Ibid., p. 10.
93. *Nainsī rī Khyāt*, pp. 3-8.
94. Hukum Singh Bhati, ed., *Sagat Rāso by Girdhar Āsiā*, Udaipur, 1987, p. 1, v. 2, '*sūrajvaṁśa sarahiyai, bhuj dhara je sitradhara guru dhara gahilota tanau, sāhī chāi to saṁsār*'.
95. Ibid., v. 3, '*kahī māhī sāhī gahalot kula vāplā hātha kodivaris sāhu sirahāra sesaudiā, sasa avara cauvīs*'.
96. Ibid., v. 4, '*cauvīsain jala cadīva dhara mevār sādhira citrakoṭa cala uddhārana, hinduā chat hamīra*'.
97. Ibid.

98. Ibid., v. 5, '*hinduā chat pratāpai hamīra, nagendra vaṁśa cādiva niral kalaṅkīyān rāi kedār rāṇā | pāpīyān rāi prayāga pramāṇa | vārāṇasa hātiyārān viśeṣa | maduanā rāṇā gaṅgā maheśa | dhuraisya vīrada uddhārana dhīra. hinduā chat pratāpahamīra ||*'.
99. Ibid., v. 6, '*jina hamīra ghara janamiau cho setala rāṇā | jina bhaggo ṛṇo padhdhārāi, sāh amī suratāṇa*'.
100. Ibid., v. 7, '*ṣetala laso janamio, nara nikalaṅka naresa | jina, mokālsī janamio, muggata gaṅgāmaheśa*'.
101. Ibid., vv. 8-10, '*mokalarāṇā mokala kumbho janamio, kahī avatāra kiśana lārī caurā sī gaḍha liā, vāpra chaurāsī vana, sunnahipura samuhī, ani navalāsī ana*'.
102. Ibid., vv. 11-12, '*rāṇā kumbha ghara rāimala, tehā tano pṛthīmalla, lāllāu mārī today liāu, pauha uḍānoapalla || acala bandhava sangrāmsī, sāhī be suratāna | canderī cittor galī, peho bandhī sāṅgāpana*'.
103. *Annals*, vol. I, p. 181.
104. Ibid., p. 262.
105. Ibid., p. 181.
106. Ibid., p. 184.
107. Ibid., p. 185.
108. Ibid., p. 186.
109. Ibid.
110. Ibid.
111. Ibid.
112. Ibid.
113. *Prācīna Rājasthānī Geet*, vol. I, photo-stated copy available at the library of Sahitya Sansthan, Udaipur.

'*morī mār lio mevāḍe, bhāme bhujā tana*
gaja bhīm
rām lihā kim lope rāval, sāt samand
bachā kidhī sīmā
nyāya sāsatra lopio nājāve, khatriān
gurutaya adag khāmī
bāpe lidhī āp bāha bal,
jojon koḍa pacās.'

Translation: Rāval Bāppā, who killed Morī to conquer Mewar, was very powerful. If he wished, he could have taken his arms on the other banks of the seas. But he did not like to transgress his ancestor Śrī Rāmacandra's orders. Therefore, in spite of his great arms, he did not extend the boundary of his kingdom beyond these banks of the seas. Rāval Bāppā considered himself as powerful as Bhīma. Bhīma used to topple the elephants with his own hands. But Rāmacandra's prestige could not be transgressed. And that is why he defeated Citrang Morī and confined the boundary of his kingdom up to the midst of the seven seas. The Rajputs having adorned (borne?) the arms have never deviated from the path of justice. Therefore, Bāppā Rāval also extended his territorial sway over fifty crore *yojana* of land on his own. When powerful Bāppā of the Guhila lineage (*vaṁśa*) brought the distant forts and kings under his control, everybody eulogized him by declaring that if Bāppā disregarded Rāmacandra's prestige then he would have definitely extended his sway beyond the seas.

For Kumbha see Laxmilal Joshi, *Mevāḍ ke Kahāvaten*, Ajmer, 1978, p. 144.

kumbha:
kāl pare to kumbha dhanī, meha
barse to majurī ghanī.

Translation: Mahārāṇā Kumbha was so good a ruler that his subjects did not fear even in the time of crisis. Because once it rained good, the state used to offer employment liberally.

APPENDIX

MUHAṆOT NAINSĪ RĪ KHYĀT: SĪSODĪYĀN RI KHYĀT[1]

ANCESTORS OF BĀPPĀ RĀVAL

Brahmā
Vijaipān
Devaśarmā
Agnyaśarmā
Vijaiśarmā
Khemśarmā
Rikhīśarmā
Jagśarmā
Narśarmā
Gajśarmā

Jayśarmā
Vāsuśarmā
Keśavśarmā

Rājśarmā
Vīrājśarmā
Harakhśarmā
Picaśarmā
Vedaśarmā
Hṛdaiśarmā
Narśarmā
Harśarmā
Dharmaśarmā
Viśvaśarmā
Vardevśarmā
Kampatiśarmā

Pītaśarmā
Hemvarṇaśarmā

Rājaśarmā
Galavdevśarmā
Galavśarmā

Govindśarmā
Govardhanśarmā

Vakyaśarmā
Vīraṭśarmā

Nityānandaśarmā
Vanśarmā

Āditya brāhmaṇa kings[2]

Godsiditya
Ajāditya
Grahāditya
Mādhavāditya

Vijayāditya

Jalāditya	Keśavāditya
	Nagāditya
	Bhogāditya
	Bhagāditya
	Grahāditya
Jalmallāditya	Devāditya
Padmāditya	Ambāditya
Devāditya	Bhogāditya
Hemāditya	
Kalāditya	
Karmāditya	
Harkhamāditya	
Devarājāditya	
Vikramāditya	
Janakāditya	
Nemakāditya	
Mehendrāditya	
Gañjamāditya	
Gaṅgādharāditya	
Govindāditya	
Gaṅgādharāditya	
Govindāditya	
Gaṅgāditya	
Mardanāditya	
Ghanāditya	
Ranāditya	
Venāditya	

Sūryavaṁśāvalī

The genealogical list of the Guhila kings of Mewar begins with god Brahmā and ends with an account of Mahārāja Rājasiṁha's reign. Therefore, it seems to have been composed finally by the seventeenth century. It provides a list of the first batch of ancestors of the Guhilas, the Āditya line of kings, the *rāvals* and the *rāṇās*. The manuscript is titled *Sūryavaṁśāvalī*. A detailed account of this list is given below.

	Queen Mother
Rājā Śrī Padmāditya	Jādava Princess Jaivantā Bāī
Rājā Śrī Śivāditya	Rāṭhoḍ Sudīr Bāī
Rājā Śrī Nāgāditya	Jādav Mānamati
Rājā Śrī Bhogāditya	Demāde Morānyābāī
Rājā Śrī Devāditya	Paḍihār Sahīmatī and
	Queen Solankhnī Sobhāgvatī

Rājā Śrī Āśāditya	
Rājā Śrī Kālabhojāditya	Morīna Ratnāvalī Bāī
Rājā Śrī Grahāditya	Paḍīhār Jasodā Bāī
Rājā Śrī Khummāṇa Rāval	Raj Bāī
Rāval Govind (Gogunda)	Pemāl Bāī
Rāval Mahendra	Jādava Ramā Bāī
Ālūrāval	Solankhnī Śīlā Bāī
Sīharāval	Rāṭhoḍ Ratnāvalī Bāī
Śrī Sāgar Kumār Rāval	Devdī Sambhābāī
Salvāhana Rāval	Paramār Koḍāmde
Naravāhana Rāval (Rājya Citrakūṭa)	Rāṭhoḍ Jaibantā Bāī
Rāval Ambaprasāda (Rājya Citrakūṭa)	Cāhamāna Suhāgde
Rāval Kīrat brahmā (Rājya Citrakūṭa)	Jādav Ratnāvalī Bāī
Narabrahmā Rāval	Paramār Mānabhāvalī
Naraberāval	Nāraṅgde
Uttamarāval	Solankhnī Sambhā Bāī
Karṇāditya Rāval (Rājya Citrakūṭa)	Paramār Lacchā Bāī
Bhavsiṁha Rāval (Rājya Citrakūṭa)	Hāḍī Kanakavalī
Gamtrasiṁha Rāval	Paramār Amarāvalī
Haṁsarāj	Rāṭhoḍ Gaṅgā Bāī
Jogarāj Rāval (Rājya Āhaḍa)	Paramār Pāhapāvatī
Beraḍā Rāval (Rājya Citrakūṭa)	Cāhamāna Kanaka Bāī
Bairāsī Rāval (Rājya Citrakūṭa)	Hāḍī Pura Bāī
Tejasīrāval (Rājya Citrakūṭa)	Rāṭhoḍ Lacchā Bāī
Samarasiṁha Rāval (Rājya Citrakūṭa)	Solankhnī Ramā Bāī
Karaṇa Rāval (Rājya Citrakūṭa)	Cāhamāna Pṛthā Bāī
Rāṇo Rāhap (Rājya Citrakūṭa)	Solankhnī Kodāmade Bāī
Narapati Rāṇo (Rājya Citrakūṭa)	Paramār princess
Dinakara Rāṇo (Rājya Citrakūṭa)	Pratihār Nāraṅgde Bāī
Jasakaraṇa Rāṇo (Rājya Citrakūṭa)	
Nāgapāla Rāṇo (Rājya Citrakūṭa)	Paramār Jamnādo Bāī
Puraṇapāla Rāṇo (Rājya Citrakūṭa)	Pratihar Bhāgavatī Bāī
Prathīmala Rāo (Rājya Citrakūṭa)	Solankhnī Purabāī
Bhunagsiṁha Rāṇo (Rājya Citrakūṭa)	Yādava Bāī Manmatī
Bhīmasiṁha Rāṇo (Rājya Āhaḍa)	Bhāṭayānī Pura Bāī
Jaisiṁha Rāṇo (Rājya Citrakūṭa)	Paramār Gaṅgāde Bāī
Līkhamsī Rāṇo (Rājya Kailvāde)	Rāṭhoḍ Lāl Bāī
Arsī Rāṇo (Rājya Kelvāde)	Tomar Dhana Bāī
Ajesīrāṇo (Rājya Kelvāde)	Rāṭhoḍ Dina Bāī

RĀJĀVALĪ BAHI

	Queen Mothers
Rājā Śrī Padmādatjī	Jādava Jevatā Bāī
Rājā Śrī Sevādatjī	Rāṭhoḍ Sūraj Bāī
Rājā Śrī Haridatjī	Cāhuvan Rāj Bāī
Rājā Śrī Surājditajī	Patāmde Paramārade Bāī
Rājā Śrī Somadatjī	Jādava Jamnāde
Rājā Śrī Śāladatjī	Kanakāvatīde Bāī
Rājā Śrī Keśavadatjī	Kamlāvatī Bāī; Queen Yādava Mānmatī; Son Nāgadatjī
Rājā Śrī Nāgadatjī	Yādava Mānmatī Bāī (Rājya Nāgdā)
Rājā Śrī Bhogādatjī	Morāndemāde Bāī
Rājā Śrī Devadatjī	Paḍīhār Savatī Bāī
Rājā Śrī Āśādatjī	Solankhnī Sobhāgvatī Bāī
Rājā Śrī Kālabhojajī	Mokhanā Ratnāvatī Bāī
Rājā Śrī Garādatjī	Paḍīhār Jasodā Bāī

RĀJYA

Rāval Bapojī	Vās Ghāse	Paramār Patāmde Bāī
Rāval Śrī Khūmāṇjī	Khāmnor	Rāṭhoḍ Rāj Bāī
Rāval Govindjī	Gogunda	Paramār Pemā Bāī
Rāval Mahindrajī	Machīdgarh	Jādava Rāma Bāī
Rāval Śrī Ālūjī		Solankhnī śāla Bāī
Rāval Śrī Sīhajī	Citrakoṭ	Rāṭhoḍ Ratnāvatī
Rāval Śrī Kālabhojājī		
Rāval Śrī Sagat Kanwarjī	vs 562 Citrakoṭ	Devaḍī Sambā Bāī
Rāval Śrī Matrakhjī		
Rāval Śrī Śālivāhanjī	vs 487	Paramār Kodāmde
Rāval Śrī Naravāhanjī	vs 618 Citrakoṭ	Rāṭhoḍ Jaivatā Bāī
Rāval Ambāprasādjī	vs 686 Citrakoṭ	Chāvan Sobāghde Bāī
Rāval Kīrtibhramjī	vs 691 Citrakoṭ	Jādava Ratnāvatī Bāī
Rāval Śrī Narabhramjī	vs 732 Citrakoṭ	Paramār Manbhāvatī Bāī
Rāval Śrī Khemarajī		
Rāval Śrī Narbhejī	vs 743 Citrakoṭ	Tāvar Nāgarde Bāī
Rāval Śrī Bhavasiṁhajī		
Rāval Śrī Utamjī	vs 779 Citrakoṭ	Solankhnī Sabā Bāī
Rāval Śrī Bhairavjī	vs 796 Citrakoṭ	Paḍīhār Padmāvatī Bāī
Rāval Kanadejī		
Rāval Śrī Kīratsiṁhajī		
Rāval Śrī Hasarājjī		
Rāval Śrī Jomadrājjī		

Rāval Śrī Vīradrājjī		
Rāval Śrī Vansīrājjī		
Rāval Śrī Tejasiṁha	vs 1066 Citrakoṭ	Rāṭhoḍ Lachmī Bāī
Rāval Śrī Jasvāranjī		
Rāval Śrī Surbhānjī		
Rāval Śrī Haspāljī		
Rāval Śrī Bājesiṁhajī		
Rāval Śrī Arasījī		
Rāval Śrī Barbādjī		
Rāval Śrī Depāljī		
Rāval Śrī Bajesiṁhajī		
Rāval Śrī Bhachudjī		
Rāval Śrī Dugārsiṁhajī		
Rāval Śrī Pujojī		
Rāval Śrī Partāpjī		
Rāval Śrī Samarsījī	vs 1106 Citrakoṭ	
Rāval Śrī Karansiṁhajī	vs 1155	
Mahārāṇā Śrī Rābjī	vs 1201 Citrakoṭ	Solankhnī Kodāmde Bāī
Mahārāṇā Śrī Narapatjī	vs 1262 Citrakoṭ	Paramār Surde Bāī
Mahārāṇā Śrī Dinkaranjī	vs 1295 Citrakoṭ	Paḍīhār Araṅgde Bāī
Mahārāṇā Śrī Jaskaranjī	vs 1301 Citrakoṭ	Solankhnī Jaimātā Bāī
Mahārāṇā Śrī Nāgapāljī	vs 1306 Citrakoṭ	Puvār Jivānde
Mahārāṇā Śrī Puranpāljī	vs 1311 Citrakoṭ	Paḍīhār Bhagvatī Bāī
Mahārāṇā Śrī Prathīpāljī	vs 1315 Citrakoṭ	Solankhni Pura Bāī
Mahārāṇā Śrī Bhurunsiṁhajī	vs 1319 Citrakoṭ	Jādava Bhānvatgī Bāī
Mahārāṇā Śrī Bhīmasiṁha	vs 1322 Citrakoṭ	Bhāṭānī Pura Bāī
Mahārāṇā Śrī Jayasiṁha	vs 1326 Citrakoṭ	Paramār Gaṅgāde Bāī
Mahārāṇā Śrī Gadaḷakhamansiṁha	vs 1331 Kelvāḍe	Rāṭhoḍ Queen Mother
Mahārāṇā Śrī Arsījī	vs 1346 Kelvāḍe Chittaur	Tāvar Dhana Bāī
Mahārāṇā Śrī Ajesiṁhajī	vs 1346 Kelvāḍe	Rāṭhoḍ Danade Bāī
Mahārāṇā Śrī Hamīrasiṁha		

NOTES

1. *Nainsī rī Khyāt*, p. 9.
2. Ibid., pp. 10-11.

CHAPTER VII

Conclusion

In conclusion, I briefly present the main points emerging from the present study. My main objective was to trace the emergence and development of a regional state, the Guhila state of Mewar, in early medieval and medieval India. I attempted to underline in the beginning how the study of state formation has become necessary in view of the prevailing historiography which emphasizes political fragmentation of the state brought about by the collapse of empires and thus denies the processes of continuous state formation from local roots at regional levels.

I would like to emphasize that the phenomenon of regional state formation is a slow process, details of which can be ascertained only by studying a region in depth. However, regions are usually not geographically homogeneous. Differences in geographical features give rise to variations in the human organization of space, and hence the proliferation of multiple nuclear zones in areas which became significant historically. A study of the topography of space presents us with the cultural map of a region showing distinct units which get integrated through the process of state formation under a dynasty. Thus, in order to ascertain the role of a dynasty in integrating various areas into a state, a geographical study of the region becomes necessary. Since Mewar consists of two sub-regions, I began my study with a geographical profile of the Mewar hills and the upper Banas plain.

From a topographical study of the region my study moved on to the role of the Guhila dynasty in converting the disparate zones of a region into a state in terms of a single politico-administrative unit over a period of time. Three distinct stages can be discerned in the growth of the Guhila state following its initial emergence in Nāgdā-Āhaḍa in the seventh century. It is evident that both local Guhila states—that of Nāgdā-Āhaḍa as well as that of Kiṣkindhā trued to integrate local chiefs in the *sāmanta* hierarchy through ranking and through the distribution of roles and services. The local Guhila states began their political career on an economic base that was largely and was complimented by small-scale trading activities. Penetration of state-society into the tribal areas by the local Guhila state of Nāgdā-Āhaḍa is testified by the opening up of mines and by the brāhmaṇical appropriation of the goddess of the forest dwellers, Araṇyavāsinī, to facilitate the exercise of Guhila royal power in the peripheral areas. Similarly, land grants to migrating brāhmaṇas legitimized royal power in the local state of Kiṣkindhā.

The second stage saw the consolidation of Guhila power at Nāgdā-Āhaḍa and the territorial integration of the southern part consisting of the upper Banas plain and the Mewar hills (that is the state of Kiṣkindhā) by the tenth century. Territorial integration was accompanied by the exapansion of the material resource base of the Guhila state. The earlier rural base was transformed into an urban exchange-centre at Āṭapura, which had become the seat of the Nāgdā-Āhaḍa Guhila state, by the tenth century. Attempts to legitimize the Guhila state by using religion also become evident for the first time in the tenth century. Royal patronage of the Pāśupata sect and the construction of the temple of Ekaliṅga at Nāgahṛda (Nāgdā) are politically significant as strategies of integration of local as well as migrant Rajput chiefs (who appear for the first time in this period).

I have also argued that the tenth-century records of the Nāgdā-Āhaḍa Guhilas testify to an enhanced political and social status. This is evident from their renewed claims of respectable ancestry, the prestigious matrimonial and administrative alliances they entered into, and finally, from the very mention of the Guhila power of Medapāṭa in the epigraphical records of their contemporary states, in the tenth century. The integration of the southern part of the Mewar hills and the northern middle Mahi basin, and the termination of Paramāra and Caulukyan sway over the latter indicate the connection of this region with the Nāgdā-Āhaḍa dynasty and point to the growing political power of the Guhila state. In spite of Pratihāra sway over southern Rajasthan and Chittaurgarh, no Pratihāra record has so far been discovered in the heart of Mewar hills (district of Udaipur)—the core of the Guhila state till the first half of the thirteenth century. The Pratapgarh inscription from the southern part of the upper Banas plain was issued in the reign of Pratihāra Mahendrapāladeva II only by the local Cāhamāna and Guhila rulers. Nor is any Pratihāra record reported from Chittaurgarh. The records of the late eleventh century confirm the expansion of Guhila power to the north beyond the Aravallis in the region of Marwar. Thus, it is not surprising that the Guhilas called themselves sovereigns of Medapāṭa (Mewar) by the early twelfth century in their own records.

The final stage in the development of the Guhila state was its crystallization in the thirteenth century when the Guhilas took over Chittaurgarh, the ancient landmark of Mewar and thus claimed sovereignty over the whole of Mewar. Now the Guhilas were associated with Citrakūṭa. Their records project the legendary Bāppā's possession of the fortress back into the remote past. That is why we see a shift in the role of Guhadatta who is projected as the progenitor Bāppā's son in the thirteenth century. The thirteenth-century Guhila state in fact drew legitimation from the regional cult of Ekaliṅga through the medium of the motifs of progenitor Bāppā and his preceptor, Hārītarāśi, the Pāśupata *ācārya*. The shift of the capital to Chittaurgarh during the Guhila Tejasiṁhas' reign is evident from his epigraphs. Guhila genealogy was restructured in thirteenth-century records and acquired a new form. From a brāhmaṇa origin, the Guhilas began to claim *brahma-kṣatra* status, which in turn allowed them to claim larger territoriality and social linkages with leading contemporary, kṣatriya royal families.

However, the mere possession of Chittaurgarh did not enable the Guhilas to retain power in Mewar beyond the thirteenth century. This was threatened by the Khalji intrusion in the early fourteenth century. The Hāḍās, Paramāras or Sānkhlās, Solaṁkīs, Kherāḍās, etc., were the other local chiefs with important strongholds in the eastern and northeastern upper Banas plain. It was imperative for any state of Mewar to forge close ties with them to incorporate their forts in a second line of defence for Chittaurgarh and the extended core of the Guhila state. Therefore the Guhilas of the fifteenth century forged matrimonial alliances with most of these chiefs who came to constitute a major factor in their political structure and contributed to the military might of the state. Thus, Guhila matrimonial alliances with a number of contemporary Rajput ruling families in the medieval period were actually an essential part of their military policy. For instance, their matrimonial alliances with the Hāḍās of eastern Mewar or Kherāḍās of Jahāzpur contributed to the territorial integration and control of forts strategic to Chittaurgarh. Similarly, marriage alliances with the Rāṭhaurs of Marwar or Khīcīs of Gagraun extended the Guhila line of defence in the northern and southeastern directions respectively.

Interestingly fortifications of peripheral areas did not necessarily mean that hinterlands had been politically integrated for all time to come. The list of Kumbha's forts in Merwara, Bhomat, core of Mewar hills, Oghna-Panarwa and hill-passes testify to continuing royal attempts to control tribal areas in the hinterland. A discussion of territorial integration remains incomplete without exploring the relationship between the tribal population of Mewar hills, the Bhils, and the state-society. The subject has been totally neglected by the numerous monographs available on the history of Mewar. The crux of the relationship seems to have been the symbolic recognition of the Bhils (traditions mention application of *ṭīkā* of blood on the forehead of the succeeding Guhila king by the Bhil chief of Oghna-Panarwa—a practice supposedly discontinued from the fourteenth century onwards) and the Bhil acceptance of the Guhilas as their political masters. This inauguration ritual which took place on formal occasions as well as numerous bardic traditions point to a political relationship between the Guhilas and the Bhil chiefs. But the silence of the official sources on the importance and proximity of the core-area Bhils indicates their subordinate position in the Guhila state. 'Peasantization' of the core-area Bhils, control over routes of communication in the hilly and forested terrain by Bhils, local Bhil militias and labour at the mining centres, were all important resources for the Guhila state. Such interaction over a long period of time were bound to bring significant changes in the so-called egalitarian tribal society. Bhil chiefs of Oghna-Panarwa claimed Solaṁkī Rajput origin around the sixteenth century. The emergence of such elite groups in Bhil society points towards caste formation, a social process that accompanied the phenomenon of state formation.

My examination of the evidence shows that the administrative structure, initially dominated by the Rajputs, came to incorporate non-Rajput social groups such as the Jains by the thirteenth century. The Jains controlled most of the contemporary trade in western India and served the Guhila state as administrative personnel (often as the chief treasurer of the chief minister). They provided the state with one of the main sources of state revenues. Their assimilation into the Rajput political structure is evident from their new title of Rājaputra. The Guhila state patronized Jain religious establishments between the thirteenth and fifteenth centuries. However, if the Guhilas had to integrate this wealthy community into the state, the Jains too depended on the state for furthering its economic interests through political connections. At this stage, most Rajput chiefs and their retainers were involved in building a strong military apparatus in the context of the growing political instability from the thirteenth to the fifteenth century. Royal references to an increasing number of fortresses by the fifteenth century point towards the importance of Rajput personnel in the control of new areas such as Merwara within Mewar or strategic points in Hāḍāvatī or Gagraun.

Besides the Jains, brāhmaṇas, and some other non-Rajput social groups like the Ṭāmṭarāḍas of Nāgdā contributed to the development of the Guhila state in the same period. The brāhmaṇas were particularly active in legitimizing Guhila rule in the fifteenth century in areas beyond the traditional frontiers of Guhila domain, as is evident from royal land grants made to brāhmaṇas for the first time in Rāṇā Kumbha's reign. The Guhila dynasty had managed to rule for a long period as a unified royal family in which proliferating branches of the family had moved away without fragmenting royal power and by the fifteenth century, this tradition of long-lasting Guhila dynastic rule was appropriated by a chiefly family from Chittaurgarh to maintain the status of Mewar as a leading regional power of western India.

The present case study of the process of state formation in Mewar also explored the ideological apparatus of the state. The genealogical claims and origin myths as well as the symbiotic relationship between the monarchy and the cult centres were explored in detail. This particular aspect of state formation has remained largely neglected in the historiography on Mewar. Since the emergence of local states has been viewed only in terms of the breakup of an empire, the political importance of local religious and cultural traditions has been side-tracked in the existing works on Mewar. At the most, religious studies have been utilized to highlight the 'exploitation' of the masses by the ruling class. An enquiry into the relationship between the Guhila monarchy and local cult centres necessitated a study of the Pāśupata institutions and the Pāśupata *ācāryas*. My study reveals that the reciprocal relationship between the temporal and the divine, the Guhila king and the deity Ekaliṅga—a relationship which seems to have grown up on a strong base of Pāśupata influence—cannot be traced back to the earliest stage of Guhila rule in Mewar. The seventh-century Guhila states did not patronize religious sects and one finds no evidence of the predominance of any one sect in Mewar. However, Śaiva *ācāryas* appear to have been patronized by the Guhila of Kiṣkindhā in the eighth century, indicating the popularity and influence of the Śaivas who had a strong institutional (*maṭha*) base. Belonging to one of the Śaiva sects, the Pāśupata *ācāryas* got the temple of Ekaliṅga constructed by Guhila kings at Nāgdā. The Guhilas were the patrons of the Pāśupatas and in turn the Pāśupata *ācāryas* legitimized royal power through the Ekaliṅga cult and by introducing the legend of Bāppā and Hārītarāśi. This dialectic between the state and the cult of Ekaliṅga reached its zenith in the late fifteenth century when the Guhilas declared themselves *Ekaliṅgajinijasevaka* metaphorically surrendering temporal power to the regional cult. The popular tradition of various local goddesses (Araṇyavāsinī, Ghaṭṭavāsinī, Vaṭayakṣiṇidevī, etc.) were also integrated into the dominant cult of Vindhyavāsinī and used for legitimization of the state by the fifteenth century. Similarly, genealogical and origin myths graduated from relatively simple claims to highly prestigious ones in the medieval period. Like the state itself, the ideology underwent a slow process of transformation, spanning centuries.

My study of the history of a regional state, in Mewar, from the tenth to the fifteenth centuries confirms some of my basic arguments about the political processes of early medieval India. Local level ruling-class families developed into regional dynasties through the process of the integration of local chiefs and other prominent social groups into the emerging political structure through the mechanism of ranking in the *sāmanta* hierarchy and through the distribution of administrative roles and services.

The political process of state-formation ran *in tandem* with accompanying economic, social and religious processes. The basis of the accompanying economic process was the spread of rural agrarian settlements due to individual as well as royal initiatives which contributed to the growth of landlords and met the growing needs of the state for revenue. This process culminated in the expansion of some rural settlements into urban trading centres, intensifying the growth of the regional economy and royal mobilization of additional resources. The other major aspect of the economic processes was the 'peasantization' of the local tribes, with the spread of cultivation as well as the operation of local mines. The process of Rajputization that ran parallel to the process of peasantization in western India which culminated in caste formation formed the basis of the social process.

Royal affiliation to regional cults or *tīrtha* facilitated emergence of a central pantheon into which most of the local cults and *tīrthas* were incorporated. Hence, regional state formation also ran parallel to the formation of a regional religious traditions.

Finally, in my study, I have attempted to demonstrate that some of the processes of state formation in regional contexts cut across the traditional divide between the periods of early medieval and medieval India. For instance, the emergence of Delhi Sultanate did not bring to an end the process of legitimization of the Guhila state of Mewar. As I had argued at the very outset, it was in the fifteenth century that the epithet of Ekaliṅga came to be used for Guhila kings. The zenith of the process of territorial expansion and consolidation of Guhila power and the crystallization of a new political structure occurred in the fifteenth century. Even if the territorial extent of the state of Mewar fluctuated in the medieval period, the political structure so attained lent stability to the polity of Mewar.

Bibliography

PRIMARY SOURCES

I. Inscriptions

Altekar, A.S., ed., Nandsā-Yupa Inscription, AD 226, *EI*, vol. XXVI, pp. 25ff.

Banerji, Adris, A Chittaurgarh Fragmentary Inscription in the sub-circle office of Archaeological Survey (Chittaurgarh) AD sixth century, in his *Archaeological History of South-eastern Rajasthan*, Varanasi, 1471, p. 118.

Bhandarkar, D.R., ed., Another Bijolia Rock Inscription of Cāhamāna Someśvara, AD 1168-1169, PRAS, WC, March 1915, p. 35.

———, Ekaliṅgajī Temple Inscriptions of the time of Guhila king Naravāhana, AD 971, *Bom. Br. RAS*, vol. XXII, pp. 151-65.

———, Menal Stone Inscriptions of Cāhamāna Queen Suhadevī (queen of Pṛthvīrāja II), AD 1168, PRAS, WC, 1905-6, pp. 57 and 60.

———, Six Small Stone Inscription from Bijolia (Mandākinī *tīrtha*), AD 1287-1388, PRAS, WC, 1905-6, p. 56.

———, Āhaḍa Fragmentary Inscription of the time of Guhila king Śaktikumāra, tenth century AD characters, PRAS, WC, 1905-6, p. 60 (no. 2233).

———, Āṭapur Inscription of Guhila King Śaktikumāra, AD 977, *IA*, vol. XXXIX, pp. 186-91.

———, Chittaurgarh Fragmentary Inscription, AD 1245-6, PRAS, WC, 1905-6, pp. 61-2.

———, Hathibada Brahmi Inscription, beginning of first century BC, *EI*, vol. XXII, pp. 198-205.

———, Deoli Plates of Kṛṣṇa III, AD 940-41, *EI*, vol. V, pp. 188-97.

———, Karhad Plates of Kṛṣṇa III, AD 959, *EI*, vol. IV, pp. 278-90.

Chhabra, B. Ch., Alauddin Khilji's Inscriptions from Chittaurgarh, *ARIE*, 1955-6, Appendix C, no. 126.

Chakravarti, N.P. and B. Ch. Chhabra, eds., *Rājapraśasti Mahākavyam*, AD 1662, *EI*, vol. XXIX, pp. 1-90.

Desai, Z.A., ed., Two Persian Inscriptions of the Reign of Muhammad-bin Tughlaq from Chittaurgarh dated AD 1320 and 1325, *EIAPS*, 1955-6, pp. 67-70.

Gai, G.S., ed., A Digambar Jain Inscription from Chittaurgarh of the reign of Jaitrasiṁha, *ARIE*, 1962-3, no. B-836.

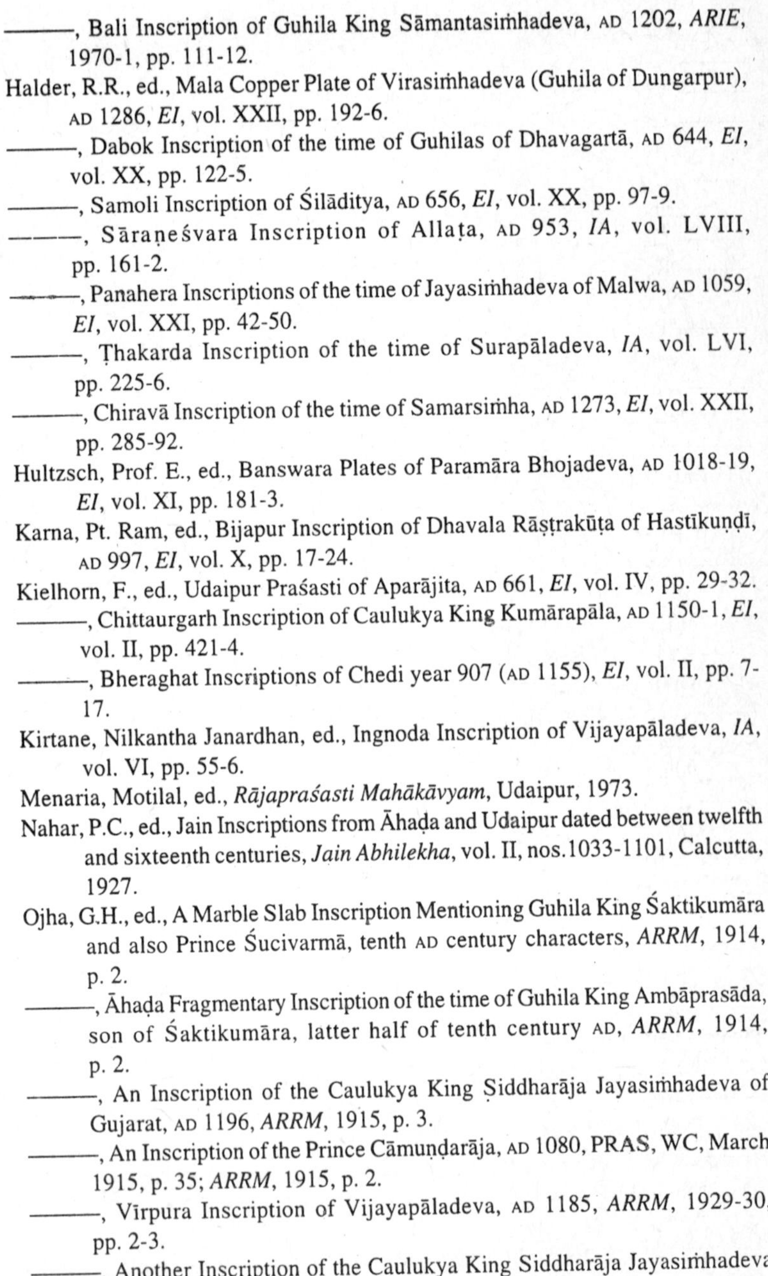

———, Bali Inscription of Guhila King Sāmantasiṁhadeva, AD 1202, *ARIE*, 1970-1, pp. 111-12.

Halder, R.R., ed., Mala Copper Plate of Virasiṁhadeva (Guhila of Dungarpur), AD 1286, *EI*, vol. XXII, pp. 192-6.

———, Dabok Inscription of the time of Guhilas of Dhavagartā, AD 644, *EI*, vol. XX, pp. 122-5.

———, Samoli Inscription of Śilāditya, AD 656, *EI*, vol. XX, pp. 97-9.

———, Sāraṇeśvara Inscription of Allaṭa, AD 953, *IA*, vol. LVIII, pp. 161-2.

———, Panahera Inscriptions of the time of Jayasiṁhadeva of Malwa, AD 1059, *EI*, vol. XXI, pp. 42-50.

———, Ṭhakarda Inscription of the time of Surapāladeva, *IA*, vol. LVI, pp. 225-6.

———, Chiravā Inscription of the time of Samarsiṁha, AD 1273, *EI*, vol. XXII, pp. 285-92.

Hultzsch, Prof. E., ed., Banswara Plates of Paramāra Bhojadeva, AD 1018-19, *EI*, vol. XI, pp. 181-3.

Karna, Pt. Ram, ed., Bijapur Inscription of Dhavala Rāṣṭrakūṭa of Hastīkuṇḍī, AD 997, *EI*, vol. X, pp. 17-24.

Kielhorn, F., ed., Udaipur Praśasti of Aparājita, AD 661, *EI*, vol. IV, pp. 29-32.

———, Chittaurgarh Inscription of Caulukya King Kumārapāla, AD 1150-1, *EI*, vol. II, pp. 421-4.

———, Bheraghat Inscriptions of Chedi year 907 (AD 1155), *EI*, vol. II, pp. 7-17.

Kirtane, Nilkantha Janardhan, ed., Ingnoda Inscription of Vijayapāladeva, *IA*, vol. VI, pp. 55-6.

Menaria, Motilal, ed., *Rājapraśasti Mahākāvyam*, Udaipur, 1973.

Nahar, P.C., ed., Jain Inscriptions from Āhaḍa and Udaipur dated between twelfth and sixteenth centuries, *Jain Abhilekha*, vol. II, nos.1033-1101, Calcutta, 1927.

Ojha, G.H., ed., A Marble Slab Inscription Mentioning Guhila King Śaktikumāra and also Prince Śucivarmā, tenth AD century characters, *ARRM*, 1914, p. 2.

———, Āhaḍa Fragmentary Inscription of the time of Guhila King Ambāprasāda, son of Śaktikumāra, latter half of tenth century AD, *ARRM*, 1914, p. 2.

———, An Inscription of the Caulukya King Ṣiddharāja Jayasiṁhadeva of Gujarat, AD 1196, *ARRM*, 1915, p. 3.

———, An Inscription of the Prince Cāmuṇḍarāja, AD 1080, PRAS, WC, March 1915, p. 35; *ARRM*, 1915, p. 2.

———, Vīrpura Inscription of Vijayapāladeva, AD 1185, *ARRM*, 1929-30, pp. 2-3.

———, Another Inscription of the Caulukya King Siddharāja Jayasiṁhadeva of Gujarat (n.d.). But it should be dated around the last decade of twelfth century AD, PRAS, WC, March 1915, p. 35.

———, Chittaur Inscription of Samarasiṁha, AD 1287, *URI*, vol. I, p. 177.

———, Chittaur Stone Inscription of Samarasiṁha, AD 1274, *URI*, p. 176.

———, Chittaur Stone Inscription (found near river Gambhiri), *URI*, AD 1267, p. 176.

———, Dungarpur Inscription of the time of Mahārājādhirāja Sīhadeva (Guhila Prince of Dungarpur) AD 1234, *ARRM*, 1915, p. 3.

———, Ghaghsa (Chittaurgarh) Record, AD 1265, *URI*, p. 170.

———, Kankroli Road-Station Inscription of the time of Samarasiṁha, AD 1298-99, *URI*, p. 177.

———, Pratapgarh Inscription of the time of Pratihāra King Mahendrapāladeva II, AD 942-6, *EI*, vol. XIV, pp. 176-88.

———, Āhaḍa Fragmentary Inscription of the time of Guhila King Naravāhana, date falls in the period AD 953-77, *ARRM*, 1914-18, p. 2.

———, An Inscription of Paramāra Prince Cāmuṇḍarāja (Paramāra of Vagod), AD 1078, PRAS, WC, March 1915, p. 35; *ARRM*, 1915, p. 2.

———, Dungarpur Inscription of Caulukya King Bhīmadeva, AD 1196, *ARRM*, 1915, p. 2.

———, Dungarpur Inscription of the same Prince Sāmantasiṁhadeva, AD 1178-9, *ARRM*, 1915, p. 3; also see, D.R. Bhandarkar, ed., PRAS, WC, 1915, p. 35.

———, Jagat Inscription of Guhila Sāmantasiṁhadeva of Mewar (founder of Guhila house of Dungarpur), AD 1171-2, *ARRM*, 1915, p. 3.

———, Jagat Inscription of Jayasiṁhadeva (son of Dungarpur Guhila Prince Sīhadadeva and grandson of famous Jaitrasiṁhadeva of Mewar Nāgdā-Āhaḍa house), AD 1249, *ARRM*, 1915, p. 3.

———, Two Inscriptions of Guhila Mahāsāmantādhipati of Nāgdā, AD 1000 and 1008, *ARRM*, 1936, p. 2.

Peterson, Peter, ed., 'A Stone Inscription of King Naravāhana in the Temple of Nātha (Udaipur)', in *A Collection of Prakrit and Sanskrit Inscriptions*, Bhavnagar Archaeological Department, n.d., pp. 69-72.

———, 'Sāraṇeśvara Temple Inscription of Guhila King Allaṭa, AD 953', in *A Collection of Prakrit and Sanskrit Inscriptions*, Bhavnagar Archaeological Department, n.d., pp. 67-9.

Shyamaldas, Kaviraj, ed., Chittaurgarh Inscription of Samarsiṁha, AD 1274, *Vir Vinod*, vol. I, Delhi, 1986, pp. 392-6.

———, Achaleśvara Inscription of Samarasiṁha, AD 1285, *Vir Vinod*, vol. I, Delhi, 1986, pp. 397-401; also see *IA*, vol. XVI, pp. 345-53.

———, Inscription of Kāyastha Vījada from Chittaurgarh of AD 1287, *Vir Vinod*, vol. I, Delhi, 1986, p. 401.

———, Jain Inscription, AD 1421 from the Temple of Śāntinātha at Zawar, *Vir Vinod*, vol. I, Delhi, 1986, pp. 401-2.

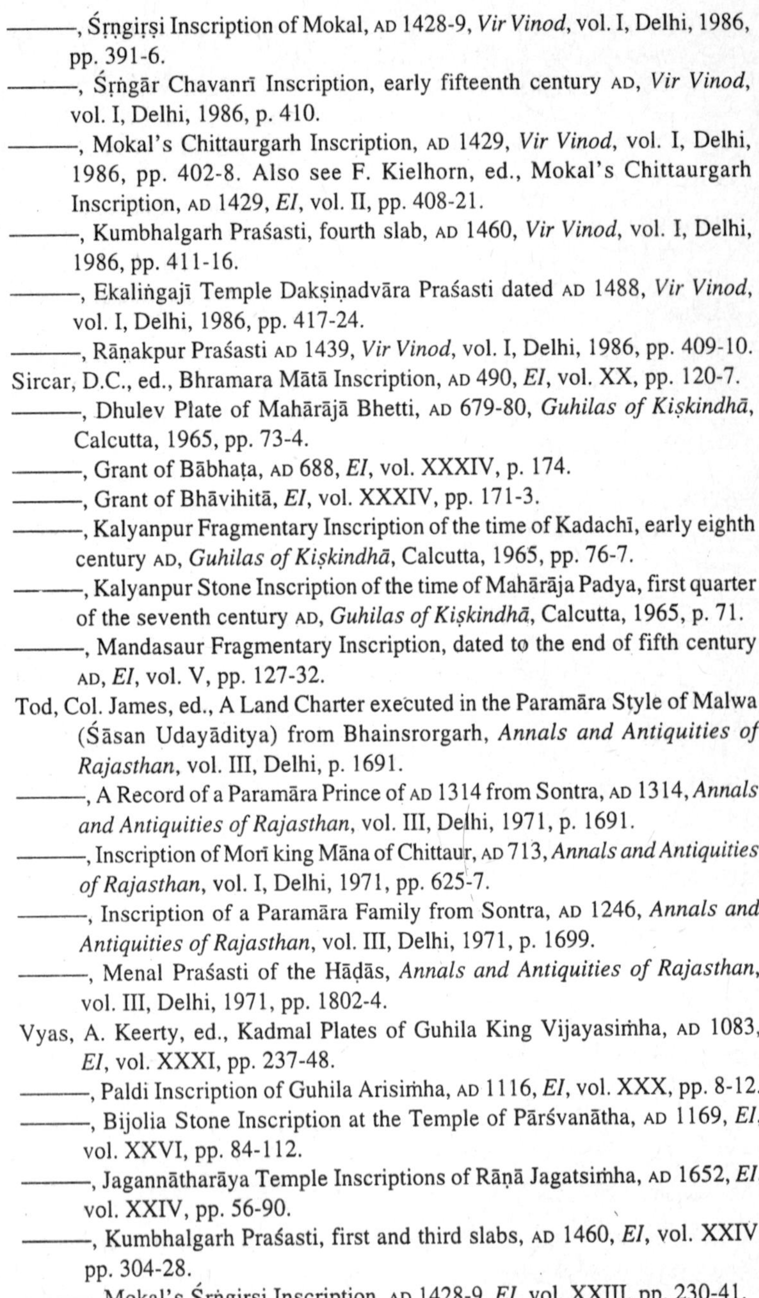

———, Śṛṇgiṛṣi Inscription of Mokal, AD 1428-9, *Vir Vinod*, vol. I, Delhi, 1986, pp. 391-6.

———, Śṛṅgār Chavanrī Inscription, early fifteenth century AD, *Vir Vinod*, vol. I, Delhi, 1986, p. 410.

———, Mokal's Chittaurgarh Inscription, AD 1429, *Vir Vinod*, vol. I, Delhi, 1986, pp. 402-8. Also see F. Kielhorn, ed., Mokal's Chittaurgarh Inscription, AD 1429, *EI*, vol. II, pp. 408-21.

———, Kumbhalgarh Praśasti, fourth slab, AD 1460, *Vir Vinod*, vol. I, Delhi, 1986, pp. 411-16.

———, Ekaliṅgajī Temple Dakṣiṇadvāra Praśasti dated AD 1488, *Vir Vinod*, vol. I, Delhi, 1986, pp. 417-24.

———, Rāṇakpur Praśasti AD 1439, *Vir Vinod*, vol. I, Delhi, 1986, pp. 409-10.

Sircar, D.C., ed., Bhramara Mātā Inscription, AD 490, *EI*, vol. XX, pp. 120-7.

———, Dhulev Plate of Mahārājā Bhetti, AD 679-80, *Guhilas of Kiṣkindhā*, Calcutta, 1965, pp. 73-4.

———, Grant of Bābhaṭa, AD 688, *EI*, vol. XXXIV, p. 174.

———, Grant of Bhāvihitā, *EI*, vol. XXXIV, pp. 171-3.

———, Kalyanpur Fragmentary Inscription of the time of Kadachī, early eighth century AD, *Guhilas of Kiṣkindhā*, Calcutta, 1965, pp. 76-7.

———, Kalyanpur Stone Inscription of the time of Mahārāja Padya, first quarter of the seventh century AD, *Guhilas of Kiṣkindhā*, Calcutta, 1965, p. 71.

———, Mandasaur Fragmentary Inscription, dated to the end of fifth century AD, *EI*, vol. V, pp. 127-32.

Tod, Col. James, ed., A Land Charter executed in the Paramāra Style of Malwa (Śāsan Udayāditya) from Bhainsrorgarh, *Annals and Antiquities of Rajasthan*, vol. III, Delhi, p. 1691.

———, A Record of a Paramāra Prince of AD 1314 from Sontra, AD 1314, *Annals and Antiquities of Rajasthan*, vol. III, Delhi, 1971, p. 1691.

———, Inscription of Morī king Māna of Chittaur, AD 713, *Annals and Antiquities of Rajasthan*, vol. I, Delhi, 1971, pp. 625-7.

———, Inscription of a Paramāra Family from Sontra, AD 1246, *Annals and Antiquities of Rajasthan*, vol. III, Delhi, 1971, p. 1699.

———, Menal Praśasti of the Hāḍās, *Annals and Antiquities of Rajasthan*, vol. III, Delhi, 1971, pp. 1802-4.

Vyas, A. Keerty, ed., Kadmal Plates of Guhila King Vijayasiṁha, AD 1083, *EI*, vol. XXXI, pp. 237-48.

———, Paldi Inscription of Guhila Arisiṁha, AD 1116, *EI*, vol. XXX, pp. 8-12.

———, Bijolia Stone Inscription at the Temple of Pārśvanātha, AD 1169, *EI*, vol. XXVI, pp. 84-112.

———, Jagannātharāya Temple Inscriptions of Rāṇā Jagatsiṁha, AD 1652, *EI*, vol. XXIV, pp. 56-90.

———, Kumbhalgarh Praśasti, first and third slabs, AD 1460, *EI*, vol. XXIV, pp. 304-28.

———, Mokal's Śṛṅgiṛṣi Inscription, AD 1428-9, *EI*, vol. XXIII, pp. 230-41.

Vyas, Nathulal, ed., Kadmal Copper Plate Inscription of Tejasiṁha, AD 1259, *Shodh Patrika*, VS 2010, p. 53.

———, Sītaladevī Temple Inscription (Gogunda) of the Reign of Rāṇā Khetā of AD 1366, *Shodh Patrika*, VS 2010, pp. 56-7.

II. Reports on Numismatic Sources

Alexander Cunningham, *Coins of Medieval India, seventh century AD to Muhammadan Conquests*, Varanasi, 1967.

III. Archaeological Surveys, Explorations and Excavations

Archaeological Survey of India, *Annual Report*, 1903-4, 1925-6.

Bhandarkar, D.R., *The Archaeological Remains and Excavations at Nāgarī*, Calcutta, 1920.

Carllyle, A.C.L., ed., *Report of a Tour in Eastern Rajputana*, Archaeological Survey of India, 1871-2.

Indian Archaeology—A Review, Archaeological Survey of India, 1956-7 to 1970-1.

Sankalia, H.D., S.B. Deo and Z.D. Ansari, *Excavations at Ahar* (*Tāmvavatī*), Poona, 1969.

Progress Reports of the Archaeological Survey, Western Circle, 1905 to 1921.

IV. Texts

Sanskrit Texts

Dalal, C.D., ed., *Jayasiṁhasūri's Hammīramadamardana*, Gaekwad Oriental Series, no. X, Baroda, 1920.

———, *Lekhapaddhati*, Gaekwad Oriental Series, no. 19, Baroda, 1925.

Jinavijayamuni, ed., *Jinaprabha Sūri's Vividhatīrthakalpa*, Shantiniketan, 1934.

———, *Jain Pustaka Praśasti Saṁgraha*, pt. I, Bombay, 1943.

———, *Jinapāla's Kharataragacchabṛhadgurvāvalī*, Bombay, 1956.

Kirtane, N.J., ed., *Nyāyacandra Sūri's Hammīramahākāvyam*, Bombay, 1879.

Kothari, Dev, ed., *Amarakāvyam of Raṇachoḍa Bhaṭṭa*, Udaipur, 1985.

Nahar, P.C., ed., *Jinavijayajī's Kharataragacchapaṭṭāvalī Saṁgraha*, Calcutta, 1956.

Sharma, Premlata, ed., *Rāṇā Kumbha's Saṅgītarāja*, Delhi, 1963.

———, *Ekaliṅgamāhātmyam*, Delhi, 1976.

Sūtradhāra, Maṇḍana, *Prāsādamaṇḍana and Rājaballabha Maṇḍana*, Calcutta Sanskrit Series, no. 32, Calcutta, 1948.

English Translations

Beal, S., *Si-Yu-Ki: Buddhist Records of the Western World*, Hiuen Tsiang's Accounts, rpt., Delhi, 1969.

Rajasthani Texts

Hukum Singh Bhati, ed., *Girdhar Āsiā's Sagat Rāso*, Udaipur, 1987.

Lakshmi Kumari Chundawat, ed., *Bagḍāvat Devanārāyaṇa Mahāgāthā*, Jaipur, 1993.

Murārīdān rī Khyāt in *Rajasthan Prachya Vidya Pratisthan Granthanka*, no. 15657 (Hindi trans.).

Paliwal, Devilal, ed., *Baḍvādevīdān Khyāt*, Udaipur, 1985.

———, *Jhulnā Mahārāṇā Pratāp Singhjī rā*, in *Mahārāṇā Pratāp Smṛti Grantha*, Udaipur, 1969.

———, *Rāṇāji rī bāt*, in *Baḍvādevīdān Khyāt*, Appendix, Udaipur, 1985.

———, *Sūryavaṁśāvalī in Baḍvādevīdan Khyāt*, Appendix, Udaipur, 1985.

Sakaria, Badri Prasad, *Nainsī rī Khyāt* (2nd edn.), Jodhpur, 1984.

Sharma, Giridharlal, ed., *Rājasthānī Bhīl Geet* (1st edn.), vol. II, Udaipur, 1956.

Swami, Pt. Narottamdas, ed., *Bānkīdās rī Khyāt*, Jodhpur, 1956.

Persian, Arabic and Turkish Texts with English Translations

Basu, K.K., *Yahyabin Ahmad Sirhindi's Tarikh-i-Mubarakshahi*, Eng. trans., Baroda Oriental Institute, 1932.

Beveridge, H., *Akbar Nama of Abul Fazal*, Delhi, 1973.

Briggs, J., *Muhammad Qasim Ferishta's Tarikh-i-Ferishta*, in *Bibliothica Indica*, Calcutta, 1913.

Elliot, H.M. and John Dowson, *History of India As Told by its Historians*, vol. III, Allahabad, 1973, pp. 67-92.

———, *History of India As Told by its Historians*, vol. IV, Allahabad, 1973, pp. 218-87.

Fuller, Maj. A.R., *Ziauddin Barani's Tarikh-i-Firuzshahi*, Extracts translated in English from *Bibliothica Indica*, Calcutta, 1862.

Habib, Muhammad, *Amir Khusrau Khazain-ul-Futh*, Madras, 1931.

Hussain, Agha Mahdi, *Rehla or Travels of Ibn Batuta* (Eng. trans.), Baroda, 1953.

SECONDARY SOURCES

Books

Adhya, G.L., *Early Indian Economics : Studies in the Economic Life of Northern and Western India, c. 200 BC-AD 300*, Bombay, 1966.

Altekar, A.S., *State and Government in Ancient India*, 3rd edn., rpt., Delhi, 1972.

Anderson, Perry, *Lineages of the Absolutist State*, London, 1974.

Asopa, J.N., *Origin of the Rajputs*, Delhi, 1976.

Banerjee, A.C., *Lectures on Rajput History*, Calcutta, 1962.

———, *State and Society in Northern India, AD 1206-1526*, Calcutta, 1982.

Banerjee, J.N., *Puranic and Tantric Religion*, Calcutta, 1966.

Banerji, Adris, *Archaeological History of south-eastern Rajasthan*, Varanasi, 1971.

Bayley, E.C., *The Local Muhammadan Dynasties: History of Gujarat*, Delhi, 1st Indian rpt, 1970.

Begde, Prabhakar V., *Forts and Palaces of India*, Delhi, 1982.

Bhanawat, Mahendra, *Rājasthān kī Gaṇagaur*, Udaipur, 1977.

Bhati, Hukum Singh, *Rājasthān ke Mertiyā Rāṭhaur* (*AD 1458-1707*), Jodhpur, 1986.

Bhatia, Pratipal, *The Paramāras* (*AD 800-1305 Century*), Delhi, 1970.

Bloch, Marc, *Feudal Society*, vol. II, tr. L.A. Manson, Chicago and London, 1962.

Chakraborti, Haripada, *Pāśupata Sūtram*, Calcutta, 1970.

Champion, T.C., ed., *Centre and Periphery—Comparative Studies in Archaeology*, London, 1989.

Chattopadhyaya, B.D., *Aspects of Rural Settlements and Rural Society in Early Medieval India*, Calcutta, 1990.

———, *The Making of Early Medieval India*, Delhi, 1994.

———, *Representing the Other? Sanskrit Sources and the Muslims, eighth to fourteenth century*, Delhi, 1998.

Chaudhary, A.K., *Early Medieval Village in North-Eastern India, AD 600-1200*, Calcutta, 1971.

Chaudhary, G.C., *Political History of Northern India from Jain Sources c. AD 650-1300*, Amritsar, 1963.

Claessen, H.J.M. and Peter Skalnik, eds., *The Early State*, The Hague, Mouton, 1978.

———, *The Study of the State*, The Hague, Mouton, 1981.

Claessen, H.J.M. and P. Van de Velde, eds., *Early State Dynamics*, Leiden, 1987.

Cohen, Ronald and Elman R. Service, eds., *Origins of the State: The Anthropology of Political Evolution*, Philadelphia, 1978.

Coomaraswamy, A.K., *Spiritual Authority and Temporal Power in the Indian Theory of Government*, rpt., Delhi, 1978.

Dave, P.C., *Grasias*, Delhi, 1960.

Day, Upendra Nath, *Medieval Malwa: A Political and Cultural History, AD 1401-1562*, 1st edn., Delhi, 1965.

———, *Mewar under Mahārāṇā Kumbha*, Delhi, 1978.

Deliege, Robert, *The Bhils of Western India: Some Empirical and Theoretical Issues in Anthropology in India*, Delhi, 1985.

Deyell, John S., *Living Without Silver: The Monetary History of Early Medieval North India*, Delhi, 1990.

Dhabai, R.K., 'Regional Structure of Mewar', M.Phil. Dissertation (unpublished), Centre for Studies in Regional Development, Jawaharlal Nehru University, 1975.

Dhaky, M.A., *Studies in Indian Temple Architecture*, Delhi-Bombay, 1975.

Dirks, Nicholas B., *The Hollow Crown, Ethnohistory of an Indian Kingdom*, Cambridge, 1987.

Doshi, J.K., *Social Structure and Cultural Change in a Bhil Village*, Delhi, 1974.

Eisenstadt, S.N., *The Political System of Empires*, New York, 1969.

Eschmann, A., H. Kulke and G.C. Tripathi, *The Cult of Jagannath and the Regional Tradition of Orissa*, Delhi, 1978.

Fox, Richard G., *Kin, Clan, Raja and Rule: State-Hinterland Relations in pre-Industrial India*, Bombay, 1971.

———, *Realm and Region in Traditional India*, Delhi, 1977.

Fried, Morton, *The Evolution of Political Society*, New York, 1967.

Gahlot, Sukhvir Singh and Banshi Dhar, *Castes and Tribes of Rajasthan*, Jodhpur, 1989.

Ganguly, Kalyan Kumar, *Cultural History of Rajasthan*, Delhi, 1983.

Ghoshal, U.N., *A History of Indian Political Ideas*, London, 1966.

Gopal, Lallanji, *Economic Life of Northern India, c.* AD *700-1200*, Varanasi, 1965.

Grigson, Wilfred, *The Maria Gonds of Bastar*, London, 1949.

Hall, K.R., *Trade and Statecraft in the Age of the Colas*, Delhi, 1980.

Handa, Devendra, *Osian: History, Archaeology, Art and Architecture*, Delhi, 1984.

Inden, Ronald, *Imagining India*, Delhi, 1990.

Ingold, Tim, David Riches and James Woodburn, eds., *Hunters and Gatherers: History, Evolution and Social Change*, Oxford-New York, 1988.

Jain, K.C., *Jainism in Rajasthan*, Sholapur, 1963.

———, *Ancient Cities and Towns of Rajasthan (A Study of Culture and Civilization)*, Delhi-Varanasi-Patna, 1972.

Jain, V.K., *Trade and Traders in Western India:* AD *1000-1300*, Delhi, 1990.

Jha, D.N., ed., *Feudal Social Formation in Early India*, Delhi, 1987.

Kaushik, Neelam, *Rājasthan ke Cūṇḍāwaton kā Itihāsa*, Jaipur, 1988.

Kolff, Dirk H.A., *Naukar, Rajput and Sepoy: The Ethnohistory of the Military Labour Market in Hindustan, 1450-1850*, Cambridge, 1990.

Kosambi, D.D., *An Introduction to the Study of Indian History*, Bombay, 1956.

Kulke, Hermann, *Kings and Cults, State Formation and Legitimation in India and Southeast Asia*, Delhi, 1993.

Lahiri, Nayanjot, *The Archaeology of Indian Trade Routes, up to c. 200* BC, Delhi, 1992.

Law, B.C., *Historical Geography of Ancient India*, Paris, 1954.

Lorenzen, David N., *Kāpālikas and Kālāmukhas, Two Lost Śaivite Sects* 2nd edn., Delhi, 1991.

Maity, S.K., *Economic Life of Northern India in the Gupta Period (c.* AD *330-550)*, 2nd edn., Delhi-Varanasi-Patna, 1970.

Majumdar, A.K., *Chaulukyas of Gujarat: A Survey of the History and Culture of Gujarat from the Middle of the Tenth to the end of the Thirteenth Century*, Bombay, 1956.

Majumdar, R.C., *The Age of Imperial Kanauj*, Bombay: Bharatiya Vidya Bhavan Series, 1964.

Majumdar, R.C., ed., *The Age of Imperial Unity*, Bombay: Bharatiya Vidya Bhavan Series, 1960.

Misra, S.C., *The Rise of Muslim Power in Gujarat: A History of Gujarat from* AD *1298 to* AD *1442*, Bombay, 1963.

Misra, V.C., *Geography of Rajasthan*, Delhi, 1967.

Misra, V.N., *Pre- and Proto-history of the Berach Basin, South Rajasthan*, Poona, 1967.

Naik, T.B., *Bhils: A Study*, Delhi, 1956.

Nandi, R.N., *Religious Institutions and Cults in Deccan*, Delhi, 1973.

Nath, Y.V.S., *Bhils of Ratanmal*, Baroda, date not printed.

Nilakantha Sastri, K.N., *The Colas,* 2nd edn., rpt., Madras, 1975.

Ojha, G.H., ed., *Udaipur Rājya kā Itihāsa*, vols. I-II, Ajmer, 1930.

———, *Dungarpur Rājya kā Itihāsa*, Ajmer, 1936.

———, *Early History of Rajputana*, vol. I, 2nd edn., Ajmer, 1937.

———, *Pratāpgarh Rājya kā Itihāsa*, Ajmer, 1940.

Poulantzas, N., *State, Power and Socialism*, London, 1980.

Puri, B.N., *The History of the Gurjara-Pratihāras*, Bombay, 1957.

Ray, H.C., *Dynastic History of Northern India*, vol. II, Calcutta, 1936.

Raychaudhuri, G.C., *History of Mewar*, Calcutta, date not printed.

Raychaudhuri, H.C., *Political History of Ancient India,* 6th edn., Calcutta, 1953.

Roy, Kumkum, *The Emergence of Monarchy in North India: Eighth-Fourth Centuries B.C. as Reflected in the Brāhmaṇical Tradition*, Delhi, 1995.

Rudolph, Susanne and Lloyd I. Rudolph, *Essays in Rajputana, History, Culture and Administration*, Delhi, 1984.

Schomer, Karine, et al., eds., *The Idea of Rajasthan: Explorations in Regional Identity*, vol. I, *Constructions* and vol. II, *Institutions*, Delhi, 1994, rpt. 2001, Pb. in 1 volume.

Sharda, Harbilas, *Mahārāṇā Kumbha*, Ajmer, 1922.

———, *Mahārāṇā Sāṅgā*, Ajmer, 1930.

Sharma, Dasharath, *Early Chauhan Dynasties, A Study of Chauhan Political History, Chauhan Political Institutions and Life in the Chauhan Dominions from c.* AD *800 to 1316*, Delhi, 1959.

———, *Rajasthan Through the Ages*, Bikaner, 1966.

Sharma, G.C., *Administrative System of the Rajputs*, Delhi, 1979.

Sharma, G.D., *Rajput Polity*, Delhi, 1977.

Sharma, R.S., *Aspects of Political Ideas and Institutions in Ancient India* (3rd revd. edn.), Delhi, 1991.

———, *Indian Feudalism, c. 300-1200*, Calcutta, 1965.

———, *Material Culture and Social Formations in Ancient India*, Delhi, 1983.

———, *Social Changes in Early Medieval India, c.* AD *500-1200*, Delhi, 1969.

———, *Urban Decay in India (c. 300-c. 1000)*, Delhi, 1987.

Shyamaldas, Kaviraj, *Vir Vinod*, vols. I-II, Delhi, 1986.

Singh, R.B.P., *Jainism in Early Medieval Karnataka c.* AD *500-1200*, Delhi, 1975.

Sircar, D.C., *Indian Epigraphy*, Delhi, 1965.

———, *The Guhilas of Kiṣkindhā*, Calcutta, 1965.

———, *Indian Epigraphical Glossary*, Delhi, 1966.

Sircar, D.C., ed., *Land System and Feudalism in Ancient India*, Calcutta, 1966.

Somani, Ram Vallabh, *Mahārāṇā Kumbha*, Jodhpur, 1968 (Hindi).

Spate, O.H.K. and A.T.A. Learmonth, *India and Pakistan, A General and Regional Geography*, 3rd edn., London, 1967.

Stein, Burton, *Peasant State and Society in Medieval South India*, Delhi, 1980.

———, *New Cambridge History of India: Vijayanagara*, vol. I, no. 2, Delhi, 1991.

Thapar, Romila, *Ancient Indian Social History, Some Interpretations*, Delhi, 1978.

———, *Cultural Trasanctions and Early India, Tradition and Patronage*, Delhi, 1994.

———, *Exile and the Kingdom: Some Thoughts on the Rāmāyaṇa*, Bangalore, 1978.

———, *From Lineage to State: Social Formations in the Mid-First Millennium* B.C. *in the Gaṅgā Valley*, Bombay, 1984.

———, *Mauryas Revisted*, S.G. Deuskar Lectures on Indian History, 1984, Calcutta, 1987.

Tod, James, *Annals and Antiquities of Rajasthan*, ed. William Crooke, rpt., vols. I-III, Delhi, 1971.

———, *Travels in Western India*, Delhi, 1971.

Vaidya, C.V., *History of Hindu Medieval India*, vols. I-II, Pune, 1924.

Wink, Andre, *Al-Hind: The Making of the Indo-Islamic World*, Leiden, 1990.

Yadava, B.N.S., *Society and Culture in Northern India in* A.D. *12th Century*, Allahabad, 1973.

ARTICLES

Agrawala, R.C., 'Dramma in Ancient Indian Epigraphs and Literature', *Journal of the Numismatic Society of India*, vol. XVII, no. 2, 1955, pp. 64-82.

———, 'Some more Unpublished Sculptures from Rajasthan', *Lalit Kala*, no. 10, Plate XX, Fig. 4.

———, 'Two Standing Lakulīśa Sculptures from Rajasthan', *Journal of Oriental Institute*, vol. XIV, nos. 1-4, Baroda, 1965, pp. 386-90.

Banerji, J.N., 'Lakulīśa—The Founder or the Systematization of Pāśupata Order', *Proceedings of the Indian History Congress*, Jaipur, 1951, pp. 33-7.

Bhandarkar, D.R., 'Foreign Elements in the Hindu Population', *Indian Antiquary*, vol. XL, 1911, pp. 7-37.

———, 'Peasant State and Society in Medieval South India: A Review Article', *Indian Economic and Social History Review*, vol. XVIII, pts. 3-4, 1981, pp. 411-26.

Bhattacharya, S., 'Political Authority and Brāhmaṇa-Kṣatriya Relations in Early India—An Aspect of the Power-Elite Configuration', *IHR*, vol. X, nos. 1-2, 1983-4, pp. 1-20.

Bhattacharjee, J.B., 'Dimasa State Formation in Cachar', in Surajit Sinha, ed., *Tribal Politics and State Systems in Pre-Colonial Eastern and North-Eastern India*, Calcutta, 1987, pp. 177-211.

Carneiro, Robert L., 'Political Expansion as an Expression of Principle of Competitive Exclusion', in Ronald Cohen and Elman R. Service, eds., *Origins of the State: The Anthropology of Political Evolution*, Philadelphia, 1978, pp. 205-23.

Castairs, Morris, 'The Bhils of Kotra Bhomat', *The Eastern Anthropologist*, vol. VII, nos. 3-4, 1954, pp. 169-81.

Chakravarty, Chintaharan, ed., 'Pāśupatasūtra', *Indian Historical Quarterly*, vol. XIX, no. 3, June 1943, pp. 270-1.

Champakalakshmi, R., 'Religious Conflict in the Tamil Country: A Reappraisal of Epigraphic Evidence', *Journal of the Epigraphical Society of India*, vol. V, 1978, pp. 69-81.

———, 'Growth of Urban Centres in South India: Kuḍāmukku-Pālaiyar, the Twin-city of the Colas', in *Studies in History*, vol. I, no. 1, 1979, pp. 1-29.

Chattopadhyaya, B.D., '"Reappearance" of the Goddess or the Brāhmaṇical Mode of Appropriation: Some Early Epigraphic Evidence bearing on Goddess Cults', G.-D. Sontheimer Memorial, *An Integrated View of Indian Culture* (unpublished symposium paper), Delhi, 1994.

———, 'Introduction: The Making of Early Medieval India', in his *The Making of Early Medieval India*, Delhi, 1994, pp. 1-37.

———, 'Irrigation in Early Medieval Rajasthan', *Journal of the Economic and Social History of the Orient*, vol. XVI, 1973, pp. 298-316; reprinted in his *The Making of Early Medieval India*, Delhi, 1994, pp. 38-56.

———, 'Markets and Merchants in Early Medieval Rajasthan', *Social Science Probings*, vol. II, no. 4, 1985, pp. 413-40; reprinted in his *Making of Early Medieval India*, Delhi, 1994, pp. 89-119.

———, 'Origin of the Rajputs: The Political, Economic and Social Processes in Early Medieval Rajasthan', *Indian Historical Review*, vol. III, 1976, pp. 59-72; reprinted in his *The Making of Early Medieval India*, Delhi, 1994, pp. 57-8.

———, 'Political Processes and Structure of Polity in Early Medieval India', Presidential Address, Ancient Indian Section, Indian History Congress, 44th Session, Burdwan, December 1983; reprinted in his *The Making of Early Medieval India*, Delhi, 1994, pp. 183-222.

———, 'Trade and Urban Centres in Early Medieval North India', *Indian Historical Review*, vol. I, 1974, pp. 203-19; reprinted in his *The Making of Early Medieval India*, Delhi, 1994, pp. 130-54.

———, 'Urban Centres in Early Medieval India: An Overview', in R. Thapar and S. Bhattacharya, eds., *Situating Indian History* 1986, pp. 8-33; reprinted in his *The Making of Early Medieval India*, Delhi, 1994, pp. 155-82.

Cherry, J.F., 'Power in Space: Archaeological and Geographical Studies of the State', in J.H. Wagstaff, ed., *Landscape and Culture: A Geographical and Archaeological Perspective*, London, 1992, pp. 146-72.

Craddock, Paul T., Freestone, Gurjar Middleton and Willies, 'The Production of Lead, Silver and Zinc in Early India', in A. Hauptmaun, E.P. Perinicka and G.A. Wagner, eds., *Old World Archaeometry*, Bochum: Deutsches Bergalu Museum, 1989, pp. 51-68.

David P. Henige, 'Some Phantom Dynasties of Early and Medieval India: Epigraphic Evidence and the Abhorrence of a Vacuum', *Bulletin of the School of Oriental and African Studies*, vol. 38, pt. 3, 1975, pp. 525-49.

De Casparis, J.G., 'Inscriptions and South Asian Dynastic Tradition', in R.J. Moore, ed., *Tradition and Politics in South Asia*, Delhi, 1979, pp. 103-27.

Desai, Devangana, 'Art under Feudalism in India', *IHR*, vol. I, pt. I, 1974, pp. 78-85.

———, 'The Patronage of the Lakshmana Temple at Khajuraho', in Barbara Stoler Miller, ed., *The Powers of Art: Patronage in Indian Culture*, Delhi, 1992, pp. 78-85.

Divanji, P.C., 'Lakulīśa of Karvan and His Pasupata Cult', *Journal of Gujarat Research Society*, vol. XVII, January 1955, pp. 267-74.

Dumont, Louis, 'The Conception of Kingship in Ancient India', in his *Religion, Politics and History in India: Collected Papers in Indian Sociology*, Paris-The Hague, Mouton, 1970, pp. 63-88.

Fried, Morton, 'On the Concepts of "Tribes" and "Tribal Society"', Paper Presented at meeting of the Division, Department of Anthropology, Columbia University, New York, 24 January 1966, Proceedings, pp. 527-40.

Gopal, Lallanji, 'Sāmanta—its Varying Significance in Ancient India', *Journal of the Royal Asiatic Society of Great Britain and Ireland*, pts. I-II, 1963, pp. 21-37.

Guha, A., 'Tribalism to Feudalism in Assam: 1600-1750', *IHR*, vol. I, no. I, 1974, pp. 65-76.

Halder, J.C., 'Power and Authority in Indian Tradition', in R.J. Moore, ed., *Tradition and Politics in South Asia*, Delhi, 1979, pp. 60-85.

Hooja, Rima, 'Contacts, Conflicts and Co-existence: Bhils and non-Bhils in South-eastern Rajasthan', in Bridget Allchin, ed., *Living Traditions:*

Studies in the Ethnoarchaeology of South Asia, Cambridge, 1995, pp. 125-42.

Jaiswal, Suvira, 'Caste in the Socio-Economic Framework of Early India', Presidential Address to Ancient Indian Section, Indian History Congress, 38th Session, Bhuvaneswar, 1977.

———, 'Studies in Early Indian Social History: Trends and Possibilities', *Indian Historical Review*, vol. 6, pts. 1-2, 1979-80, pp. 1-63.

Jha, D.N., 'Early Indian Feudalism: A Historiographical Critique', Presidential Address to Ancient Indian Section, Indian History Congress, 40th Session, Waltair, 1979.

———, 'Relevance of "Peasant State and Society" in Pallava-Cola Times', *IHR*, vol. VIII, nos. 1-2, 1981-2, pp. 74-94.

Jha, Vishwa Mohan, 'The Artless Pirennian, Review of Wink's *Al-Hind*', *IHR*, vol. XVIII, nos. 1-2, pp. 93-103.

Kosambi, D.D., 'On the Development of Feudalism in India', *Annals of the Bhandarkar Oriental Research Institute*, vol. XXXVI, pp. 258-69.

———, 'Origins of Feudalism in Kashmir', *Journal of the Bombay Branch of the Royal Asiatic Society*, 1956-7, pp. 108-20.

Krader, Lawrence, 'The State in History', *Studies in History*, vol. IV, no. 2, 1982, pp. 167-80.

Kulke, Hermann, 'Early State Formation and Royal Legitimation in Tribal Areas in Eastern India', in R. Moser and M.K. Gautam, eds., *Aspects of Tribal Life in South Asia, I: Strategy and Survival,* Berne, 1978, pp. 29-38.

———, 'Fragmentation and Segmentation versus Integration? Reflections on the Concept of Indian Feudalism and the Segmentary State in Indian History', *Studies in History*, vol. 4, no. 2, 1982, pp. 237-63.

———, 'Royal Temple Policy and the Structure of Medieval Hindu Kingdom', in A. Eschmann, H. Kulke and G.C. Tripathi, eds., *The Cult of Jagannatha and the Regional Tradition of Orissa*, Delhi, 1978, pp. 125-38.

———, 'The Early and the Imperial Kingdom: A Processual Model of Integrative State Formation in Early Medieval India', in his *The State in India AD 1000-1700*, Delhi, 1995, pp. 233-62.

Majumdar, B.P., 'Lakulīśa Pāśupatas and their Temples in Medieval India', *Journal of the Bihar Research Society*, vol. XXXIX, March-June 1953, pp. 1-9.

Malcolm, J., 'Essay on the Bhils', *Transactions of Royal Asiatic Society of Great Britain*, vol. I, 1827, pp. 65-91.

Mukhia, H., 'Was There Feudalism in Indian History?', Presidential Address to Medieval Indian Section, Indian History Congress, 40th Session, Waltair, 1979.

Nandi, R.N., 'Origin and Nature of Śaivite Monasticism: The Case of Kālāmukhas', in R.S. Sharma and V. Jha, eds., *Indian Society: Historical Probings* (in memory of D.D. Kosambi), Delhi, 1974, pp. 190-201.

Narayanan, M.G.S. and Kesavan Veluthat, 'Bhakti Movement in South India', in D.N. Jha, ed., *Feudal Social Formation in Early India*, Delhi, pp. 348-75.

Perlin, Frank, 'The Pre-Colonial Indian State in History and Epistemology: A Reconstruction of Societal Formation in the Western Deccan from the Fifteenth to the Early Nineteenth Century', in H.J.M. Claessen and Peter Skalnik, eds., *The Study of the State*, The Hague, 1981, pp. 275-302.

Price, Barbara J., 'Secondary State Formation', in Ronald Cohn and Elman R. Service, eds., *Origin of State—The Anthropology of Political Evolution*, Philadelphia, 1978, pp. 161-86.

Sanyal, Hiteshranjan, 'Mallabhum', in Surajit Sinha, ed., *Tribal Politics and State Systems in Pre-Colonial Eastern and North-Eastern India*, Calcutta, 1987, pp. 73-142.

Seneviratne, Sudarshan, 'Kaliṅga and Andhra: The Process of Secondary State Formation in Early India', in H.J.M. Claessen and Peter Skalnik, eds., *The Study of the State*, The Hague, 1981, pp. 317-38.

Sharma, R.S., 'Decay of Gangetic Towns in Gupta and Post-Gupta Times', *PIHC*, 33rd Session, Muzaffarpur, 1972, pp. 94-104.

———, 'How Feudal was Indian Feudalism?', in T.J. Byres and Harbans Mukhia, eds., *Feudalism and Non-European Societies*, London, 1985, pp. 19-43.

———, 'Landgrants to Vassals and Officials in Northern India, *c*. AD 1000-1200', *Journal of the Economic and Social History of the Orient*, vol. 4, 1961, pp. 70-105.

———, 'Origins of Feudalism in India (*c*. AD 400-650)', *Journal of the Economic and Social History of the Orient*, vol. 1, no. 3, 1958, pp. 297-328.

———, 'Problem of Transition from Ancient to Medieval Indian History', *The Indian Historical Review*, vol. I, no. 1, 1974, pp. 1-9.

———, 'The Kali Age: A Period of Social Crisis', in S.N. Mukherjee, ed., *India: History and Thought, Essays in Honour of A.L. Basham*, Calcutta, 1982, pp. 186-203.

Stein, Burton, 'State Formation and Rajput Myth in Tribal Central India', *Man in India*, vol. 42, no. 1, 1962, pp. 35-80.

———, 'Integration of the Agrarian Order', in R. Frykenberg, ed., *Land Control and Social Structure in Indian History*, 1969, pp. 175-216.

———, 'The Cola State', *Studies in History*, vol. 4, no. 2, 1982, pp. 265-306.

———, 'The Segmentary State in South Indian History', in R.G. Fox, ed., *Realm and Region in Traditional India*, Delhi, 1977, pp. 3-51.

Thapar, Romila, 'Social Mobility in Ancient India with Special Reference to Elite Groups', in *Ancient Indian Social History: Some Interpretations*, Delhi, 1978, pp. 122-51.

———, 'State Formation in Early India', *International Social Science Journal*, vol. XXXII, no. 4, 1980, pp. 655-70.

———, 'The State as Empire', in H. Claessen and P. Skalnik, eds., *The Study of the State*, The Hague, 1981, pp. 409-26.

Veluthat, Kesavan, 'Royalty and Divinity: Legitimization of Monarchical Power in the South', *PIHC*, 39th Session, Hyderabad, 1978, pp. 241-9.

Yadava, B.N.S., 'Immobility and Subjection of Indian Peasantry in Early Medieval Complex', *IHR*, vol. 1, no. 1, 1974, pp. 31-63.

Ziegler, Norman P., 'Marwari Historical Chronicles: Sources for the Social and Cultural History of Rajasthan', *IESHR*, vol. 13, 1976, pp. 219-50.

Other Publications

Gupta, C.S., ed., *Rajasthan: Fairs and Festivals*, Census of India, vol. XIV, pt. VII-B, 1961.

Rajasthan District Gazetteers

(i) Banswara, 1879.
(ii) Bhilwara, 1975.
(iii) Dungarpur State, 1908.
(iv) Chittaurgarh, 1977.
(v) Udaipur, 1979.
(vi) Erskine, Maj. K.D., ed., Mewar Residency, *Rajasthan Gazetteers*, vol. II-A and vol. II-B, Ajmer, 1908, reprinted in 1992, Gurgaon.
(vii) *The Imperial Gazetteer of India*, vol. XXIV, 1908.

Index